SEEKING SECURITY

Many academic criminal lawyers and criminal law theorists seek to resolve the optimum conditions to be met by a criminal law fit to serve a liberal democracy. Typical wish lists include a criminal law that intervenes against any given individual only when there is a reasonable suspicion that s/he has caused harm to the legally protected interests of another or was on the brink of doing so. Until there is conduct that gives rise to a reasonable suspicion of criminal conduct by an individual, s/he should be allowed to go about his or her business free from covert surveillance or other forms of intrusion. All elements of crimes should be proved beyond any reasonable doubt. Any punishment should be proportionate to the gravity of the wrongdoing and when the offender has served this punishment the account should be cleared and good standing recovered. *Seeking Security* explores the gap between the normative aspirations of liberal, criminal law scholarship and the current criminal law and practice of Anglophone jurisdictions. The concern with security and risk, which in large part explains the disconnection between theory and practice, seems set to stay and is a major challenge to the form and relevance of a large part of criminal law scholarship.

Seeking Security

Pre-Empting the Commission of Criminal Harms

Edited by

G R Sullivan

and

Ian Dennis

• HART •
PUBLISHING

OXFORD AND PORTLAND, OREGON

2012

Published in the United Kingdom by Hart Publishing Ltd
16C Worcester Place, Oxford, OX1 2JW
Telephone: +44 (0)1865 517530
Fax: +44 (0)1865 510710
E-mail: mail@hartpub.co.uk
Website: http://www.hartpub.co.uk

Published in North America (US and Canada) by
Hart Publishing
c/o International Specialized Book Services
920 NE 58th Avenue, Suite 300
Portland, OR 97213-3786
USA
Tel: +1 503 287 3093 or toll-free: (1) 800 944 6190
Fax: +1 503 280 8832
E-mail: orders@isbs.com
Website: http://www.isbs.com

British Library Cataloguing in Publication Data
Data Available

ISBN: 978-1-84946-166-5

Typeset by Hope Services, Abingdon
Printed and bound in Great Britain by
Lightning Source UK Ltd

Preface

The essays in this volume are based on papers given at a conference entitled 'Seeking Security: Pre-Empting the Commission of Criminal Harms', held at University College London (UCL) on 2–3 September 2010. The conference was organised by the Centre for Criminal Law of the UCL Faculty of Laws. The aim was to explore the numerous issues for the criminal law presented by ever-increasing demands in recent years for 'security', in the form of coercive measures against risks of the future commission of criminal harms.

Thanks are due to Kingsley Napley for their generous financial support for the Centre. Thanks also to Lisa Penfold, the Faculty's Events Manager, for her immaculate organisation of the conference. Finally, thank you to all the speakers and participants for making the conference such a stimulating and enjoyable occasion.

Ian Dennis, Director of the Centre for Criminal Law, UCL

August, 2011

Contents

Contributors

Larry Alexander, Warren Distinguished Professor of Law, University of San Diego

Ian Dennis, Professor of Law, University College, London.

R A Duff, Professor, Law School, University of Minnesota; Emeritus Professor, University of Sterling.

Kimberly Kessler Ferzan, Professor of Law, Rutgers University School of Law.

Jeremy Horder, Edmund-Davies Professor of Criminal Law and Criminal Justice, King's College London.

Peter Ramsay, Lecturer in Law, London School of Economics.

Jonathan Rogers, Senior Lecturer in Law, University College London.

AP Simester, Professor of Law, National University of Singapore; Fellow, Wolfson College, Cambridge.

John Stanton-Ife, Senior Lecturer in Law, King's College London.

GR Sullivan, Emeritus Professor of Law, University College London.

Malcolm Thorburn, Canada Research Chair in Crime, Security and Constitutionalism; Associate Professor, Queen's University, Kingston.

Shlomit Wallerstein, CUF Lecturer and Fellow, St Peter's College, University of Oxford.

Martin Wasik, Professor of Law, Keele University.

Lucia Zedner, Professor of Criminal Justice, Faculty of Law and Corpus Christi College, University of Oxford and Conjoint Professor, Faculty of Law, UNSW, Sydney.

Table of Cases

Table of Legislation

NATIONAL LEGISLATION

United Kingdom

Australia

Germany

Hungary

India

Israel

Singapore

United States

EU LEGISLATION

INTERNATIONAL LEGISLATION

Seeking Security: An Introduction

G R SULLIVAN AND IAN DENNIS

IMAGINE A LIBERAL, democratic society governed by persons with broad and deep commitments to equality before the law, the autonomy of individuals, to tolerance of divergent lifestyles and who only resort to coercive measures for matters of great public importance and as a very last resort. In such a society, the presumption of innocence should have resonance beyond proof of guilt at a criminal trial. The governance of such a society would be permeated with a disposition to trust individuals, to assume, unless there is good reason to think otherwise, that any given man (D) is honest and well disposed to others. It would go with the grain of such a society to have a limited, circumspect criminal law, predominately concerned with preventing and punishing conduct which wrongfully harms or threatens imminent harm to persons other than the defendant. Coercive state interventions would not be made against D unless there was a reasonable suspicion that D had caused a wrongful harm or was on the brink of doing so. Should it be proved beyond reasonable doubt that D's conduct caused or imminently threatened wrongful harm to another without any justification or excuse for doing so, punishment proportionate to the wrong committed by D would be warranted. The requirement that punishment be justified and limited to the gravity of the wrong done by D is entailed by respect for D's personhood and autonomy. He is punished to the extent that he deserves. Social benefits that may flow from the just punishment of D, such as public protection and general/individual deterrence, should not influence the quantum of punishment imposed on D.

Anyone with even a slight acquaintance with the criminal law and its practice in England and Wales is aware that the picture of criminal law and punishment offered above is a travesty. This applies not only for England and Wales but for the Anglophone world in general.[1] Punishment extending well beyond any retributivist pay back is commonplace. Conduct subjected to punishment will frequently comprise of acts and omissions which did not pose any imminent

[1] McSherry, Norrie and Bronitt (eds), *Regulating Deviance: The Redirection of Criminalisation and the Futures of Criminal Law* (Oxford, Hart Publishing, 2009).

threat of causing wrongful harm.[2] Why then waste any time with travesties? That question is deflected rather than answered by observing that the majority of academic criminal lawyers and criminal law theorists argue for a criminal law and punishment limited to wrongs that cause or threaten imminent harm and which are punished according to their gravity. There is an enormous gap between the normative aspirations of a large part of criminal law scholarship and the reality of criminal law and punishment, and there is very little chance that the gap will close.[3]

One reason why academic critiques of criminal law and punishment have so little purchase on contemporary legislators, policymakers (and even judges) arises from a commitment to diminish the risk of future harms.[4] For these officials it is not enough for the criminal law to confine itself to harms already done, supplemented by only limited rights of intervention in respect of imminent threats of harm. For them, the criminal law must be used proactively in the cause of harm prevention. That entails the application of the criminal law to conduct which threatens not only imminent harm but harm at some uncertain distance from realisation. This concern with harm prevention is unassailably legitimate.[5] Who could disagree that prevention is better than cure, particularly in the case of harms for which there is no cure? However, a serious engagement with diminishing the risk of harm through the criminal law and its processes entails the end of trust as the default relationship in interactions between subject and state. Assuming that persons are generally peaceable and well disposed is not a useful operational disposition for risk preventers. The first task of a risk preventer is to ascertain the seriousness of the kind of risks he or she is obliged to address. That requires gathering information about the proclivities and intentions of whole classes of persons who in general are peaceful and well disposed.

One source of information comes from the constant surveillance of persons in the general population when outside their places of abode. The House of Lords Select Committee on the Constitution reported that

[2] For instance s 5 of the Terrorism Act 2006 provides that any person will commit an offence if with the intention of committing an act of terrorism or assisting an act of terrorism, 'he engages in *any conduct* (emphasis supplied) in preparation for giving effect to his intention'. The maximum penalty for this offence is life imprisonment.

[3] The essays in this volume will demonstrate that convictions for offences which may carry long terms of imprisonment can occur in circumstances where there may be disputation whether one or more of the fundamental elements associated with serious crimes such as harm, wrong and culpability are present. Furthermore, indeterminate sentences in the interests of public safety are frequently passed. The concern with security that in large part explains these phenomena seems unlikely to abate.

[4] For an informed (and sobering) assessment of the likely risks to the UK from terrorist threats, see Omand, *Securing the State* (London, Hurst, 2010), particularly chs 6–8. For a breezier and more optimistic assessment see Gardner, *Risk: The Science and Politics of Fear* (London, Virgin, 2008) ch 9 (crime in general) and ch 11(terrorism).

[5] As Dennis (ch 8 of this volume) and Horder (ch 4 of this volume) observe, the intervention of the criminal law on the basis of risk is of very long standing.

> successive UK governments have gradually constructed one of the most extensive and technologically advanced surveillance systems in the world [which] represents one of the most significant changes in the life of the nation since the end of the Second World War.[6]

Malcolm Thorburn, in the opening chapter of this volume, questions the legitimacy of general surveillance. Drawing on the German idea of 'informational self determination', he argues that an effective protection of privacy precludes any general dissemination of information relating to specific individuals. That D, say, spends a lot of his time at a mosque associated with a fundamentalist version of Islam is a fact that he is entitled to keep to himself. By contrast, Thorburn asserts a strong entitlement on the part of the state to have the wherewithal to identify any person within the jurisdiction. He finds no grounding for a privacy right to keep one's identity secret and finds no argument in principle against a state insisting that persons subject to its jurisdiction carry means of identification. However, beyond that he allows very little room for a state to seek information on D for crime prevention purposes if there is no specific evidence pertaining to D giving rise to a reasonable suspicion that he may have committed a crime. That D is a Muslim fundamentalist may increase the probabilities that he is sympathetic to certain causes promoted by terrorist means. For Thorburn, that does not entitle the state to monitor and track D's activities and communications to test the possibility of criminal associations. Indeed, Thorburn considers that such surveillance breaches D's right to privacy and might render any resulting criminal trial unfair. Thorburn's paper raises serious questions for English law on the compatibility of certain information gathering techniques used by the police and security services with articles 6 and 8 of the European Convention for Human Rights.

Shlomit Wallerstein addresses the entitlement of the state to assistance from its subjects in obtaining information about the risk of criminal harms. In general terms, English law does not oblige subjects to make known to officials their knowledge of crimes committed, let alone mere suspicions of crimes that might be committed. However, as with so much else, the position changes with terrorism. It is an offence to fail to disclose information which may be of material assistance to the prevention of an act of terrorism.[7] As Wallerstein observes, the persons most frequently prosecuted for this offence are close relatives of the suspected terrorist. That fact engages a major reservation about imposing a general duty of this kind encompassing suspicions about all manner of crimes. A plural democracy should tailor the demands for information backed by criminal sanctions with due recognition of the constraints imposed by private loyalties and commitments. Wallerstein does not argue for a general duty, but

[6] *www.parliament.uk*; Constitution Committee – Second Report, *Surveillance, Citizens and the State* (2009).

[7] Terrorism Act 2000 s 38B. Wallerstein also discusses s 330 of the proceeds of Crime Act 2002 which obliges persons who are employed in the regulated sector for financial services to report suspicions of money laundering.

she does contend that that it is legitimate to impose such a duty even on close relatives in the case of suspected acts of terrorism.

That the matter suspected must be some *act* of terrorism at least confines the range of things suspected to violence or threats of violence. But of course, many terrorist offences embrace and severely punish conduct far in advance of any perpetration of a terrorist act.[8] There are also many similar 'prophylactic' offences in other parts of the criminal law.[9] The broader the swathe of conduct covered, the larger the territory for surveillance and monitoring. This expansion brings with it intractable questions relating to the very basics of criminal liability. The further away from the instantiation of any concrete harm, the more vacuous the conduct element of the crime will be. The focus will be on the intent with which the act remote from any harm is done. D may sit in his house conceiving some dreadful crime he has every intention to carry out. If he is a competent and determined criminal, the world becomes a less safe place from the moment he resolves the details of his criminal project. However, even if we put to one side questions relating to proving the criminal intentions of persons merely thinking things through in their own homes, what has D done or omitted to do that deserves censure and punishment?

It is very tempting to say that if D at no point strays from the routines of normal life, his conduct should not comprise the external elements of any crime. However that will not do. D may draw back a curtain to let in more light. Alternatively he may be giving a signal for the start of a terrorist attack. Andrew Simester accepts in general terms the social utility of prophylactic offences such as proscribing possession of firearms or excessive quantities of fertiliser. However, as he observes, the further the conduct strays from the ultimate harm that animates the offence, the greater the potential for intrusion into innocent lives. He maintains that there are tokens of conduct that are inherently innocent where the distant possibility of future wrongdoing cannot be taken to undermine the non-wrongfulness of the conduct at issue. He instances connecting to the internet as the kind of activity he has in mind. However, he concedes that where the future wrongdoing is sufficiently grave, even conduct of this inherently innocent kind may yet be allowed to constitute the *actus reus* of a criminal offence, provided the terms of the proscription do not contravene any rights that may be regarded as fundamental. Simester's chapter nicely illuminates the many dimensions of the intractable difficulties of setting limits based on firm, unyielding principle to the scope of prophylactic offences.[10] It is a problem that has bedevilled the law of attempts, giving rise to interminable disputation as to the scoping of liability for attempts.[11] These difficulties equally attend the

[8] See n 2 above.

[9] Horder in ch 4 of this volume gives interesting examples of these offences.

[10] See further Simester and von Hirsch, *Crimes, Harms and Wrongs: On the Principles of Criminalisation* (Oxford, Hart Publishing, 2011) chs 4 and 5.

[11] Duff, *Criminal Attempts* (Oxford, Oxford University Press, 1996) ch 2; Clarkson, 'Attempt: the Conduct Requirement' (2009) 29 *Oxford Journal of Legal Studies* 25.

increasing number of substantive offences that punish conduct much more anticipatory than the broadest conceptions of when a crime defined in terms of causing harm may be said to have been attempted.

Jeremy Horder is far less troubled by what he terms 'anticipatory offences'.[12] He considers that a focus on risk is a 'civilising move'[13] away from the 'fire brigade'[14] model of the criminal law. As examples of this approach he approves of recent offences aimed at protecting vulnerable groups such as children, adults in social care and animals, all of whom may be in environments which expose them to serious risks of repeated harms. These offences do not depend on proof of mistreatment or cruelty, but lay down systems and procedures which must be followed on pain of criminal sanction.[15] Horder makes the entirely reasonable claim that such offences are likely to be far more effective in decreasing the incidence of harm to the vulnerable by contrast with offences that are engaged after the event. He contrasts the anticipatory approach with what he terms 'minimalism' which confines criminal law interventions to realised harms and the immediate threat of harms. He makes the interesting observation that some prominent minimalists are not all that they seem to be in that after a sharp delineation of their minimalist position they make concessions to the anticipatory approach sufficiently far reaching as to undermine their minimalist credentials. For Horder, of course, these concessions are all to the good, although he recognises the risk that the anticipatory approach risks an overly punitive approach to conduct that does not warrant such treatment. He is content however 'that enforcement authorities working with offences that reflect the anticipatory perspective tend to press criminal charges only in cases where there has been serious fault'.[16]

Larry Alexander and Kimberley Ferzan may be described as arch minimalists.[17] For them the only basis for just punishment is retributivist desert. They see desert as the product of two factors. First, D must do or omit to do something which, based on his assessment of the circumstances, will unleash an irrevocable risk to the legally protected interests of others. Second, D must lack any justification or excuse for unleashing a risk that he takes to be irrevocable. (On the Alexander/Ferzan view of culpability, it does not matter whether or not D does create a risk to the legally protected interests of others provided that he thinks he has created a risk.)

The minimalism of this approach can be illustrated by envisaging D a violent paedophile who is in a public park where children are playing. He has in his possession a kitchen knife, masking tape and rope (all non-contraband items) and the plain clothes policemen who are keeping D under surveillance are aware that

[12] See ch 4 of this volume at 79.

[13] At 100.

[14] At ibid.

[15] One example Horder provides is s 9 of the Animal Welfare Act 2006 which prescribes the conditions in which animals must be kept.

[16] At 101.

[17] However, see Duff in ch 6 of this volume who demonstrates that the Alexander/Ferzan formula does allow some surprisingly early interventions.

he plans to kidnap a child. D is now very close to a group of children absorbed in their play. Suppose a criminal jurisdiction which has a criminal code drafted in compliance with the limits on early intervention proposed by Alexander and Ferzan.[18] If D is to be arrested for a criminal offence, the police officers must stay their hand until D has taken hold of a child because only then can D be said to have placed himself in the red zone. Up until that point D is free to resile from his atrocious project.

In favour of the Alexander/Ferzan take on minimalism is its simplicity and clarity: one avoids the labour that comes with the intractable task of formulating prophylactic offences which are compatible with retributivism. More fundamentally, Alexander and Ferzan argue that their version of minimalism is the only version that can be squared with retributivism. Until D thinks that he has unleashed an irrevocable risk to the legally protected interests of others beyond his power of recall, he has done nothing that on his own estimation has adversely altered the state of the world. Intentions are revisable. Up to the point of no return, there is no harm or risk of harm for which he may hold himself responsible and culpable. If he does renounce his intent nothing as it were has happened. Likewise, up to the point of irrevocability something has yet to happen.

Even if it is accepted that retributivism requires the minimalism set down by Alexander and Ferzan, any society preoccupied with diminishing unacceptable risks might well reject such a limited criminal law. It is unlikely in the extreme that the electorate would accept a law that stayed its hand until the gunman was squeezing the trigger or wait until the bomber had begun the process of detonating the bomb. If retributivism necessitates that degree of forbearance, then many people would say so much the worse for retributivism. For Antony Duff there is no need to renounce retributivism for this reason, because, if properly understood, it does allow interventions prior to unleashing irrevocable risks. According to Duff, 'we can be morally culpable for actions that fall far short of irrevocably unleashing a risk'.[19] Indeed for him a person can be culpable for forming an 'illegitimate intention'.[20] The culpability that arises at the point of D resolving an intention to perpetrate a wrong is, for Duff, confirmed and aggravated when D takes steps to bring to fruition his illicit intention. He instances D conceiving a scheme to defraud V. He does work on the scheme but his fraudulent intentions are discovered well before the last act stage of the plan. As Duff observes, V's feelings towards D are unlikely to lighten should it be pointed out to him that it remained possible for D to abandon his plan at a point where there was no harm done to V. Moreover, even if D's scheme was not discovered but abandoned and confessed to by D because of a genuine change of heart, it would be asking a lot of V to relinquish all of his hard feelings about D.

[18] Alexander and Ferzan have given detailed consideration to the specifics of, to use their formulation, a culpability based code: *Crime and Culpability: A Theory of Criminal Law* (Cambridge, Cambridge University Press, 2009) ch 8.

[19] This volume at 139.

[20] At 133.

To reconcile prophylactic offences with the strictures of retributivism in the manner of Duff is an attractive prospect. However, there are difficulties. To be sure, it is natural to think less of a person who conceives a fraudulent scheme to which he or she intends to give effect. But the criminal law as a system of public ordering should not be concerned with the state of a person's soul but with the things that person has overtly done or failed to do. What constitutes a wrong for the purposes of the criminal law should reflect this public dimension of legitimate criminalisation. Returning to the fraudulent D, suppose D aspires to obtain employment with V plc in order to defraud this company. To further this fraudulent project, he researches in detail the scope and nature of V's business from publicly accessible sources. Before he can apply for a position with V, his fraudulent intent is revealed by way of a boastful email to an honest friend. What has D done that is wrong in terms of the institutional purposes of the criminal law? The difficulties here are not merely the ancillary issues of intrusion, privacy and problems of proof, important though these matters are. They go to the heart of what things can be legitimately criminalised. To use Simester's expression, we are back to criminalising 'inherently innocent conduct', such things as buying airline tickets or maps of the London underground. We are back to the possibility of using preventative detention in the guise of retributivist punishment.

One means of escape from these difficulties is to seek public security through means other than the criminal law. The most obvious and drastic way of doing that is civil internment but without dilating on the obvious any peacetime government would be loath to go that route even in the case of persons suspected to be dangerous terrorists. The control order regime for all its controversial features[21] falls well short of anything that can be described as internment. Something almost as unsettling as internment would be a general jurisdiction to detain persons considered to be dangerous, a detention that need not require a criminal conviction. The former Labour Government at one time had well advanced plans for the civil incarceration of persons who in the jargon had severe anti-social personality disorder,[22] plans that were shelved not least because of the opposition of the NHS psychiatrists who would have been allocated a gate keeping role in that enterprise. A long standing jurisdiction to detain dangerous persons has existed under mental health legislation. The current legislation[23] allows, subject to a civil process, the indefinite detention of, among others, persons who are mentally disordered and if left at liberty might be threatening in the sense that they might harm others. Although treatment for the patient's condition must be available, the treatment need not aspire to anything more than seeking to achieve some form of calm and stability. The mentally disordered include those with learning disability.

[21] Considered by Dennis in ch 8 of this volume.

[22] *Managing Dangerous People with Severe Personality Disorder: Proposals for Policy Development* (London, Home Office, 1999).

[23] Mental Health Act 1983 (as amended).

John Stanton-Ife scrutinises the current legislation from the perspective of a question raised by Baroness Hale in her academic capacity:[24] 'have we created a crime of antisocial mental disorder?' Stanton-Ife's response to the question that the Baroness herself did not answer is ultimately negative. However, it is a close run thing. He notes the stigma that is associated with being 'sectioned' with a consequent loss of liberty that might be of long duration. He observes that the threat to others is merely one of 'harm' which includes psychological harm. Most disturbing of all perhaps is that among those detained will be persons who have sufficient understanding to be well aware of what is happening to them, what it entails, and who wish to remain at liberty. As Stanton-Ife observes, persons not considered mentally disordered, who may yet be far more dangerous than persons subject to detention under mental health act legislation, remain free in all aspects of their lives while those detained under the legislation must endure treatments they do not want and which are not necessarily in their own best interests. He accepts that some mentally disordered persons lack responsiveness to reason and that in their case compulsory detention may be a regrettable necessity. However, he insists that mental disorder of itself provides no reason for compulsory detention and that too few obstacles lie in the way of detaining persons who are capable of a measure of autonomy, notwithstanding a mental disorder.

In the course of his evaluation of the compulsory detention of mentally disordered persons, by way of comparison and contrast, Stanton-Ife subjects to scrutiny the antisocial behaviour order (ASBO) regime[25] and concludes that such orders make for 'a subversion of the criminal law'.[26] In coming to that verdict he joins a long running chorus of disapproval of the ASBO, a chorus that contains some very prominent voices.[27] Ian Dennis, in his careful appraisal of civil preventative orders, can be said to turn the volume down. While he endorses some of the criticisms, he advises a sense of perspective. Although civil preventative orders flourished and proliferated under the former Labour Government, in concept they are in no sense novel. As he points out, the jurisdiction to bind over for breach of the peace has for centuries subjected to sanction socially disruptive conduct which need not of itself fulfil the requirements of any criminal offence. This capacity to prevent rather than cure was eulogised by Blackstone[28] and those sentiments are echoed by Horder in this volume. Dennis notes that many ASBOS are issued post conviction as an adjunct to the sentence, and for other orders anti-social behaviour causing, 'harassment, alarm and distress' must be proved to the criminal standard. This does not negate the fact that breach of an order constitutes a serious criminal offence and may make criminal, by a two step process, conduct not otherwise criminal. Yet the preventative

[24] *Mental Health Law*, 5th edn (London, Sweet and Maxwell, 2010).
[25] Crime and Disorder Act 1998 s 1; Anti-Social Behaviour Act 2003.
[26] This volume at 145.
[27] For a recent critique see Simester and von Hirsch (n 10) ch 12.
[28] 4Bl Comm., chapter xviii, 251.

rationale backing these orders is powerful, and conduct that causes alarm, harassment and distress raises a red flag. Enactment of the currently tentative proposal to limit the consequences for breach of an ASBO to civil law sanctions[29] would do much to mollify all but the most intransigent critics of these orders.

The order most uncomfortably reminiscent of the techniques employed by authoritarian regimes is the control order.[30] The problem that these orders address is grave. There may be reliable intelligence that D has committed terrorist offences and/or is minded to commit such offences or offer material support to those that will do so. But D cannot be deported as he might be a UK subject or tortured in the country to which he is returned. To bring D to open trial may be seriously detrimental to general security by exposing valuable informants and other covert means of gathering intelligence. Consequently, D my find himself placed under virtual house arrest by the terms of a control order imposed after a hearing where the decisive evidence was of the closed variety, beyond effective challenge by D and his lawyers. Or at least that was the case. In *Secretary of State for the Home Department v AF (No 3)*,[31] the House of Lords ruled that before D was subjected to a control order he had to be given sufficient information to enable him to instruct his lawyers effectively. As Dennis explains, this infusion of due process into the control order regime threatens its very continuance. In cases where the open evidence establishes a reasonable suspicion of terrorist connections, closed hearings with accredited counsel are unnecessary. Where closed evidence is decisive, the hearings are likely to be found unfair.

Control orders were created and defended as essential to combating the terrorist threat. But as Dennis relates, the numbers of such orders are few: as of the end of 2010, eight orders were in force, all against UK subjects. The 48 orders that have been imposed since the inception of the regime in 2005 have led to a spate of litigation causing Dennis to ponder the financial cost of sustaining this regime. While it seems plausible that the regime has increased security by ending freedom of movement and communications of individuals suspected of terrorist connections, Dennis very reasonably surmises that there has been a countervailing loss of the intelligence which might have been acquired had the suspects been left at liberty but under close surveillance. Scepticism about the utility of ASBOS is also in order. The prime target for these orders were those aged between 10 and 17: 65 per cent of these child defendants breached the conditions of their orders, on average 4.2 times. Both control orders and ASBOS are under review.[32] It will be interesting to see if there is realistic reform grounded in the realities of what is achievable in security terms in a manner commensurate with constitutional values, or whether the other imperatives which have influenced criminal justice policy for over two decades will prevail.

[29] *More Effective Responses to Anti-Social Behaviour – A Consultation* (Home Office, 2011).

[30] Prevention of Terrorism Act 2005 s 3.

[31] *Secretary of State for the Home Department v AF (No 3)* (2009) UKHL 28; [2009] 3 ALL ER 643.

[32] *Review of Counter- Terrorism and Security Powers* (Cm8004, The Stationery Office (TSO), 2011). See n 29 above for proposals relating to ASBOS.

Security requires the incarceration of dangerous persons. Retributivism in all its versions requires the length of incarceration to be tethered to desert. An obvious tension arises between a concern with public safety and the strictures of retributivism when a dangerous person has paid his or her dues but remains in prison on account of the danger that the person poses or is taken to pose. As alluded to already, some form of retributivist posture is the critical stance of most Anglophone academic criminal lawyers and criminal law theorists. For them preventative detention of persons convicted of crimes is simply a moral mistake, something that should be castigated. Meanwhile, the world goes about its business. In England and Wales for example, any offender who has been convicted of a specified (but wide) range of violent and sexual offences and is judicially assessed to be likely to commit further specified offences of significant risk to members of the public will, depending on the offence he or she has committed and his or her previous convictions, receive a life sentence, or indefinite imprisonment for public protection or an extended sentence.[33] If we add those prisoners who have received the mandatory life sentences for murder,[34] we fully account for the thousands of prisoners serving time beyond their due.

Release may be a distant and uncertain prospect for many of these prisoners. For prisoners serving life terms or imprisonment for public protection, the sentencing judge will fix a minimum term assessed on retributivist grounds. After that term has expired, the prisoner can apply to the Parole Board for a release date. Essentially, the prisoner must prove he or she no longer constitutes a risk to particular persons or persons generally. Attendance at vocational and anger management courses is helpful to show a commitment to new ways but the availability of such courses is contingent. Any protestation of innocence will jeopardise the prospect of release. Besides all that, the Parole Board is very busy working through a backlog of cases.[35] In terms of orthodox penal theory, there is grave injustice here. Yet it is remarkable how little impact this system of indeterminate detention has made on the conscience of the general public. To be sure, in newspapers such as *The Guardian* and *The Independent* there has been plenty of discussion of expanding and overcrowded prisons and penal populism. However, even in those havens of liberal thought, there has been no defence of the proposition that given that a prisoner has served his or her retributivist term, the prisoner should thereupon be released even if there is reason to think he or she remains dangerous. This commonplace of classic retributivism has no hold on any significant segment of public opinion.

Peter Ramsey addresses the current lack of purchase of retributivism in the public sphere. The obvious point of opposition to retributivism is utilitarianism, but as Ramsey comments there is no sense that those who advocate and apply preventative detention do so with a sense that they are overriding deonto-

[33] Criminal justice Act 2003 pt 12 as amended by the Criminal Justice and Immigration Act 2008.

[34] Murder (Abolition of Death Penalty) Act 1965; Criminal Justice Act 2003 s 269 sch 21.

[35] In March 2011, the Parole Board published a business plan for the period 2011–15 which acknowledges the extent of the backlog.

logical restraints on punishment in the interests of a greater good. There is a sense that what is being done is appropriate not merely expedient. Ramsey notes the salience of the precautionary principle in modern governance and administration. Applied to penal contexts, it has led to an elevation of the interests of persons at risk of criminal harms over the proportionate punishment of wrongdoers. The application of precautionary principles to wrongdoers, with an inflationary effect on punishment, has been underpinned and fortified by extending the conception of wrongdoing to include not merely the harms done by D but any disposition on his part to occasion harm even to unidentified victims at some unspecified future time. Ramsey notes the withering away of any aspirations in penal practice to reform adult, serious offenders and re-integrate them back into mainstream society. Rather, if an offender is assessed as risky that sets the offender apart and obliges him or her to demonstrate as a condition for release that he or she is not risky. According to Ramsey, one influence on the public acceptance of indefinite detention has been the resurgence of religious beliefs which emphasise the fallen and corruptible nature of humankind. In penal contexts, this cashes out as a pre-occupation with the prevention of sin at the expense of redemption. Ramsey's chapter on imprisonment on the basis of adverse risk assessment seeks to explain rather than justify or condemn the practice. Of one thing he is sure, namely that no significant changes will be made to the practice by refighting the battles between retributivism and utilitarianism.

By contrast, Lucia Zedner powerfully asserts the continuing relevance of retributivist principles to the just operation of the penal system. For her, the incarceration of persons beyond the limits of just deserts contravenes any fair reading of the entailments of the presumption of innocence. A served term of imprisonment determined by retributivist principles clears the account. From that point the prisoner, like any other subject in good standing, is entitled to be presumed innocent. Continued incarceration of the prisoner is tantamount to punishment for some unproved wrong. That is her fundamental objection to indeterminate detention, but she also objects to the flawed practice of prevention. She is highly critical of the senior judiciary who have interpreted the relevant statutes in a manner which endorses the priority of any discernible risk of future harm to persons unknown over the freedom of the prisoner before them.[36] Because of these interpretations, the judges are aware that the risk that licences further imprisonment may be unfounded in fact even if present on some actuarial calculation to be found in the statute. As she puts it, judges have imposed on themselves the 'duty to get it wrong'[37] if such errors considered within the process overall can be said to advance general security. She draws a contrast between the willingness of the judges to endorse and fortify statutory presumptions of risk notwithstanding the injustice thereby caused, with the serious

[36] She is particularly critical of the judgment of Lord Bingham in *A and Others v Secretary of State for the Home Department* [2004] UKHL 56.

[37] Chapter 10 of this volume at 219.

reservations of prominent mental health professionals as to the methods and ethics of the risk assessment procedures found in recent legislation.

The contribution of Martin Wasik to the indeterminate detention debate is of particular interest, given that Wasik is not only a prominent criminal law/justice academic but also sits as a sentencing judge. His conclusion, following a meticulous examination of the legislation and its interpretation, has particular weight: 'the provisions were poorly drafted and over-inclusive, and have perpetrated great injustice'.[38] Although far from an enthusiast for the continuance of preventative provisions, Wasik recognises the political realities. He lays down the minimum conditions that must be satisfied if indeterminate sentences are to have a vestige of legitimacy. The current offence must very serious not merely of itself but when placed in the context of the nature and extent of the previous convictions of the prisoner. The penal regime under which such sentences are served must be designed to offer the prisoners the opportunity to demonstrate they no longer constitute a risk to the public and must be funded in a manner that gives practical effect to that aspiration.

So far we have looked at the pursuit of greater security by way of the processes of the criminal law, civil law preventative measures and imprisonment. However, sometimes effective crime prevention may require immediate and direct action on the part of state officials and even by private subjects. Jonathan Rogers offers a rethinking of the use of force in self defence and crime prevention. In the case of state officials he is particularly concerned with the excusatory weight the current law gives to D's subjective beliefs as to dangers confronted and with what he instinctively thought to be necessary to deal with the perceived dangers. Offering a careful examination of incidents which culminated in the use of fatal force employed by way of reaction to dangers apparent to D but unfounded by the facts, Rogers concludes that the current law is insufficiently concerned with why D erred in the way that he did. From his study of these fatal incidents, Rogers considers that the current law allows too much latitude to the use of force with a punitive motivation or with an attitude of indifference to the safety of others. As he believes that the presence of these attitudes should lead to a forfeiture of any defence, he argues that courts should be receptive to evidence that may reveal their presence, evidence which could include an extraordinary pattern of similar but unsubstantiated complaints against D. While the kind of evidence that could be adduced would need the most careful consideration, Rogers is clearly right to be uneasy about the current form and application of the current law of justifiable/excusable force, particularly the matter of the routine vindication of police officers whose conduct has been the subject of complaint. And, as he notes, his concerns carry over to private persons employed in the security industry and, one might add, those troublesome cases involving the use of fatal force to defend homes and possessions.

[38] Chapter 11 of this volume at 262.

Robert Sullivan's chapter engages with questions relating to the forceful treatment of innocent persons by state officials who believe such interventions to be necessary in order to prevent or mitigate large scale and imminent terrorist attacks. One class of innocents considered are persons who seem destined to die along with many other innocent persons should the terrorists carry out their attack but who also will be killed by the preventative measures state officials are minded to employ. In other words should the highjacked passenger plane be destroyed before it is flown into the densely populated skyscraper? An affirmative answer is given essentially on the grounds that numbers should matter even for deontologists when the prospects for the rescue of the persons killed were reasonably estimated as much bleaker than for the persons whose rescue is sought by means of the intervention. Indeed, where the prospects for rescue for one group seem set at zero, numbers may cease to matter if there are reasonable prospects for the rescue of the other group. Of course these conclusions will be hotly contested by those who believe that any deontologist worthy of the description must favour an unwavering proscription of the direct and intentional killing of innocent persons.

Consideration is also given to the forceful interrogation of various classes of persons who might have information or whose harsh treatment might release information which would prevent or mitigate a large scale and imminent terrorist attack. The absolute proscription of torture[39] on any members of these classes is defended. Particular issue is taken with theorists who maintain that even a deontologist can excuse or even justify torture *in extremis* in a manner compatible with core deontological commitments. These attempts to turn the flank of the absolute proscription are found wanting. Acknowledgment is made of the fearful prospect of terrorist attacks of a magnitude and impact far greater than anything achieved so far.[40] What measures should be considered legitimate in response to truly existential threats should be openly debated by politicians, officials and the public. While debate about 'ticking bomb' scenarios is a staple of academic papers and student seminars, there has been nothing approaching a serious debate about these unsettling matters in Parliament.

Returning to the beginning of this introduction, a depiction of a society based on liberal values with a limited, circumspect criminal law based on retributive principles was described as a travesty if it were offered as a true picture of the criminal law of England and Wales. Of course, many criminal trials will be for harms fully realised, harms which will be punished in a manner which reflects the gravity of D's conduct. But this is far from always the case. The conduct punished may have done no harm at all, if harm is conceived as implying a concrete event having a detrimental impact on to a legally protected interest. The punishment endured may far surpass any sanction based on a retributivist calculation. This challenges major suppositions of legitimate criminalisation.

[39] UN Convention on Torture 1984; Criminal Justice Act 1988 s 134.

[40] See n 4 above.

With disturbing frequency, particular trials culminating in long terms of imprisonment raise unresolved issues relating to harms, wrongs, culpability and punishment.[41] Although there is considerable criticism of this state of affairs, in academic settings these criticisms evoke little by way of positive response from the general public officials, legislators and the judiciary. This is likely to be the way it is unless some unforeseen and beneficent changes in the state of the world enhance our sense of security.

[41] One may note the recent sentence of 12 years imprisonment for incitement to murder imposed on one Bilal Zaheer Ahmad who posted a message on an Islamist extremist website urging Muslims to 'raise the knife of jihad' and kill MPs who voted in favour of the Iraq war.

1

Identification, Surveillance and Profiling: On the Use and Abuse of Citizen Data

MALCOLM THORBURN*

I INTRODUCTION

OVER THE LAST 30 years, the dominant response to crime in most Western countries has turned away from the rehabilitative ideal and toward an approach that David Garland has termed 'the culture of control'.[1] Under the old rehabilitative ideal, governments treated offenders as citizens toward whom we might feel some sympathy. It was assumed that offenders turned to crime because of some identifiable cause: perhaps as a result of general social concerns such as poor living conditions, economic inequality, racial discrimination or perhaps as a result of something more specific to the offender such as drug addiction or mental health problems. Under the old rehabilitative ideal, governments tried to identify the relevant problems and to ameliorate them; they would fight crime by eliminating what they took to be the causes of crime. However, the contemporary culture of control is considerably less ambitious. Governments no longer worry quite as much about the root causes of deviance; instead, they largely take for granted that some people will constitute persistent threats to the security of others.[2] Rather than seeking to ameliorate the conditions

* Thanks to the Social Sciences and Humanities Research Council of Canada for research support, to Noémi Paquette for valuable research assistance, to the participants in the workshop at University College London (and especially to the organisers, Ian Dennis and Bob Sullivan) and to Larissa Katz and David Lyon for helpful comments and advice on an earlier draft.

[1] David Garland, *The Culture of Control: Crime and Social Order in Contemporary Society* (Chicago, University of Chicago Press, 2001). Of course, I do not mean to suggest that the rehabilitative ideal has died altogether, nor do I mean to deny that some aspects of the 'culture of control' have roots that go back more than 10 or 20 years. Nevertheless, the shift in emphasis in crime control strategy across an array of jurisdictions over the past 10 or 20 years is remarkably consistent.

[2] A reason often cited for moving away from the rehabilitative ideal toward a 'culture of control' is the perceived rise in crime rates. Oddly, however, the culture of control seems to be coming to be at a time when most crime rates are either stable or on the decline. However, this is not new. Michel Foucault pointed out that the same phenomenon was present in eighteenth century France when the

of potential offenders, the principal crime-fighting strategy is to monitor potential offenders as closely as possible, to structure the environment in ways that make crime more difficult to carry out, and to put in place an array of pre-emptive measures to prevent *them* from threatening *our* security.

This volume is dedicated to the topics of 'seeking security' and 'pre-empting harm' – the hallmarks of the culture of control. Although this approach includes a wide array of practices, I concern myself in this chapter with only one small part of that story. I consider some of the ways in which Western governments now collect and use data about ordinary citizens as part of their larger effort to pre-empt the causing of criminal harms. In recent years, this topic (usually under the title 'surveillance studies') has been the object of more detailed discussions than almost any other in the criminological and broader sociological literature.[3] In much of that literature, however, the collection of citizen data is treated as a single, monolithic phenomenon.[4] However in this chapter, I argue that we ought to draw a fairly clear analytical distinction between three quite different ways in which governments collect and use citizen data as part of their crime control efforts: what I call (somewhat idiosyncratically)[5] *identification, surveillance* and *profiling. Identification* is a core state function, and involves regulating and guaranteeing the identity of individuals; *surveillance* is concerned with capturing specific information about our activities; and *profiling* is an attempt to give specific content to what particular persons or classes of persons are like – their preferences, their practices, their personal histories, etc – in order to anticipate future behaviour. Governments often try to elide the important distinctions between these three practices and to introduce elements of surveillance and profiling under the cover of an identification scheme. The recent effort to introduce national identification cards in the UK is one example of this phenomenon.[6] Although there is often substantial overlap between these three methods in practice, we can achieve significant analytical clarity in our

culture of discipline was on the rise: 'Alors que les historiens d'aujourd'hui constatent une diminution des grandes bandes des malfaiteurs . . . [l]a plupart des observateurs [contemporains] soutiennent que la délinquence augmente . . .' (*Surveiller et punir: naissance de la prison* (Paris, Gallimard, 1975) 92.

[3] See David Lyon, *Surveillance Studies: an Overview* (Cambridge, Polity Press, 2007) [Lyon, *Surveillance Studies*] for a good overview of the literature.

[4] For example, David Lyon, *Identifying Citizens: ID Cards as Surveillance* (Cambridge, Polity Press, 2009) [Lyon, *Identifying Citizens*], which is probably the leading book on the subject, treats them all as aspects of the single phenomenon of surveillance. That said, Lyon is careful to distinguish identification cards (which are largely the tools of identification *simpliciter*) and the database that governments usually try to attach to them (which are the tools of surveillance and profiling).

[5] The term 'surveillance' is often used in the sociological literature to refer to all three of these practices. It should be clear from the outset, then, that I am not using this term in the usual way.

[6] The UK National Identity Cards Act 2006 c 15 identified four purposes for establishing and maintaining the national identity register: (1) national security, (2) crime control, (3) immigration and illegal working controls and (4) the delivery of public services. I shall argue below that the control of fraud – with respect to illegal working, illegal immigration, benefits fraud and private fraud – might all be legitimate targets of an identification scheme. The loosely-defined 'crime control' and 'national security' purposes, however, suggest that a broad scheme of surveillance and profiling are also part of the national identity cards scheme.

discussions if we keep in mind that they are at least in principle distinct – so our acceptance or rejection of one need not necessarily require us to accept or reject the others.

According to many of the leading theories of the state, citizen *identification* is a crucial part of the state's basic function.[7] Just as the state must register property titles and guarantee the authenticity of currency and regulate markets simply in order to allow individuals to interact freely, so too must it regulate and guarantee the identity of individuals simply in order to make private interactions juridically possible.[8] According to this view of the state's role, our privacy is not directly engaged by the state's practice of identifying citizens. There is an important division of labour at work between the user (either the state or a private individual) who brings information about an individual as an input to the system and the identification scheme that merely allows the user to attribute that information to that individual across time and space. An identification scheme need not contain any specific information about individuals except a single identifying feature (such as a fingerprint, iris scan, etc) and his place of residence. For this reason, I argue that the creation of a national identification system, if it is designed *purely* for the purpose of ascertaining an individual's identity, should not be cause for alarm.

By contrast, when the state engages in surveillance or profiling, it is likely inter alia to invade our privacy in important ways, for they are both concerned with ascertaining and using specific information about individuals. *Surveillance* is concerned with capturing specific information about our activities with or (more usually) without our consent. States do this by actually watching us (through human agents or through cameras) or by monitoring the activities of our 'data doubles' through the mandatory disclosure of data about our banking, our use of government services, our internet use and the like.[9] As such, it can pose a significant threat to what in German constitutional jurisprudence is called our right to 'informational self-determination' – that is, our right to decide how we shall present ourselves to others. This is true even in situations where it seems that we have no privacy to lose, such as when we are walking down a public street. For even then, although we have chosen to

[7] It is the core of what is often referred to as the state's traditional regulatory power (referred to traditionally as the 'police power'). See Markus Dirk Dubber, *The Police Power: Patriarchy and the Foundations of American Government* (New York, Columbia University Press, 2005).

[8] For a fuller treatment of the Kantian argument for the connection between the state's regulatory powers and its role of securing the necessary conditions for individual freedom, see Arthur Ripstein, *Force and Freedom: Kant's Legal and Political Philosophy* (Cambridge, MA, Harvard University Press, 2009).

[9] There is an enormous literature on the ways in which governments are able to act much more easily toward their citizens by means of a system of identification documents. Rather than conferring benefits and imposing burdens on actual natural persons, these benefits and burdens can simply be added to the data profile of that person within a database associated with a certain identification card. One of the most powerful discussions of this form of governance is James C Scott, *Seeing like a State: How Certain Schemes to Improve the Human Condition have Failed* (New Haven, CT, Yale University Press, 1999).

make our actions public to a certain class of persons (viz, those who are present in the street with us), this still does not mean that we have chosen to disclose our activities to anyone who might look at surveillance footage of us walking by.

Finally, *profiling* is concerned not only with identifying the same person over time and with capturing specific information about that person; it goes further by trying to give specific content to what particular persons are like – their preferences, their practices, their personal histories, etc – in order to anticipate who poses a significant threat to the security of the state and of other citizens and therefore who should be subject to further monitoring and (where necessary) pre-emptive security measures. I shall argue that profiling not only threatens each person's right to 'informational self-determination', but it also threatens a cornerstone of our criminal justice system: the right to be presumed innocent.

Drawing on this initial tripartite distinction, I go on to distinguish two ideal types of citizen-state relations, (which I shall refer to as 'common law' and 'civil law').[10] These cultures take opposite positions on the legitimacy of each form of data collection discussed above. In the common law world, there is a long history of broad popular resistance to government identification card programmes. Canada and the US, for instance, have never undertaken national citizen identification programmes, and with the exception of the two world wars, the UK has never had a national citizen identification programme either. Although there was a detailed plan in place in the UK to create a national identification card, it has been abolished by the new Conservative-Liberal Democrat Coalition Government that came to power after the election of 6 May 2010. By contrast, in much of continental Europe, it is commonplace for citizens to be issued (and often, to carry) some sort of citizen identification document. However, when the topic changes from identification to surveillance and profiling, attitudes in the two legal regimes are turned on their heads. As David Lyon points out, '[t]he UK population, though wary of . . . national identification cards, seems in general to be content with the massive colonization of the streets by CCTV'.[11] The surveillance and profiling measures that are now quite common in Britain, the US and Canada – collecting and storing ANPR (Automatic Number Plate Recognition) camera data, communications data, sharing data about citizens across government departments and even between government and private

[10] The use of 'ideal types' is a common method of sociological analysis at least since the time of Max Weber. (Indeed, as HH Gerth and C Wright Mills point out, through the apparatus of ideal types, Weber 'merely intended to bring to full awareness what social scientists and historians had been doing when they used words like "the economic man, feudalism," etc'. From *Max Weber: Essays in Sociology* (London, Routledge, 1948) 59.) It provides a way of organising disparate sociological phenomena for analytical purposes. However, a crucial part of this analysis is our recognition that it is a treatment of ideal types only. Significant adjustment must be made to our analysis in order to make sense of the messy reality of the real world.

[11] Lyon, *Surveillance Studies* (n 3 above) 39.

industry[12] – are generally regarded with great suspicion and are often found to be unconstitutional in much of continental Europe.[13]

After setting out these two different cultures of state-citizen relations, I argue that there are good reasons to prefer many aspects of the civil law approach to their common law alternatives. First, well-designed national identification schemes can provide significant benefits (both to citizens in their private affairs and to government in the administration of benefits schemes and much else besides) without significantly affecting citizens' legitimate privacy interests. For example, the massive problems of illegal migrants in the US are almost unheard of in Germany, largely because of its clear and well-functioning national identification system.[14] Indeed, the United Nations Convention on the Rights of the Child asserts that everyone has the right to have his identity registered at birth.[15] Surveillance and profiling schemes, by contrast, often involve serious invasions of citizens' privacy interests and may also raise important concerns about equal treatment under the law, as well.

There is a second reason to prefer the civil law approach to the collection of citizen information by governments. That is, because the common law seems to focus on the question of whether individuals have a 'reasonable expectation of privacy' in a certain piece of information, it often treats the question of data privacy as an all-or-nothing affair. One either does or does not have a reasonable expectation of privacy. If one does, then it ought not to be available to the state; and if one does not, then the state may do with that information just as it would like. As a result, the common law approach is unable to make much sense of many of the most common threats to privacy that occur in the contemporary world. In many cases today, it makes little sense to talk about individuals having a 'reasonable expectation of privacy' *tout court* in any particular piece of information; instead, it makes more sense to try to define its legitimate audience carefully. For example, our medical information may be disclosed – but only to those who have legitimate medical reasons to obtain it; and our movements on the street may be observed – but only by those who happen to be in the area at

[12] Eg, the British Government has just announced a new plan to hire private credit agencies to track the spending habits of welfare recipients in Britain in order to track fraudsters: BBC Online,'Benefits Fraud: Cameron Defends use of Credit Rate Firms' (10 August 2010), available at www.bbc.co.uk/news/uk-10922261.

[13] In an important decision of the Hungarian constitutional court, for example, the Government's storage of personal information under a single identifier that allowed all information to be accessed together was found to violate each person's right of informational self-determination. Following this decision, the Hungarian Parliament then created separate identifiers for each type of personal information in Act No XX of 1996.

[14] Dita Vogel, 'Identifying Unauthorized Foreign Workers in the German Labour Market' in Jane Caplan and John C Torpey (eds), *Documenting Individual Identity: The Development of State Practices in the Modern World* (Princeton, Princeton University Press, 2001). Of course, this is not to deny that there are very significant problems in the way that *Gastarbeiter* (guest workers) in Germany are treated.

[15] United Nations Convention on the Rights of the Child art 7(1): 'The child shall be registered immediately after birth and shall have the right from birth to a name, the right to acquire a nationality and as far as possible, the right to know and be cared for by his or her parents.'

the time. The problem in all these cases and many more is not disclosure as such, but disclosure to the wrong audience. The civil law approach to data privacy, which focuses more squarely on the management of personal information (especially the collation of data and the reasons and the specific audience for its disclosure) rather than on its non-disclosure *tout court*, offers an attractive alternative to the all-or-nothing common law approach.[16]

II POPULATION DATA VERSUS PERSONAL DATA

States have been collecting information about their populations for as long as there have been states.[17] However, if we are to make any progress in setting out a normative framework to help us to distinguish legitimate from illegitimate data collection schemes, we will need to set out some normatively significant differences among them. As a first cut, we may distinguish programmes that collect data about *populations* and programmes that collect data about *individuals*. Most modern countries conduct a national census from time to time to collect data that is essential to a variety of government functions. In early American history, for instance, the census was used primarily to re-draw electoral boundaries. The first census in modern Britain was conducted in 1801 in order to ascertain the country's readiness for war against Napoleon – the size of both its wealth and of its citizenry who might serve in the armed forces. Today, governments use census data to assist them in making policy in a wide range of areas, from questions of economic development to the targeting of resources to disadvantaged groups to the anticipation of demographic shifts that could affect the size and makeup of the labour pool and demand for government benefits. However, such data about populations is almost always taken anonymously because it is interesting only as data about a *population* as a whole.[18] It is of no particular significance to the census-taker that it is this or that person who will soon be retiring and needing pension benefits – only the fact that there will be a certain number of such people in a certain location and that they will therefore make economic demands on the government of a certain size. For this reason, the privacy concerns at stake in *population* studies such as a national census are radically different from the collection of data about *individuals*.[19] Further, such

[16] This point is developed most fully by Helen Nissenbaum, *Privacy in Context* (Stanford 2010).

[17] Indeed, the practices of data collection – along with the collection of taxes and the formation and funding of armies – have often been key parts of the process of state formation. See, for example, Michael J Braddick, *State-Formation in Early Modern England c. 1550–1700* (Cambridge, Cambridge University Press, 2000).

[18] Indeed, in their famous decision of 1983, the *Bundesverfassungsgericht* (German Federal Constitutional Court) held the German census law to be unconstitutional partly on the grounds that it failed adequately to distinguish between the collection of anonymous census data and personal data about identifiable individuals.

[19] Notwithstanding this important difference, governments in the US and, most recently, Canada have argued that the collection of population data by the state is an invasion of privacy. See Brenda Bouw and Steven Chase, 'Canada's Stat Crunchers Join Census Fight' *Globe and Mail* (2 August

data are interesting to crime control in quite a different way from individual-specific data. They tell us only about the best use of police resources; they do not tell us anything about whom, specifically, to investigate.[20]

We may set aside for the purposes of this chapter the collection of information about populations; our concern is with the collection of data about identifiable individuals. However, even within this category, there are a variety of different sorts of data-collection regimes. I shall turn to them now.

III IDENTIFICATION

One of the central theses of this chapter is that programmes of identification are importantly different from surveillance and profiling. In order to see how, we must remind ourselves of how basic the problem of identification is to the establishment of a functioning legal system. In pre-modern societies, problems of identity arose only sporadically. In traditional societies where the set of people with whom we interacted was small and stable, we could usually rely on direct personal experience to tell us who was who, who lived where, and who owned what. Of course, there were problems at the margins with itinerant populations (who were often the targets of special rules about identity)[21] and special problems of identity sometimes arose when individuals went off to war (such as those raised in the book and film *The Return of Martin Guerre*),[22] but pre-modern conditions did not give rise to what Michael Ignatieff calls a 'society of strangers'.[23] However with modernisation came the mass migrations of populations within a jurisdiction (through urbanisation, industrialisation, etc) and consequently the broadening of the class of persons with whom each person might interact.[24] In place of direct knowledge and trust (or, where appropriate,

2010), available at www.theglobeandmail.com/news/politics/canadas-stat-crunchers-join-census-fight/article1659883/?cmpid=nl-news1.

[20] Of course, census data collection can, and frequently has been, hijacked for political ends. See, for example, Anat Leibler and Daniel Breslau, 'The Uncounted: Citizenship and Exclusion in the Israeli Census of 1948' (2005) 28 *Ethnic and Racial Studies* 880.

[21] There were a number of rules attached to itinerant populations such as traders, actors, pilgrims and others in late Medieval Europe. See Valentin Groebner, 'Describing the Person, Reading the Signs in Late Medieval and Renaissance Europe: Identity Papers, Vested Figures, and the Limits of Identification, 1400–1600' in Jane Caplan and John Torpey (eds), *Documenting Individual Identity: The Development of State Practices in the Modern World* (Princeton, Princeton University Press, 2001) [Groebner, *Describing the Person*].

[22] Nathalie Zemon Davis, *The Return of Martin Guerre* (Cambridge, Harvard University Press, 1983).

[23] Michael Ignatieff, 'State, Civil Society and Total Institutions: A Critique of Recent Social Histories of Punishment' in Stanley Cohen and Andrew Scull (eds), *Social Control of the State: Historical and Comparative Essays* (Oxford, Martin Robertson, 1983).

[24] I do not mean to suggest that there was a clear break between 'pre-modern' societies that were entirely stable and 'modern' ones that are highly mobile. Indeed, because rural communities in France at the time of the Revolution were still quite stable, they saw little need for the new programmes of identification initiated in Paris. As a result, they were very reluctant to incur the significant expense of implementing them. See Gérard Noirel, 'L'identification des citoyens. Naissance de l'état civil républicain' (1993) 13 *Genèses, sciences sociales et histoire* 3.

distrust) of each person, there arose a need for 'tokens of trust' – mechanisms that would allow strangers to interact without incurring the significant cost of investigating one another's identity.

However, what exactly do we need to know in order to be certain of the identity of the people with whom we are dealing? First, it should be clear that we are not interested in their identity in the thick sense that might include their religious, ethnic and national affiliations, their sexual orientation and other markers of their deepest commitments.[25] We are concerned, instead, with the much thinner notion of identity that can apply as much to inanimate objects of property as it can to persons.[26] The thin notion of identity that concerns us is what David Lyon refers to (rather chillingly) as a 'body badge'[27] – a marker of some kind that allows us to do the following three things: (a) to distinguish individuals from one another; (b) to identify the same individual over time; and (c) to locate individuals when necessary. If we are engaged in a commercial transaction, for example, we need to be able to find the other party to the agreement should anything go wrong. However, it is not only for commercial purposes that the identity of others is important. We also need to have some way to identify and to locate individuals who have committed criminal wrongs. It is also important to be able to identify individuals who have legal commitments elsewhere to children, to spouses, etc which they might have shirked.[28] Indeed, for the proper functioning of almost every area of law, it is crucial that we be able to keep track of who is who and who is where. It is important to be clear, however, that a system of identification need not contain anything more than the barest information about each person. As David Lyon's expression 'body badges' is meant to suggest, the idea of identification is, at its root, simply a mechanism for branding human bodies so that we can track them over time and space. To apply a badge to a body does not require us to know anything about the bearer's propensities, preferences, personal history, etc. (But of course, as we shall see, governments have found it almost impossible to resist the temptation of connecting a system of 'body badges' to an ever-increasing set of data about each person – and these collections of data represent significant threats to our personal privacy.)

[25] This sense of 'identity' is often associated with the writings of GWF Hegel. See Charles Taylor, *Sources of the Self: The Making of the Modern Identity* (Cambridge, Harvard University Press, 1992).

[26] In this way, then, this thin, legal conception of identity does not fully track our deeper metaphysical concerns about personal identity. A seminal treatment of the metaphysical issues of personal identity is Derek Parfit's *Reasons and Persons* (Oxford, Oxford University Press, 1986). The law has other mechanisms for dealing with these deeper issues, such as the law of mental disorder in criminal law or the statutes of limitations more generally.

[27] Lyon, *Identifying Citizens* (n 4 above) 110ff.

[28] Indeed, the concern over bigamy was the dominant theme in post-war efforts to maintain a national identification scheme in the UK. See Jon Agar, 'Modern Horrors: British Identity and Identity Cards' in Jane Caplan and John C Torpey (eds), *Documenting Individual Identity: The Development of State Practices in the Modern World* (Princeton, Princeton University Press, 2001).

There are a number of different possible ways to solve these problems of identity. Quite early on, we can see a divergence between common law practices in Britain and the more statist approach adopted in much of continental Europe. The traditional common law approach to questions of identity – as with so much else – is for the state to do very little, allowing individuals to solve these problems for themselves informally; the common law's role is simply to give formal recognition to the informal realities on the ground. One can think of the common law approach to identity by way of analogy to its approach to the registration of ownership of land. Rather than setting out a government-run registry of titles that is legally dispositive of who owns what, the traditional common law approach is simply to give legal recognition to the strongest claim among a set of informal claims to a particular parcel of land.[29] The relativity of title in land law finds its parallel in the doctrine of 'repute' in the traditional common law approach to personal identity. The Government in England did little to regulate naming practices even into the nineteenth century. The state did not regulate the names that parents could give their children, the conferral of family names through the generations, or how a person might change his name over the course of his life.[30] Instead, it allowed people to present themselves to others as they saw fit and it relied on private parties to do their own work both to determine whether or not to trust those with whom they had dealings and also to track down their debtors through what might be a long series of name changes and other changes in identity. A person's identity for the purposes of the common law was established by repute: whatever he was generally taken to be by others in the community. This situation led Jeremy Bentham to complain: 'It is to be regretted that the proper names of individuals are on so irregular a footing [that they] only imperfectly accomplish their object in a great nation.' There was no way for strangers in Britain to be sure of the identity of the people with whom they were dealing. As a result, suspicion could fall on innocent people who happened to have the wrong name[31] and the guilty could escape the law by assuming a new name. To remedy this situation, he proposed that the entire population be tattooed on the forearm with name, date and place of birth. Bentham argued that such a programme 'would be a new spring for morality, a new source of power for the laws, an almost infallible precaution against a multitude of offences'.[32]

[29] A classic case of the relativity of title under the common law is *Armory v Delamirie* (1722) 1 Strange 505.

[30] Jane Caplan (n 14 above) cites an English judicial pronouncement from 1890 to this effect: 'there is no law to prevent a man assuming any name he likes.'

[31] The list of those who were put on US 'no-fly' lists, detained and questioned on grounds of mistaken identity include the late US senator Edward Kennedy and Catherine Stevens, the wife of the late US senator Ted Stevens (in the latter case, this was apparently because she was mistaken for the singer and Islamic activist Cat Stevens).

[32] Jeremy Bentham, 'Principles of Penal Law' in John Bowring (ed), *The Works of Jeremy Bentham* (Edinburgh, Tait, 1838) vol 1 pt 2, 557.

As is typical of Bentham's approach to so many issues, he cut to the conceptual root of the problem, but in a way that seemed to make his proposed solution as unattractive as possible. As his suggestion of a system of universal tattooing makes vividly clear, the core idea in a system of identification is simply that we need some way to ensure that the person we are dealing with today is the same as the person we dealt with yesterday (and distinct from others with whom he might be confused) – a problem that can be nicely solved (as it is with cattle) with a physical branding on the body itself. As is also typical of Bentham, however, his solution to the problem of identification was so obviously distasteful that it made the whole idea of a universal programme of identification seem almost revolting. Of course, there are also other methods of identification available to us – ones that many civil law legal systems (and, eventually, even the common law world) adopted. Rather than 'writing on' human bodies in order to identify them, these systems 'read off' our bodies – our physical description, our faces, our fingerprints, our irises, etc.

By contrast with the highly informal arrangements that obtained in common law countries, the state in many European countries – most notably France and Germany – took an active role in establishing and guaranteeing the identity of citizens to one another, just as it took an active role in registering and enforcing property claims. The basic idea in both areas of the civil law is the same: rather than having individuals sort out questions of identity or title among themselves informally, the state can set out a single, authoritative mechanism by which such questions are to be answered. Also, in order to ensure that the state's answer is in fact authoritative, it must use the coercive power of the state to require everyone to abide by its answers. Quite early in the history of the French Revolution, for example, the French state enacted laws forbidding citizens to change their names from the ones they were given at birth.[33] Further, the state also regulated the choice of name that parents might bestow upon their children (forenames were limited to calendrical and historical names) and required all public documents to refer to individuals by their full registered name only. In some states of Germany (such as Saxony), the authorities also required that no child should be given the same name as any other living person in the jurisdiction. However, it is not enough for the state simply to keep tidy records; it must ensure that the records it keeps actually govern the interactions of citizens. One way to ensure that people actually use the names recognised by the state is Bentham's radical programme of mass tattooing. No continental writers seem to have endorsed Bentham's suggestion, but the German philosopher JG Fichte famously suggested that it would be necessary for each citizen to carry an identification card with a description or picture of the bearer. He wrote:

[33] This was enacted in the law of 6 Fructidor, An II (23 August 1794) – a law that remained in place until 1993! See Jane Caplan, 'Protocols of Identification,' in Jane Caplan and John C Torpey (eds), *Documenting Individual Identity* (n 14 above).

> The principal maxim of every well-constituted police power must be the following: *every citizen must be readily identifiable, wherever necessary, as this or that particular person*. Police officers must be able to establish the identity of every citizen, which can only be accomplished as follows. Everyone must always carry an identity card with him, issued by the nearest authority and containing a precise description of his person; this applies to everyone, regardless of class or rank. Since merely verbal descriptions of a person always remain ambiguous, it might be good if important persons (who therefore can afford it as well) were to carry accurate portraits in their identity cards, rather than descriptions. [. . .] But . . . police officers must be prohibited – on pain of punishment – from demanding to see identity cards out of mere whim or curiosity, but may do so only when it is necessary to verify a person's identity . . .[34]

It is noteworthy that in Fichte's ideal police state, it is important for the police to be able to identify citizens 'as this or that particular person', but he makes no mention of storing data about each citizen's past conduct, preferences, membership in organisations, etc in order to allow the police to create citizen profiles. It should be clear that these two issues – identification and profiling – may be kept quite distinct. A scheme for introducing national identification cards (the basic tool of most identification schemes) may in principle be distinguished from a scheme for attaching massive databases of personal information to those cards (the basic tool of surveillance and profiling).

Now, once we have a single, authoritative determinant of identity, it is important that such a system not be liable to fraud. Indeed, as we have seen with many of the criticisms of the proposed (and now defunct) national identification scheme for the UK, one of the great challenges in creating an identification scheme is to ensure that the cure for identity fraud is no worse than the disease. For although it might be fairly easy to pose as someone else when there are no working systems of identification in place, it might be even easier to do so if one is able to steal another's proof of identity. The physical description of individuals proposed by Fichte is clearly liable to this sort of problem, as are (to a lesser extent) photographs of the bearer. A puzzle that has plagued almost every modern system of identification is how to guarantee that there is a one-to-one relationship of identity card to card-holder. A common nineteenth century method was *Bertillonage*, named after its inventor Alphonse Bertillon. This was a system of measurements of the body that could serve to identify an individual quite accurately. Although Bertillon's system is rarely, if ever, used today, we can see vestiges of it in the narrative description of a person's physical appearance in many forms of identification (hair: brown; eyes: blue; etc). Bertillon's ideas were replaced in many areas with fingerprinting. In many countries, governments have been reluctant to use fingerprinting technology because of its historical association with crime control (thereby suggesting that all citizens are

[34] Johann Gottlieb Fichte, *Foundations of Natural Rights According to the Principles of the Wissenschaftslehre*, Frederick Neuhouser (ed) and Michael Baur (tr) (Cambridge, Cambridge University Press, 2000) 295–96.

criminal suspects).[35] Today, however, technological advances have opened up an array of new methods by which we may identify citizens: in addition to electronic forms of the traditional photographs and fingerprints, they also include encrypted passwords, iris scans, DNA registers and even full body scans. In many of the new biometric identification systems now being contemplated, a number of such identification methods are now being included.[36]

Keeping in mind the purposes that a system of identification must serve, however, we should remind ourselves that a one-to-one correspondence of card to card-holder is still not sufficient to make the system function properly. We also need some way of locating individuals in order to hold them to their legal responsibilities. Once again, this is a characteristically modern problem. In pre-modern times, most people lived and died in the same place where they were born, so it was not difficult to locate those with whom we had dealings. Indeed, there were often complex systems of identification cards in place only for those classes of persons who were 'of no fixed address', such as beggars, actors, Roma (or 'Gypsies', as they were then called), pilgrims, and so on.[37] Thus, in Medieval France, everyone other than the nobility was required to show identification when he was outside his home county.[38] Nowadays, however, it is commonplace for people to move from one place to another within a country and, increasingly, from country to country. Traditionally, the common law offered no solution to this problem; in recent years, however, the Government of the United Kingdom has begun to use a variety of mechanisms to track the location of individuals: CCTV and automatic number plate recognition (ANPR) cameras, as well as the collection of flight records. For many years, of course, UK nationals have needed a valid passport containing name and place of birth in order to leave and re-enter the UK. The traditional civil law solution to that problem, by contrast, is fairly straightforward: as part of each person's identification card, the bearer's address must also be recorded by the state.

The federal law on citizen registers in Germany (the *Melderechtsrahmengesetz*)[39] is a good example of a contemporary effort to provide a complete record of all citizens, their names and addresses. It is also a good illustration of the fact that, although in principle distinct, governments rarely keep identification programmes and profiling programmes entirely separate in practice. Under that law, the governments of the various German *Länder* (states) are required to maintain public registers of citizens which record each person's full legal name, date and

[35] In Germany, for example, the state decided to use photographic identification cards instead of fingerprints because of the association of fingerprinting with criminal suspicion. See Andreas Donatsch, 'Identifizierung von Tatverdächtigen' cited in Marita Häuser, 'Your Passport Please! An Overview of the History of ID Documents' in *The Future of Identity in the Information Society* (FIDIS) *D13.3: Study on ID number policies*, 2007.

[36] In a sense, then, Bertillonage has been revived. See Pierre Piazza's website www.projetbertillon.com/.

[37] Groebner, *Describing the Person* (n 21 above).

[38] ibid.

[39] The *Melderechtsrahmengesetz*, available at www.gesetze-im-internet.de/mrrg/index.html.

place of birth, citizenship and address. In addition to this, however, these public registers also include information on each person's religious affiliation, family status, employment status, doctoral degree (!) and a number of other items.[40] The register thus provides a determinative statement of each person's legal identity: her name and address. In addition to these crucial features, however, the registers also include a number of features that are not essential to the task of identifying individuals as this or that person, but are important only for giving a more detailed picture of that person's affiliations and commitments. As such, they straddle the line between pure identification and a form of profiling.

A more familiar and much more extreme version of the same problem is at work in the now-defunct UK National Identity Cards Act 2006. Although it was billed as a scheme of identity cards, designed to detect fraud in illegal employment, collection of government benefits and the like, there was a great deal more at work in the scheme than that. In addition to these purposes, the Act was explicitly designed to address the amorphous concerns of 'national security' and 'crime control'. The most important parts of the scheme were not the cards themselves, but the massive National Identity Register that was to include thousands of pieces of personal information about each resident of the UK in a single database, accessible across a wide range of government departments.[41] The National Identity Cards Act was about surveillance and profiling first and foremost.

IV SURVEILLANCE

Nowadays, governments are interested in doing more than simply identifying citizens. More and more, they are interested in accumulating as much data about their citizens as they can by means of one sort of 'surveillance' technique or another.[42] To some extent, this can be explained as a predictable instinct by all bureaucracies to accumulate data quite irrespective of any use they might be able to make of it.[43] However, there are also a number of uses to which such surveillance data are often put. First is the deterrent value that the collection of data is sometimes thought to have upon prospective offenders.[44] The mere

[40] See *Melderechtsrahmengesetz* § 2.

[41] Thus, the central feature of the now-defunct identification scheme in the UK was to be a database of personal information on each citizen. It is this collection and sharing of personal data, rather than the existence of identification cards as such that is rightly the object of most of the criticism of the scheme.

[42] The term 'surveillance' has become a term of art. It does not refer only to the direct observation of our behaviour by state officials or even our observation by video cameras and the like. Increasingly, it is concerned with the observation of what are sometimes called our 'data doubles' by other means. Thus, requirements on banks to inform officials of transfers over a certain amount constitute a form of surveillance simply because they convey crucial information about our conduct to the state for the purpose of monitoring. See Lyon, *Surveillance Studies* (n 3 above).

[43] Gary T Marx, in particular, has analysed the way in which police forces tend to accumulate citizen data without any apparent purpose in mind.

[44] The empirical support for this assumption, however, is not altogether clear. See Lyon, *Surveillance Studies* (n 3 above).

presence of data-collection mechanisms such as CCTV cameras, for example, is often thought to deter those who might engage in 'crimes of opportunity'. The installation of CCTV cameras, then, might be thought of as part of a larger strategy of 'situational crime control' – along with burglar alarms, security guards, secure locks, and the like.

A second motivation for the increased monitoring of everyday life is its (real or imagined)[45] usefulness ex post facto in helping to identify perpetrators of past crimes. The surveillance video of the abduction of James Bulger, for example, is often raised as an example of the usefulness of video evidence of crime as a forensic tool. At present, CCTV cameras mostly produce hours of unwatched footage. If such cameras were matched with reliable facial recognition technology, however, they would produce immensely more useful data. However, that is not yet the case. It is certainly clear, however, that some sorts of surveillance measures – such as the use of ANPR cameras to identify drivers who run red lights or drive in excess of the speed limit – are already highly effective tools for the limited class of offences that they are designed to address.[46] Another form of surveillance for crime detection has arisen largely in response to new technologies. Whereas in earlier times, a police constable walking the streets might have been able to observe most forms of suspicious activity taking place, this is clearly no longer true. The proliferation of electronic means of communication – telephones, of course, but also email, text messaging, internet chat rooms and much more – have made it possible for potential offenders to conspire together and to develop and even carry out their criminal plans without leaving their homes. For police officials to become aware of some criminal activities at all, it is essential that they be able to monitor some sorts of private communications in order to ensure that they are not being used for the perpetration of criminal offences. Telecommunications data is now collected within the European Union;[47] so is information about bank transfers and some other financial and business dealings.

Third, some forms of surveillance are defended on the grounds that they allow police to identify those who are already suspects for earlier offences. For example, governments across the West have argued that they need access to passenger flight data from airlines in order to help them to identify and to

[45] Once again, the forensic usefulness of such video footage is often overstated. See Lyon, ibid. See also the analysis by Liberty, which suggests that even though it might help to being some prosecutions, there is little evidence to suggest that it reduces crime rates overall: www.privacyinternational.org/article.shtml?cmd[347]=x-347-61925&als[theme]=Video%20Surveillance&headline=CCTV%20Frequently%20Asked%20Questions#3.

[46] Although some initial tests of ANPR cameras in the UK suggested an alarmingly high rate of false positives, this rate has been reduced dramatically with subsequent upgrades and refinements.

[47] Directive 2006/24/EC of the European Parliament and of the Council of 15 March 2006 on the retention of data generated or processed in connection with the provision of publicly available electronic communications services or of public communications networks and amending Directive 2002/58/EC. But see the decision of the German Constitutional Court holding the German law enacting this directive to be unconstitutional: BVerfG, 1 BvR 256/08 vom 2.3.2010, Absatz-Nr. (1 - 345).

apprehend suspects who might be fleeing the jurisdiction or who might attempt to engage in criminal activities (such as hijackings) on board aircraft.[48]

What are we to make of all these burgeoning surveillance technologies? One of the most illuminating sources of normative guidance in these matters over the past 30 years has been the *Bundesverfassungsgericht* (German Federal Constitutional Court). In their sweeping decision of 1983, in which they struck down the federal census law, they set out the framework for a new and quite compelling way to understand the privacy rights of citizens, based on the concept of 'informational self-determination'.[49] In a trilogy of recent decisions concerning online searching of computers, ANPR systems and telecommunications data retention, the Constitutional Court applied these principles of 'informational self-determination' to the context of present-day concerns.[50]

The German Constitutional Court's decision in the census case emphasised the influential sociological systems theory of Niklas Luhmann.[51] Fundamental rights, according to Luhmann, serve to differentiate society into different sub-systems. Privacy rules serve to ensure that sensitive information from one context does not migrate to others. That is, privacy law is not concerned with protecting some special stock of information (or decision-making power) that is 'private' in some absolute sense from exposure or regulation. Rather, it is a relational notion that prevents information from flowing across boundaries in whatever direction. For example, privacy on this view is no less concerned with the flow of information from the work context to the home context than vice-versa. Human rights generally, but the right to privacy especially, are concerned with preserving the distinction between different sub-systems in society. Our right to privacy, according to Luhmann, allows us to maintain those separate identities and, thus, to live the complex and segmented life that modernity promises us.[52]

[48] In Canada, (as in most countries), the Government has actually requested much broader powers with respect to passenger flight data, using it to identify any potential criminal suspect, and not only those who are considered to be dangerous to their fellow airline passengers.

[49] A helpful English-language discussion of this decision may be found in Gerrit Hornung and Christoph Schnabel, 'Data Protection in Germany I: The Population Census Decision and the Right to Informational Self-Determination' (2009) 25 *Computer Law & Security Report* 84.

[50] A helpful English-language discussion of these decisions may be found in Gerrit Hornung and Christoph Schnabel, 'Data Protection in Germany II: Recent Decisions on Online-Searching of Computers, Automatic Number Plate Recognition and Data Retention'(2009) 25 *Computer Law & Security Report* 115 .

[51] Niklas Luhmann, 'Theoretische und praktische Probleme der anwendungsbezogenen Sozialwissenschaften: Zur Einfuhrung' in Wissenschaftszentrum zu Berlin (ed), *Interaktion von Wissenschaft und Politik. Theoretische und praktische Probleme der anwendungsorientierten Sozialwissenschaften* (Frankfurt, Campus, 1977).

[52] Although the German Court used the language of Luhmann's systems theory, we could rephrase the Court's concern in Michael Oakeshott's language of modes of relation, each of which takes a persona (rather than a natural person) as its object. The point is that privacy is concerned with protecting our right to keep different spheres of our life separate from one another. See Michael Oakeshott, 'The Rule of Law' in *On History and Other Essays* (Liberty Fund). Although Oakeshott makes good sense of this idea of privacy and its centrality to the rule of law, this idea does not seem to have been picked up in the English-language case law.

In order to put the German decisions in context, it is important to see the common law tradition against which they can be seen to be working. The contrast between the German and the common law tradition of privacy is set out most clearly by James Q Whitman in 'The Two Western Traditions of Privacy: Dignity vs. Liberty'.[53] In that article, Whitman is concerned with the law of privacy more generally, and not only with the protection of personal information from the state. But in so doing, his treatment provides a clear insight into the governmental treatment of personal information in both traditions. He argues that the principal difference between the traditions is their focus on dignity *vs* liberty. Americans, when they think of privacy, think of the protection of private spaces (where, in American constitutional jargon, we have a 'reasonable expectation of privacy') from search, and the protection of certain intimate decisions (our choice of sexual partner, whether or not to have an abortion, to name our children as we like, etc) from government interference, and our liberty to tell the government as little about ourselves as we like (not having to register our place of residence with the state, or indeed, to carry any form of personal identification). Civilians, by contrast, think of privacy in terms of the protection of our dignity primarily by what the German Constitutional Court calls the right to 'informational self-determination'. That is, we have the right (subject to justifiable infringement[54]) to oversee and control which and what kind of information is openly accessible. Whitman suggests that the German dignity tradition arises not from a reaction to the destruction of any meaningful conception of privacy under the Nazis, but with an older tradition of aristocratic dignity (which was legally protected in the common law world, too)[55] that has since been expanded in Germany to cover all citizens.

If we take the Anglo-American approach to privacy seriously, we tend to fetishise certain decisions and certain forms of information and exclude others. Just as the American and Canadian Supreme Courts have done, we might tend to believe that there are certain places that are entitled to almost total protection from invasion by the state – paradigmatically, the home – but almost all other places are due no respect whatsoever. Thus, we might be led to the conclusion drawn by the US Supreme Court that our conduct 'in public' (such as on a public street) is due no privacy protection whatsoever. For this reason, the US Constitution's protection against unreasonable search and seizure affords no protection to citizens against CCTV monitoring – even if it amounted to total surveillance of their every move while outside the home. That is, as a number of American observers have remarked, the Anglo-American approach to privacy and surveillance seems to lead to a *reductio ad absurdum*.[56]

[53] James Q Whitman, 'The Two Western Traditions of Privacy: Dignity vs. Liberty' (2004) 113 *Yale Law Journal* 1130.

[54] Like almost all rights under the German Basic Law (*Grundgesestz*), the right to informational self-determination is subject to justified infringement.

[55] For example, the laws protecting 'great persons of the realm' against slander.

[56] Chris Slobogin, 'Public Privacy: Surveillance of Public Places and the Right to Anonymity' (2002) 72 *Mississippi Law Journal* 213, 233. He writes: 'Meaningful legal strictures on government

V PROFILING

The focus of my concern in this section is the collection of information about citizens in order to create citizen profiles – slotting citizens into what Gary T Marx calls 'categories of suspicion'[57] – for the sake of predicting their future conduct. In order to create these categories of suspicion, it is not enough simply to collect data about citizen behaviour through surveillance. It is also necessary to collate large quantities of data and subject them to meta-analysis in order to find suspicious patterns of behaviour. Under the UK Anti-terrorism, Crime and Security Act and the American USA Patriot Act, government agencies are now much freer to share information about individuals than they once were.[58] Police use such apparently benign information about individuals (and sometimes even about their relatives)[59] such as the telephone numbers we call on a regular basis; the internet sites we visit; the email addresses from which we receive and to which we send emails; the size and nature of banking transactions; and our use of various government services. The UK also has in place a large and expanding DNA database (which already contains over two million samples) and there are plans afoot in the UK to use the nationwide system of ANPR cameras to track driving patterns in order to create an even more complete profile of almost every resident of the UK.[60] Finally, in the UK especially, the Government has contemplated giving access to law enforcement agencies to information about a citizen's use of a broad array of government services: health services, welfare benefits, immigration status, and the like. Once all these data are available to police, they must then sort through them using 'data mining' techniques in order to detect suspicious patterns.

use of public surveillance cameras in Great Britain, Canada and the United States are non-existent.' He also points out that although a number of courts have suggested that particularly intrusive public surveillance might offend the fourth amendment, none has actually held this in their reasons (236). See also Elia Zureik et al, *Surveillance, Privacy and the Globalization of Personal Data* (Montreal, McGill-Queen's Press, 2010).

[57] Gary T Marx, *Undercover: Police Surveillance in America* (Berkeley, University of California Press, 1988).

[58] For example, in the UK, s 36 of the Immigration and Asylum Act 1999 formerly required officials to destroy any fingerprints collected during the course of an investigation once that case had been resolved. Section 36 of the Anti-terrorism, Crime and Security Act has now removed this requirement.

[59] One of the more controversial policing methods to come about recently is 'family DNA searching'. There, police officers compare DNA found at a crime scene with the DNA it has on file. They are not looking for an exact match. Rather, they are simply looking for a close enough match that they can then identify the suspect as a close family member of the person whose DNA was identified by the test. This method is now fairly common in the UK. It is still highly controversial in the US. However, it was used in the recent high-profile case of the serial killer referred to as the 'Grim Sleeper'. See Natasha Singer, 'In Fighting Crime, How Wide Should a Genetic Net Reach?' *The New York Times* (24 July 2010), available at www.nytimes.com/2010/07/25/business/25stream.html?src=busln.

[60] For more details on the expansion of these programmes and the dismantling of barriers between organisations, see Benjamin J Goold, 'Privacy, Identity and Security' in Benjamin J Goold and Liora Lazarus (eds), *Security and Human Rights* (Oxford, Hart Publishing, 2007).

Profiling schemes give rise to the most serious normative challenges of all. For not only do such schemes involve the collection of masses of data, much of it without the consent of the person under surveillance, they also involve a further concern that touches on one of the central issues in Anglo-American criminal law: the presumption of innocence. Although the creation of 'categories of suspicion' does not in itself defeat the presumption of innocence as we understand it to operate at trial (for it may not actually be adduced at trial as evidence of guilt), it threatens the normative foundations upon which this presumption is based. The presumption of innocence, at root, is a normative commitment on the part of the criminal justice system to treat each person as a free agent, capable of acting in ways that are entirely at odds with his past conduct. Regardless of what our actuarial tables might tell us about a particular person, the criminal justice system is committed to treating each person as though we knew almost nothing of his past – demanding proof beyond a reasonable doubt from his accusers that he actually committed the particular acts of which he stands accused.[61] Evidence of his association with dubious characters, of his membership in suspect organisations and even of his prior criminal acts is generally excluded from consideration – for in every case, they tend to colour our judgment about the accused's guilt even though, strictly speaking, they are not evidence of his guilt on the particular charge. The presumption of innocence is not directly at issue here because we are not concerned with profiling being used as a substitute for proof of guilt at trial. Nevertheless, the same basic normative commitment ought to animate our approach to policing.[62] That is, we ought to treat all citizens equally until we have good reason to suspect them individually of wrongdoing. The practice of profiling often[63] threatens that commitment.

Some of the most powerful and effective critiques of many of these profiling techniques comes from Bernard Harcourt's recent book, *Against Prediction*.[64] In that book, Harcourt argues that profiling, despite its promise of rationally allocating scarce police resources toward monitoring those who are genuine threats and away from those who are not, in fact fails on a number of fronts. Harcourt suggests that it might actually fail even on its own terms, as a crime-fighting

[61] Perhaps no words in the history of English criminal law are better known than Viscount Sankey's famous speech in *R v Woolmington* [1935] AC 462: 'Throughout the web of the English Criminal Law one golden thread is always to be seen, that it is the duty of the prosecution to prove the prisoner's guilt . . .'

[62] I have discussed this idea of the presumption of innocence and non-partisanship in policing in 'Reinventing the Night-Watchman State' (2010) 60 *University of Toronto Law Journal* 425.

[63] Of course, this is not always the case. For example, if a pattern of telephone calls suggests that an individual is dealing in drugs, it would not violate norms of equal treatment to investigate further. However, many forms of profiling do not track actual criminal conduct but only proxies for it (such as race, associations with others who have a criminal past, etc) – and this latter form of profiling clearly does violate such norms. Thanks to Bob Sullivan for pressing me on this distinction.

[64] Bernard Harcourt, *Against Prediction: Punishing and Policing in an Actuarial Age* (Chicago, University of Chicago Press, 2007).

strategy.[65] However, Harcourt's harshest critiques are normative ones. He argues that policing one group much more heavily than another – even if it is much more likely to commit criminal offences – violates norms of equal treatment according to which our likelihood of being apprehended are the same, no matter who we are. If we focus most of our policing energies on some but not others, members of the highly policed group will be much more likely to be apprehended for reasons that have nothing to do with their actual likelihood of criminality. Further, he argues that as we move closer to an actuarial model of criminal justice, our ideas of just punishment are also becoming distorted in such a way that we actually take just punishment to be whatever we can anticipate will prevent a certain person from offending, rather than simply the punishment that is proportionate to the seriousness of the offence.

Harcourt's colleague at the University of Chicago law school, Lior Stahilevitz, has suggested that profiling should actually be welcomed by racial minorities and others who have traditionally been targets of unjustified police suspicion. Strahilevitz's argument is that if police have access to specific information about each person, this will allow the police to draw subtler contrasts between those whose past conduct suggests that they are likely to commit certain sorts of criminal offences and those who merely share the same racial heritage (or other irrelevant characteristic).[66] However, this argument seems too quick. For although Strahilevitz is right to suggest that the full disclosure of one's personal history might allow some who previously were the victims of unfair discrimination to escape from it (for they can now show that, despite their racial heritage, their past conduct suggests that they have no criminal propensities), it nevertheless allows individuals to be treated differently based on predictions about their future conduct. Although we might allow credit rating agencies to charge more for loans to those who have a history of defaulting on their debts, it is less clear that we should allow the police and other public servants to treat citizens differently – even based on a criminal past. For the key distinguishing feature of police and public services generally is that they ought to serve all equally, regardless of our backgrounds. The presumption of innocence is born of a deeper assumption built into our legal system that each of us is free to choose to act differently in the future than we did in the past. Although private actors might be free to charge more to 'bad credit risks', it is not open to the public service to do the same.

[65] Harcourt suggests that if the reactions of prospective offenders to increased policing are not consistently elastic, then moving police resources from one place to another might actually backfire. For although it might seem to be plausible to move police resources from a low-crime area to a high-crime area (or from policing a low-crime demographic and toward policing a high-crime demographic), this might backfire if the high-crime group is considerably less elastic in its reaction to increased policing ibid.

[66] Lior Stahilevitz, 'Reputation Nation: Law in an Era of Ubiquitous Personal Information' (2008) 102 *Northwestern University Law Review* 1667. Strahilevitz develops this argument further in his forthcoming book, *Information and Exclusion* (New Haven, CT, Yale University Press, 2010).

VI (TENTATIVE) CONCLUSIONS

My central aim in this chapter has been to draw initial distinctions among the various governmental techniques of data collection and management we see at work in most Western countries. The central distinction I have drawn is between systems of identification on the one hand, which are purely formal mechanisms that identify each person and allow those who have specific information about that person to identify the person in question over time and through space, and systems of surveillance and profiling on the other hand, that are concerned with the accumulation and management of personal data. I have drawn this distinction in order to disentangle a number of issues that are often conflated in recent discussions about identification systems. First, those who object to the expansion of the state's powers of surveillance all too often point to the existence of identification documents as the central normative issue in these schemes. However this, I have argued, misses the point. It is not identification cards as such that are the most serious problem; indeed, they are in an important sense a distraction from the much more worrisome collection of citizen databases through surveillance and profiling.

Second, once we see that identification schemes are formal tools that can be used by anyone with information about a person to help track that person through time and space, it becomes clear that such a system does not require us to centralise the substantive information about each person in the Government's possession. Each government department may use the identification scheme to track citizens for their own purposes – they need not have access to information about citizens that is irrelevant to their purposes.

Third, those (especially in North America) who object to identification schemes often get caught up on the common law's concern with those places where we have a 'reasonable expectation of privacy.' However, as the example of CCTV surveillance of public streets makes clear, we always have *some* privacy interest in information about us, even if we have chosen to make it quite widely available to the public. Civil law conceptions of privacy, focused on keeping our different *personae* separate, provide a more useful set of concepts through which to make sense of these issues.

I conclude with a note of caution about the sorts of practical conclusions one can draw from the fairly abstract analysis I undertake here. As in most things, the devil is in the details: many programmes that are put forward as 'mere identification schemes' (and therefore, on my analysis, benign), in fact have a significant profiling component to them (or, through a sort of 'mission creep', may quickly come to be used for this purpose). And many practices in the common law and civilian legal systems do not conform to the 'common law' and 'civil law' ideal types I put forward here. Further, there are a host of other important normative issues surrounding the administration of such programmes that lie beyond the scope of this chapter, such as the use of identification documents as instruments of government action, the transparency of the Government's administration of each programme, the history of corruption or prejudice among the civil servants charged with administering the system, and so on. With these qualifications in mind, however, the treatment of the two cultures of state-citizen relations set out here may be of use – albeit as only one tool among many – when considering the legitimacy of citizen data collection measures.

2

On the Legitimacy of Imposing Direct and Indirect Obligations to Disclose Information on Non-Suspects

SHLOMIT WALLERSTEIN*

WHAT INFORMATION CAN the state legitimately require from persons who have knowledge concerning the involvement of others in criminal activity? This is the question at the centre of this chapter. Information can be collected either from testimonies of what people know of or else it can be extracted from physical and electronic evidence (eg an address book, a list of items or tools found on a premises). Consequently, obligations concerning the disclosure of information can take one of two forms: direct or indirect. Direct obligations impose duties on persons to actively reveal, by speech or in writing, information known to them concerning the involvement of another in criminal activity. These may include an obligation to come forward with such information alongside a duty to respond to direct questions from the police or to testify in court. Indirect obligations entail passive disclosure of information. That is, the provision of information without actually requiring direct positive physical engagement by speech or in writing. Rather, indirect obligations to disclose require citizens not to obstruct the police who are carrying out its own investigation and allow the police access to material evidence (physical and electronic) found in their possession or control. In answering the question we must consider both types of obligations to disclose.

Over the years English law has undergone important changes. In the early days it imposed a direct obligation to disclose information voluntarily, requiring citizens to come forward whenever they are in possession of information concerning the involvement of others in criminal activity. Acknowledging the difficulties that such an obligation creates, it abolished this obligation and for many years it maintained a more limited direct obligation to disclose information only in testimonies in court alongside the imposition of indirect

* I wish to thank Mr Nick Barber for his valuable comments and to the participants of the workshop on 'seeking security'.

obligations to disclose. Yet, in the last two decades there has been some erosion in this principled approach and new exceptions to the general principle have been introduced.

The chapter examines the existence of both direct and indirect obligations to disclose information in English law and attempts to set out the various considerations that ought to be taken into account in assessing the legitimacy of such obligations. Section I sets out the background for the discussion and presents the offences of misprision of felony and misprision of treason that were previously recognised at common law. These offences created a direct obligation to disclose information regarding felonies and acts of treason respectively. However, as part of a more general revision, the Criminal Law Act 1967 abolished the offence of misprision of felony. Section II discusses the various reasons in support of this move and points to the difficulties that such obligations create in a liberal democratic society. The section examines the violation that such obligations pose to personal autonomy and liberty. It points to the problematic nature of constraints which are not based on choice and personal responsibility for harm done, the danger that compliance with such obligations may pose to a person and the type of suspicious and fearful atmosphere that duties to disclose may bring about. The article then goes on to present the new (current) regime (section III). The general arrangements impose only a very limited direct obligation in relation to testimonies in court, but recognise an indirect obligation under strict conditions. However, two exceptions have been created in recent years – the first involves the imposition of a direct obligation to disclose information in relations to money laundering and the second involves the imposition of both direct obligation to disclose information relating to terrorist activity and the expansion of the indirect obligation in the context of terrorism. Finally, section IV examines the possibility to justify this more nuanced approach – both in terms of the general principle and in terms of its exceptions. First, it is argued that indirect obligations to disclose cause less difficulties than a direct obligation to disclose and can be more easily justified. Second, it is argued that a distinction must be drawn between people who involuntarily found themselves in a position where they gain information, and those who choose to engage in an activity that may expose them to such information, and between those who are not helping the criminal and those that, although inadvertently, help the criminal. Where a person chooses to engage in certain activity and his or her conduct helps a criminal activity, it is legitimate to impose obligations to disclose. Third, it is submitted that distinct objectives for information-gathering may result in the creation of different regimes of disclosure-obligations. Gathering information is important for the conviction of the guilty.[1] However, this may not be the only aim. A further aim that the state has is gathering intelligence in order to prevent crime before it occurs. This aim is of special importance in the context

[1] A Ashworth and M Redmayne, *The Criminal Process*, 4th edn (Oxford, Oxford University Press, 2010) 22–23.

of counter-terrorism.[2] The prominence given by the state to each of the aims, clearly affects the powers granted to the police, and other law enforcement agencies, and may well affect the legitimacy of the information that the state may require from its citizens. Fourth, it is argued that the seriousness of the crime may impact on the legitimacy of such obligations. The article concludes by pointing to some of the possible effects that special relationships may have on the legitimacy to impose information to disclose.

The discussion in this article concentrates on the legitimacy, or justifiability, of the imposition of duties to disclose information on people who are not, themselves, involved in criminal activity. It is not concerned with duties to disclose imposed on persons who are engaged or suspected of being engaged in criminal activity, and are being asked to provide information about their accomplices. Although some of the concerns that a duty to disclose raise may be similar to both categories, this latter category raises further considerations which are unique to it regarding personal involvement in the crime and subsequently their own responsibility, and to the issue of self-incrimination. As such it deserves a separate discussion that cannot be accommodated here.

I THE OLD LAW

Since the thirteenth century, Common Law has recognised offences of failure to disclose information about offenders who committed serious crimes: an offence of misprision of felony and an offence of misprision of treason. The offence of misprision of felony consisted of concealing or procuring the concealment of a felony known to have been committed. It was sufficient to show mere silence without any endeavour to bring the offender to justice where there is a reasonable opportunity available to do so.[3] Thus, for example, in the case of *Aberg*,[4] the accused, a nurse who ran a private nursing agency, was convicted for misprision of felony for knowingly concealing an escaped prisoner.

Yet, the elements of the offence remained vague[5] for many years until the case of *Sykes v DPP*[6] (1961) in which the House of Lords considered the offence at length. The Court set out the specific elements of the offence, but its scope of application was left unclear. Lord Morton held that the offence applies to all those who fail to report a known felony, even when a person *reasonably* thought

[2] Note that these two aims are not intended to correspond to the two models of Herbert Packer's two models of evaluating the criminal process (the due process and the crime control). (See H Packer, *The Limits of the Criminal Sanction* (Stanford, Stanford University Press, 1968).)

[3] 1 Hawk. C 59, s 2; *Sykes v DPP* [1962] AC 528; JW Cecil Turner, *Russell* on *Crime*, 12th edn (London, Stevens Publishing,1964) vol 1, 168–71; *Stephen's Digest of the Criminal Law*, 9th edn (London, Sweet & Maxwell, 1950) 158 art 209. See also Criminal Law Revision Committee Seventh Report – Felonies and Misdemeanours (1965) (Cmnd 2659).

[4] *Aberg* [1948] 2 KB 173, 32 Cr App R 144.

[5] See eg the speeches of Lord Westbury in *William v Bayley* (1866) LR 1 HL 200, 220, and Lord Goddard CJ in *Aberg* [1948] 2 KB 173, 176.

[6] *Sykes v DPP* [1962] AC 528; 45 Cr App R 230.

that in the circumstances it was not his or her duty to inform the police,[7] while Lord Denning thought that some limitations should be imposed, stating that:

> Non-disclosure may sometimes be justified or excused on the ground of privilege. For instance, if a lawyer is told by his client that he has committed a felony, it should be no misprision in the lawyer not to report it to the police, for he might in good faith claim that he was under a duty to keep it confidential. Likewise with doctor and patient, and clergyman and parishioner. There are other relationships, which may give rise to a claim in good faith that it is in the public interest not to disclose it. For instance, if an employer discovers that his servant has been stealing from the till, he might well be justified in giving him another chance rather than reporting him to the police. Likewise with the master of a college and a student. But close family or personal ties will not suffice where the offence is of so serious a character that it ought to be reported . . .[8]

This lack of clarity and the potential wide and unlimited scope of application of the offence attracted criticism from leading academics.[9]

The second offence was misprision of treason. It occurs when a person who knows that another person has committed an act of treason does not, within a reasonable time, give information to the appropriate authority.[10] Like the offence of misprision of felony, it is sufficient to show mere silence without any endeavour to bring the offender to justice where there is a reasonable opportunity available for him or her to do so. At common law the punishment is life imprisonment and forfeiture of the offender's goods and land. However, there is no known prosecution for this offence in modern time.

The two offences thus defined are limited to the disclosure of information *after* a felony has been committed. There is some early authority, from the eighteenth century, that suggests that the scope of the offence was extended to include the case of one who knows of a felony, or treason, that is planned but not yet carried out, and fails to disclose this information.[11] However, there is no later reference to this extension and in setting the elements of the offence in *Sykes* the House of Lords did not mention this extension.

Alongside these two offences, the law imposed a general obligation to testify in a court of law when summoned by the court. As such, a person may be required by the court to disclosure of any information he or she may have concerning the involvement of others in criminal activity. This obligation is supported by a criminal offence of perjury – for lying under oath,[12] and contempt of court – for refusing to give evidence.[13]

[7] *Sykes v DPP* [1962] AC 528, 570.

[8] *Sykes v DPP* [1962] AC 528, 564.

[9] See Glanville Williams in his comment on the case in (1961) *CLJ* 142, 143 for the opinion that their Lordships' lack of positive endorsement of Lord Denning's privileged-relationships-exception should be read as leaving these exceptions outside the law of misprision of felony.

[10] *Stephen's Digest of the Criminal Law*, 9th edn (London, Sweet & Maxwell, 1950) 158 art 208.

[11] Hawkins, *Pleas of the Crown*, 8th edn (London, S Sweet,1824) vol 2 ch 29 s 23.

[12] Perjury Act 1911 s 1.

[13] Contempt of Court Act 1981, *cf Montgomery* [1995] 2 Cr App R 23.

II THE ABOLITION OF MISPRISION OF FELONY

With the abolition of the distinction between felonies and misdemeanours, the Criminal Law Act 1967 abolished the offence of misprision of felony.[14] Though, failure to report a known act of treason still amounts to an offence, at common law, of misprision of treason. The Criminal Law Revision Committee which recommended the changes provided a very short explanation stating that:

> With the abolition of felony it is desirable that the law . . . should be reconsidered. There are obvious objections to making a person criminally liable for not reporting to the police any minor offence of which he happen to know. The present law of misprision is also open to objection in that it does not require that the omission to give information of the felony should be dishonest, and that it contains no clear limitations as regards offences omitted even by near relatives.[15]

The Committee went further and explained that even in the case of withholding information from the police in response to direct questions, where there is a strong argument for criminalising such conduct based on the principle that 'citizens have a duty to help a police officer to discover and apprehend offenders', 'public opinion would be unlikely to agree to an offence of consisting or refusing to answer questions by the police about the commission of offences'.[16] They recognised that conferring such a power on the police should not be taken lightly and should be limited to the most serious situations.[17]

The Committee's main reason for rejecting the concept of an imposition of a general duty to disclose – 'the obvious reasons' – leaves the reader a little uncertain. For one thing, apparently it is not all that obvious. It was only five years earlier that the House of Lords held that the offence of misprision of felony is *not* obsolete and the debate as to the appropriateness of such offence seemed to be limited to its details and to its correct scope. However, more importantly, it is unclear what those 'obvious reasons' are that the Committee had in mind. One can think of a number of different reasons for rejecting the idea of an imposition of a general duty to disclose. A possible hint to what was in the Committee's

[14] Though a new offence of concealing information about a crime that has been committed in return for a bribe or where an individual (actively) provides false or misleading information to the police was introduced in s 5. *cf* Roydhouse, *The Criminal Law and Criminal Justice Act 1967* (London, Butterworth, 1968) 19.

[15] Criminal Law Revision Committee Seventh Report – Felonies and Misdemeanours (1965) (Cmnd 2659) para 39.

[16] ibid para 42. Although it is important to distinguish between the permitted refusal to answer and between the provision of false information aimed at misleading the police. The latter is considered a criminal offence (Criminal Law Act 1967 s 5).

[17] The Committee compares it with a similar power that was recognised at the time in the Official Secrets Act 1920, which dealt with offences related to secret information, and even there, such power was subject to permission from the Secretary of State.

Note, that the discussion in limited to disclosure of information that is not self-incriminating. The disclosure of self-incriminating information raises further issues related to the right not to self-incriminate oneself.

mind could be drawn from their later comment about public opinion's rejection of an offence that would consist of refusal to answer questions by the police. Perhaps, they thought of what Lord Lloyd referred to (years later) as the general concern that even if individuals have a moral obligation to help the police this should not be turned into a legal obligation.[18]

This position resonates with the conventional claim against the introduction of a general duty to (easy) rescue and the concerns raised against 'bad Samaritan law'. The gist of the claim raised is that such a duty to rescue is an imposition on, if not a violation of, personal autonomy and liberty.[19] As Andrew Ashworth explains:[20]

> Each person is regarded as an autonomous being, responsible for his or her own conduct. One aim of the law is to maximise individual liberty, so as to allow each individual to pursue a conception of the good life with as few constraints as possible. Constraints there must be, of course, in modern society: but freedom of action should be curtailed only so far as is necessary to restrain individuals from causing injury or loss to others. Setting these outer limits to freedom of action is, however, much more acceptable than requiring certain actions of a citizen, especially at times and in circumstances which may be inconvenient and may conflict with one's personal goals . . .

Similarly, an imposition of a duty to disclose requires a person to act in a specific way although he or she is not responsible for the harm (or offence) either as principal or accomplice and it requires a very specific type of action, which may be in conflict with his or her pursuit of personal goals. Supporters of social responsibility would argue that unlike a duty to rescue that requires an individual to act in a certain way at a specific time (ie save life when seeing another in peril), a duty to disclose information does not pose the same level of intrusion on one's autonomy and liberty as it provides a more flexible requirement of informing the police within a 'reasonable time' which enables a person to accommodate it more comfortably and reduces the conflict with other personal goals. As such the level of interference is minimal and justified. Yet, even if there is a little more flexibility it still creates a burden on a citizen, which may be time consuming and as such conflicts with other activities.

This notion of violation of one's liberty is reflected in art 5 of the European Convention of Human Rights (ECHR). Recently the European Court of Human Rights, discussing the power to 'stop and search' in the case of *Gillan and*

[18] Lord Lloyd of Berwick, *Inquiry Into Legislation Against Terrorism* (1996) Cm 3420 para 14.21, 14.24. Lord Lloyd considered this in the context of his review of counter-terrorism legislation and the legitimacy of a duty to disclose information about terrorist activity. This will be discussed in the following sections in greater details.

[19] For a more detailed debate about the duty to rescue, see eg A Ashworth, 'The Scope of Criminal Liability for Omissions' (1989) *QLR* 424; J Dressler, 'Some Brief Thoughts (Mostly Negative) About Bad Samaritan Laws' (2000) *Santa Clara Law Review* 971; L Alexander, 'Criminal Liability for Omissions: An Inventory of Issues' in A Simester and S Shute (eds), *Criminal Law Theory* (Oxford, Oxford University Press, 2002) 121; N Cobb, 'Compulsory Care-Giving: Some Thoughts on Relational Feminism, the Ethics of Care and Omissions Liability' (2008) 39 *The Cambrian Law Review* 11.

[20] A Ashworth, 'The Scope of Criminal Liability for Omissions' (n 19 above) 427.

Quinton v United Kingdom, held that holding someone for 20 minutes for a search amounts to deprivation of their liberty, because during this time they could not do anything else.[21] Analogously, requiring a person to disclose information means that during the time the person reports the information to the police, he or she is also unable to do anything else, and this may take much longer than just 20 minutes.

Moreover, in terms of liberty, criminal law should recognise a person's choices rather than allow liability to be governed by chance, and the obligation to disclose information is created by chance, upon a person who becomes aware of another's involvement in criminal activity, and may well prefer not to become involved at all.[22]

Both a duty to rescue and a duty to disclose involve the imposition of a duty to act on a person who is not responsible for the harm on the basis of some concept of social responsibility or solidarity.[23] However, even those who argue for the imposition of a duty to rescue for reasons of social responsibility and solidarity recognise that the duty should be limited to cases of 'easy rescue' and should not require a person to put him, or herself, at risk.[24] Yet, a duty to disclose ought to be compared not with a case of an easy rescue but rather with a case of a rescue which may place one in risk for his or her own wellbeing. Disclosing information of another's involvement in criminal activity may place that person at risk of retaliation by the criminal or his or her friends. This kind of threat may extend for many years, as may be the case where the offender, upon completing his or her (possibly long) sentence, comes out of prison and wishes to take revenge on those who he or she considers responsible for him or her being caught. Often, it may further place not only the person's life at risk but also that of his or her close family. In such circumstances the police would not always be able to offer effective protection.[25] It would, therefore, be unjustified to demand from a person to put his or her personal safety at serious risk for the benefit of society, especially where the person is not responsible for the harm (or the offence) nor did he or she choose to gain the knowledge they have (of another's involvement in criminal activity).

We should further point to the fact that a duty to disclose goes further than a duty to rescue. In a society that is based on the equation of individual autonomy with negative liberty (ie liberty not to do certain things) and therefore rejects even the imposition of a duty to easy rescue, it seems unfair to impose a duty to act to achieve 'lesser' objectives. A duty to rescue is limited to instances

[21] *Gillan and Quinton v United Kingdom* (App No 4158/05), Judgment of January 12, 2010 ECtHR. However it should be noted that the Court did not decide whether this violation of the right to liberty amounts to violation of art 5 of the ECHR.

[22] For this argument in the context of a duty to rescue see Ashworth (n 19 above) 427–28.

[23] See Ashworth's argument from social responsibility in support of the imposition of a duty to rescue in his article, ibid 431–33.

[24] ibid 432.

[25] At other times the only effective protection is going into the witness protection programme and this may require the witness to go undercover and change his and his family's whole way of life.

where there is a need for an immediate response to save another's life. A duty to disclose – insofar as it refers to disclosure of information concerning a crime that has already been committed – does not entail an element of imminent peril and there is no one in need of saving. It is 'just' about catching a person after the harm or injury has already been done. If saving life is an insufficient reason to impose a duty, it seems unlikely that bringing a person to justice ought to be sufficient to impose such duty. Insofar as the duty to disclose may require the disclosure of information about planned crimes that are yet to be carried out, than it seems unjustified to require a person to try and prevent harm (by disclosure of information) that is still in the future (and as such is not inevitable) while there is no requirement to prevent harm that is imminent by coming to the rescue of a person in peril.[26]

Alternatively, maybe the reason public opinion would object to the imposition of such a duty is due to the feeling that this duty encourages individuals to spy on their neighbours, and requires us to 'snitch' on them or on our family or friends. This is a behaviour that is often connected with totalitarian regimes rather than liberal democracies and is generic of 'police states'.[27] This creates an atmosphere of fear and suspicion. A vivid example is the recent broadcasting of an anti-terror radio advertisement encouraging people to report to the police any suspicions they may have about local people who avoided company, kept their windows covered and eschewed bank cards for cash. This advertisement was met by angry public reaction which critically viewed it as encouraging the creation of a police society (and note, that the advertisement did not impose a duty but only 'encouraged' people to report).[28]

This is also closely connected with the speculative basis for intervention that heightens the jeopardy of false accusations, which will inflict damage to persons and to the legitimacy of the criminal process.[29] Indeed, ruling on the legitimacy of the anti-terror advertisement mentioned above, the Advertising Standards Authority (ASA) recognised that this might affect many people who behave in a suspicious, yet innocent way.[30]

A further argument noted by the Criminal Law Committee concerns the tension and damage that such a duty may cause to family relationships. Contrary to the position taken by Lord Denning in *Sykes*, family relationships seem to cause more difficulties and deserve, at the very least, separate attention.[31] The duty to disclose places a person in a conflict of loyalties: it requires a mother to

[26] Although admittedly, such contradictory results may be explained by different policy considerations, which are engaged by a duty to rescue on the one hand and a duty to report serious crimes on the other.

[27] C Walker, 'Conscripting the Public in Terrorism Policing: Towards Safer Communities or a Police State?' (2010) *Crim LR* 441, 442.

[28] See www.guardian.co.uk/uk/2010/aug/11/asa-anti-terror-hotline-advert (11 August 2010).

[29] C Walker, 'Conscripting the Public in Terrorism Policing' (n 27 above) 442.

[30] See www.guardian.co.uk/uk/2010/aug/11/asa-anti-terror-hotline-advert (11 August 2010).

[31] See eg the Criminal Law Revision Committee's own view, above n 15; G Williams (n 9 above) 143.

inform about her son's conduct, and a brother to inform about his sister's criminal activity. There are strong public reasons not to place individuals in such conflict of interests and weaken family connections.[32] Going back to the discussion above, such requirement would remind many of the behaviour which was common in East Germany during the 1970s and the 1980s where, under the control of Stasi, people often reported on their parents or siblings.

A duty to disclose information may further undermine a whole range of 'professional' relationships, such as relationships with physicians, therapists, lawyers, confessions based on religious obligations, as well as journalistic work which often depends on source-confidentiality. As noted by Lord Denning, these types of relationships are all valuable to society and depend on confidentiality. A duty to disclose information that has been acquired in the course of these relationships would undermine them.[33]

Finally, such an obligation has the potential of violating the basic human right of privacy, which is protected under art 8 of the ECHR. This is so because, in the context of a direct obligation, it may require a person to disclose the context in which he or she became aware of another person's involvement in criminal activity. In the context of indirect obligation – it requires one to cooperate with the police and allow them to enter into his or her premises to search and seize material, and possibly require them to then provide explanation for the material seized.[34]

III THE NEW REGIME AND THE EXCEPTIONS TO THE GENERAL RULE

A The General Principle

Since the abolition of the offence of misprision of felony, generally the law does not require citizens to disclose information concerning the involvement of others in criminal activity to the police or other enforcement agencies, and although the offence of misprision of treason still exists, in practice, to date, there has been no prosecution for this offence. In line with the general obligation to help the police, the police may question people about their knowledge regarding the involvement of others in criminal activity,[35] but as said above, there is no legal requirement to answer these questions and provide any information and an

[32] Thus, eg, the law recognises a marital privilege that prevents the court from compelling one spouse to testify against the other concerning confidential communications made during marriage.

[33] Lord Denning talks about these in terms of 'a claim of right made in good faith'. I do not subscribe to this specific description of the reason for confidentiality in these relationships. Rather, I think that these claims are an essential element in these relationships and the relationships are valuable to society for a range of reasons. *cf* G Williams (n 9 above) 143.

[34] This will be discussed in greater detail below.

[35] Note that this does not amount to detention and the questioning is not a police interview. An interview is defined in Code C 11.1A as 'a questioning of a person regarding their involvement or suspected involvement in a criminal offence or offences'. Such interviews of suspects are then subject to strict limitations.

individual may end the questioning at any time. That is, in practice, the police have no more powers to require us to answer their questions than any other citizen. The only direct obligation that still exists is the requirement to respond to direct questions while giving testimony in court. It is more limited in scope because it only comes into play once the police completed an independent investigation and the testimony only corroborates their conclusions. The aim, of course, is to ensure the conviction of the guilty, but admittedly even this duty is open to some of the criticisms discussed in the previous section and first and foremost the exposure of the witness to personal risk to life.[36]

At the same time, the law created a regime that does require people to provide information, including information about the involvement of others in criminal activity, indirectly. That is, although individuals are not required to volunteer such information, the police are granted a range of powers that enables them to collect material found in the control or possession of those people, and require their co-operation.

As part of the pre-trial process, police are granted a range of powers that enable them to collect information on their initiative and require citizens to co-operate. The police powers that may affect people who are not themselves involved, or suspected of being involved in criminal activity are concerned with the powers of 'entry search and seize', which are generally granted either through the consent of the person entitled to grant entry, or by warrant which is ordinarily issued by a magistrate who examines compliance with the following five conditions, set out in section 8 of the Police and Criminal Evidence Act 1984 (PACE):[37]

(1) An indictable offence has been committed.
(2) There is material in the premises which is likely to be of substantial value to the investigation of the offence.
(3) The material is likely to be relevant evidence.
(4) The material does not consist of or include 'items subject to legal privilege', 'excluded material' or 'special procedure material'.
(5) It is not practicable to communicate with a person entitled to grant entry and access to the material, or such access would not be granted without a warrant, or the purpose of the search may be frustrated or seriously prejudiced unless immediate access is secured.

[36] Indeed, in recognition of this, the police may provide special protection if needed and the law recognises a special offence, at common law, of contempt of court for those who intimidate or harass witnesses (including former witnesses) (*A-G v Judd* [1995] COD 15; *A-G v Butterworth* [1963] 1 QB 696). This, however, does not relieve the witness from the obligation to give evidence in court.

[37] See also PACE, Code B. Further powers to search are granted where a person is arrested for an indictable offence, based on reasonable ground, a constable may enter and search any premises where the person was at the time of or immediately before the arrest for evidence relating to the offence for which he was arrested (PACE s 32(2)(b)).

As is evident from the second and fourth conditions, a search warrant may be issued not only with regard to premises of a suspect, but of any other person where material which is valuable to the investigation of the offence may be found (including information which is stored in any electronic form and is accessible from the premises), even if the owner of the premises is not, him or herself involved in the criminal enterprise.

Special arrangements exist with regards to three types of material: excluded material, special procedure material and material covered by legal privileges. 'Excluded material' involves material held by a person in confidence owed to a third party and may take the form of one of three types: personal records, human tissue or tissue fluid or journalistic material held in confidence consisting of documents or records other than documents.[38] 'Legal privileges material' include communications made in connection with the giving of legal advice to a client between a lawyer and a client; or a lawyer and a person representing the client and communications made in connection with or in contemplation of legal proceedings and for the purpose of such proceedings between a number of people identified in the statute.[39] 'Special procedure material' is a sweeping-up category of material meriting special protection but falling outside the scope of the other two categories.[40] Where the material required involves any of these three categories of special procedures the warrant is issued, subject to stricter conditions, by a Circuit judge,[41] and 'legal privileges material' may never be subject to any warrant or seizure.[42] This procedure, according to the court, provides a careful balance between the public interest in the effective investigation and prosecution of crime and the interests of citizens in protecting their personal and property rights.[43]

In recent years two exceptions to the general principle have been created. Both impose a direct duty to disclose information. The first involves information relating to money laundering and the second concerns information relating to counter-terrorism. In the later exception, the law also extended some of the obligations connected to what I term 'indirect' provision of information.

[38] PACE s 11.

[39] PACE s 10.

[40] PACE s 14. The section sets out the specific types of material that would fall into this category.

[41] Generally there are two gateways to get a warrant: the first is wider but does not apply to 'excluded material'. It requires that in addition to the conditions required for 'ordinary' search warrant it is proven that it is in the public interest, having regard to the likely benefit to the investigation and the circumstances under which the person holds the material, that it should be produced or that access should be granted (PACE sch 1 para 2). The second gateway set in PACE sch 2 para 3 is narrower but permits access to both 'excluded material' and 'special procedure material'.

[42] PACE ss 10, 18 and 19 and the Terrorism Act 2000 sch 5 pt 1. It may be subject to a 'seize and sift' power under the Criminal Justice and Police Act 2001 s 50 where it is not reasonably practical to separate the legally privileged material from other material, but even then the police will not be able to actually read/listen to the legally privileged material.

[43] *Crown Court at Lewes, ex parte Hill* (1991) 93 Cr App R 60; *R (Bright) v Central Criminal Court* [2001] 1 WLR 662.

B The First Exception – Money Laundering

The first exception to the general principle set out above is the creation of a direct duty to disclose information relating to money laundering. The duty is imposed on the regulated sector,[44] to disclose information relating to Money Laundering (Proceeds of Crime Act 2002 section 330). Persons working in the regulated sector who know, suspect or have reasonable grounds for knowing or suspecting that another person is engaged in money laundering on the basis of information which came to them as part of their work in the regulated sector and enables them to identify the person and/or the whereabouts of any laundered property are duty-bound to disclose the identity of the person, the whereabouts of the laundered property and all the relevant information on which the knowledge or suspicion is based. Failure to disclose is a punishable offence.

C The Second Exception – Counter-Terrorism

The second exception to the general principle against the imposition of direct duty to disclose information relates to terrorism. Initially, The Prevention of Terrorism (Temporary Provisions) Act 1976 section 11 and its later version, The Prevention of Terrorism (Temporary Provisions) Act 1989 (hereafter: the PTA) section 18 created an offence of failure to disclose information related only to Northern Ireland terrorism. In an inquiry into the legislation against terrorism, Lord Lloyd recommended the repeal of this offence both because of the general concern that even if individuals have a moral obligation to help the police, this should not be turned into a legal obligation (a claim which resonates with the arguments against the introduction of a general duty to rescue discussed above), and because such prosecution is used most often against members of the families of suspected terrorists, putting them in an impossible position of conflicting loyalties.[45] These recommendations were only partially accepted: the old offence was scrapped and a new offence relating to all terrorist activity was introduced in the Terrorism Act 2000. The offence was directed at banks and other businesses requiring them to disclose information relating to the financing of terrorism.[46] Yet, in the aftermath of the terrorist attacks on 9/11 in the US, the general offence of failure to disclose information, which may be of material assistance to the prevention of an act of terrorism (widely defined in section 1 of the Terrorism Act 2000) or in securing the apprehension, prosecution or con-

[44] Defined in Proceeds of Crime Act 2002 sch 9.

[45] Lord Lloyd of Berwick, *Inquiry Into Legislation Against Terrorism* (1996) Cm 3420 para 14.21 and 14.24.

[46] Terrorism Act 2000 s 19. The explanatory notes note that 'in response to Lord Lloyd's recommendation the Government decided that suspicions arising in home life which were previously covered by section 18 of the PTA will not be replicated' (*Explanatory Notes to The Terrorism Bill as introduced to the House of Commons on 2nd December 1999* [Bill 10]).

viction of another person in an act of terrorism was reintroduced as section 38B of the Terrorism Act 2000.[47] Interestingly, the duty to disclose set out in section 38B is wider than the general duty to disclose previously recognised in the (now abolished) offence of misprision of felony, and its sister offence of misprision of treason. As noted above, the latter offences only require disclosure of information concerning crimes that have already been committed, whereas the offence in section 38B also requires disclosure of information relating to terrorist acts that are being planned but have yet to be carried out.

Alongside the creation of a direct duty to disclose, the legislature extended the powers of the police so that the requirements for indirect disclosure of information through a requirement of compliance with the police's search and seizure powers have also been extended. The Terrorism Act section 37 and schedule 5 introduced a variant of the 'entry, search and seizure' powers. They differ from the 'ordinary' powers in a number of ways.[48] First, the common trigger for these powers is 'terrorism investigation', that is, search warrants are granted by a judge if the warrant is requested for a terrorist investigation and complies with the conditions similar to the conditions for ordinary search warrant (ie existence of reasonable grounds that there is material of substantial value for investigation, necessity, etc). The second change is the extended complimentary powers to seize and sift (material) elsewhere where it is not practicable to do so at the place of search. The main change is in lowering the threshold for seizure. The 'ordinary' arrangements set out in the Criminal Justice and Police Act 2001 sections 50, 51 and 55 require reasonable suspicion that the seized material is relevant evidence in relation to the offence that justified the search. The power under section 1 of the Counter-Terrorism Act 2008 does not set a similar demand and instead is based on what a police officer 'thinks' is necessary.[49] It is worth noting that this extension does not apply to legally privileged material, which may not be removed, and if it was, must be returned immediately.[50] A further change is the extended powers where the search warrant is for non-residential premises, whereby it is not necessary to show that the warrant 'is necessary in the circumstances of the case'. In certain circumstances search warrants (for any premises) may be issued by a superintendent and, in cases of emergency, by any constable. A third important change concerns the production and access to excluded or special procedure material (only legally privileged material is completely excluded, paragraph 8). By schedule 5 paragraph 5, a judge may issue a warrant to access such material in pursuit of terrorism investigation. There is no need to notify the owner and it is not necessary to show that the material has a potential of becoming evidence for a court case. The conditions for giving the warrant are: the existence of a reasonable ground to

[47] The new section was inserted by the Anti-Terrorism, Crime and Security Act 2001 s 117.

[48] This list of differences is not exhaustive. It only brings the main changes that are of relevance to the current discussion.

[49] See the debate in the House of Lords, Hansard, HL vol 704, col 339 (9 October 2008).

[50] Counter-Terrorism Act 2008 s 3.

believe it is of substantial value to the investigation and reasonable ground for believing it is in the public interest to produce the material. The warrant will require access be given to the material, or its production within a given time to a constable, or a statement to best of knowledge where the material is. These powers have raised special concerns in cases involving journalistic material.[51] Finally, there are some ancillary powers, one of which may have special relevance to the category of persons at the centre of this chapter: By paragraph 13, at a constable's request, a circuit judge may issue an order requiring a person specified in the order to provide an explanation of any material seized, produced, or made available under paragraphs 1, 5 or 11.[52] This is accompanied by an offence set out in paragraph 14 of knowingly or recklessly giving false or misleading information. Thus, although an order may impose direct obligation to disclose information (though only in response to an initiative of the police), the scope of the offence is limited to instances where a person actively provides false or misleading information, but does not extend to keeping silent. This position, if taken on its own (ie ignoring the general duty to disclose set out in section 38B), seems to reflect the general principle according to which one is not required to disclose information to the police, but the provision of false or misleading information is an offence.[53]

IV THE JUSTIFIABILITY OF THE NEW REGIME

In the last section we presented the existing regime, in the UK, concerning the obligation to provide information regarding the involvement of another in criminal activity. The question then, is whether given the concerns (discussed in section II) that such an obligation entails, the current regime, including its exceptions, can be justified.

A number of considerations may justify the imposition of a duty to disclose in certain circumstances.

A Distinguishing Direct from Indirect Obligation to Disclose Information

The discussion in previous sections suggests that there is a difference between the two forms of obligations: direct and indirect. Direct obligation requires a person to provide information to the police either by coming forward of his or

[51] See eg *R v Middlesex Guildhall Crown Court ex parte Salinger* [1993] QB 564; *Re Jordan* [2003] NICC 1. For a fuller discussion of these cases see C Walker, *Blackstone's Guide to The Anti-Terrorism Legislation*, 2nd edn (2009) 109–11 and in Walker, 'Conscripting the Public in Terrorism Policing' (n 27 above) 449–50.

[52] With the exception of 'legally privileged material'.

[53] Of course, if a person is ordered to provide an explanation of any material seized as part of his or her testimony in a court of law and maintains silence, that person may be found in contempt of court – in line with the general separate obligation to disclose information in testimonies in court.

her own volition, or by answering questions put to him or her by the police or as a witness in court. Indirect obligation entails a duty of passive provision of information by requiring a person to co-operate with the police and to avoid obstructing them in their investigation to obtain evidence (and through it information) that exists independently. The current regime clearly distinguishes between these forms of obligation: while the legislator generally avoids an imposition of direct obligation to disclose information, it creates a range of indirect obligations of disclosure.

This distinction is important because many of the concerns raised against the imposition of direct obligation to disclose are either irrelevant or else lose some of their weight in the context of indirect obligation to disclose. Indirect obligation may be considered as less intrusive and as such does not violate one's autonomy and liberty to the same extent as a direct obligation to disclose would. Indirect obligation does not impose an active duty on the citizen to come forward. Rather it imposes a passive duty: to allow the police to enter into the premises and conduct a search. Thus, the reduction in one's liberty is more limited in line with the imposition of outer restrictions on one's liberty. One is not asked to do X (preventing the person from doing anything else but X), but rather he or she are required not to do Y (allowing them to do anything else but Y). Admittedly, when police officers knock on one's door to conduct a search the owner/occupant needs to be present (or would wish to) and so he or she would be unable to go about their planned day. Yet, even the ECHR in article 5 recognises that the right to liberty is not an absolute right and convicting the criminal is a legitimate public interest. Thus, when it is done in accordance with the law, which must provide the necessary safeguards, the right to liberty may be interfered with.

Note, that such legislation can also respond to other concerns. By setting out strict conditions (as English law does), which ensure that search warrants will only be issued where there is a reasonable suspicion that relevant material may be found on a premises, the legislator also removes the concern raised by Walker about the speculative basis and the jeopardy of false accusation.

Imposing a passive duty also means that it does not impact one's choices to the same extent as a direct obligation would, and does not base criminal liability on some random 'chance' that a person came across some information.

Importantly, it removes (or at the very least dramatically reduces) the risk to one's life and wellbeing involved in coming forward with information. It is the police initiative that does not require any positive contribution from the individual (he or she does not have to provide them with information). It is limited to seizing physical material that is not dependant on his or her words or statement. As such the individual will not be considered to be the 'snitch' and the one 'responsible' for the offender being caught. The offender is more likely to think that it is the result of his or her own doing (in leaving a trail of evidence) or an element of 'bad luck' on his or her part.

Lastly, adopting this approach embraces the view that it is the job of the police to gather the information (and evidence) and while citizens have an obligation to help the police they are not expected to spy on their neighbours. In essence, what the indirect obligation to disclose is saying is that it recognises that it is the job of the police to conduct the investigation but it must also mean that citizens need to provide the police with a practical way of investigating. At the very least this must mean that citizens may not obstruct the police, even if they are not required to actively help them. Technically, this position is not undermined even by the existence of a direct obligation to testify in court as the trial only takes place after the police have completed its (independent) investigation. However, arguably not too much can be made of this distinction because the conviction inevitably relies on the findings of the court, and as such giving evidence in court may still be considered as 'snitching'.

B Personal Choice and Participation in Crime

One of the concerns regarding the imposition of a direct duty to disclose information discussed in section II was the claim that one ought to be responsible only for those things that he or she chooses to do and with regards to harm that he or she causes. Thus, an important distinction can be made between the imposition of a direct duty to disclose which applies to everyone and between the imposition of such duty to people who make a choice to enter into a certain relationship or position. Indeed, in the context of duty to rescue we do not think it problematic nor as negating one's liberty to impose such duty on persons who assume a particular responsibility. Thus, we demand from a railway worker to care for the passengers[54] or a lifeguard or a police officer to rescue another person, and in some cases, even if that means putting him or herself at risk. Similarly, it seems less problematic to impose a direct obligation to disclose on members of identified groups of people where joining these groups is a matter of choice.

A second aspect of the idea of choice is concerned with the personal involvement in the criminal conduct of a person who knows of another person's involvement in a criminal activity. The whole discussion about the imposition of a duty to disclose assumes that the person is not participating in the criminal activity. Clearly, where one is participating in the criminal activity inadvertently and at some point becomes aware of the criminal nature of the activity, that person becomes partly responsible for any harm done from that point on because of the choice he or she makes to continue their involvement after becoming aware of the crime. Similarly, if the person suspects that 'something fishy' is going on and chooses not to follow up on his or her suspicions, than that person is responsible

[54] *Pittwood* (1902) 19 TLR 37, though arguably the source of this duty was not because he was hired to protect the public, but rather because he was hired to discharge a duty to the public that was owed by his employer. See A Simester, J Spencer, G Sullivan and G Virgo, *Simester and Sullivan's Criminal Law – Theory and Doctrine*, 4th edn (Oxford, Hart Publishing, 2010) 73; *Smith* (1869) 11 Cox CC 210.

for the subsequent harm, and this responsibility is based on the choice he or she made not to inquire into his or her suspicions. This is the underlying reason at the basis of the criminal law doctrine regarding a closed (or blind) eye.

Thus, the first exception to the general rule discussed in section III – the imposition of a duty to disclose information relating to money laundering, can be justified on the basis of these two considerations. This obligation was imposed on a small identifiable group of people who chose to work in the 'regulated sector'.[55] When a person chooses to work in the regulated sector he or she could be considered as voluntarily undertaking this duty in the same way that a railway worker or a police officer are considered to voluntarily undertake a duty to care for others.

More importantly, the personal involvement of a person in the regulated sector or the involvement of the institution for which that person works differs from the personal involvement in the criminal conduct of a person who knows of another person's involvement in criminal activity. Knowledge of another's involvement in, say, acts of terrorism, does not in and of itself actively contribute to the terrorist conduct physically, or even psychologically or mentally.[56] So, a person may have such knowledge and yet not take part in the terrorist enterprise. However, those working for the regulated sector actively help (even if unknowingly) to launder the money. They transfer the money, invest it, etc and as such enable criminals to conceal and launder their money. Consequently, it is legitimate to require them to report any suspicions (or knowledge) they might have about the origin of the money.

The law, however, has extended the scope of the 'closed eye' doctrine because it requires disclosure of information even where a person does not suspect the illegal origin of the money but ought to have suspected it (ie negligence). Yet, this extension can be justified by one's professional role, which may justify the imposition of higher standard of practice,[57] coupled with that person's potential involvement in the crime. Indeed, it is this active involvement which is at the basis of the duty as is apparent from the explanatory notes of this offence which state that: 'The clause reflects the fact that persons who are carrying out activities in the regulated sector should be expected to exercise a higher level of diligence in handling transactions than those employed in other businesses.'[58]

It may be argued that any justification for the imposition of a direct obligation to disclose on the regulated sector must take into account a further concern unique to this sector – the regulated sector's obligations to their clients requiring them to carry out their clients' instructions promptly. An obligation to disclose information, coupled with the need to suspend any action (with the

[55] As opposed to the general direct obligation imposed in the context of terrorism in s 38B of the Terrorism Act 2000.

[56] Since the terrorist may be unaware of the person's knowledge of his or her involvement.

[57] Similar to the higher standard imposed on, say, physicians (see *R v Adomako* [1995] 1 AC 171 (HL)).

[58] Proceeds of Crime Bill – Explanatory Notes Introduced in the House of Commons on 18th October 2001 para 455.

money) until the fulfilment of these statutory duties may cause severe damage to (legitimate, non criminal) clients.[59] The response to this concern is two-folded – first, it is submitted that this is but one of a range of possible special relationships which give rise to concerns of conflict of interests. There is nothing unique about the regulated sector's duty towards its clients. A parent may have similar duties towards his or her child, or a therapist towards his or her patient. Moreover, as long as the bank fulfils its statutory duties promptly it is legitimate to avoid carrying out the client's instructions. Clients must know that instructions are not carried out immediately but only after the necessary check-ups are done (in as short a time as possible). No client has a protected right to have his or her instructions fulfilled immediately regardless of the law. Put a different way, it appears that these two conflicting duties – to the client and to the state – can be balanced, and where a correct balance is struck the courts will provide the banks with the necessary protection.[60]

C The Objective for which Information is Required

The third consideration that may justify an imposition of a direct and/or indirect duty to disclose information is the objective for which the information is required. Criminal investigations after a crime has been committed are first and foremost interested with information to enable the conviction of the guilty. It is in this context that the offence of misprision of felony has been developed: to deal with the concealment of criminals, and it is in this context that the obligation to testify in court was imposed. Indeed, this is the most important role, if not the only role, of the criminal process.[61] However, this is not the only objective. At times, gathering information is useful for crime prevention before it occurs in the first place. Inevitably, the relative importance of these distinct objectives may change with regards to different types of crime and presumably, different ends may result in different scopes of justifiable duties. Things that may not be justified on the basis of one objective may be considered reasonable for the achievement of another objective.

Thus, for example, in the context of terrorism one of the most important elements for counter terrorism is intelligence gathering. The need for intelligence is often explained by the fact that detection at an early stage allows prevention and contingency planning. It also enables the criminal prosecution, which is important because politically this is the most persuasive way of disposing the accused and the least likely way to provoke internal or international criticism.

[59] For a fuller discussion on the regulated sector's obligation toward their clients and the conflict of interest this places the banks, see M Egan, 'The Role of the Regulated Sector in the UK Anti-Money Laundering Framework: Pushing the Boundaries of the Private Police' (2010) 6(2) *JCER* 272, especially 283–85 and the cases discussed there.

[60] See eg the cases discussed in M Egan's article (n 59 above).

[61] See Ashworth and Redmayne, *The Criminal Process* (n 1 above) 22–23.

Finally, as Walker points out, a wealth of information allows the Government to criticise rebels, to gauge the strength of the political opposition it faces and to make cogent reforms.[62] In other words, the regime created to deal with terrorism is not just about convicting the criminal. Rather, the main aim is the prevention of harm in the first place because the kind of damage that terrorism may bring about may be devastating to the state. Even the use of the criminal process to convict the criminal has strategic and political basis rather than the 'simple' explanation (such as desert or deterrence), which is usually given in the context of 'ordinary' crime. So, when assessing the justifiability of the special arrangements in the context of terrorism, one must bear in mind the specific objectives of the information gathering.

The objective for which the information is required should not simply justify the imposition of any duty (direct or indirect) to disclose, but could potentially also shape the scope of a duty to disclose information. Thus, if it is considered that convicting the guilty is insufficient to justify an imposition of a direct duty to disclose information, but that the need to prevent crime (or a certain type of crime) is sufficient, a duty to disclose may be justified only with regards to information concerning planned crimes that are yet to be carried out. This justification can be extended to information disclosed even after the crime has been committed where the crime reported is preparatory in nature (as are many anti-terrorist offences), as it may still help in the prevention of the subsequent harmful crime (yet to be committed). However, where the information concerns a substantive crime that has already been committed and it is no longer possible to prevent the harm, no such obligation exists. Indeed, Israeli criminal law recognises an offence where 'a person who, knowing that a person designs to commit a felony, fails to use all reasonable means to prevent the commission or completion thereof.'[63] Discussing this offence Justice Heshin explained that:

> The role of the police is to protect public order and its security, and as part of this obligation to prevent the commission of crimes. However, the police do not know everything about anything and is not found at every place at any given time. Naturally it is unable to prevent crimes, which it is unaware of in advance. In such circumstances the citizen is asked to help the authorities to prevent crimes if he or she is aware that another is planning a crime. What is required from the individual is not much: usually it is sufficient to inform the police, even by a phone call. Indeed, with very little trouble a citizen may prevent harm – sometimes very serious harm – to another individual and to society; Harm that is far greater than the burden it imposes on that person. There are those who see it as his or her obligation as part of the social contract of living as part of a community but I see no need to go into this issue . . .[64]

[62] C Walker, *The Prevention of Terrorism in British Law*, 2nd edn (Manchester, Manchester University Press, 1992) 10 and the references in fn 40.

[63] Israeli Criminal Code 1994 s 262.

[64] Criminal Appeal 3417/99 *Margalit Har-Sheffi v The State* (Supreme Court). The translation is mine (SW).

Likewise, the exceptional regime for terrorism created by English law, appear to shape the duty in-line with the objective by imposing a duty to disclose information about planned terrorist attacks (ie before they are carried out). One might argue that based on this explanation the extension of the duty to include an obligation to disclose information after the terrorist attack cannot be justified (or more accurately, can only be justified where the crime involved is preparatory in nature). However, the division between planned crimes versus crimes that have been committed is not always a simple one to make. As already noted, many of the terrorist offences involve prohibitions of conduct that is preparatory in nature. Furthermore, even in terms of offences that cause direct harm, in the context of terrorism there is still a strong element of crime prevention even after a terrorist attack has taken place. Given the strong religious, political and/or ideological convictions of the offenders there is a very high likelihood that they will go on to commit a further crime unless stopped. There is also a need to identify the wider terrorist network to which they belong in order to prevent further attacks from taking place. Therefore, it might still be necessary to extend such duty to disclosure of information post terrorist attacks for reasons of prevention.

D The Severity of the Harm

The last consideration that needs to be accounted for in any assessment is the severity of the harm. Clearly, the seriousness of the crime impacts on the relative weight that is to be given to the objective of crime prevention. The more serious the crime the more important it is to prevent it. This seems to be one of the underlying presumptions of the UK Government which has continuously justified many of its counter-terrorism measures on the basis that there is 'a public emergency threatening the life of the nation'.[65]

However, arguably, this should also be relevant in discussing the objective of convicting the guilty. Thus, for example, in the offence of misprision of treason English law still recognises the obligation to disclose information relating to treason where the offence has already been committed.[66] As can be seen, thus far the seriousness of the crime has been used only with regards to crimes against the state (terrorism and treason), but arguably, this may be used even further to justify imposition of direct duties to disclose information relating to other serious crimes (eg people trafficking, murders and other heinous crimes).

[65] 'Counter–Terrorism Policy and Human Rights (Seventeenth Report): Bringing Human Rights Back In', House of Lords and House of Commons Joint Committee on Human Rights (HL Paper 86 HC111, March 2010) 3.

[66] See also the comment made by the Criminal Law Revision Committee report on the abolition of the offence of misprision of felony, above n 15.

E Special Relationships and the Duty to Disclose

One of the questions that remain open is the issue of special or 'privileged' relationship. As we have seen in section II, this category brings together many different types of relationships that are valuable for different reasons. Clearly, there is no one solution that would fit the concerns of all those relationships. It is also unclear what approach should be taken in dealing with these relationships: should they be protected across the board? Are they similarly affected by both direct and indirect obligations? How should the seriousness of the offence and the different objectives for the collection of information impact on them? Take for example relatives – in the first place it is not obvious why the conflict of loyalties that a duty to disclose would create is more important than a conflict faced by very good friends. If this conflict is something that society should care about, should the seriousness of the crime involved matter? Although many think family relationships matter,[67] the extent to which they matter diverge: the legislator, for example, recognises marital privilege in the context of giving evidence, yet the duty to disclose information regarding terrorist activity does not take into account these relationships. In fact, most of the convictions for failure to disclose information relating to terrorism have been of family members of terrorists.[68] However, others may think that it is not reasonable to expect a person to report on his or her sibling, parents or children even when the offence involved is terrorism. Yet, when it comes to family relationships there seem to be much less conflict of loyalties where the obligation involved is indirect as the person is not 'put on the spot' and is not required to voluntarily reveal any information.

Compare this with the lawyer-client relationship. Clearly, if the end for which information is needed is the conviction of the guilty it is essential that due process is kept and that trial is conducted properly. To this end it is essential that any information given or held by the offender's lawyer is kept confidential. In this context both direct and indirect obligations to disclose information would cause similar damage. However, should the same stand if the aim is prevention of harm? The current law takes the view that this does not matter and carefully

[67] See eg the comments made by the Criminal law Revision Committee in their report on the abolition of the offence of misprision of felony, (above note 15); G Williams (n 9 above); Lord Lloyd of Berwick in his *Inquiry Into Legislation Against Terrorism* (1996) (n 45 above).

[68] Following the attempted London bombing of 21 July 2005, convictions for failing to disclose information (among other offences) of people who were linked to these attacks included: Yeshiemebet Girma, wife of 21 July bomber Hussein Osman, Mulumbet Girma (Yeshi's sister) and her former partner Mohammed Kabashi, and Esayas Girma (Yeshi's brother) (*Girma* [2010] Cr App R (S.) 28 (p 172); Fardosa Abdullahi, who was previously engaged to a bomber, Yassin Omar, (*The Times*, 12 July 2008, p 34); Siraj Ali who was in the care of the same foster parents as 21 July bomber Yassin Omar, Abdul Sherif, brother of bomber Hussein Osman and Wahdi Mohamed, brother of 21 July bomber Ramzi Mohamed (*R v Sherif (Abdul)* [2009] 2 Cr App R (S) 33; Sabeel Ahmed, brother of Kafeel Ahmed who planted care bombs outside London nightclubs, and later died following a car bombing of Glasgow Airport in 2007 (*The Times*, 12 April 2008, p 9).

protects lawyer-client confidentiality in all cases. Theoretically, however, it is possible to construct a duty to disclose information and ensure that such information would not be used for conviction of the criminal. The information may be used by the police in order to prevent harm to people and/or property but may not be admissible in court.[69]

At the same time when it comes to a journalist, the value of freedom of speech and the importance of revealing the truth may negate the imposition of any duty to disclose information: direct and indirect and whether the objective is conviction of the guilty or prevention of harm. Yet the legislator and the court have not always been forthcoming in protecting the confidentiality of journalists' information.

Other relationships may raise different concerns with regards to the different justificatory considerations.[70] It is an open question whether the law should recognise them in the first place, and if so to what extent and how reasonable it is to demand a separate consideration of each type of relationship. Should it also include informal but valuable conduct such as that suggested by Lord Denning between the employer and her employee or between a Master of a college and his student? The fear of course, is that this would become an ever-expending list of special relationships.

The decision to impose an obligation to disclose information raises questions about the relationships between the individual and the society they live in, and among individuals in society. There is no one answer that strikes the correct balance between the competing interests and values in all cases. What may count as legitimate may vary from country to country. This article sets out the range of considerations that ought to be taken into account in assessing the justifiability of the imposition of a duty to disclose information, but their relative strength and their application has to be done on a careful case by case analysis.

[69] A similar approach has been suggested in relation to information gained in urgent interviews (otherwise known as 'public safety interviews') conducted by the police as part of an investigation of suspects of terrorist offences. The law permits the police to delay the provision of legal advice and conduct an urgent interview with suspects of terrorist offences where there is reasonable reason to believe that delaying the interview may result (among other things) in physical injury to another person (ie situations of 'a ticking bomb') (see Terrorism Act 2000 sch 8, although urgent interviews are not limited to terrorist offences and may be permitted in other circumstances as well). Given that the aim of such an interview is the prevention of imminent harm and in order to give the suspect an incentive to co-operate with the police, some argue that any information gained by the police as part of this interview should not be admissible in court in a trial against the suspect. NB, that this position has been rejected by the Court of Appeal which held that the admissibility of safety interviews and their fruit, in evidence in subsequent trial should be decided on a case-by-case basis in accordance with the principles governing a fair trial (*R v Ibrahim* [2008] 2 Cr App R 23 at para 35–36.

[70] For example, the relationship between the regulated sector and their clients discussed earlier.

3

Prophylactic Crimes

AP SIMESTER*

IT HAS BECOME increasingly common for legislatures to regulate harmful conduct on an anticipatory basis, very often by criminalising activity which is preliminary to that conduct, thereby seeking to pre-empt opportunities for the harmful conduct to be perpetrated at all. This kind of crime, which I call prophylactic,[1] is not new. Theft criminalises 'appropriation', whereas the underlying harm being aimed at is permanent deprivation. Anti-Social Behaviour Orders (ASBOs) may criminalise a person's entry into designated locations by way of preventing disruptive behaviour once there. The formation of a conspiracy to defraud is a crime even though the plan is never implemented.[2] English law knows a crime of 'going equipped' – merely being out and about with instruments of burglary.[3] Possession of an unlicensed firearm is an offence notwithstanding that the real concern is their misuse. And so on.

The spectre of terrorism introduces few, if any, distinctive theoretical problems into the field of prophylactic offences. To be sure, some writers have claimed that modern terrorism is different, in as much as it constitutes a truly existential threat to the social and legal orders of a targeted jurisdiction.[4] Yet this claim is for the moment controversial. Western Europeans will recall many acts of terrorism across the past four decades that did not pose such a risk. Until there are very cogent reasons for thinking that the terrorist threat has reached that stage, acts of terrorism should be treated as criminal conduct in the ordinary way. Moreover, even if existential threats were real, it would not follow that exceptional

* I am grateful to the conference organisers for the opportunity to present an early draft of this essay, and to participants for many helpful comments. Particular thanks to Bob Sullivan for written feedback and suggestions, and to the Singapore MoE Tier One Research Grant (number R241000092112) for research travel support.

[1] *cf* AP Simester and A von Hirsch, *Crimes, Harms, and Wrongs: On the Principles of Criminalisation* (Oxford, Hart Publishing, 2011) § 5.2 (hereafter *Simester and von Hirsch*).

[2] See, eg AP Simester et al, *Simester and Sullivan's Criminal Law: Theory and Doctrine*, 4th edn (Oxford, Hart Publishing, 2010) § 9.3 (hereafter *Simester and Sullivan*).

[3] *cf* Theft Act 1968 s 25(1): 'A person shall be guilty of an offence if, when not at his place of abode, he has with him any article for use in the course of or in connection with any burglary, theft or cheat.'

[4] For example, P Bobbitt, *Terror and Consent: The Wars for the Twenty-First Century* (New York, Alfred A Knopf, 2008).

criminal-law responses should be adopted. If and when that juncture is reached, the way forward may well be to address such dangers by emergency mechanisms of the kind appropriate to other radical events such as natural disasters, the spread of a virulent, non-treatable disease, or international war. At least in the context of making wrongs criminal, it is a moral mistake to think that, when existence is threatened, the gloves may come off and anything goes.

(Indeed, the same caveat holds for non-criminal measures, such as quarantine. Detention is not a legal 'black hole', a zone where anything goes: it need not deprive an individual of all rights, but only of freedom. Mistreatment of detainees can, and should, remain illegal. Moreover, the justification of emergency detentions implies originating and terminating conditions, eg based on the ongoing health risk, that are intrinsically bound to the reasons why that detention is justified; and which are not at the discretion of the officials who administer it.[5])

So terrorism does not seem to introduce a new and unprecedented category of risk. However, it does generate pressure for the state and its agencies. In many ways, that's why it's interesting. The potential for harm and disruption to citizens' lives is apparently very great, and the advantages of early intervention considerable. Moreover, as with inchoate offences, there is widespread agreement that convictions should not depend on the harm's occurrence. Indeed, many people think that those who try to hurt others are just as evil, just as deserving of punishment, as those who succeed. Whatever the truth of that moral equivalence view, few would contest that conduct which directly risks causing harm to others may be sufficiently wrongful and in principle eligible for criminalisation; subject always to the normal checks and balances supplied by considerations such as autonomy, free speech, and the like.

In turn, as the risks increase, one may think that waiting for those risks to crystallise, waiting until people are concretely endangered, is already too late. We need to intervene before that. Public concern with 'security', ie freedom from the risk of harm,[6] generates a call for the state to enact prophylactic offences. Perhaps it even generates an obligation to enact them. Surely, the state is sometimes justified in enacting crimes like 'going equipped'. All the more so then when the risks of carnage become greater.

Yet prophylactic crimes raise difficult normative issues. They are likely to generate over-criminalisation, since they frequently prohibit conduct that in itself creates no risk of harm. Possessing a pistol is never itself harmful.

[5] See AP Simester, 'Necessity, Torture and the Rule of Law' in V Ramraj (ed), *Emergencies and the Limits of Legality* (Cambridge, Cambridge University Press, 2008) 289, 310–12.

[6] Given this equivalence, I'm not sure that I see room for normative work to be done by a separate 'obligation of security': V Tadros, 'Justice and Terrorism' (2007) 10 *New Criminal LR* 658, 679ff. It would be otherwise if dangerousness were equated to being *perceived* as a risk, as Peter Ramsay suggests: 'Precaution as a Sentencing Principle' (this volume), 207; but that equation should not be made. Compare also the text at and following n 12 below.

Moreover, its prohibition may require us – notably,[7] members of the Olympic shooting team – to forego options that are themselves valuable. Post-prohibition, there are now all sorts of harmless activities that morally upright citizens might reasonably want to pursue, and which they cannot; for reasons that have nothing to do with them. Taken to extremes, prophylactic crimes have the potential severely to undermine liberty. The threat of criminal liability could become as much a threat to the security of citizens as the harms they are designed to safeguard against.[8]

There are two main ways in which the prevention of harm can be extended into the realm of prophylactic crimes. The first is to deploy ulterior *mens rea* formulations, in order to criminalise a variety of preparatory conduct that is in some way directed toward begetting the ultimate harm. As we shall see, some more recent legislation adopts this technique. The second is to refine the *actus reus*, so as to proscribe some more specific step that is typically taken toward committing a substantive crime: gun possession offences are an example of this very common device. One can, and should, combine the two.[9] Each method typically engages slightly different normative worries, and there is much variation in the kinds of problems they throw up. However, all prophylactic offences share a common form: doing X is declared to be a crime in order to reduce the likelihood that Y will be done.

The difficulty is to identify any principled limits. Morally legitimate criminalisation must negotiate a wide variety of *kinds* of constraint, and prophylactic offences – like all crimes – should in principle satisfy them all. But very few of those constraints are trumps, factors that exclude a candidate crime altogether. Rather, they are factors to be *weighed* against the decision to proscribe, a decision involving judgments of degree. Even autonomy is, fundamentally, a weighting factor. As such, it becomes harder to draw a normative line in the legislative sand, especially in the context of terrorism offences.

I A SPECTRUM OF PROPHYLACTIC OFFENCES

Let us assume that Y, the ultimately harmful activity, is of such a nature that it may justifiably be prohibited through the criminal law;[10] say, that it falls straightforwardly within the scope of the Harm Principle. There is a range of activities prior to Y at which the state might be tempted to intervene, and nothing in the Harm Principle that requires the prohibited activity, X, *in itself* to be harmful. Consider Joel Feinberg's classic formulation:[11]

[7] See, eg, 'Shooters Seek Handgun Law Change' news.bbc.co.uk/sport2/hi/other_sports/ olympics_2012/4162498.stm.

[8] *cf Simester and Sullivan* (n 2 above) § 2.

[9] Compare s 474.14 of the Criminal Code Act 1995 (Aust), noted below in § I.

[10] For discussion of this constraint, see *Simester and von Hirsch* (n 1 above) § 5.2.

[11] J Feinberg, *Harm to Others* (New York, Oxford University Press, 1984) 26.

> 'It is always a good reason in support of penal legislation that it would be effective in preventing (eliminating, reducing) harm to persons other than the actor (the one prohibited from acting) and there is no other means that is equally effective at no greater cost to other values.'

It is the prevention, not the occurrence, of harm that counts here. Rather than mandating that X be harmful, Feinberg demands only that its criminalisation will prevent harm. In many ways, therefore, the important question to ask is, what if this act were always permitted? Would harm result?

However, one can extend this thought too far, and I think that Jeremy Horder does so in his chapter for this volume when he adopts John Gardner and Stephen Shute's analysis:[12]

> 'It is no objection under the harm principle that a harmless action was criminalized, nor even that an action with no tendency to cause harm was criminalized. It is enough to meet the demands of the harm principle that, if the action were not criminalized, *that* would be harmful.'

It does not follow from the fact that Y is harmful that X is wrong – even if Y is known to be correlated to X, so that the occurrence of X means that Y is predictably more likely. Sometimes, the prospect that Y may occur supplies *no reason at all* why X is wrong. Yet a properly understood Harm Principle requires, inter alia, that X be wrong.

Typically, grounding the wrong in a further harm presents problems of imputation. However, it is also worth noting, in the context of security-based offences, that it is even more problematic to rely on the reactions of the public to satisfy the Harm Principle. As a general proposition, such reactions – even of fear – do not make a person's conduct wrong. Hence they do not by themselves establish a case for criminalisation. Suppose that two teenagers, D and E, walk down the street wearing trainers and hoodies. F, a middle-aged person, crosses the street in order to avoid them. D and E do nothing wrong, and F has no right to be protected from the source of her fear.

I cannot go into the details of these complex issues here. They are considered elsewhere.[13] It suffices for the moment to acknowledge that, subject to certain conditions, the Harm Principle is compatible with criminalising conduct that is not directly harmful. Yet, how remote can the conduct legitimately be? Broadly speaking, the range of candidate activities for prohibition lies along a spectrum, ranging from what George Orwell once called 'thoughtcrimes'; through what criminal lawyers call 'preparatory' conduct; via incomplete *attempts*; then *complete* attempts; to, ultimately, the harmful activity (Y) itself. Consider the following hypothetical offences:

[12] J Gardner and S Shute, 'The Wrongness of Rape' in J Horder (ed), *Oxford Essays in Jurisprudence*, 4th series (Oxford, Oxford University Press, 2000) 193, 216; J Horder in ch 4 of this volume.

[13] *Simester and von Hirsch* (n 1 above) chs 3–5. For specific criticism of the analysis by Gardner and Shute from which Horder draws, see ibid, § 3.2(c).

1. Intending to commit the murder of some other person.[14]
2. Walking down any public road while intending to murder another.
3. Walking down Oxford Street, London, while intending to murder another.
4. Eating muesli (in order to get fit, say) in order to carry out a murder in the future.[15]
5. Entering Oxford Street, London, with intent while there to murder another.
6. Doing anything with intent *thereby* to murder another.

Some of these examples certainly look problematic. As we shall see below, the first three are exposed to additional objections, beyond those of remoteness. At the same time, many wide-ranging offences that fall well short of attempts – complete or incomplete – are being deployed nowadays. Individuals in England and Wales have been prohibited from entering defined areas under Anti-Social Behaviour Orders,[16] and from leaving their own house outside permitted hours under Control Orders.[17] Under Australian federal law, it is now an offence to connect to the internet with intent to commit a serious offence:[18]

474.14 Using a telecommunications network with intention to commit a serious offence

(1) A person is guilty of an offence if:

(a) the person:

(i) connects equipment to a telecommunications network; and

(ii) intends by this to commit, or to facilitate the commission of, an offence (whether by that person or another person); and

(b) the offence is:

(i) a serious offence against a law of the Commonwealth, a State or a Territory; or

(ii) a serious offence against a foreign law.

The maximum penalty for the offence is that corresponding to perpetration of the ulterior intended offence. An extreme example of this kind of legislation in the UK is supplied by section 5 of the Terrorism Act 2006, which enacts an offence punishable by life imprisonment:

5. Preparation of terrorist acts

(1) A person commits an offence if, with the intention of –

(a) committing acts of terrorism,[19] or

[14] I use 'murder' rather than 'kill' just to exclude the thought of potential defences.

[15] Thanks to Bob Sullivan for this example.

[16] See, eg, AP Simester and A von Hirsch, 'Regulating Offensive Conduct Through Two-Step Prohibitions' in *Incivilities: Regulating Offensive Behaviour* (Oxford, Hart Publishing, 2006) 173.

[17] See, eg, L Zedner, 'Preventive Justice or Pre-Punishment? The Case of Control Orders' (2007) 60 *Current Legal Problems* 174.

[18] Criminal Code Act 1995.

[19] Lucia Zedner observed in discussion that such an offence is exposed to additional remoteness objections, in that Y ('acts of terrorism') is, as currently defined under English law, very open-ended and comprises conduct that it not itself harmful or wrongful either. This important point is incidental here.

(b) assisting another to commit such acts,

he engages in any conduct in preparation for giving effect to his intention.

(2) It is irrelevant for the purposes of subsection (1) whether the intention and preparations relate to one or more particular acts of terrorism, acts of terrorism of a particular description or acts of terrorism generally.

Many of the worries about crimes like these are familiar, and I shall not rehearse them in close detail. My project is, rather, an exploratory one: to investigate in the following sections whether there might be any *general* normative limits upon the scope of prophylactic offences.

II LIMITED NON-NEGOTIABLE CONSTRAINTS

It is sometimes said that there is at least one in-principle constraint upon criminalisation, which is that actions are only (morally speaking) legitimately criminalised when they are wrongful, in the sense that they ought not to be done.[20] I think this is right, for reasons to which we return in section III. However, this requirement, while important, is not by itself an adequate safeguard against unjustified criminalisation. Each of the activities in our list of hypothetical offences is a problematic candidate for criminalisation. At the same time, it is at least arguable that each of these involves wrongful activity.[21] Indeed, if it is wrongful to intend to murder a person, then they all do – being just subsets of the mental activity described in example (1). And it certainly seems plausible that people ought not to hold intentions to kill other persons.

Thoughtcrimes, such as example (1), are not unknown to the law. The Statute of Treasons 1351 includes within the ambit of treason, 'When a Man doth compass or imagine the Death of our Lord the King, or of our Lady his Queen or of their eldest Son and Heir.' Similar formulations can still be found in the legislation of other nations.[22] Equally familiar are the reservations about their enactment, including some concerns that cut across ordinary criminalisation-limiting principles like the Harm Principle. Without an *actus reus*, it is arguable that we cannot ensure the prohibited event, the mental state, is voluntary; which, in turn, deprives us of any assurance that the agent is morally responsible for the

[20] In practice, the criminal law frequently prohibits actions that are not pre-legally wrong. Such cases present a challenge to the proposition advanced here. I think that challenge can in principle be met, in as much as the law plays a role in creating (typically, giving specific form to) reasons for and against doing a particular activity. For discussion, see *Simester and von Hirsch*, § 2.3(b).

[21] This point is subject to the line of reasoning explored below, in § V, where it is suggested that, arguably, for certain 'inherently innocent' activities, doing X cannot be made wrongful by the fact that it is motivated by Y. In such cases, even though 'doing X with intent then to Y' may name something wrongful, the wrongfulness would rest just in the intention to Y; it would not make doing X wrongful.

[22] See, eg, s 121A of the Penal Code (Singapore): 'Whoever compasses, imagines, invents, devises, or intends the death of or hurt to or imprisonment or restraint of the President, shall be punished with death, or with imprisonment for life and shall, if he is not sentenced to death, also be liable to fine.'

event.[23] She may be 'responsible' for it in various other senses; after all, the thought is hers. However, to be eligible for *blaming* judgments in respect of the event, it must lie within her voluntary control. In turn, since the criminal law is a blaming system, its prohibitions should be restricted to events that are voluntary. Perhaps there is inadequate control over thoughts or even intentions for blaming judgments to be appropriate.[24]

This is not to suggest, as some writers have, that there must always be a formal 'act' requirement in crimes. So-called 'situational' and 'possession' offences are not conceptually wrong.[25] It is enough that there be some *actus reus* event over which the agent has control, that it is not impossible for the agent to prevent.[26] Still, even that minimum could suffice to exclude crime (1).

Other worries about thoughtcrimes, however, are more negotiable. They go too far in restricting the autonomy of subject-citizens. They transgress upon a realm that should be treated as private. They require policing and enforcement mechanisms that are too intrusive and too unreliable. They are likely to lead to problems of discretionary and discriminatory enforcement. These are all valid objections, and it is hard to imagine any thoughtcrime that might be justified in the light of them. Yet they are largely contingent.[27] Their assessment requires the kind of weighing and balancing exercises contemplated by writers like Feinberg under standard formulations of the Harm Principle,[28] when considering the legitimacy of state intervention. It is surely safe to generalise that thoughtcrimes are so invasive a prohibition that their benefits, if any, are always outweighed by their costs in terms of individual freedom. They are overbroad, paradigmatically so. However, that generalisation emerges as a conclusion, a product of the calculus of criminalisation.

Let us, then, add a further element. Consider the second and third examples. We should remain concerned, of course, about their breadth. In the second example, D now has a means of avoiding criminal liability, although it might ask too much that he should do so. But does the same hold for the third case?

[23] AP Simester, 'On the So-called Requirement for Voluntary Action' (1998) 1 *Buffalo Criminal LR* 403. I assume, for the sake of argument, that mental 'acts' are possible. There is also the practical problem of identifying what kind of mental act a given thought may be – an intention, a wish, a conjecture, etc. See, eg, G Dworkin and D Blumenfeld, 'Punishment for Intention' (1966) 75 *Mind* 396, 401.

[24] For an interesting discussion of this large question, see D Husak, 'Does Criminal Liability Require an Act' in RA Duff (ed), *Philosophy and the Criminal Law: Principle and Critique* (Cambridge, Cambridge University Press, 1998) 60, § IV.

[25] ibid 409–13.

[26] *Simester and Sullivan* (n 2 above) § 4.3(ii). The 'event' in question may involve a non-occurrence, as when D fails to report for duty at 7am because he sleeps through his alarm. This is not, as Michael Moore once claimed, 'literally nothing at all': *Act and Crime: The Theory of Action and its Implications for Criminal Law* (Oxford University Press, 1993) 28. It describes an event involving a non-doing, not a non-event.

[27] Admittedly, concerns about privacy might support a further in-principle generalisation, that conduct should be (even if indirectly) other-affecting before it is eligible for criminalisation. That famous issue need not be resolved here.

[28] Feinberg, *Harm to Others* (n 11 above) 216.

Again, the contingent objections may be open to us. On the standard analysis espoused by Feinberg, the moral case for criminalisation should always consider the gravity and likelihood of the harm-to-be-prevented, weighing that against the social value of the conduct to be prohibited and the degree of intrusion upon citizens' lives that prohibition would entail. The more grave and probable the harm, the more likely that criminalisation is warranted. The more costly the prohibition, in terms of valuable options lost to citizens,[29] the stronger the case against criminalisation. Arguably, and perhaps even fairly clearly, the crimes here look overbroad. Their potential benefits do not justify the liberty-restrictions they impose.

However, if that's all that is wrong about crimes like these, they aren't ruled out altogether. Justifying their enactment simply needs fine-tuning. If the threat is severe enough, as terrorism is often thought to be, and if the conduct element is sufficiently narrowed – say by narrowing the proscription to the most vulnerable street – then, eventually, the checks and balances might weigh in favour of prohibition.

The standard, weighting approach to criminalisation is a necessary step in the justification of crimes, in as much as proscriptions are not warranted unless the matter is appropriately serious. But it is not sufficient. It envisages analysis whereby the various factors are stacked up against each other in order to determine which pile has the greater weight. Perhaps I should be left free to walk down Oxford Street if there is a remote chance I might injure someone. Maybe not, however, if the potential harm is more serious, eg when there is the same chance of causing many deaths. And so on. Major restrictions on liberty are undesirable but, on a weighting approach, that just means some more extreme risk is needed to justify them. Provided the stakes are high enough, potentially anything goes.

III SUPPLEMENTARY CONSTRAINTS ON PROPHYLACTIC CRIMES

So, what additional considerations might constrain the morally legitimate reach of the criminal law? Let me suggest some supplementary, in-principle constraints upon crimes of this sort.

A Wrongful Action

When seeking to pre-empt risk, there is a variety of ways in which the state can regulate conduct. Notoriously, the UK has used devices such as Control Orders simply to corral individuals,[30] so that it can restrict and monitor their move-

[29] *cf* also the pragmatic and rule-of-law considerations noted in respect of thought crimes.

[30] Prevention of Terrorism Act 2005. The system of Control Orders is to be replaced by one of 'Terrorism Prevention and Investigation Measures': HC Deb 26 January 2011, vol 522, cols 306–09.

ments. Even this was not particularly novel. Internment and quarantine orders are familiar, if controversial, techniques available to the state outside the criminal law. However, if we want morally loaded, condemnatory tools to regulate behaviour, we should normally use the criminal law. The blaming judgments embedded in criminal law are part of its distinctive character. Criminalisation speaks in moral terms to subject-citizens, to wrongdoers potential and actual. Through criminal proscriptions, the state makes an official declaration concerning the normative status of the proscribed behaviour. Subsequently, through conviction and punishment, it makes an official declaration about the wrongfulness of the defendant's conduct.

This official moral condemnation of activity and actor generates a truth-constraint. When labeling conduct as wrongful, and when labeling those it convicts as culpable wrongdoers, the state should get it right. In particular, the criminal law contains a general limiting principle that D should not be convicted of an offence unless he is responsible for a wrong.[31] Any formal judgment of blame, including the finding of guilt on which the conviction is based, must be predicated upon norm-violating conduct. One cannot blame a person unless that person does something that, all things considered, she ought not to do.[32]

The wrongdoing requirement establishes a prima facie barrier to many prophylactic crimes in particular. Notice that it is the *prohibited* action (X), rather than the later potential action (Y), that must be wrongful. In the context of prophylactic crimes, this generates a problem: it needs to be shown why the prospect of future wrongdoing makes it wrong for the defendant to act as she does. It may be wrong to kill someone, and indeed to intend to kill someone, but there is nothing wrong with walking down the street or connecting to the internet. We can't blame a person for doing *that*; in which case, we shouldn't be criminalising the activity (at least, not under that description).

B A Nexus Requirement

In the context of ulterior intent offences, of course, that's a bit too simplified. What is being prohibited is not walking down the street, *simpliciter*, but walking down the street with intent to kill. And there is definitely *something* wrong with that.

Even so, there is potential for difficulty about the location of the wrong. By contrast with examples (4) and (5), what is really objectionable about examples (2) and (3) is that what's wrong – the intention – is not sufficiently connected to the *actus reus*, so that walking down the street is still not something for which D can be blamed. In order for the wrongfulness requirement to be satisfied, the

[31] *cf* Simester, 'The Mental Element in Complicity' (2006) 122 *LQR* 578, 579–80; also now *Simester and von Hirsch* (n 1 above) pt I.

[32] This point is prior to the (further) requirement that the person be at fault for doing it. *cf Simester and von Hirsch* (n 1 above) § 2.3(a).

conduct must be wrongful, or at least wrongful when done with the relevant ulterior intent. This means that we must be able to give reasons *ex ante* why a person should not perpetrate that conduct. In examples (2) and (3), the mere existence of an intention to kill does not supply reasons why one should refrain from walking down streets, let alone Oxford Street in particular. As such, we have no grounds morally to condemn a person who does so. And there is no case for criminalisation.

There are three different aspects of what are sometimes called 'remoteness' problems. They need to be separated out in this discussion. First, the nexus requirement, which I have set out here, addresses the connection between risks of Y and the doing of X, such that *doing X with the intent to do Y* becomes a wrong. Its point is that the connection is established when there is a nexus between the doing of X and the intent to do (or, perhaps, facilitate) Y. If I am walking the streets today, having resolved to murder my brother tomorrow, that connection is lacking – unless my actions today are part of my project for tomorrow.

This first point helps us to analyse Larry Alexander's and Kimberly Ferzan's example of Roger, the would-be art thief, who intends to steal the Mona Lisa; but only if it is in the Metropolitan Museum of Art in New York (most unlikely), and only if it is not heavily guarded.[33] Alexander and Ferzan themselves favour restricting criminalisation to completed attempts or endangerments, arguing that 'it is only at the time the actor engages in the act that unleashes a risk of harm that he believes he can no longer control . . . that he has performed a culpable action.'[34] That strikes me as too restrictive: incomplete attempts can be wrongful, and in turn culpable. At the same time, merely entering the museum does not seem wrongful, and perhaps not wrongful even when done by someone who happens to have a conditional intention to steal the Mona Lisa. What makes it wrongful (subject to other aspects of remoteness, noted below) is that Roger enters the museum *in order* to steal the Mona Lisa, in the unlikely event that it's there. A key issue, in other words, is *why* Roger enters the museum. Without that nexus, entering the museum seems unproblematic.[35]

It might be wrongful, none the less. Sometimes, a connection can be supplied in other ways, eg because D's act of doing X supplies the means for D, or another, subsequently to do Y. In these kinds of cases it may be legitimate to proscribe X without incorporating an ulterior intention requirement; a controversial example is the criminalisation of gun possession. Even here, however, it is not sufficient that X merely raises the probability that Y may occur. More is required. This second type of 'remoteness' problem raises issues of imputation. As was noted earlier, their discussion lies outside the scope of this chapter.[36]

[33] L Alexander and K Ferzan, *Crime and Culpability: A Theory of Criminal Law* (New York, Cambridge University Press, 2009) 203.

[34] ibid 197.

[35] Even so, the nexus requirement is very accommodating. It does not, for example, rule out the muesli example: see section IV below.

[36] See *Simester and von Hirsch* (n 1 above) chs 4–5.

The third type of 'remoteness' issue is more familiar, under that rubric, to criminal lawyers. Even though the nexus requirement is satisfied, entry to the museum in order to steal might still be counted as too 'remote' from the crystallised harm to warrant criminalisation. In the language of inchoate criminal liability, it is 'mere preparation' rather than 'attempt'. This problem is raised by my hypothetical examples (4) and (5), and will be discussed below, in section IV.

C Arbitrary Dispensations

Finally, beyond discussing their shared defect, we should also note the difference between examples (2) and (3). The latter is restricted to Oxford Street rather than any public road. Prima facie, the Oxford Street limitation lacks any rationale related to the ultimate harm that motivates enactment of the offence. It might be different if Oxford Street were a well known murder hotspot; perhaps Downing Street might be an appropriate limitation in the context of terrorist offences. Failing some consideration of that kind, however, the limitation is arbitrary. Why are people walking down Bond Street with like intent getting away with it?

Limitations of this type can, of course, abet the case for criminalisation by reducing the scope and intrusiveness of prohibitions, as well as the costs of policing and the need for invasive methods of surveillance. However, such payoffs do not warrant a free choice among filtering elements to include in the offence.[37] Arbitrary elements can violate requirements of fairness in the distribution of convictions and punishment. It is unfair to single out one person rather than another for punishment, when both are equally deserving, unless there are good reasons – which may in part be institutional – for distributing such burdens unevenly. Without more, the Oxford Street rule violates this constraint.

IV PREPARATORY OFFENCES

Consider, now, the UK and Australian offences we noted earlier. Those offences do not fall foul of the nexus constraint, because they maintain a connection between the *actus reus* and the source of the wrongfulness. What is criminalised is conduct that is itself directed toward subsequent wrongdoing. Hence they more closely resemble examples (4) and (5) of our hypothetical list:

4. Eating muesli in order to carry out a murder in the future.
5. Entering Oxford Street, London, with intent while there to murder another.

[37] See AP Simester, 'Is Strict Liability Always Wrong' in *Appraising Strict Liability* (Oxford, Oxford University Press, 2005) 21, 47–48.

They are, in other words, *preparatory* in nature. Preparatory offences are narrower in scope than the general class of prophylactic offences, in as much as X is prohibited only because its commission is directed toward the perpetration of Y. Here, the difficulty is a more familiar variety of remoteness. Unless we restrict ourselves to complete-attempt offences like example (6), is there any general constraint on criminalisation that rules out offence (4)?

One general worry about liability for preparatory conduct is that, unless and until done, or at least risked, by D herself, the anticipated harmful wrong (Y) is not D's responsibility and, consequently, it is prima facie unsuitable for the censuring response of the criminal law. D's own behaviour is harmless. It becomes a candidate for criminalisation only because there might be an autonomous subsequent decision (by D or another) to engage in further behaviour that does or risks harm. Rather like ASBO prohibitions on entering certain areas, to impose criminal liability on D in such situations is a form of situational harm prevention. It treats D as being other than a morally responsible agent, capable of deliberation and self-control: as someone who lacks the insight or self-control to resist the later temptation.

Antony Duff raises a related concern when he suggests that preparatory crimes eliminate the *locus poenitentiae*, within which citizens can make up their own minds whether to go through with envisaged wrongdoing.[38] That thought similarly rests on the idea that the state should treat its citizens as responsible agents. Perhaps, though, we can take the underlying idea in a slightly different direction, one that focuses on the lack of trust and respect exhibited by a state that pre-emptively regulates conduct – whether through the criminal *or* the civil law. Jeremy Waldron captures the thought strongly: law may be mandatory, but it is not brute. When it coerces people, 'they will not be herded like cattle or broken like horses; they will not be beaten like dumb animals or treated as bodies to be manipulated'.[39] At the core of any decent legal system is a commitment to respect the dignity of those it governs, to treat them as reasoning human beings. Preparatory crimes undermine that commitment.

To a greater or lesser extent, of course, this is true for all incomplete attempts as well as acts of preparation. Apart from the kinds of complete attempts contemplated in example (6), even the traditional inchoate offences are prophylactic: they need not lead directly to the ultimate harm, but include what are mere steps along that path. All the more so for conduct that does not cross the preparation threshold into the realm of actualised attempt.[40]

[38] RA Duff, *Criminal Attempts* (Oxford, Oxford University Press, 1996) 386–89. One restriction upon Duff's objection is that, *if* doing X with intent to Y is wrongful, there is already wrongdoing at this preparatory point; and its criminalisation is compatible with treating persons as responsible wrongdoers. We return to the question of wrongfulness later in the text.

[39] J Waldron, 'Torture and Positive Law: Jurisprudence for the White House' (2005) 105 *Columbia LR* 1681, 1727.

[40] *cf* the striking case of *Campbell* (1990) 93 Cr App Rep 350 (CA), in which D, carrying an imitation firearm, was arrested just before entering a post office that he intended to rob. His conviction for attempted robbery was quashed, on the ground that he was at that stage merely getting into position to commence the *actus reus* of robbery (ie theft by force).

One might be tempted to think of preparatory offences simply as throwing up problems of imputation, of the kind we mentioned earlier. That thought is right insofar as they do raise a common question: whether the state may legitimately compel D to give up options merely because harmful wrongs might later occur. The imputation of remote harms requires that there be something more than predictability or correlation in order to make that later prospect (of Y) a ground for prohibiting D's conduct (X), such that X becomes wrongful conduct. As we noted in section III, however, in the case of preparation there does appear to be a normative link between X and Y, in that the doing of X is *directed toward* facilitating the subsequent, albeit potential, perpetration of Y. This nexus does seem to be sufficient to make the prospect of Y at least the business of D; to pick D out as involved in, and responsible for, the perpetration of Y.

But is the prospect of Y enough to make doing X wrong? And if so, when? There seems no reason to object to a person's eating cereal. It certainly isn't wrong in and of itself. A good example of this worry is the modern UK law of theft, the *actus reus* of which can be committed by one who appropriates another's property even with that other's consent.[41] Imagine the following facts:[42]

> While shopping, D notices a pair of shoes. Each shoe has a price tag attached, but one tag reads £6.99, the other £4.99. She picks up the shoes in order to take them to the cashier, hoping that the cashier will only notice the lower (as D knows, incorrect) price.

As the law stands, this is a consummated theft – complete at the moment D touches the shoes, well before she approaches the cashier. But her doing so is (i) authorised and (ii) merely preparatory, a precursor to approaching the cashier. Touching a pair of shoes inside a shoe shop is not theftuous behaviour. Prima facie, it is in no way wrongful. As such, it should not be criminal.

Much the same, it seems to me, applies to a person who connects to the internet as a prelude to criminal behaviour. Sometimes, even where a person's behaviour (in doing X) is by itself innocent, liability as an attempt (to do Y) may be appropriate, but not until then.

V POSSIBLE CONSTRAINTS ON PREPARATORY OFFENCES

Section 5 of the Terrorism Act 2006 does seem to proscribe acts of cereal eating, eg when done as part of a fitness programme in preparation for committing a terrorist act. Morally speaking, the section probably overreaches, extending the criminal law beyond its legitimate bounds. On balance, the prohibition seems too invasive of privacy and autonomy. It generates rule of law worries, such as the potential for discriminatory enforcement. In addition to these

[41] *Gomez* [1993] AC 442 (HL); *Hinks* [2001] 2 AC 241 (HL). The *actus reus* must be perpetrated dishonestly and with intention permanently to deprive. See *Simester and Sullivan* (n 2 above) ch 13.

[42] *cf Dip Kaur v Chief Constable for Hampshire* [1981] 2 All ER 430 (CA).

standard concerns we noted in section II, preparatory offences frequently involve significant problems of evidential uncertainty. Proof of an actor's intentions is typically greater at the point of preliminary conduct, which is likely to be morally ambiguous in character. This is one of the controversies surrounding the English law of theft. The *actus reus* of theft is now so preliminary that the gist of the offence rests on dishonesty – and it is highly undesirable that such an amorphous concept should become so central to liability.

From an *ex ante* perspective, evidential uncertainty can also expand the effective scope of a prohibition. Someone wanting to avoid being accused of a preparatory crime might have to forgo even innocent behaviour for fear of its being misconstrued. Perhaps, in the current political climate, farmers should stop buying fertiliser. Apparently, school dinner ladies are well advised not to give children biscuits.[43] And the police themselves have advertised that paying for transactions in cash, or keeping one's curtains drawn, can be suggestive of terrorism.[44]

These kinds of considerations play a significant, indeed crucial, role when assessing the justification of preparatory offences. However, as we observed in section II, such factors are negotiable. Their importance might be outweighed if the stakes are high enough. The criminalisation of cereal eating with intent might, on the standard analysis, be legitimate. Of course, that conclusion is unlikely in practice – and it is a strength of the standard analysis that it is responsive to the interests of *both* potential defendants and potential victims. Even so, it is worth considering whether there are other lines that we might draw in the sand, as it were, to divide legitimate from illegitimate preparatory offences.

A The Attempt-Preparation Divide in Inchoate Offences

One boundary is familiar, and I shall just mention it here. Where the *actus reus* content of X is unspecific, the dividing line between incomplete attempts and 'mere preparation' does a considerable amount of work in the criminal law. That division, however, is not a clear one. In some respects, this is a significant payoff of Alexander's and Ferzan's preference to criminalise only complete attempts:[45] at least the distinction between complete and incomplete attempts is clearly meaningful. The risk posed by the former is present: by the latter, potential. In comparison, the borderline between incomplete attempts and preparation may seem arbitrary. Yet there seems reason to refrain from that conclusion, just as touching a pair of shoes inside a shoe shop is not already an attempt to steal them. The distinction may be fuzzy, but it is not meaningless, in as much as it seeks to capture the point at which D has *embarked* upon *commission* of her intended crime. Of course there are some cases that are difficult to categorise on

[43] 'Dinner Lady's Child Grooming Warning Over Biscuit' *Belfast Telegraph* 8 October 2010.

[44] See, eg, 'Anti-Terrorist Hotline Ad Banned for being "Offensive"': www.bbc.co.uk/news/uk-10929203.

[45] Above n 33 ch 6.

this basis. Arguably, that simply reflects the truth that they are genuinely hard cases, not that the distinction is empty. Moreover, the difference also seems to inform the principles of self-defence, a point to which we return in section VI.

B Motive-Dependent Wrongfulness?

Is there any other line that we can potentially draw between entering Oxford Street and eating cereal? Perhaps, although the matter is far from certain. In the rest of this section, we consider one possible ground of differentiation. Recall that these offences criminalise doing X as preparation for Y. It follows, as we noted in section III, that doing X with the requisite intention must be wrongful. We should therefore ask whether it is wrongful to eat cereal, or to enter Oxford Street, by way of preparation (and not attempt) to murder?

Our answer depends, of course, on when a bad intention can make an otherwise innocent activity wrongful. To this underlying question, different responses may be offered,[46] although the most plausible analysis seems to be that, wherever it is wrong to do Y, it is prima facie wrongful to do X in furtherance of Y. Yet that has not always been the approach of the law. Arguably, one can draw a distinction between (i) behaviour that is not wrongful and is not made wrongful by the intentions with which it is done, and behaviour that is either (ii) in itself wrongful (eg killing) or is (iii) capable of being made wrongful when done for certain kinds of reasons. For convenience, let us term these three categories of behaviour 'inherently innocent', 'inherently wrongful', and 'morally ambiguous'.

This kind of distinction was a feature of the former English law of indecent assault. In *Court*,[47] D placed a 12-year-old girl, fully clothed, across his knees and beat her on the buttocks. The House of Lords ruled that such conduct, if a disciplinary measure, was a mere assault; but if done for sexual gratification, the assault was indecent. Their Lordships distinguished three types of conduct for these purposes: (a) conduct which is inherently decent; (b) conduct which is inherently indecent; and (c) conduct which may or may not be indecent. If an act is 'inherently decent', it cannot constitute an indecent assault even if D's motive in perpetrating the act is sexual: thus touching a woman's shoe,[48] whatever the underlying fetish, would be at most a simple battery. At the other end of the spectrum, conduct might be indecent by its very nature, irrespective of motive. Thus where D, a doctor, takes a vaginal sample from V under the guise of diagnosis – but in truth for the sake of his private research – the non-consensual assault is inherently indecent.[49]

[46] At the conference on which this book was based, for example, Antony Duff gave three different answers in response to consecutive questions on this difficult issue: assuming it is wrong to do Y, then (i) it is wrong to do X in order then to do Y; (ii) it is wrong to do X solely in order then to do Y; (iii) it is wrong unreasonably to do X in order then to do Y.

[47] *Court* [1989] AC 28.

[48] *cf George* [1956] Crim LR 52.

[49] *Court* [1989] AC 28, 44 (Lord Ackner). *cf Tabassum* [2000] 2 Cr App R 328.

The facts of *Court* fell within type (c). Sometimes, as in that case, the character of an action cannot be determined by reference to its external, *actus reus* features alone. The same applies in tort law: if D picks up P's wallet lying in the street, having it in mind to take it to the nearest police-station, D's *conduct* (the act of a responsible citizen) is different in kind from that of a person who picks up someone else's wallet in order to keep it (a tortious conversion,[50] as well as a theft). And, of course, outside the law: if D approaches V with fist clenched, the nature of D's conduct and the appropriateness of V's reaction may depend on whether D intends genuinely to attack V or to act out her role in a stage production; or, indeed, to demonstrate a legal nicety to D's class of undergraduates.

If that's right, the implications for criminalisation are potentially significant. As we noted earlier, a criminal prohibition constitutes, inter alia, an official pronouncement that the activity is morally wrongful – qua activity, and not just on particular occasions. Where the proscribed activity is not wrongful, it follows that the state is not telling the truth and criminalisation is prima facie unjustified.[51] Hence the state should not prohibit, and label as criminal, type (i) behaviour – ie, inherently innocent conduct, such as a customer's authorised handling of shoes in a store. Or eating cereal. The thought here is that eating cereal is simply not wrong, and its normative status – qua eating cereal – cannot be infected by the further intentions with which it is done.[52]

In turn, if category (i) is populated at all, it follows that the open-ended proscription in section 5 of the Terrorism Act 2006, of '*any conduct* in preparation for giving effect to his intention', is illegitimate. Necessarily, the class of activities proscribed includes conduct that is inherently innocent, and reference to D's intention cannot save it from doing so. Open-ended conduct may legitimately be proscribed qua *attempt*, incomplete or complete; but not in its own right.[53]

Section 474.14 of the Australian legislation is not quite so easily disposed of. Whether it is legitimate depends mainly on whether connecting to the internet (say) is inherently innocent or morally ambiguous. If the latter, then the *mens rea* requirement of the offence may suffice to restrict its application to activities that are indeed wrongful; a conclusion that is not available under the UK offence because of the sheer breadth of the *actus reus*.

Arguably, connecting to the internet is like picking up the telephone, switching on a computer, eating cereal, or indeed walking down the street. It is the kind of everyday activity that should be regarded as inherently innocent. The prospect of future wrongdoing doesn't seem to supply any significant reason why we should not do those activities, any reason that we might remark upon. The risk of facilitating such wrongdoing is too ancillary, especially where the

[50] *Police v Moodley* [1974] 1 NZLR 644. The examples here are taken from the first edition of *Simester and Sullivan* (n 2 above) § 12.2(i)(b).

[51] Note the proviso: prima facie. The possibility of over-inclusive proscriptions on the basis of necessity is noted below, in section VI.

[52] *cf* n 21 above.

[53] Implicitly, this line of argument requires us to sustain the distinction between incomplete attempts and mere preparation, noted earlier in this section.

conduct is otherwise quotidian and harmless. Activities such as walking down the street generate no specific risks of wrongdoing, in as much as there is no reason, *ex ante*, to think that a person doing X may be preparing for Y.

Even ordinary activities have the potential to facilitate crime. If D buys a car, it is always possible that D may drive the car in such as manner as to injure others, and may even do so deliberately. Yet no-one seriously suggests that car sales should therefore be prohibited. This is not just a matter of probabilities. Everyday activities standardly have legitimate purposes: cars are *meant* to be driven, just as pavements are meant to be walked upon. D has no independent reason for desisting from use of the car – driving per se is neither wrongful nor harmful. By way of illustration, contrast the purchase of a police radar detector, which might legitimately be considered for prohibition as a form of preparatory conduct, in as much as their core function is illegitimate.[54] One cannot regard the use of radar detectors as incidental or ancillary, and unconnected to its purchase.

Obviously, there will be borderline cases. Sometimes, an activity may be morally ambiguous because it has multiple standard purposes, some innocent and some not: for example, carrying a crowbar. Here, a *mens rea*-specific offence may be appropriate, so that D offends only if actually carrying the crowbar for the purposes of burglary.

C A Negotiable Matter?

As will be apparent, the 'everyday' nature of an activity is bound up with our social understanding of that activity. To a considerable extent, that understanding is conventional, and may well differ across societies. The possession of handguns, constitutionally protected in the USA, seems to be in this category. Within the UK, the social understanding of handguns tends to associate their use with violence and wrongdoing; perhaps reflecting the traditionally more crowded nature of domestic housing, which permits few opportunities for recreational use. Legitimate uses are exceptional rather than core. Insofar as this is true, their supply can be more clearly understood as associating the possessor with the wrongdoing they facilitate.

It is likely, in turn, that the risks associated with their use may come to inform the social understanding of an activity. This has seemingly occurred for drink-driving, and may well be true in the case of handguns. A question therefore arises whether we are back to the realm of negotiable, rather than in-principle constraints; whether, as with factors such as autonomy, the wrongfulness constraint just imposes a restriction of degree, since an activity might come to be seen as wrongful once the stakes get high enough.

Two factors contraindicate. The first is practical. In the case of a genuinely ordinary activity, one that is associated with everyday, innocent purposes, it is

[54] *cf Simester and von Hirsch* (n 1 above) § 5.2(c)(iii).

hard to see how the distant possibility of future wrongdoing will overwhelm those associations so as to corrupt the activity's *inherent* standing. Even now, connecting to the internet is understood to be just what it (predominantly, overwhelmingly) is: connecting to the internet, and not as a form of conduct facilitating wrongdoing. In itself, it remains an inherently innocent activity.

The second is structural. The exploratory analysis here involves two steps: first, determining whether an activity is inherently innocent; second, excluding the criminalisation of those activities. The in-principle constraint, against criminalising activity that is not wrongful, constitutes the second step. The question whether an activity is inherently innocent may be itself borderline (*cf* handguns); but if it is innocent, the scale of contingent risks becomes irrelevant.

VI NECESSITOUS OVER-INCLUSION

A final thread of constraint arises from the limitations of necessity. Suppose that a prohibition contravenes one of the restrictions we have explored. It is prima facie illegitimate. Nonetheless, it may be justified by reference to necessity. Driving on a UK motorway at speeds greater than 70 miles per hour may not always be dangerous; but the pragmatic needs of enforceable regulation, required in order to safeguard against the abstract dangers of driving too fast, may warrant an over-inclusive rule. Few writers contend that this line of argument is *never* available to justify prohibitions of morally innocent conduct by reference to the harms at which those prohibitions are directed.

Of course, as a preliminary matter, it needs to be shown that the over-inclusive prohibition is genuinely necessary to prevent the relevant potential harm. Australian legislation contains an extensive range of specific offences involving computer misuse, and it is hard to see how the section 474.14 crime offers any kind of vital complement to that repertoire. More importantly, though, there may be limits to the *kinds* of acts that necessity can justify.

A Necessity Rather than Self-Defence

Notice first that preparatory offences are analogous to necessity rather than self-defence (or defence on behalf of another). While I can only sketch the difference here, it is a significant one.[55] Actions taken in self-defence can be preemptive too, but only when the risk being addressed is a crystallised, active threat – only when a threat has passed beyond incipience, when it is no longer looming and the attack has commenced. Self-defence thus contains a line analogous to the attempt-mere preparation divide in inchoate crimes. Partly, this is

[55] See further W Chan and AP Simester, 'Duress, Necessity: How Many Defences?' (2005) 16 *King's College LJ* 121; AP Simester, 'Wrongs and Reasons' (2009) 72 *MLR* 648, 651–54.

for rule of law reasons, in as much as persons acting in self-defence do not, in the urgency of the moment, have recourse to official protection when responding to a wrongful attack.[56] Preparatory offences, by contrast, pre-empt at leisure. Partly, too, the difference is that self-defence is right-defending. It is action taken to suppress a wrongful threat to some entitlement of the victim's. At the stage of preparatory conduct, the wrongfulness resides in D's intention, rather than action; so there is nothing 'concrete', as it were, for the self-defence to address.

One of the central features of justified acts taken in self-defence is that, because they are right-defending, the defender does not wrong his victim. Self-defence operates to justify the infliction of harm by showing that the action was *not* a wrong. It denies that P's right to life was violated, because P's right does not exclude self-protection as a reason for action, even lethal action, on behalf of those whom P threatens. D has a general duty not to take lives; a protected reason not to kill that excludes all sorts of reasons in favour of killing.[57] But it doesn't exclude this one. She doesn't have a general duty not to kill in self-defence. And there is no tortuous obligation to compensate P in such cases.

Necessity, however, is different. A necessitous action is justified by a reference to considerations that are extraneous to the victim's right – the basis for breaching that right does not address V's own conduct, and is grounded instead in the needs of others. Suppose, for example, that D breaks into P's house in order to call an ambulance on behalf of E, who is lying injured outside. D can cite the necessity of E's predicament as overriding her duty not to violate P's property rights. Her conduct is morally permissible and, in turn, no crime. However, this does not mean that the property-damage wrong goes away. Unlike self-defence, there will normally be a duty to pay damages for any loss that P suffers. Necessity, unlike self-defence, involves a justified (ie permissible) wrong.

B Excluded Reasons for Criminalisation: Fundamental Rights?

Preparatory offences do not protect V from D's conduct. They protect V *from what might be done.* They are justified by reference to V's needs, not D's wrong. Hence, they are necessitous in nature.

The payoff is that necessity is not always available, even in circumstances where self-defence would be. In particular, some reasons for perpetrating an act (including a coercive act of prohibition) may be excluded, under certain or even all circumstances, from consideration altogether. Absent V's consent, for

[56] *cf* Indian Penal Code s 99(3): 'There is no right of private defence in cases in which there is time to have recourse to the protection of the public authorities.'

[57] Rather than being outweighed, it is possible for some reasons favouring an act that is in need of justification to be *excluded* altogether from consideration; in which case they add no weight to the case for doing that act. For a kidney-transplant example, see below in the text. More generally, see J Raz, *Practical Reason and Norm*, 2nd edn (Princeton, Princeton University Press, 1990) § 1.2.

example, it supplies *no reason at all* in favour of removing one of V's kidneys that transplanting the kidney into T's body will save T's life. The 'reason' is excluded from consideration; its exclusion is part-and-parcel of the very importance of our rights to personal autonomy and integrity – that they are not amenable to this kind of calculation. Being excluded altogether, it isn't helped when we multiply the number of beneficiaries. We still get zero. Similarly, the *in extremis* concessions of writers like Michael Moore, allowing torture if the stakes are sufficiently high, should be resisted.[58]

Analogous exclusions may well apply, I suspect, to open-ended legislation. It is one thing to restrict the liberty to drive. It is quite another to restrict freedom to walk down public streets; and, I think, communicative rights that are dependent on the internet. In as much as it does not respond to D's own conduct, necessity should not normally be available to justify the violation of D's fundamental rights; indeed, this is part of what it means for rights to be fundamental. This is not to conclude that one can never directly attack the subject matter of fundamental rights. One can sometimes deliberately kill, for example, for the sake of self-defence; but not for the sake of necessity.[59] A claim of necessity is a claim justifiably to *use* a person in some way, which is why it involves a wrong. And where the wrong is fundamental, the justification fails.

VII IN CLOSING

Prophylactic offences can be a good idea. Especially when narrowly specified, they can offer helpful guidance to citizens regarding how to abide by the law. Don't possess automatic firearms or, say, more than 100 sacks of fertiliser. However, as we get further away from the harm such offences are ultimately designed to prevent, the potential for abuse, for over-extension into the innocent lives of citizens, increases dramatically. Let's hope that walking down a street with intent to commit a crime is never criminalised. However, some pretty comparable things have been. Even as the spectre of terrorism creates pressure to extend the anticipatory reach of the criminal law, a corresponding pressure arises to push back; to safeguard the liberties of citizens whose actions are not wrongful. Many of the ideas in this chapter are speculative. Perhaps, however, we would be safer from the state if we adopted at least some of them.

[58] M Moore, 'Torture and the Balance of Evils' (1989) 24 *Israel LR* 280. This argument is made more fully in Simester, 'Necessity, Torture and the Rule of Law' (n 5 above).

[59] See, famously, *Dudley and Stephens* (1884) 14 QBD 273.

4

Harmless Wrongdoing and the Anticipatory Perspective on Criminalisation

JEREMY HORDER

I INTRODUCTION

WE HAVE A shared interest in deterring people from engaging in wrongful harm-doing. Only if (amongst other things) enough is done to deter such activity, can the conditions be secured in which people can reliably be expected to participate in important kinds of collective commitment, such as a commitment to live by the rule of law and participate in a culture respectful of human rights.[1] In that regard, it may prove necessary or desirable to use state coercion and the stigmatising and punitive nature of the criminal law in particular, to deter wrongful harm-doing. However, in using the criminal law to deter such activity, in the interests of shoring up important collective commitments, law creators should ensure that the criminal law respects values constitutive of those commitments, such as the value of the rule of law. Taking this moral background for granted, different views may nonetheless be taken about the kind of activity on which it is more, or less, justifiable for the criminal law to focus when it is performing its deterrent (preventative) function. I will distinguish two standpoints on how to understand the relative justifiability of instances of criminalisation: the 'harm-done' and the 'anticipatory' perspectives (defined in section II). Those who adopt the former perspective purport to take a restrictive, 'minimalist' view of the justifiability of criminalisation, unlike those who adopt the latter perspective. However, I will seek to show how the integrity of the minimalist harm-done perspective is not very strictly maintained even by its supposed supporters. I suggest that this is an implicit recognition of the fact that there are sound arguments for giving at least equal status to the anticipatory perspective in any theory of the justification for criminalisation.

[1] See generally, John Finnis, *Natural Law and Natural Rights* (Oxford, Clarendon Press, 1980) ch 6; Jeremy Horder, *Excusing Crime* (Oxford, Oxford University Press, 2004) ch 1.2.

II ANTICIPATORY AND HARM-DONE PERSPECTIVES ON CRIMINALISATION: AN OUTLINE

On one view, the key to ensuring that the criminal law is kept within acceptable limits, in performing its preventive function, is to make harmful wrongdoing itself the primary focus. I will call this view the 'harm-done' perspective on the relationship between harm prevention and the criminal law.[2] From this perspective, the criminal law's concern with harm merely intended or foreseen, or with the simple posing of unwarranted risks of harm, is less justifiable and should thus be a more limited, secondary focus. Why? Sir John Smith argued that inchoate offences extend the ambit of the criminal law without adding much benefit in terms of general deterrence.[3] We do better, he later added, to focus on cases of wrongdoing to which our negative reaction is stronger for retributive reasons: when a harmful result has thereby been caused.[4] To such arguments against inchoate offences and offences of unjustified risk-taking, Andrew Ashworth has added the view that such offences create the danger of excessive use of state power.[5] On this view, proof of harm done requires proof of 'open and objective facts' whereas, for example, the reliance of inchoate offences on proof of fault as a constituent element creates the temptation for the prosecution to rely on evidence of confessions or previous misconduct unsupported by 'objectively incriminating' facts.[6] For Ashworth, if criminal liability is too readily extended to cover something so vague and so remote from harm done as preparatory conduct, mere possession, and so on, this threatens the rule-of-law requirement that there must be fair warning of when one's conduct may involve criminality.[7] Such an expanded focus, so the argument runs, risks surprising people unfairly by fixing them with criminal liability for, say, conspiracy, encouraging crime, or posing risks of unjustified harm, when they may have done little more than possess bad intentions or unduly risk-positive attitudes.[8] In order to

[2] Someone who adopts the harm-done (or the anticipatory) perspective may also set great store by additional conditions for criminalization, such as fault requirements.

[3] JC Smith, 'The Element of Chance in Criminal Liability' (1971) *Crim LR* 73.

[4] JC Smith, 'Some Problems of the Reform of the Law against Offences Against the Person' (1978) 31 *CLP* 13. Our stronger negative reaction may stem from the fact that, once the deed is done, there is no scope for 'thinking better of it', or for abandonment: see Andrew Ashworth, 'Defining Criminal Offences without Harm' in PF Smith (ed), *Criminal Law: Essays in Honour of JC Smith* (London, Butterworths, 1987) 16.

[5] Andrew Ashworth, *Principles of Criminal Law*, 6th edn (Oxford, Oxford University Press, 2009) 16. Ashworth's point has force, in this respect, whether or not the inchoate crime in question involves proof of fault on the part of the offender.

[6] Ashworth (n 5 above) 16–17.

[7] Ashworth (n 5 above) 468.

[8] This argument does not apply with such force to attempts to commit crimes, narrowly construed, because the offender cannot complain about having been taken by surprise when he or she was on the brink of committing the offence intentionally. Especially when the offender has done all he or she can do to being about the commission of the offence, attempts to commit crimes are the easiest of the inchoate offences to retain as an exception to the view that the focus of the criminal law should be on actual harm-doing: see Sir Rupert Cross, *The English Sentencing*

avoid this, putting it metaphorically (if slightly misleadingly), from the harm-done perspective there is in fact something morally and legally to be said for taking official censuring action only after the horse has bolted: after the harm has been done.[9]

It would be possible to take issue with or pose questions about these arguments individually. Even inchoate offences require the objective fact of something done (which may include, for example, an identifiable civil wrong such as trespass). Further, the suspicion with which inchoate offences are regarded by both Smith and Ashworth is hard, albeit not impossible, to square with their commitment to eliminating or sharply reducing the element of chance in whether criminal liability is incurred.[10] That is because one of the main sources of that element in the criminal law comes from offences the commission of which depends on wrongful harm done. More broadly, in just what sense need harm – and wrongful harm in particular – involve, to use Ashworth's words, 'objectively incriminating' or 'open and objective' facts?[11] However, putting these points to one side, I want to broaden my focus. I suggest, from what can be called the 'anticipatory' perspective on criminalisation, that it may be as important (and sometimes more important) for the criminal law to prohibit wrongful inchoate or risk-posing conduct, as it is for it to prohibit harm wrongfully done. This thesis can be defended, notwithstanding concerns we may all have with the breadth of the criminal law and with the need in that regard to respect the value of the rule of law.

First, there are instances in which placing a criminal prohibition on the harm-doing itself would for some reason be wrong, whereas it is perfectly justifiable to impose a prohibition on conduct that encourages and assists, or unjustifiably increases the risk of, the occurrence of the doing of such a harm. An example is the criminalisation of assisting or encouraging suicide,[12] even though the commission of suicide, the harm done, is not itself a criminal offence because when that harm is knowingly and freely self-inflicted it is not permissibly criminalised

System, 3rd edn (Oxford, Clarendon Press, 1981) 151–57, cited by Ashworth (n 5 above) 20. It follows that in the ensuing discussion contrasting the harm-done and anticipatory perspectives, I will tend to focus on criminalisation of harmless wrongdoing broader in scope than an attempt to commit an offence.

[9] There will be an understandable temptation to view this as the 'just deserts' or retributive perspective (see Smith (n 4 above)), but I deliberately avoid presentation of the argument in such terms. What I describe as the 'harm-done perspective' can be understood in purely preventative or deterrent terms, and may have nothing to do with 'just deserts'. From a 'just deserts' perspective, making D suffer punishment may have intrinsic value of some kind, whether or not the wrong D did that justifies the infliction of that punishment is substantive or inchoate.

[10] Smith (n 3 above); Andrew Ashworth, 'Taking the Consequences' in Stephen Shute, John Gardner and Jeremy Horder (eds), *Action and Value in the Criminal Law* (Oxford, Oxford University Press, 1993).

[11] The courts have struggled unsuccessfully to develop something like this notion when seeking to determine whether a defendant found unfit to plead has done 'the act' at issue: see *Antoine* [2001] 1 AC 340 (HL).

[12] Suicide Act 1961 s 2(1).

under the harm principle.[13] Another example of a similar sort might be the criminalisation of the knowing sale of alcohol to intoxicated persons, even though it is not an offence to cause harm to oneself through intoxication.[14] In such cases, the anticipatory perspective is, morally speaking, to be preferred to the harm-done perspective on criminalisation because the normative considerations inspired by the harm principle favour criminalisation of the inchoate or risk-posing conduct, whilst at the same time ruling out the criminalisation of the harm-doing itself. The criminalisation of the inchoate or risk-posing conduct is justified insofar as it may be effective in reducing the incidence of the harm done, whilst honouring the right to self-determination means that there is nonetheless a reason to seek to reduce such harms other than by criminalisation of the harm-doing actions themselves. Accordingly, there is good cause to reject the over-generality of the principle, well articulated by Douglas Husak, according to which, in order to rein in the permissible scope of criminalisation when no harm has been done:

> [A] nonconsummate offense proscribing an act-type that creates a risk of some undesirable state of affairs cannot be justified unless a consummate offense proscribing an act-type that intentionally causes that very state of affairs would be justified as well.[15]

I respectfully suggest that, in setting out this general principle, Husak overlooks the liberal justification that exists in some cases for using coercion to reduce the incidence of undesirable harm done by targeting only certain kinds of conduct that unjustifiably increase the risk of its occurrence, and not the harm-doing itself. Such a justification may be found in cases where principles focused on dignity and self-determination rule out criminalisation of the latter but not the former. That one should be free from criminality in engaging in action that, through causing harm to oneself, will make one's life go badly (or even extinguish it), does not entail that others should be free from criminality in engaging in conduct likely to lead one down that road.

Second, there are instances in which criminalisation of the harm done would not be wrong normatively speaking (it is not ruled out by, for example, the harm principle); but, even so, conditions clearly favour criminalisation of the wrongdoing that may lead to harm, whether or not the harm-doing is itself prohibited. One kind of example involves deception-related offences where, by way of contrast with the offences of fraud under the Fraud Act 2006 (where economic

[13] For a general discussion, see Joel Feinberg, *The Moral Limits of the Criminal Law: Harm to Self* (New York, Oxford University Press, 1986) vol 3.

[14] Licensing Act 2003 s 141(1). In both instances, a failure to prohibit the activity in question (assisting or encouraging suicide; sale of alcohol to intoxicated persons) would almost certainly lead to greater numbers of instances in which irreparable harm was needlessly done. For an examination of this argument, as a justification for criminalisation, see text at n 89 below.

[15] Douglas Husak, 'The Nature and Justifiability of Nonconsummate Offences' (1995) 37 *Arizona LR* 151,170. It may be, of course, that Professor Husak did not have it in mind that this principle should cover instances where the harm done is self-inflicted, or consensually inflicted by another, but I hope I do him no disservice by taking him to be supporting an exception-less version of the principle.

harm is specifically at issue), the range of potential harms to which the deception in question may lead is wide or indeterminate. In such cases, no good purpose may be served by seeking to narrow the range of legally relevant harms to which the deception in question must lead, by specifying them in the definition of the offence; it may make more sense simply to focus on the deceptive conduct itself. Two examples are wilfully and falsely pretending to be a doctor or surgeon,[16] and wearing an article of police uniform that makes the wearer so closely resemble a member of the police as to make the wearing of the article calculated to deceive.[17] In such cases, there may simply be an insufficiently substantial reason to insist that harm – which may take many forms in this context, from obtaining services or money, to the infliction of grievous harm – must be done, before criminal liability can arise.[18] There may not even be a strong reason to create a separate offence to cater for instances in which harm has been done, given that any harm done can be accounted for in sentencing or by charging other offences.[19]

Another kind of example arises when it will prove manifestly preferable to give priority to deterring and punishing failures to establish and maintain adequate harm-prevention systems (systemic failures), over and above the criminalisation of harm-doing stemming from such failures, even if the latter remains perfectly justifiable. Giving priority to harm-prevention may be preferable for one or both of at least two reasons in such instances.[20] It may too frequently be unacceptably difficult for the prosecution to show in the relevant context that an individual instance of harm done (such as falling victim to an aggressive form of cancer developed whilst working for a particular employer) was caused by a systemic failure (rather than by a purely unfortunate work-related accident). Additionally, in the absence of a primary focus in point of retribution and deterrence on the maintenance of adequate harm-prevention systems, there may be too great an incentive to maintain (cheaper) less effective systems in the vain hope that no harm will be done. Common illustrations involve a focus on formalised organisational activity, as is the case with the offences under the Health and Safety at Work Act 1974 (aimed at employers),[21] or with the offences under the 2009 regulations made pursuant to the Health and Social Care Act 2008 (aimed at health or social care providers).[22] However, such examples include

[16] Medical Act 1983 s 49.

[17] Police Act 1996 s 90(2).

[18] That being so, such instances also bring the anticipatory perspective into conflict with Husak's 'consummate criminal harm' principle: see n 15 above.

[19] See, eg, *Richardson* [1998] 2 Crim App R 200.

[20] For an examination of this thesis, as it applies to corporate criminal liability, see J Gobert, 'Corporate Criminality: Four Models of Fault' (1994) *Legal Studies* 393.

[21] See the discussion in the text at n 82 below. These offences are, of course, now backed up when death has been caused by the substantive offence of corporate manslaughter, but this offence is not intended to play a leading role in deterring and punishing unsafe or unhealthy practices in the workplace.

[22] The Health and Social Care Act 2008 (Registration of Regulated Activities) Regulations 2009. Section 5 of these regulations places an obligation on health care providers, backed by a criminal

informal individual activity, as in the case of offences concerned with the domestic environment in which pet-keeping takes place.[23] Clearly, in all such instances, it would not be wrong to make harm-doing stemming from systemic failure a criminal offence.[24] However, in the particular context, certain key factors – such as difficulties of proof in point of causation; the need to deter poor practice generally, and so on – point unequivocally in favour of priority being given to the risk-based offence.

More broadly, even when, normatively speaking, there are compelling reasons to prohibit harm actually done, it may still be at least as important to prohibit inchoate or unacceptably risky conduct that may lead to the prohibited harm-doing in question. This is because, given the generation of some additional deterrent effect through their creation and enforcement, prohibitions on inchoate or risky conduct may help to reduce the occurrence of the relevant harm-doing.[25] Thereby, inchoate or risk-focused liability can do as much or more through harm-prevention to shore up our collective commitments, notwithstanding any risks of over-criminalisation.[26] Rhetorically, from the anticipatory perspective, someone might ask: what kind of harm-prevention system insists that we are on the right path to inspiring faith in our collective commitments, including a commitment to live in a culture respectful of human rights under the rule of law, if we must wait for, say, murders, rapes, thefts, and so forth, to actually be committed (or, for that matter, attempted) before invoking the criminal law to achieve legitimate deterrence objectives? Surely, if we could deter and prevent at least some such crimes by making it possible to use the criminal law against those who, say, conspire to commit the wrongful harm in question, against those who assist or encourage its commission, and against those who

offence, 'so far as reasonably practicable, [to] ensure that the patients . . . are protected against identifiable risks of acquiring . . . an infection by . . . the effective operation of systems designed to assess the risk of and to prevent, detect, treat and control the spread of, a health care associated infection . . .'.

[23] See the Animal Welfare Act 2006 s 9, discussed in the text below at n 112.

[24] Peter Glazebrook, for example, has argued in favour of such offences where breaches of health and safety leading to harm done are concerned: see his, 'A Better Way of Convicting Business of Avoidable Deaths and Injuries' (2002) *CLJ* 405.

[25] It is true that insofar as people are deterred by the existence of the substantive crimes of murder, or rape, they will also be deterred from, say, attempting murder or rape. So, it might be said, no extra deterrent effect is achieved by creating such inchoate offences. However (*pace* Smith, n 4 above), whilst that argument might hold true for an inchoate offence bound up with the commission of the substantive offence itself, like attempt, I suggest that it has far less force with conduct more remote from the substantive offence, such as the formation of conspiracies or acts of assistance or encouragement. Offences focused on such conduct may add independently to the deterrent effect the law wishes to secure.

[26] In a broader sense of 'anticipatory perspective', there is obviously a reason to ensure that inchoate offending does not occur, as well as to ensure that substantive offending does not occur. However, I will confine myself here to the merits of criminalising inchoate as well as substantive offending. Whether, properly understood, the anticipatory perspective justifies criminalising conduct that leads to inchoate offending, or if it does, whether that justification is too weak to overcome a host of objections to extending the reach of the criminal law in such a way, is addressed by Ashworth (n 5 above) ch 2.4.

unjustifiably pose risks of its occurrence, we should do that as well? Too narrow a concern only with harm done might, ironically, undermine respect amongst the law-abiding for the very values of the rule of law and respect for human rights that motivate some theorists to work within a predominantly harm-done perspective. In section III, I will be concentrating on cases in which the normative considerations in favour of criminalising harm done are very strong, because it is in such cases that the anticipatory perspective on criminalisation can be too easily downplayed.

III MINIMALISM: WHO REALLY BELIEVES IN IT?

Any intelligent system of criminal law must embody a set of priorities. So far as Anglo-American criminal law is concerned, a number of criminal law theorists set these priorities by employing the harm-done perspective.[27] They would like to make more than trivial wrongful harm (culpably) done the central case of criminal wrongdoing. For them, other kinds of conduct may legitimately be criminalised, but only if more restrictive conditions are met than apply to the instances exemplifying the central case. Few have done as much to develop this particular version of central case analysis as Andrew Ashworth. For him:

> [T]he *building blocks* of criminalisation decisions are that the conduct in question must be harmful, wrongful, and of public concern – three key elements which are contestable in their application to given facts, but which are crucial dimensions.[28]

This way of understanding the criminal law's priorities from the harm-done perspective is what Ashworth calls 'minimalism'. The minimalist element to it is explained by the restrictive approach Ashworth believes that we should take to criminalising conduct going beyond the 'building blocks' (mentioned in the passage just cited). As he put it in the fifth edition of his *Principles of Criminal Law:*

> [M]inimalism has no difficulty in accepting the criminalisation of direct, victimising wrongs that harm individuals; but as one moves away from those *clear cases*, it demands stronger justifications for criminalising (as distinct from using civil or administrative strategies).[29]

What kind of conduct falls outside the 'clear cases'? Ashworth's main focus is on two kinds of example. First, there are the so-called inchoate offences, such as

[27] Alongside Ashworth, another theorist who favours the harm-done perspective is Douglas Husak: see his *Overcriminalisation* (New York, Oxford University Press, 2008), and Douglas Husak (n 15 above).

[28] Ashworth (n 5 above) 39 (my emphasis). For a similar view, see Douglas Husak (n 27 above).

[29] Andrew Ashworth, *Principles of Criminal Law*, 5th edn (Oxford, Oxford University Press, 2006) 31 (my emphasis). This passage is erased from the 6th edition, but his thesis has not significantly changed. As Ashworth says in the later edition (n 5 above, 38), 'conduct that is not harmful in itself should not attract liability, or (as with inchoate offences) at least not unless it is accompanied by an intention to encourage, assist or commit a substantive offence.'

conspiracy, attempt or assisting and encouraging crime. For Ashworth, there should be only restricted scope for such offences in a civilised system of criminal law because they do not involve wrongful harm done, even if they are of public concern. An agreement to commit an offence is not in itself harmful; neither is taking aim at someone with a gun, nor urging one person to stab another, even though all such conduct is clearly connected to the ultimate commission of a substantive offence. Ashworth argues that there is only, 'a limited (preventative) role for the criminalisation of conduct more or less remotely connected with the occurrence of harmful consequences',[30] and so, 'the more remote an offence becomes from the actual infliction of harm, the higher the degree of fault necessary to justify criminalisation'.[31] Additionally, in that regard, he has argued that, 'the law [of inchoate offences] should stretch further against crimes of violence than against mere property offences'.[32] It is obvious that a good deal of the existing law falls short of these ideals. Inchoate offences apply with equal legal force to both violent and property crime and some are not restricted to instances in which (as Ashworth would prefer[33]) D intended to commit the offence.[34]

Second, much more clearly falling outside Ashworth's conception of the clear or central cases fit for criminalisation are pieces of conduct (including, for convenience's sake, within the notion of 'conduct' instances of possession, and so forth) harmless in themselves that do not amount to inchoate offences because – loosely speaking – they are not engaged with the commission of a substantive offence as the intended or anticipated result. There are many examples of such harmless conduct being criminalised. Indeed, as Ashworth has himself demonstrated,[35] probably at least half of modern criminal legislation is focused on such conduct. Well-known examples where conduct that does not in itself cause harm but which is subject to criminalisation include speeding and dangerous driving,[36] and the possession of firearms or ammunition without a certificate.[37] There are also thousands of extraordinarily diverse offences, intended to provide support for a variety of regulatory schemes that do not involve harm done. To give at random two relatively recent examples, it is now an offence to remove a bovine animal from a semen collection centre except in order to kill it,[38] and to fail to comply, as a person in charge of a fishing boat, with a require-

[30] Ashworth (n 5 above) 40.
[31] ibid 456.
[32] ibid 469.
[33] ibid 38.
[34] For example, in relation to assisting or encouraging crime, contrary to the Serious Crimes Act 2007, in a very broad, non-definitional sense, it is sufficient, with respect to some piece of wrongful harm, whether or not yet done, that D has willed either the end or, aware of the possible end, has willed the means (namely the conduct element of the offence).
[35] Andrew Ashworth, 'Is the Criminal Law a Lost Cause?' (2000) 116 *LQR* 225.
[36] Road Traffic Act 1991 s 2.
[37] Firearms Act 1968 s 1(1).
[38] Transmissible Spongiform Encephalopathies (England) Regulations SI 2008 No 1881 sch 3.5(3)(a).

ment imposed by a British sea-fishery officer to weigh fish.[39] Some of these instances of conduct harmless in itself involve the posing of direct risks of harm, as in the case of dangerous driving or the abandonment of hazardous waste. However, other instances involve posing no such risk, and may depend on further actions or events to occur before any risk is posed or harm done.[40] Classic examples are offences that punish selling dangerous things without a licence, where the concern is with the increased incidence of harm needlessly done if an unregulated market for the thing in question is allowed to develop;[41] but there are other kinds of analogous example. Unlicensed possession or abandonment of something potentially hazardous is frequently criminalised when the concern is not harm done intentionally by the possessor or by someone into whose hands the things falls. Instead, the concern is (as the perpetrator may know perfectly well when taking possession of or when abandoning property) with harm that may be done unintentionally through mishap, lack of handling expertise, or through the consequences of loss of possession.[42] Some of these offences are, no doubt, questionable when considered in terms of the proportionality of the state's response: is it really appropriate, for example, to make it a criminal offence (not just a civil wrong[43]) simply to abandon a vehicle, irrespective of whether such conduct amounts to the common law offence of public nuisance?[44]

Such offences may seem to have been created simply to serve bureaucratic convenience, but that is not true of the criminalisation of all harmless wrongdoing where the risk of harm done is indirect. An example is the recently-created offence of paying for the sexual services of a prostitute subjected to exploitation, contrary to section 53A of the Sexual Offences Act 2003:[45]

[39] Sea Fishing (Recovery Measures) Order 2008/2347, 8-(1).

[40] For an innovative discussion, see Andrew von Hirsch, 'Extending the Harm Principle: "Remote" Harms and Fair Imputation' in AP Simester and ATH Smith (eds), *Harm and Culpability* (Oxford, Oxford University Press, 1996) 264–65.

[41] Restrictions on the sale of some medicines and drugs are an obvious example. For further analysis of criminal law and markets, see the ground-breaking work of Peter Alldridge, *Relocating Criminal Law* (Dartmouth, Aldershot, 2000).

[42] See, for an intriguing example, the Department for Environment, Food and Rural Affairs (DEFRA) publication, 'Who Needs a Crayfish Licence?', available at www.defra.gov.uk/foodfarm/fisheries/freshwater/crayfish.htm#LEG.

[43] So far as abandoned shopping trolleys are concerned, for example, the costs of removing them can be recovered by the local authority from the owner: see the Environmental Protection Act 1990 s 99, available at www.defra.gov.uk/environment/quality/local/legislation/ cnea/documents/trolleys.pdf.

[44] Refuse Disposal (Amenity) Act 1978 s 2.1. The reason given by DEFRA for criminalisation was, indeed, a harm-related one: 'Abandoned vehicles are a blight on local neighbourhoods, a health risk and can attract anti-social behaviour and crime', but its force seems weak in this context: see http://www.defra.gov.uk/environment/quality/local/abandoned/vehicles/index.htm.

[45] An offence introduced by the Policing and Crime Act 2009 s 14. For a sympathetic understanding and broader explanation of the context of such offences, see Michelle Dempsey, 'Sex Trafficking and Criminalisation: In Defense of Feminist Abolitionism' (2010) 158 *University of Pennsylvania Law Review* 1729.

> A person (A) commits an offence if –
>
> A makes or promises payment for the sexual services of a prostitute (B);
>
> A third person (C) has engaged in exploitative conduct of a kind likely to induce or encourage B to provide the sexual services for which A has made or promised payment
>
> . . .

To be committed by A, the offence requires proof that A has made or promised payment for the sexual services of a prostitute. This wrongdoing is A's essential contribution to the conduct elements of the offence.[46] Second, the offence requires proof that exploitative conduct likely to influence or encourage B to provide sexual services as requested have been engaged in by C. This is C's necessary contribution to the conduct elements of the offence.[47] Most importantly, the offence does not require that B has in fact been acting under the influence of exploitation, when providing or agreeing to provide the sexual services to A. The focus of the offence is thus harmless wrongdoing committed by persons such as A, in circumstances where it provides an incentive for persons such as C to seek to satisfy demand for sexual services by exploiting others, perhaps by harmful means (if need be).[48] To explain the offence in this way is not necessarily to justify its creation in the exact form that it takes, all things considered. My point here is simply that 'prophylactic' offences are not confined in English law to serving the industry or sector-specific priorities of the modern bureaucratic state. What is the minimalist approach to such offences? In principle, Ashworth is very clear about the matter. In his view, there is no case for using the criminal law to deter and punish harmless wrongdoing (although it may be subject to civil sanctions) whatever the public concerns about it may be, unless it is accompanied by an intention to commit an offence involving harm done. Were it otherwise, the conduct would not be sufficiently closely connected to wrongful harm done to warrant criminalisation:

> [C]onduct that is not harmful in itself should not attract liability, or (as with the inchoate offences) at least not unless it is accompanied by an intention to encourage, assist, or commit a substantive offence. This would rule out most offences of possession, which do not require evidence of any further intent. In particular, cases in which

[46] On the nature of such conduct as wrong in itself, but not necessarily harmful in itself, see John Gardner and Stephen Shute, 'The Wrongness of Rape' in Jeremy Horder (ed), *Oxford Essays in Jurisprudence*, 4th Series (Oxford, Oxford University Press, 2000) 193, 207, 'In our view . . . sex industry workers typically are being objectified by their clients and consumers, and this is indeed an attack on their humanity . . . But the sex workers' right to sexual autonomy, where their consent is genuine, serves to license the abuse'.

[47] I incline to the view that 'exploitation' is wrongful but not necessarily harmful, although it may be effected through harmful means (such as the use of violence), as the definition of 'exploitative conduct' in the new s 53A(3) inserted into the 2003 Act makes clear. Resolution of the issue is not crucial one way or another respecting the point currently under consideration.

[48] This explanation of the offence may not be a full one because it makes the justification for the offence look unduly 'individualist', focused on the sum of the goods of individual persons liable to exploitation be persons such as C, and ignoring certain common goods that may also be protected or promoted by the legislation; but I will not go into that question here.

> the occurrence of harm depends on a further decision by the actor or another (eg to fire the gun unlawfully) are unsuitable for criminalisation.[49]

On the contrary, in Ashworth's view, the criminal law should be reserved for, 'the most serious invasions of interests'.[50] Implemented in full, such an approach would have a dramatic effect in reducing the reach of criminal law. To give a range of examples, it would cease to be a criminal offence to be found in possession of nuclear or any other kind of weapons without a licence, to issue prescription drugs well past their use-by date, to sell rotting meat, or to impersonate a surgeon. Naturally, it is possible to justify remaining a steadfast minimalist in the face of such examples. A steadfast minimalist could insist that the conduct in question can be treated in a similar way to parking in a forbidden place, by being made subject to regulatory civil penalties, or other analogous non-criminal measures. Ashworth himself on occasions relies on such arguments.[51] However, it seems that Ashworth is not an especially steadfast minimalist after all.

Speaking of possession offences, immediately following the passage just cited, he says that in the context of modern societies it would be 'foolish' not to criminalise unregistered possession of firearms, explosives and the like:

> The social context could be used as a basis for arguing that abstaining from possession of certain dangerous articles, like guns and explosives ought to be recognised as a duty of citizenship . . . The question is whether it is justified [to criminalise such conduct] . . . and in answering this question one should have regard to the magnitude of the harm as well as the likelihood of its occurrence.[52]

This concession does a great deal to weaken the case for minimalism as a moral 'building block' setting limits to criminalisation decisions. It is not just that whether or not something is a harm of genuine 'magnitude,' and that whether or not some activity involves a 'likelihood' of harm done, are matters beset by vagueness, making it in practice impossible for legislators to know just when they have overstepped minimalist boundaries. It is also that this concession detaches the building blocks for criminalisation decisions from any special foundational link with harm actually done. As Ashworth himself concedes, the concession makes a different question central to criminalisation decisions: how much 'preventable victimisation' (his term) will in fact be prevented by having prohibitions on harmless but risky conduct?[53] In that regard, the argument in the passage just cited is reminiscent of the attempt a century ago to keep tortuous liability for harm caused through a negligent breach of a duty of care confined to duties relating to 'things dangerous in themselves' such as, to use Ashworth's examples, guns and explosives. Of such attempts, Scrutton LJ famously remarked:

[49] Ashworth (n 5 above) 38.
[50] ibid 32.
[51] ibid 32–33.
[52] ibid 38.
[53] ibid 39.

> Personally, I do not understand the difference between a thing dangerous in itself, as poison, and a thing not dangerous as a class, but by negligent construction dangerous as a particular thing. The latter, if anything, seems the more obvious danger of the two; it is a wolf in sheep's clothing instead of an obvious wolf.[54]

These observations are just as important to a criminal context as they are to a civil law context. They do a good deal to explain, for example, the use of criminalisation to deter and punish inaccurate labelling of products or animals.[55] Inaccurately labelled products or animals are not dangerous in themselves, but a mis-labelled product or animal may very well turn out to be a 'wolf in sheep's clothing' (perhaps especially in the case of a wrongly labelled sheep[56]). The same point could be made about conduct that is not dangerous in itself, such as the making of false or misleading statements, which may nonetheless influence consumer behaviour to the consumer's detriment.[57] Once one admits that criminalisation may be justified depending on how much 'preventable victimisation' will result, it becomes hard to see how there can be any 'building blocks' for criminalisation at all. In reality, criminalisation decisions must commonly turn on multiple questions of contested judgment in which assessments of seriousness jostle for attention with consideration of proportionality, marginal utility, projected impact (short, medium and long-term), side-effects (good, bad and indifferent), and so on. On such shifting sands, secure building blocks for taking criminalisation decisions are likely to prove more of a mirage than an oasis. More significant, I suggest, for the would-be 'minimalist', should really be supervisory public law principles aimed at holding the executive to account for exercise of the power to create criminal offences, and at broadening the executive's ongoing responsibilities to include regular review of the use and continuing utility and fairness of such offences.[58]

All in all, I suggest that Ashworth is not really a wholehearted believer in minimalism at all, in the form in which he presents it; he is just someone who cares very much about over-criminalisation.[59] For one thing, he does not truly believe in the theory supposedly central to minimalism that the criminal law should be used only as a 'last resort'.[60] In a minimalist context, such a thesis strongly implies that non-criminal forms of deterrence and retribution should

[54] *Hodge Sons v Anglo-American Oil Co* (1922) 12 Lloyds Law Reports 183, 187, cited by (and sometimes wrongly attributed to) Lord Atkin in *Donoghue v Stevenson* [1932] AC 562, 595–96.

[55] See Stuart P Green, 'Why It's a Crime to Tear the Tag Off a Mattress: Overcriminalisation and the Moral Content of Regulatory Offences' (1997) 46 *Emory Law Journal* 1533. See also the offences created by the Transmissible Spongiform Encephalopathies (England) Regulations SI 2008 No 1881.

[56] See DEFRA, 'Guidance for Keepers in England and Wales: Rules for Identifying Sheep and Goats' (Dec 2009, www.defra.gov.uk/foodfarm/farmanimal/movements/sheep/documents.).

[57] See the discussion in the text below at n 97.

[58] See Law Commission, 'Post-Legislative Scrutiny' (LC 302, 1996).

[59] For a similar analysis of another would-be minimalist, Douglas Husak (n 27 above), see John Gardner, 'Over-Criminalisation: The Limits of the Criminal Law' (2008) *Notre Dame Philosophical Reviews* 03.

[60] Ashworth (n 5 above) 32–33.

always be employed first against conduct that does not in itself involve harmful wrongdoing. It is only if such measures demonstrably fail that the criminal law should be used instead;[61] but understood in such a way, the last resort thesis could lead to some counter-intuitive moral and legal conclusions. Suppose that the question is whether it should be an offence (a) to give or receive instruction or training with the intention of using that instruction or training in connection with terrorist activity,[62] or (b) to cause a nuclear explosion (an offence created as part of the implementation of the test ban treaty).[63] Is it really right – both morally and legally – to insist that such offences should not be created unless, for example, the deterrent effect of civil penalties (say, fixed fines and 'stop now' notices) for engaging in such activities has been measured first? Such an approach simply lacks much moral conviction, because it risks too much preventable victimisation and (in the case of nuclear explosions) catastrophic environmental damage as well. So, it is no real surprise to discover that, for Ashworth, the proper approach involves a far more balanced, measured assessment before legislating of, 'whether a particular kind of misconduct is more appropriately dealt with through a regulatory framework, or by civil liability, or by a civil preventative order'.[64] Such an approach avoids the unconvincing elements of an undiluted 'last resort' thesis, but is a significantly weaker constraint on criminalisation. It requires little more than what had already been stated in Ministry of Justice guidance on criminal law-creation by other departments, drawn up during the Labour Governments of 1997–2010, a period that saw well over 3000 new criminal offences introduced. The guidance suggests that departments ask themselves the question (in relation to implementation of European obligations): 'Does the obligation require, "dissuasive and proportionate" sanctions? (In appropriate circumstances this could mean the creation of criminal sanctions).'[65]

More significantly, in the present context, Ashworth sometimes combines both harm-done and anticipatory perspectives in his analysis. He says:

> The need to recognise the preventative function [of the criminal law] as one of the central functions of the criminal law is not in doubt; it would not make sense if the criminal law were purely a retrospective, blaming institution, since the seriousness with which it treats wrongs against physical safety, for example, points to the importance of preventing those wrongs from occurring. This supplies the rationale for the inchoate offences and, less strongly, for many of the possession offences.[66]

[61] For a general discussion, see Douglas Husak, 'The Criminal Law as a Last Resort' (1994) 24 *OJLS* 207.

[62] See the Terrorism Act 2006 s 6(1) and 6(2).

[63] See the Nuclear Explosions (Prohibitions and Inspections) Act 1998 s 1.

[64] Ashworth (n 5 above) 33.

[65] Ministry of Justice and Department for Business, Enterprise and Regulatory Reform [now Business, Innovation and Skills], 'Guidance on Creating New Regulatory Penalties' (26 January 2009) 3.

[66] Andrew Ashworth, 'Conceptions of Overcriminalisation' (2008) 5 *Ohio State Journal of Criminal Law* 407, 417. See also, Ashworth (n 5 above) 16. There is more than a hint here that Ashworth associates the 'harm-done' perspective with a 'retrospective' just deserts rationale for

Having appreciated this point, we are in a position to turn to an examination of the anticipatory perspective. I will consider the merits of that perspective, that include contributing positively to a system of criminal law that will do enough to prevent harm through the use of coercion to make our collective commitments worthwhile, whilst still honouring the values constitutive of those commitments.

IV THE ANTICIPATORY PERSPECTIVE ON CRIMINALISATION

A Harm Done, Deterrent Value and what Counts against Criminalisation

From the anticipatory perspective on criminalisation, any deterrent effect generated by prohibiting and punishing inchoate wrongdoing is morally more significant than the deterrent effect created when wrongful harm itself is prohibited and punished.[67] From the anticipatory perspective, the ideal is that, if and when the threat of state sanctions is needed to deter harmful wrongdoing, the deterrence or prevention can be achieved by targeting conduct at a stage when such harm is yet to be done. From the anticipatory perspective, deterrent effect created by punishing harm done is a kind of Pyrrhic victory, because it is achieved only at the cost of victims' suffering or loss. When it takes place within a liberal theory involving the commitments I set out at the very start, the pursuit of the ideal from the anticipatory perspective may clash, or be in tension, with other important goals, such as the avoidance of an over-extensive or over-intrusive criminal law;[68] but that should not obscure the significance of the ideal itself. In this respect, the moral significance of the anticipatory perspective has gone unnoticed or been downplayed for two reasons. First, it is commonly assumed, at least where one is concerned with criminal offences that also involve serious moral wrongdoing, that much of the vital deterrent effect that the criminal law provides must inevitably come from offences concerned with harm wrongfully done.[69] If, for example, the substantive offences of murder and rape come with the deterrent threat of severe sentences, there is unlikely to be any further deterrent value added by prohibitions on, say, attempting murder or rape.[70] Whilst this assumption may hold true for many of what might loosely be called 'destructive' offences – murder, inflicting grievous bodily harm, or criminal damage, for example – it is not an

criminal law and punishment; but I believe that it would be a mistake to do that: see n 9 above. Inchoate offences may fully deserve punishment in the same way as completed offences, just as both may serve deterrent functions.

[67] Hence, from the anticipatory perspective, the principal argument for having substantive offences will be the representative or fair labelling argument: see Andrew Ashworth, 'The Elasticity of Mens Rea' in Colin Tapper (ed), *Crime, Proof and Punishment* (London, Butterworths, 1981) for the original discussion of this argument.

[68] See the helpful discussion in Andrew von Hirsch (n 40 above) 259, 266.

[69] See, for example, JC Smith (n 4 above).

[70] Although, as I have already indicated, that may not be true in relation to more remote conduct such as assisting, encouraging or threatening murder or rape: see n 25 above.

assumption underpinning the structure of many 'acquisitive' offences, such as theft, fraud, and bribery. These offences are commonly defined or (in the case of theft) interpreted[71] in a wholly or substantially inchoate way, with the broadly inchoate forms of the offence carrying a very substantial burden in terms of creating a deterrent effect. In the context in which acquisitive offences arise, by way of contrast with the destructive offences, it is the element of substantive harm-doing (if any) in the offence definition that is regarded in law as adding little in the way of deterrent effect. There is a second consideration that may have contributed to the downgrading of the anticipatory perspective's moral significance. This is that proposals to create inchoate or risk-based offences have been thought to face a greater number of countervailing moral considerations militating against their creation than the substantive offences to which they relate (if any).[72] Harm-prevention only provides a good reason for creating a criminal offence. There may in any given instance be countervailing considerations that outweigh that reason. The conditions for criminalisation can be met,[73] and yet it can still be a disproportionate or (more broadly) a mistaken step to create the contemplated prohibition. It might be, for example, that even if there is no other effective way of preventing a given harm, that harm is too trivial, or the probability of its occurrence too low, to warrant the creation of criminal liability to deter it. Alternatively, the deterrent benefits of having a given offence might be outweighed by the dangers of its over-reliance on the use of official discretion and judgment to render concrete the demands of the offence, and to decide whether there has been a violation.[74] So, by way of example, whilst the existence of the offence of possessing an article in circumstances giving rise to a reasonable suspicion that the possession is for a purpose connected with terrorism[75] must be explained from anticipatory perspective, its uncertainty, its tendency to cover far more activity than it is intended to prevent, and its disproportionate character, count tellingly against its legitimacy.[76]

However, in principle, I do not believe that proposals to prohibit harmless wrongdoing that risks harm are, simply in virtue of the fact that the offences will not involve the need to show harm done, necessarily more vulnerable to defeat at the hands of such countervailing considerations. There is no reason why the anticipatory perspective cannot be as sensitive to the need for the exercise of restraint in the creation of inchoate or risk-based offences, and to the requirement for proportionality, as the harm-done perspective is in

[71] See Morris [1984] AC 320 (HL).

[72] See the list of such considerations provided by Joel Feinberg, *Harm to Others* (New York, Oxford University Press, 1984) 216.

[73] On the basic conditions for legitimate criminalisation, see ibid 26: 'It is always a good reason in support of penal legislation that it would probably be effective in preventing (eliminating, reducing) harm to persons other than the actor and there is probably no other means that is equally effective at no greater cost to to other values.'

[74] See Ashworth (n 5 above) 321.

[75] Terrorism Act 2000 s 57.

[76] See *Zafar* [2008] EWCA Crim 184, and the excellent discussion in Victor Tadros, 'Crimes and Security' (2008) 71 *MLR* 240.

relation to the creation of substantive offences. For example, respecting the criminalisation of harmless wrongdoing, John Gardner has said:

> [T]he harm principle regulates achievement as well as endeavour. The law must actually prevent the harm that it is intended to prevent, and must, moreover, do so in a way that is proportionate to the harm actually prevented. Herein lies the real power of the harm principle as a constraint on legislators. It is easy to point to a harm that one's pet legislation is designed to eradicate; it is a lot harder to show that it eradicates it.[77]

These strictures apply with as much force to prohibitions on harmless wrongdoing that risks harm as they do to offences involving proof of harm done.

Moreover, the assumption that the countervailing considerations are weightier when considering the criminalisation of inchoate conduct and risk-taking can no longer be taken for granted. More recent analysis has revealed the arbitrariness, or pointless technicality, that may be involved in insisting on proof of harm done as a condition of criminalisation in some instances, such as fraud.[78] Indeed, an insistence on proof of harm done as a condition of criminalisation can lead to absurdity. Who would be prepared to argue, from a harm-done perspective, that in point of deterrence one should give priority to (say) prohibiting harm-causing suicide bombings themselves, over and above conduct intended to assist, encourage or attempt suicide bombings? Changing perceptions about the (lesser) importance of harm done to justification for criminalisation may in the future mean that it is an insistence on harm-done that faces the more compelling set of countervailing considerations, when seeking the optimum point of deterrence through criminalisation. From the anticipatory perspective, there is an argument that the burden of deterrence through law should be carried by criminalisation of conduct prior to the point at which harm is done, even if substantive offences in some form ought to remain in some areas because of their importance to, for instance, representative or fair labelling.[79] That having been said, the main argument for explaining the importance of the anticipatory perspective is not simply a broadly pragmatic one focused on the avoidance of arbitrariness, technicality or absurdity. It is a moral argument, sensitive to the idea that a focus only on harm done will lead, in terms of deterrence achieved, to nothing but Pyrrhic victories that may threaten people's trust and confidence in the rule of law. It is no surprise, then, that even minimalists adopt the anticipatory perspective when they grant space within the limits of legitimate criminalisation for inchoate offences and limited forms of unjustified risk-taking.[80] Just how extensive that space must be is a matter worth further consideration, as an illustration of the subtlety of the way in which English law interprets and applies the harm principle.

[77] Gardner (n 59 above).

[78] See, eg *Hensler* (1870) 11 Cox CC 570, and the more general discussion in GR Sullivan, 'Fraud and the Efficacy of the Criminal Law: A Proposal for a Wide General Offence' (1985) *Crim LR* 616. See also Law Commission, 'Fraud' (LC 276, 2002).

[79] On which, see Ashworth (n 67 above).

[80] See text at n 52 above.

B The Explanatory Power of the Anticipatory Perspective: Direct Harm Risked

Legislation creating offences frequently focuses on conduct posing unwarranted risks of harm (as illustrated by some of the examples we have already encountered). The aim of such legislation, as in the classic case of the offence of 'dangerous driving',[81] is to create some of the desired deterrent effect without having to rely entirely on offences involving harm wrongfully done: an approach favoured by the anticipatory perspective. An important example we have already come across is provided by the Health and Safety at Work Act 1974, whose standards are now such a pervasive feature (at least in theory) of the management of the workplace in England. The 1974 Act reflects the anticipatory perspective in its underlying legal structure, in that liability is triggered by the maintenance of 'unsafe' working practices, and not, or not necessarily, by harm done through the maintenance of such practices.[82] Further, the need to adopt the anticipatory perspective in justifying criminalisation in this example seems demonstrated by the fact that the offence does not meet Ashworth's minimalist criteria for criminalisation of unjustified risk-taking, namely that the harm must be of great magnitude, or the risk of harm high.[83] It could be argued that this just goes to show that the maintenance of unsafe working practices should not be a criminal offence, but only a civil wrong to be met with a civil penalty. At the very least, many might agree that the Health and Safety Executive should be able to issue civil penalties (or equivalent measures) for more minor infractions of the relevant legislation. However, it is notable that the Health and Safety Executive itself has emphatically rejected the introduction of civil penalties to deal with some important kinds of transgressions under the 1974 Act;[84] and I do not know of any minimalist who makes an argument for wholesale de-criminalisation of the relevant offences. Finally, as I have already suggested, it would not normally be open to a minimalist such as Ashworth to suggest that the maintenance of unsafe working practices should, without more, be a criminal offence only if that leads to harm done.[85] That would be to make criminal liability turn on the element of chance, the 'accident' of harm in fact resulting

[81] Road Traffic Act 1988 s 2.

[82] Health and Safety at Work Act 1974 s 1. I am not suggesting that the approach taken by the 1974 Act is, in this respect, beyond criticism.

[83] See the quoted passage in the text at n 52 above, which implies the need for such a requirement. Naturally, it is possible that prosecutions are only taken in such circumstances, but that is another matter. My concern is with criminalisation in law.

[84] See, the Health and Safety Executive's (HSE) Response to DEFRA's Consultation on Civil Sanctions for Environmental Offences, www.hse.gov.uk/about us/meetings/smt/2009/020909/psepsmt0997.pdf (September 2009), 'HSE considered adopting similar options for health and safety offences, but has consistently said that they are not needed (see HSE 06/30). There are no gaps in HSE's and local authorities' enforcement tool kits and thus health and safety law is effectively enforced by existing criminal sanctions without being driven to excessive use of prosecution.'

[85] See text at n 9 above.

from unjustified risk-taking, something Ashworth is famous for criticising as an influence on criminalisation decisions.[86]

Offences contrary to the Health and Safety at Work Act 1974 involve, like offences such as dangerous driving, more or less direct risks of harm. It can be said that this makes them sufficiently close to the actual causing harm, through the posing of such risks, to be a species of endangerment-based criminalisation that the harm-done perspective can live with.[87] However, it is arguable that, whilst still honouring the values at the heart of our collective commitments,[88] a system of criminal law properly informed by the anticipatory perspective on the prevention of harm may go further.

C The Explanatory Power of the Anticipatory Perspective: Harm Risked Indirectly

An important starting-point is Gardner and Shute's explanation of the width of the harm principle:

> It is no objection under the harm principle that a harmless action was criminalised, nor even that an action with no tendency to cause harm was criminalised. It is enough to meet the demands of the harm principle that, if the action were not criminalised, *that* would be harmful.[89]

An example of this interpretation of the harm principle in action involves what Jonathan Rogers has aptly called the 'slippery slope' principle of criminalisation, under which:

> The legislature decides that if conduct which (on its facts) does not threaten a state interest thereby goes unpunished, then it is inevitable that other citizens (even if acting in good faith) will think that the conduct is, or has become, legal in a wider range of cases . . . They may consequently perform conduct which *does* threaten a state interest.[90]

Rogers' slippery slope argument is not by any means confined in its application to purely inchoate or risk-focused offences, but I will concentrate on its application to such offences here. A simple example concerns the formerly separate offences of careless driving, on the one hand, and on the other hand, inconsiderate driving.[91] 'Careless' driving is manifestly a way of unjustifiably threatening

[86] See text at n 9 above.

[87] Ashworth (n 5 above) 319, 'It is also justifiable, however, for the criminal law to penalise conduct which creates the risk of physical harm, particularly in situations where the conduct has little social utility or where the risk is well known'. See further, AP Simester and Andrew Von Hirsch, 'Remote Harms and Non-constitutive Crimes' (2009) 28 *Criminal Justice Ethics* 89.

[88] See text at n 1 above.

[89] John Gardner and Stephen Shute (n 46 above) 216.

[90] Jonathan Rogers, 'Prosecutors, Courts and Conduct of the Accused Which Engages a Qualified Human Right' (2005) 58 *CLP* 101, 119 (Rogers' emphasis). For an analogous argument in relation to the scope of excuses, see Jeremy Horder (n 1 above) ch 1.2.

[91] These are now alternative bases for proving a single offence, contrary to the Road Traffic Act 1988, as amended by the Road Traffic Act 1991.

a state interest, namely the protection of citizens from being exposed to unnecessary risks of wrongful harm done. By way of contrast, 'inconsiderate' driving may not in itself threaten this state interest. Some of the examples of the offence given by the Crown Prosecution Service indicate as much: flashing one's headlights to encourage drivers to give way; misusing lanes to gain advantages over other drivers, and so on.[92] However, to de-criminalise inconsiderate driving because, in itself, it does not threaten a relevant state interest would be to take too narrow a view of the scope of what should be prohibited, for much the reasons given by Rogers. Drivers would all too easily be led to regard their conduct as possibly inconsiderate, but not careless, when in fact it *was* careless.

Rogers' argument provides a reason (albeit a minor one) for including within the scope of criminal attempt instances of factually impossible attempts, and within the scope of assisting and encouraging crime acts capable of assistance or encouragement to criminality that in fact do nothing to assist or to encourage criminality.[93] The argument also helps to explain the criminalisation of some kinds of conduct involving (broadly speaking) the making of statements, reckless as to their truth or falsity, that do not lead to harm done. An example given by Ashworth is perjury.[94] Perjury can be committed when D makes a statement without believing that it is true, even if it is in fact true and even if no reliance is placed on it by the court.[95] Another example is an offence under section 1 of the Fraud Act 2006: fraud by false representation. A key part of the section 1 offence involves the dishonest making of a false representation, and a representation will be regarded as false if, 'the person making it knows that it is *or might be*, untrue or misleading'.[96] It follows that someone could make a statement that was entirely true and that was believed to be true by the intended 'victim,' and yet, if he or she made the statement dishonestly, still commit the offence contrary to section 1 of the 2006 Act. One important justification (if not the only one) for criminalisation of such breadth centres on the cumulative consequences of tolerating the reckless endangerment of others' interests that is involved.[97] Employing Rogers' slippery slope argument, one can argue that were such conduct lawful, too many people would be likely then to assume that the law does not require that they concern themselves with the truth of statements

[92] See www.cps.gov.uk/news/fact_sheets/dangerous_driving.

[93] See respectively, the Criminal Attempts Act 1981 s 1(2), and the Serious Crime Act 2007 pt 2. The argument is that people will too easily come to believe, mistakenly, that if an attempt, or an act of assistance or encouragement could never have 'come off' for some reason, then no offence is committed. Of course, the improbability of such confusion arising in practice, or becoming widespread, means that by far the most powerful justification for criminalisation in such instances is D's engagement in the relevant conduct with the specified fault element.

[94] Ashworth (n 4 above) 14.

[95] Perjury Act 1911 s 1(1).

[96] Fraud Act 2006 s 2(2)(b) (my emphasis).

[97] Another justification focuses not on the sum of individuals' interests protected by the broader offence, but on the need to support, through judicious use of the criminal law where necessary, the public good constituted by high standards of honesty and fair dealing when other's key interests are at stake. I will not pursue the importance of this justification here.

they make, even when reliance on those statements *will* in all probability lead to a wrongful loss suffered by another.[98]

This point is, I believe, overlooked or given insufficient emphasis by those who criticise the width of the offences in the Fraud Act 2006 Act on the grounds that the wrong at the core of a criminal offence of fraud (defined in the inchoate mode) should be seen in individualist terms, as involving an intention to deceive someone through the making of the misleading statement.[99] Pursuing this line of argument, Professor Tadros has said:

> Consider misleading advertising puffs that are designed to make the product seem more appealing at a subconscious level. It may well be dishonest to say misleading things that create a subconscious response to a product. But if that is wrong, it is only a very minor wrong, and not something that should result in a criminal conviction.[100]

One may applaud the broad sentiment expressed here. However, there are a number of criticisms that might be made of this argument, specifically in the fraud context. First, whether or not the dishonest and knowing publication of misleading advertising puffs involves only a 'very minor wrong' depends on matters of fact and degree, such as the nature of the product being advertised. It might only be a minor wrong in respect of shoe sales, but does not seem so minor if what is on sale is said to be a self-help cure for a life-threatening disease, 'better than anything you can find through the National Health Service', or involves animals destined for the food chain said to be, 'as healthy as the day they were born'.[101]

Second, following on from this point, as Tadros is well aware, English law has no *de minimis* principle. So, it is as much arson to light your cigarette when you have asked me not to, as it is to burn down the Palace of Westminster. English law prefers to deal with such matters through the exercise of prosecutorial discretion.[102] This preference both reflects the perceived importance of preventing whether or not something was indeed '*de minimis*' itself becoming a question of law for satellite litigation, and does a good deal to prevent the criminality of conduct turning on arbitrary line-drawing. For that reason, we may expect to see in respect of very many offences in English law, coverage of examples – such as those involving minor wrongs – that would never in practice be subject to criminal prosecution. In that regard, there is all the difference, from a harm principle perspective, between prohibiting a moral wrong, whether or not a minor one, simply because it is morally wrong (not permitted), and prohibiting a minor moral wrong because it is intimately bound with a broader practice that unacceptably threatens harm (permitted). It is the latter that provides a justificatory reason for the breath of the 2006 Act. A useful contrast, in this

[98] See Rogers (n 90 above).
[99] Tadros (n 76 above) 953.
[100] ibid 953.
[101] An example of a criminal prohibition on advertisements for cancer cures is given below.
[102] See The Code for Crown Prosecutors, 'The Full Code Test' para 4.17.

respect, could be drawn with the numerous offences in regulatory contexts identified by the Law Commission as involving little or nothing more than the making of a false or misleading statement to a Government official.[103] An example under the Eggs and Chicks (England) Regulations 2008 SI 2008 No 1718, regulation 15(1)(c) runs as follows:

> A person is guilty of an offence if – . . .they give to an authorised officer acting in the execution of these Regulations any information which they know, or ought reasonably to know, to be false or misleading.

In this example, no harm is done, and none may directly be threatened by the making of the false or misleading statement which need not even be known to be false or misleading, let alone dishonestly made. Further, by way of contrast with offences under the 2006 Act, the wrongdoing directly affects mainly Government officials acting in a public capacity (the officials' personal or private business interests not being at risk), and not the interests of the public at large. For that reason, the use of criminal sanctions to punish and deter the making of such false or misleading statements is, as the Law Commission provisionally argues, disproportionate.[104]

It is important to note that Gardner and Shute's thesis, and the slippery slope argument, need not concern only justifications for criminalisation that addresses the risk that people will make (under-inclusive) mistakes about the limits to individual offences. Gardner and Shute's thesis is concerned with the prevention of harm *whether* or not the potential harm-doing involves offending. If it was lawful to posses firearms without a licence, the principal concern might not only or even mainly be the increased threat that these weapons could be used in a criminal enterprise. The threat of harm accidentally caused through misuse (by children, for example) could be just as great a concern.[105] Consider also, for example, the offence under section 4 of the Cancer Act 1939 of advertising to the public a cure for cancer:

> No person shall take any part in the publication of any advertisement – (a) containing an offer to treat any person for cancer, or to prescribe any remedy therefor, or to give any advice in connection with the treatment thereof . . . or (b) referring to any article, or articles of any description, in terms which are calculated to lead to the use of that article, or articles of that description, in the treatment of cancer.

This offence does not depend on the 'cure' for cancer being in reality some kind of placebo, or even on publication being sought in the knowledge that the cure is not, or might not be, all that it is claimed to be. The offence is committed even if the cure is known by the person advertising it to be fully effective. The justification for the offence is thus neither harm done, nor harm directly risked, but

[103] Law Commission Consultation Paper, Criminal Liability in Regulatory Contexts (No 195, 2010) pt 4.

[104] ibid.

[105] See the discussion in the text at n 41 to n 42.

the fact that, if a free advertising market were to develop in alleged cures for those desperate enough to try anything to arrest the course of their illness, *that* would be harmful.[106]

V CONCLUSION: THE ANTICIPATORY PERSPECTIVE AND CRIMINAL LAW'S CHANGING LANDSCAPE

Even were harm itself not 'a morally loaded and essentially contested concept',[107] the burden of justification for criminalisation would still be heavy when what is proposed is to make criminal harmless conduct, either on the grounds that it involves a risk of harm or on the grounds that, were it not prohibited, that would be harmful. That is because the criminality of the act in question will often turn almost exclusively on value judgments (by the legislator) about the likelihood of wrongful harm becoming more common if the conduct is left free from criminal consequences, or (by the regulator or tribunal of fact) about whether a risk was unjustifiably posed in an individual case. There may seem to be a particular danger that, through the way in which these value judgments are exercised, criminalisation becomes arbitrary, oppressive, or focused on goals ancillary to those envisaged by the relevant legislation.[108] I have already indicated that those who seek to justify criminalisation from an anticipatory perspective are duty-bound to be as sensitive to reasons not to criminalise conduct as those writing from the harm-done perspective,[109] even if the former may strike the balance between competing considerations in a different way.

From an anticipatory perspective, a focus on unacceptable risk posed rather than on harm done can in fact be shown up in a good light, as a civilising move away from a traditional 'fire brigade' model of criminal law to a criminal law aimed at (so to speak) preventing fire breaking out in the first place.[110] For example, the criminal law's deterrent effect can be used to coerce people in charge of the potentially vulnerable – children; those receiving adult social care; animals – into avoiding kinds of (mis)treatment that systematically expose them to harm.[111] By taking this approach, the criminal law may do much more to prevent harm than could be done by the imposition of even the most draconian penal-

[106] For an analogous example, see Human Fertilisation and Embryology Act 1990 s 4, prohibiting the unlicensed use of gametes in human reproduction. The worry here is the harm that might be done through the operation of an unregulated market appealing to people so desperate for children they will try anything to have them; see generally, Alldridge (n 42 above).

[107] Neil MacCormick, *Legal Right and Social Democracy* (Oxford, Oxford University Press, 1982) 29 and 30, cited by Ashworth (n 5 above) 30 and 52.

[108] See Ashworth (n 5 above) 468; Gardner (n 59 above).

[109] See text at n 73 above.

[110] Just as, in fact, fire prevention is now an important focus for the fire brigade itself, alongside the traditional focus on putting fires out: see www.london-fire.gov.uk/AboutUs, 'The LFB will always respond to fires and other emergencies, but our work has changed over the years with a much stronger emphasis now on fire prevention and community safety.'

[111] See the text at n 23 above.

ties for individual instances of wrongful harm-doing. For instance, in the field of animal welfare in private homes, the Animal Welfare Act 2006 heralded a shift away from a focus on proven cruelty or unnecessary suffering, to a focus on the conditions in which animals are kept. Section 9 provides that:

> (1) A person commits an offence if he does not take such steps as are reasonable in all the circumstances to ensure that the needs of an animal for which he is responsible are met to the extent required by good practice.
> (2) For the purposes of this Act, an animal's needs shall be taken to include –
> (a) its need for a suitable environment,
> (b) its need for a suitable diet,
> (c) its need to be able to exhibit normal behaviour patterns,
> (d) any need it has to be housed with, or apart from, other animals, and
> (e) its need to be protected from pain, suffering, injury and disease.

From an anticipatory perspective, the advantage of this offence is obviously that the law can intervene to punish and deter before cruelty or suffering occur, and perhaps thereby or additionally do something to coerce otherwise indifferent or careless animal owners into anticipating and avoiding sources of suffering for their pets. The focus is thus on neglectful animal-keeping and not, as it was before, largely on the adverse consequences of neglectful animal-keeping.[112]

It is, naturally, possible to argue that any civilising effects that such legislation may have will be over-shadowed by a more general negativity that accompanies them, namely that the effects must be achieved through use of the condemnatory force of the criminal law. However, it has long been noted that enforcement authorities working with offences that reflect the anticipatory perspective tend to press criminal charges only in cases where there has been serious fault, and hence a strong public interest in criminal prosecution to secure condemnation of the offender.[113] Moreover, the enforcement 'gap' that such a legitimate policy of restraint opens up, respecting less serious regulatory offending, is increasingly being plugged by modified or quasi-criminal forms of penalty whose message to wrongdoers and the wider public may be much less clearly and unambiguously condemnatory. In England and Wales, 'civil' penalties (commonly in the form of pre-set fines) can at present replace criminal proceedings in a whole variety of cases, and constitute a form of punishment without an ensuing criminal record.[114] This is so, even though the enforcement authority must often mimic the criminal process by satisfying itself *beyond reasonable*

[112] The relevant Government department (DEFRA) is responsible for issuing guidance to pet-owners on what they need to do to meet the 'reasonable steps' standard set by the Act (www.defra.gov.uk/wildlife-pets), just as the HSE issues guidance to businesses on what to do to ensure that employees are protected so far as is 'reasonably practicable' respecting their health and safety (www.hse.gov.uk/business).

[113] See, for example, Genevra Richardson, 'Strict Liability for Regulatory Crime: The Empirical Research' (1987) *Crim LR* 295; and more generally, Keith Hawkins, *Law as a Last Resort* (Oxford, Oxford University Press, 2002). Regulatory enforcement policy is, in this respect, vindicated by the overall percentages for successful convictions (often over 90% for some agencies).

[114] See for example, s 23(4) of the Anti-social Behaviour Act 2003.

doubt that an offence has been committed, and even though enforcement authorities may have a power to 'name and shame' those who have had such penalties imposed on them in a way that is roughly to acquiring a criminal record.[115] For some critics, such 'civil' measures are the Devil's work,[116] but there can be little doubt in some form that they are here to stay, and likely to proliferate.[117] Such blurring of the line between criminal and civil procedure makes it but a short step to permitting judges themselves in criminal proceedings to impose civil penalties as a form of punishment following conviction, if they believe that a penalty would be right, but a criminal record following punishment would be disproportionate. Such developments reflect a broader trend. There is an increasing willingness in a number of jurisdictions to avoid invoking the full condemnatory force of the criminal law when dealing with lower-level offending by modifying its traditional features. For example, under section 10 of the Crimes (Sentencing Procedure) Act 1999 (NSW),[118] a judge may order that a conviction is not to be 'recorded' if the offender complies with a good behaviour bond or intervention programme, thus cutting the intrinsic link between conviction and record.[119] It seems increasingly likely that criminal law theorists must be prepared to face a new world. This is a world in which not only does minimalism seem increasingly irrelevant to modern legislators, but the availability of new and morally more ambiguous forms of censure – alternatives to and modifications of 'truly criminal' proceedings, punishment and accompanying record – also threatens the traditional basis for opposing the increasing expansion of punitive laws into the anticipatory domain.

[115] See the discussion of the measures in the Regulatory Enforcement and Sanctions Act 2008, in Julia Black, 'A Review of Enforcement Techniques' in Law Commission (n 103 above) appendix A, A10 and A90.

[116] Robin R White, 'Civil Penalties: Oxymoron, Chimera, and Stealth Sanction' (2010) 126 *LQR* 593.

[117] Under the Law Commission's provisional proposals for reducing the numbers of criminal offences on the statute book (n 103 above), civil penalties are to play a much more prominent role in enforcing standards across a large range of (largely, business) activities.

[118] Crimes (Sentencing Procedure) Act 1999 (NSW) s 10 says, 'A court that convicts an offender may dispose of the proceedings without imposing any other penalty.'

[119] For a modern statement of the traditional link between conviction and record, see AP Simester, 'Is Strict Liability Always Wrong?' in AP Simester (ed), *Appraising Strict Liability* (Oxford, Oxford University Press, 2005) 35, 'Convictions are official. They condemn D on behalf of society as a whole. To say that D has a criminal record is to say that he has been labeled as a reprehensible wrongdoer . . .'.

5

Risk and Inchoate Crimes: Retribution or Prevention?

LARRY ALEXANDER AND KIMBERLY KESSLER FERZAN

I INTRODUCTION

IN *CRIME AND Culpability: A Theory of Criminal Law*,[1] we set forth our vision of what criminal law should look like if it were premised solely on the retributive goal of giving people their just (negative) deserts. We did and do endorse that retributive goal, although we do not, of course, advocate that it be pursued monomaniacly, whatever the cost to other valid social goals.[2] Offenders receiving their just punishments is a good, but it is only one good among many. We also endorsed and still endorse a retributive side-constraint prohibiting knowingly punishing offenders more than they deserve.[3] However, that side-constraint does not prohibit *risking* greater-than-deserved punishment, which all systems of criminal punishment will do to a greater or lesser extent. We did not take a stand on the optimal degree of that risk, such as that entailed by proof beyond a reasonable doubt. Our views on that issue were not central to the book's principal concerns.

In *Crime and Culpability*, we argued that negative desert, the measure of just punishment, is solely a function of the culpability of the offender.[4] We argued further that culpability is itself determined by two factors.[5] The first factor is the risks to others' legally protected interests that the actor believes his action is ''unleashing' beyond his ability to alter. Such risks from a single act can be to a variety of legally protected interests and can be of various magnitudes. The relevant question for culpability is not which legally protected interests God will perceive to be at risk from the act, nor is it which ones the so-called 'reasonable person' will perceive to be at risk. Rather, the proper question is which legally

[1] Larry Alexander and Kimberly Kessler Ferzan (with Stephen Morse), *Crime and Culpability: A Theory of Criminal Law* (Cambridge, Cambridge University Press, 2009).

[2] ibid 7–10.

[3] ibid 8–9, 12–13.

[4] ibid chs 2, 5.

[5] ibid ch 2.

protected interests of others does the *actor* believe his act is putting at risk. The same goes for the magnitude of those risks. The relevant magnitude of risk is that assessed by the actor, not what magnitude God or the 'reasonable person' would assess. (God will, of course, know precisely which legally protected interests are at risk – the ones, if any, that are ultimately actually affected – and will likewise assess all magnitudes of the risks as either one or zero, depending on which will be realised.)

The second factor in the culpability equation are the reasons the actor perceives in favour of and against imposing the risks. Those reasons are based on the facts the actor believes exist at the time of his act – discounted by the probabilities of their nonexistence that he assesses – that count in favour of or against imposing risks to others' interests. The actor does *not* have to be motivated by the facts that will justify his risky act for that act to be nonculpable; but he does have to believe those justifying facts exist. Likewise, he does not have to be motivated by the facts that count against his act for those facts to render it culpable, so long as, that is, he is aware of those facts that count against the act.

On the other hand, the *weight* the actor gives to those positive and negative facts that he perceives is immaterial, as is whether he even assesses the negative facts as negative and the positive facts as positive. Whether a fact is positive or negative in the reasons calculus, and how much negative or positive weight it carries, is not an issue on which the actor's opinion matters. What *does* matter is whether he is aware of those facts when he acts.

In essence, we reduced all culpability assessments to that of recklessness. Recklessness is commonly defined as taking a substantial and unjustifiable risk (to others' legally protected interests) while adverting to that risk. We argued that the 'substantial' prong does no real work independently of the 'justifiability' prong, which does all the work. (An unjustifiable risk is always 'substantial' no matter its magnitude.) The culpable *mens rea* of 'purpose' is merely a factor on the justifiability axis, a factor that counts against imposing risks on others. The culpable *mens rea* of 'knowledge' is at one end of the perceived magnitude of risk axis. The recklessness analysis can subsume both of those forms of *mens rea* without loss.

We not only argued that recklessness was the paradigmatic form of culpability and could subsume purpose and knowledge, but we also argued that negligence was not a form of culpability at all.[6] The negligent actor is one who perceives the riskiness of his act as lower than the 'reasonable person' would perceive it, or who perceives justifying facts that the 'reasonable person' would not perceive. As a result, the negligent actor imposes risks for reasons that would render his act nonculpable were the risks and reason as he perceives them but culpable were they as perceived by the 'reasonable person'.

We argued that the negligent actor is not culpable for his negligent act because he is the captive of his misperceptions. Those misperceptions may have been

[6] ibid ch 3.

caused by cognitive or characterological defects, but the actor cannot be deemed culpable for these. He has no control over them and their influence on his perception of the world at the time of the negligent act. His only control over his character and cognition is indirect. He can seek to improve them, though he would have to be aware of their deficiencies to have reason to do so. And those very deficiencies may blind him to their presence. His negligent act *might* be the product of an earlier reckless act – an act that he perceived created an unjustified risk that he would later fail to appreciate other risks. (He might have forgone attending a lecture on 'Japanese for the street-wise American sailor in Yokohama', realising that he was running a risk of dangerously misunderstanding Japanese women, a risk that, given his reasons for skipping the lecture, was an unjustified one.) Perhaps he is culpable for taking the reckless progenitor (of negligence) act. However, *that* culpability is separate from any culpability that attaches to his negligent act, which we argued is non-existent.

Finally, we argued that the results of reckless acts do not affect culpability and therefore do not affect retributive desert.[7] That is why a reckless act that is reckless because it creates an unjustifiable risk of a later negligent act is culpable independently of the negligent act, if any, that is its product. If the negligent act is due to an earlier reckless act, the actor should only be punished for the reckless act. And he should be punished for it even if it never leads to a negligent act. An actor who culpably imposes a risk to others' legally protected interests should be punished for that risk-imposition whether or not any harm to those interests result from the act. Results of acts do not affect the culpability and hence the negative desert of the actors.

II INCHOATE CRIMES

An inchoate crime as we defined it in *Crime and Culpability* is one in which the criminal act is prior to the act that unleashes the risk(s) of harm.[8] In other words, it is a crime that occurs while the actor still has the ability to choose to refrain from imposing the risk. On that definition, completed attempts and reckless endangerments are *not* inchoate crimes. A completed attempt is an attempt to commit a crime by an actor who believes that he has done everything necessary to commit the crime and that preventing the crime is now beyond his control. The paradigm of a completed attempt is the actor's pulling the trigger on a gun that he believes is loaded, in working order, and pointed at a vital spot on the victim. If it turns out the gun is unloaded, or jammed, or misaimed, and the victim is not harmed by the actor's pulling the trigger, the actor has committed a completed attempt of murder. Similarly, the driver who drives recklessly but manages to cause no injury to life, limb, or property has committed the

[7] ibid ch 5.
[8] ibid ch 6.

completed crime of reckless endangerment; for whether injury occurred was beyond his control once he committed the reckless act.

The paradigmatic inchoate crime is the incomplete attempt. In an incomplete attempt, the actor intends to commit a culpable act in the future and has taken some steps toward that end. (How many steps he must take and how close to committing the intended culpable act he must come are matters of controversy and vary from jurisdiction to jurisdiction.) Thus, for example, when Frankie lies in wait for Johnny to return home, at which time she intends to kill him with her .44, she has in most jurisdictions committed an incomplete attempt of murder.

Solicitation, conspiracy, and giving aid to another to assist the latter's commission of a future crime are often regarded as inchoate crimes. On our analysis, with the exception of a conspiracy in which the conspirator in question intends to carry out the future crime as the principal, these crimes, if they are truly culpable, are properly regarded as completed crimes of reckless endangerment.[9] For the actors have unleashed beyond their control risks of *others'* criminal acts by virtue of encouraging or aiding those future acts. Only if the actor retains control over whether those future crimes occur do we have a true inchoate crime.

(What we call 'lit fuse' attempts, where the actor has set up the mechanism that will unleash the risk in the near future without any further action on his part, but where he believes he can still act to prevent the realisation of that risk – as with a lit fuse – has some characteristics of a completed attempt and some of an incomplete attempt.[10] For our purposes here, it should be thought of as a completed attempt and thus as beyond the scope of this article.)

III ARE INCHOATE CRIMES CULPABLE?

In *Crime and Culpability* we argued that true inchoate crimes are not culpable and should not be punished.[11] Our arguments that negligent acts were not culpable and that results do not affect culpability were (and are) controversial, but the controversies in which they partook were longstanding and well understood ones. Our position on inchoate criminality, however, provoked a controversy that had little precedent. We think it fair to say that our position on inchoate crimes was the most controversial of all the controversial positions we took. That is the position we shall revisit and defend in these pages.

So let us return to Frankie, lying in wait for Johnny, intending to kill him with her .44. Until Frankie pulls the trigger of her .44, while aiming it at Johnny's heart, believing it to be loaded and in good working condition, and not believing she is Superwoman and faster than a speeding bullet, has Frankie committed a culpable act?

[9] ibid 223–25.
[10] ibid 220–21.
[11] ibid ch 6.

Surely there are some culpable acts Frankie may have committed. Carrying around a loaded .44 for no reason other than to kill Johnny may create an unjustified risk of death or injury through an accidental discharge. Likewise, merely driving to Johnny's house, no matter how carefully, for the sole purpose of killing Johnny, may create an unjustified risk of a traffic accident. For even if these risks are very small in Frankie's estimation, if her only reason for imposing them is a bad reason – to kill Johnny – then her driving and carrying the .44 are reckless and culpable. If she reaches the stage where she is pointing the gun at Johnny with her hand on the trigger, the risk of accidental discharge may be so high (in her estimation of the risk) that she is quite culpable for imposing the risk.

Furthermore, in addition to creating risks of accidental discharge or traffic accidents, Frankie may have culpably unleashed a risk of causing fear. For if she realises that there is a risk that someone – perhaps Johnny, or perhaps a third party – will see her lying in wait with a gun and fear for his or another's life, then Frankie will be aware that she has unleashed this risk, and she will have done so for a reason – murder – that does not justify the risk.

So there are several culpable acts that Frankie may have committed or be committing in lying in wait for Johnny. However, none of them is as culpable as a completed attempt at murder. Nor are any of the relevant risks the risk of Frankie's intentionally pulling the trigger while aiming at Johnny. In other words, these other possible culpable acts are not acts of attempted murder. Also, Frankie's intent to kill Johnny enters into the analysis of these acts' culpability only to establish that any risks Frankie perceives she is imposing are not justifiable risks.

Those who wish to make incomplete attempts criminal apart from these collateral risks they may impose and of which the attempter may be aware do so because they think Frankie's *intending* to kill Johnny (and perhaps taking some steps towards realising that intention) is what makes Frankie culpable as an attempted murderer. We rejected this, for reasons to which we now turn.

A The Centrality of Intending a Culpable Act to the Case for the Culpability of Inchoate Crimes

A retributivist case for punishing inchoate crimes such as incomplete attempts ultimately must rest on the premise that intending a future culpable act is itself a culpable act. (Remember: we are excluding from consideration the various risks of harm that an actor, such as Frankie, may have already unleashed – put beyond her ability to affect – in the course of conduct leading to the intended crime.) Why do we say that the key premise in the case for inchoate criminality is that intending a culpable act is itself a culpable act? After all, the law of incomplete attempts requires not only an intent to commit a wrong but also steps towards acting on that intent that go beyond 'mere preparation'. (Just how the line between 'mere preparation' and attempting is drawn is inherently imprecise, and its formulation varies from jurisdiction to jurisdiction; here we shall use the Model Penal Code's 'substantial steps' formulation, which is a representative one.)

The law might have two different concerns in requiring the (incomplete) attempter to have taken 'substantial steps' towards acting on a culpable intention. One concern is to corroborate that the actor really does possess the culpable intention. The Model Penal Code states that the requisite substantial steps must corroborate the actor's culpable intent. This, however, seems unnecessary, as the culpable intent must always be proved 'beyond a reasonable doubt'. Moreover, if an act requirement is added for the purpose of constraining the state and curbing abuse, such a rationale is not retributive; the act requirement is not based on what the actor deserves.

The other concern is a concern with dangerousness. The closer the actor is to executing her culpable intention, the more likely she is to execute it unless she changes her mind or someone or something intervenes to prevent her. The problem with this rationale for requiring 'substantial steps' is that dangerousness and culpability are independent of one another, and each can be present in the absence of the other. We punish people because they are culpable, whereas we restrain people, when we do so, because they are dangerous. Frankie's lying in wait for Johnny makes her more dangerous, if she retains her culpable intent, than she was when she first formed the intent to kill him – perhaps while sitting in a chair in her home, many miles from Johnny's house. However, does it make her more culpable? She is no less capable of changing her mind and relenting; and although she has sunk more costs in her plan to kill Johnny by the time she reaches his house, she still has an overriding reason to change her mind: namely, that her intended act is a culpable one. In other words, she still controls the culpability of her future conduct and still has an overriding reason to see that it is not culpable.

Here is another example drawn from *Crime and Culpability*[12] that shows that the culpable intent is what does all the real work in deeming incomplete attempts culpable. Dan intends to kill Victor, who takes a daily walk on a trail that passes under Balanced Rock. Dan purchases a jackhammer and takes it to a point alongside Balanced Rock. He plans to start the jackhammer as Victor walks by so that its vibrations will unbalance Balanced Rock and cause it to fall on Victor. However, as Dan sees Victor walking toward Balanced Rock, Dan decides to wait to execute his plan on another day because there are too many picnickers around. Dan departs, leaving his jackhammer behind.

Because Dan arguably took substantial steps towards killing Victor, and because he did not abandon his attempted murder out of a change of heart, Dan would arguably be guilty of an incomplete attempted murder in most jurisdictions and under the Model Penal Code. Now compare Dan with Dana. Dana

[12] ibid 210.

happens to be picnicking right next to the spot where Dan leaves his jackhammer. Dana also hates Victor, and when she sees him coming, she realises that she could kill him by starting the jackhammer, and she forms the intent to do so.

Surely if Dan is culpable for his incomplete attempt to kill Victor, Dana, when she forms the intent to kill Victor while sitting next to the jackhammer and Balanced Rock, is equally culpable. After all, *she is intending to kill Victor in exactly the same circumstances that Dan was in when he became guilty of the incomplete attempt*. So if Dan is culpable, so is Dana. If Dana is culpable, it can only be because of her intent to kill Victor. So we would conclude that in Dan's case as well, it is Dan's intent to kill Victor that solely accounts for this culpability.

The argument must be, then, that Frankie's intending to kill Johnny is itself culpable. Substantial steps only prove (perhaps redundantly) that the culpable intention exists. They show that it is an intention, not a mere desire or fantasy, with which we are dealing. They also show that the intention is firm enough to have led the actor to have taken various steps towards executing it. So substantial steps may play an important epistemic role. Nevertheless, it is the intention, not those steps, that has to be the culpable element if Frankie's incomplete attempt is culpable.

Still, we should note that some authors disagree with us over whether substantial steps are merely evidential. Some have argued that the more steps the actor takes towards executing his intention to commit a culpable act, the more he is 'rationally committed' to executing it and under 'rational pressure' to do so.[13] However, this is an argument that is very close to asserting that it is rational to recover 'sunk costs'.[14] In the case of an intention to perform a culpable act, it is always rational to change one's mind and desist – no matter how many steps taken and how much cost sunk. After all, the culpability of the intended act is in no way diminished by the actor's previous efforts towards committing it. ('I really shouldn't be blamed for the murder; after all, I spent an enormous amount of time planning it and enormous amounts of money on the weapon, the camouflage, the ticket to Rio . . .'). The actor will not only be acting most rationally if she changes her mind, but she is also always free to do so.

[13] See, eg Gideon Yaffe, 'Trying, Acting and Attempted Crimes' (2008) 28 *Law and Phil* 109. Yaffe does not require the step beyond intending to be a particularly important one for executing the intent. It only has to corroborate the actor's intent. However, because determining that it is such a step requires that we know the intent with which it was taken – was the purchase of the gun made for the intended killing or for marksmanship practice? – we must have independent evidence of intent. The step therefore adds nothing to an intent requirement. If one is 'rationally committed' to an illicit end by taking a step in that direction, one is 'rationally committed' to it by merely intending it.

[14] Daniel Ohana argues that the more costs the actor has sunk into her criminal plan, the more likely she is in fact to carry it out. Daniel Ohana, 'Desert and Punishment for Acts Preparatory to the Commission of a Crime' (2007) 20 *Canad J Law & Jurisp* 113, 122–23. He concludes that the actor is culpable and hence deserving of punishment for having formed the plan and made some preparations for carrying it out. ibid 124. Again, we disagree. The actor has still not unleashed an unjustified risk, given that, until she completes the last act necessary to execute her wrongful plan, she remains in complete control and can abandon it at any point, regardless of the costs she has sunk.

B Is Intending a Culpable Act Itself a Culpable Act?

If the element of an incomplete attempt that does the inculpatory work is the intent to commit the crime, we must confront the central question: *Is intending to commit a culpable act itself a culpable act?* If the answer is 'yes', then there is a retributive case for punishing inchoate crimes. If, as we argued in *Crime and Culpability*, the answer is 'no', then only acts that unleash unjustifiable risks are culpable, whereas intendings, and the inchoate crimes that they constitute, are not.

Now the case for the culpability of intending a culpable act might seem obvious. After all, if ¶ing is wrong, then would it not follow that intending to ¶ is wrong?

Surely there is something criticisable in intending a culpable act. That in itself does not show that intending the culpable act is culpable. For if ¶ing is wrong, does it follow that desiring to ¶ is wrong, or fantasising about ¶ing is wrong? Desiring or fantasising about something bad is criticisable and may reveal character defects, but it is not a culpable act. Desiring, wishing, fantasising, etc are not culpable acts because they are not acts at all, and surely not voluntary acts. Because only voluntary acts can be culpable and merit retributive responses, these attitudes toward culpable acts are not themselves culpable. So even if ¶ing is a wrong justifying retribution, desiring to ¶ is not.

Nonetheless, we did not rest the case against inchoate criminality on the ground that intending a culpable act is not a voluntary act. Instead, we assumed the contrary, namely, that intending *is* a voluntary act. Or rather, and more precisely, we assumed not that an intention, a mental state, is itself an act, but that *forming* an intention is an act, and a voluntary one. Our case against inchoate criminality accepted that intendings were different from desirings, wishings, and fantasisings in a way that made intendings potentially eligible for retributive responses.

What we should have added is that although an intention may be merely a mental state, *maintaining* an intention, like forming one, can be viewed as a voluntary act. Much of our discussion of the culpability, if any, of intending a culpable act was premised on the unstated assumption that maintaining an intention over time was potentially culpable and thus could be viewed as voluntary action.

So both forming and maintaining intentions to commit culpable acts are eligible to be deemed culpable acts, unlike desirings, wishings, and fantasisings. Nonetheless, we concluded that neither forming nor maintaining intentions to commit culpable acts were culpable acts, even if forming and maintaining such intentions were acts. We believe that conclusion is the correct one.

i The Difficulty of Distinguishing Intentions from Desires

Intentions are not the same as desires, wishes, and fantasisings. That is clear. What is less clear is how the actors in a criminal justice system – the police, prosecutor, judge, and jury – will be able to distinguish an intention to commit a culpable act from these other mental states. Remember that we are dealing with inchoate crimes – in particular, incomplete attempts. The intended culpable act will not have been committed. At best we have a confession of the defendant and conduct consistent with that confession. However, even the actor herself may have difficulty ascertaining whether she intended a future culpable act or merely desired it or was fantasising about it. Will Frankie be certain she really intends to shoot Johnny, even if she has taken a loaded gun and driven to Johnny's home? If Frankie cannot be certain she intends to shoot Johnny, can the rest of us be confident that is what she intends?

From this point on we shall assume that this epistemic worry has been overcome and that we can with sufficient confidence distinguish intentions from desires and fantasisings. Still, the murkiness of the line between intentions and these related mental states should itself give us pause about criminalising intentions.

ii A Big Worry: The Conditionality of Intentions and the Opacity of the Future

Our intentions to engage in future conduct are almost always – perhaps always – conditional. We intend to engage in that conduct in certain circumstances but not in others. Some of those conditions may be present to our minds when we form the intentions. We say to ourselves, 'I will go to the store at 3pm unless it is raining or I am at a point in the article I'm working on where I'd best not stop.' Such conditions that will defeat or trigger the intended conduct are called 'internal conditions' because they are part of the intentions as we mentally formulate them. On the other hand, most of the conditions that attach to our intentions are 'external' in that they are not present to mind when we form those intentions. We will not intend to go to the store at 3pm if we discover that our car won't start and we would have to walk, or we hear that there has been a massive accident on the road to the store, and so on. We do not consciously advert to all these defeating conditions, but our intended conduct is nevertheless conditional on whether they obtain.

In an incomplete attempt, the intention to engage in the *actus reus* of a crime is, like all intentions, conditional. Some of the internal conditions that would cancel the intention show that the intention was not an intention to engage in culpable conduct. ('I intend to kill Susan – but only if she is about to shoot Sam, or blow up the White House, etcetera.') Other internal conditions do not negate the culpability of the intended conduct but do make that conduct highly unlikely. If Roger intends to steal the Mona Lisa, but only if it is in the Metropolitan Museum of Art and not the Louvre, and only if it is not guarded, his conditional intention is culpable but very unlikely to be acted upon. The same is true if Samson intends to kill Delilah if she is ever unfaithful, but he believes (correctly) that she is and will remain faithful.

What is true of internal conditions is true of external conditions. Suppose one intends to drive from San Diego to Los Angeles in two hours time, which requires an average speed of 60 miles per hour. When one forms this intention, he does not advert to the possibility that road and traffic conditions will make 60 miles per hour an extremely unsafe speed. Nonetheless, his dispositions are such that when he sees that he cannot safely drive at that speed, he will abandon intention to arrive in two hours. Given what he now knows about the road and traffic conditions, his intention to drive to Los Angeles in two hours would be a culpable intention on which to act. However, although he did not consciously consider these adverse road and traffic conditions when he formed the intention to drive to Los Angeles in two hours, these external conditions on that intention were either always present or became present at some time prior to his driving.

The conditionality of intentions makes assessing their culpability much less straightforward than assessing the culpability of the intended acts themselves. As we have said, the culpability of the latter is a function of the risks of varying magnitudes to various legally protected interests that the actor believes his act has unleashed beyond his ability to affect, and the reasons for and against imposing those risks that the actor believes, with varying degrees of certainty, exist at the time of the act.

Consider again Roger the art thief. When he enters the Metropolitan Museum, intending to steal the Mona Lisa if it is there and unguarded, he believes the probability that those conditions will obtain and he will steal the Mona Lisa to be vanishingly low. Has he, upon entering, committed burglary (which is really a per se incomplete attempt of the target felony)? Just how culpable is Roger's entering the Metropolitan Museum with that conditional intention?

Or consider, analogously, Marge, the strong arm robber. She says to Vic, 'Your money or your life.' She is not bluffing. She intends to shoot Vic if he does not hand over his money. However, she believes it is almost certain that Vic will hand it over and that she will not have to shoot him. Marge has committed robbery. Has she also committed assault with intent to kill or attempted murder?

Or return to Frankie, en route to Johnny's house with her .44. She intends to kill Johnny if she catches him *in flagrante* with another woman. However, she has never once caught him with any other woman. She believes that it is 99 per cent likely that Johnny is not now with another woman. Still, she does intend to shoot him if he is with another woman, which is why she is carrying her .44. How culpable does her conditional intention to kill Johnny make her if she believes it is highly unlikely that the intention will be triggered?

Finally, suppose Maggie intends to drive to her child's school to pick him up, and she intends to get there in 10 minutes. If traffic is moving freely, the road is not icy, and so on, Maggie can get there in 10 minutes without recklessly endangering others. Her intention to get there in 10 minutes is not unconditional: she would not drive through a Boy Scout parade on the road, mow down pedestrians crossing at crosswalks, and so on. Still, there are some circumstances, quite unlikely but still possible, in which Maggie would drive recklessly to some degree, to which she may or may not be adverting when she forms the intention to get to the school in 10 minutes. How should we assess Maggie's culpability for so intending?

Perhaps there is a solution to this problem of the conditionality of intentions. For example, perhaps we should assess the culpability of the actor's intention by asking what probability did he attach to his acting on the intention – or, what is the same thing, what probability did he attach to the conditions obtaining that governed whether he would act? (This, of course, will be difficult and perhaps impossible for those conditions to which the actor did not consciously advert but were nonetheless present dispositionally.) Then we could ask what culpability-enhancing and culpability-mitigating conditions did the actor believe would exist at the time of the intended act, and with what probabilities. The culpability of intending the act would be the average of the culpability of the various scenarios the actor envisioned might obtain at the time of the intended act, weighted by the probabilities he assigned each scenario, and discounted by the probability he attached to his actually engaging in the intended act (the probability that the defeating conditions would not exist).

If this 'solution' appears impossibly complex – and it is – the problems of assessing the culpability of intending a (possibly) culpable future act are only beginning. For the actor may assess the relevant probabilities differently at different points in time. Take Roger the art thief, and assume he is charged, not with burglary, but with an incomplete attempt of grand larceny. Roger may, at the time he forms the intention to steal the Mona Lisa, believe that it is quite unlikely that the Metropolitan Museum possesses it. Later, he may assess that likelihood as higher (or lower). Similarly, over time he may alter his assessment of the likelihood of its being heavily guarded. Thus, Roger's estimate of the likelihood that he will ever execute his intention to steal the Mona Lisa will vary over time. Is Roger's culpability dependent on the point in time at which he is arrested? Could he have been more or less culpable if he had been arrested sooner (or later)? Is culpability assessed just at the moment of arrest, or is it the average of his culpability from the moment he formed the intention until the moment of arrest, which, too, will vary with the time of the arrest?

What goes for the actor's estimate of the probability that he will execute the culpable intention also goes for his beliefs about the culpability-relevant facts that will obtain at the time of the intended act. Those beliefs may change during the time in which the intention is held.

For instance, assume that Barb, the law school dean, decides to blow up the football stadium to protest the university's allocation of funds to the football team instead of a new law school building. At that point in time, she may not have yet considered whether she will blow up the stadium when it is full of people or when it is empty. She may be debating whether to wait until there is a home team present, or whether to ensure that it is a day when no one is in the area. However, even if Barb has resolved to blow up the stadium at a specific time, her beliefs about the attendant risks and possible justifying reasons may change several times between the time she forms the intent and the time she detonates the bomb: she may believe at one time that the stadium will be full of fans, at another that it will be empty, at another that it will be occupied only by a terrorist cell, and so on. If she were to detonate the bomb at any of these times, her culpability for doing so would vary enormously – from extremely culpable to possibly not culpable at all in the case of the terrorist cell. Again, is Barb's culpability determined by her beliefs at the time she is arrested – in which case it may be high if she is arrested at t1 but nonexistent if arrested at t2 – or is it determined by the average culpability of her intention from the time of its formation to the time of her arrest? In either case, because her beliefs about risks and reasons will change over time, her culpability level will depend on the pure fortuity of when she is arrested. (And how does one 'average' a culpable intention, as when Barb believes the stadium will be full of fans, and a justifiable one, as when she believes the stadium will contain no one but a dangerous terrorist cell?)

Indeed, not only may Barb's beliefs about risks and reasons change over time, but she simply may have formed no belief whatsoever about the degree of risk that she will ultimately impose, leaving this 'detail' to be filled in later. The ultimate risks and reasons for the intended action and therefore its culpability will be indeterminate at the moment of forming the intention.[15]

To some, our concern may seem a bit inconsistent with our approach to moral luck. Here is the potential objection to our view. If Frankie shoots at Johnny, but a bird flies in the way, we argue that the bird is irrelevant to Frankie's blameworthiness. But then, why is it not equally irrelevant that at the time that Frankie forms the intention to kill Johnny, she is unaware of the fact that a flock of birds may later block her bullet or otherwise thwart her plans?

The difference is that when an actor forms an intention as to what he will do later, he understands that his plans are open-ended. Indeed, the law's difficulty in holding that conspirators intend to kill a police officer (before they pick their

[15] One last point, suppose David has a conditional intention, the condition of which negates the criminal harm. Suppose he intends to have sex with Darlene, unless she is under the legal age. It appears that at this time, David's intent is perfectly lawful. (See Model Penal Code § 2.02(6) (1985).) However if, 'Have sex with Darlene, unless she is under the legal age' is the major premise of David's practical syllogism, the minor premise might be 'Darlene is (thankfully) over the legal age.' If so, then the conclusion David reaches is 'Have sex with Darlene.' For inchoate criminality, which intention should control – the intent in the major premise, which is legal, or the intent in the conclusion, which, if David is in error regarding Darlene's age, is illegal? Because David has not yet done what he intends to do, it is ambiguous whether he intends to have sex with Darlene (because he mistakenly believes she is over the legal age) or not to have sex with her (because he intends to have sex only if she is over the legal age).

(Of course, this problem only arises in connection with crimes that have strict liability elements or elements that require only the *mens rea* of negligence. And because we do not regard negligence as culpable – and strict liability is the antithesis of culpability – we would reject the very underpinnings of this problem.)

victim), or that an accomplice intends to aid a statutory rape (when the accomplice lends his buddy the keys to his apartment before the buddy even meets the underage girl), are motivated by the concern that until we see a situation, we do not know how we will react. We do not even know what we will intend.

Putting the concerns about conditionality of intentions and the opacity of future circumstances into a broader conceptual framework further clarifies these problems. As Michael Bratman has noted, our future intentions – our plans – are partial.[16] In other words, the conditionality of intentions is not simply a matter of there being potential circumstances that might undermine an intention. Rather, intentions are open-ended plans designed to lead to further deliberation about the specifics. Intentions structure our later means-end reasoning, and their conditionality is thus a feature of them that cannot be ignored. Any future plan may or may not lead to a future choice to risk harm to another person for insufficient reasons. An intention to go to the grocery store might lead to a culpable choice if there is heavy traffic and the actor then chooses to drive fast; but the same intention might turn out to be completely benign. How can forming the intention to go to the grocery store itself be a culpable act merely because of the former possibility?

iii Another Big Problem: The Effect of the Duration and Renunciation of Intentions

As intentions can be held for varying lengths of time, and because they can be revoked, we must ask how, if they are to be deemed culpable, their culpability is affected by these features. First, let us compare Hank and Harry. On 1 January, Hank forms the intent to kill Sally next 1 January. Later, on 1 July, Harry forms the intent to kill Sally next 1 January. On 2 July, Hank has held the intention to kill Sally for over six months, whereas Harry has done so for only a day. Is Hank more culpable than Harry?

a Assume Duration Does *Not* Affect Culpability

One view would be that the duration of maintaining the intention is immaterial to its culpability. On 2 July, Hank and Harry are equally culpable. Hank is as culpable on 1 January as he is on 2 July (barring changes in beliefs about conditions and circumstances that were discussed in the previous subsection).

However, suppose that Hank now renounces his intention to kill Sally, whereas Harry does not. What effect does his renouncing it have on his culpability, and does it matter *why* he renounces it? (If he renounces the intended act because he views it as imprudent as opposed to immoral, should that deprive his renunciation of any effect on his culpability?)

[16] See Michael E Bratman, *Intentions, Plans, and Practical Reason* (Center for the Study of Language and Information, 1987) 29.

If forming and maintaining an intention to commit a culpable act is itself a culpable act, then it is difficult to understand how the culpability that exists at that time can be expunged by later revoking the intention. The past is fixed and contains the culpable act. It cannot be altered. If Hank was culpable on 1 January for intending to kill Sally, he remains culpable for having so intended on 1 January even if he no longer intends to kill her, whether owing to prudence or conscience. Any view to the contrary would suggest our concern was not with past culpable acts but only with present character.

If the culpability of intending cannot be expunged by revoking the intent, and if the duration of maintaining the intention is immaterial, then Harry is just as culpable as Hank even if Harry revokes his intention after 30 seconds, whereas Hank has held his intention firmly for more than six months. Or if Harry is indecisive and forms the intent to kill Sally, then 30 seconds later revokes it (say, for purely prudential reasons), then forms it again, then again quickly revokes it, Harry has committed several culpable acts of intending to kill whereas Hank has committed only one. However, it seems odd to deem indecisive Harry more culpable and deserving of more punishment than steadfast Hank.

b. Assume Duration *Does* Affect Culpability

Alternatively, we might say that Hank's holding the intention to kill Sally for six months makes him more culpable than Harry, who has held the intention for a much shorter time. The problem is explaining why the duration of the intention should matter. We gave an explanation for why the duration of an act that the actor perceives to be risky matters: it matters because duration affects the degree of risk.[17] (Driving for one minute while intoxicated is less risky than driving for an hour in that condition.) However, the six month's duration of Hank's intention to kill Sally does not make the risk to Sally higher on 2 July than the risk from Harry's one day's intention.

Perhaps one could argue that the longer an intention is maintained, the more resolute that shows the actor to be; and the more resolutely an actor holds a culpable intention, the more culpable he is. Both parts of this argument are problematic, however.

First, a person can maintain an intention for a long time and yet not be resolute; for when the time comes to act on that intention, he may change his mind. On the other hand, he may act on an intention formed only a moment ago. Dan may have maintained for weeks the intention to kill Victor by causing Balanced Rock to fall on him; but when the time comes to carry through, Dan thinks better of the idea and abandons the intention. Dana, who just forms the intention to kill upon seeing Victor and the abandoned jackhammer, may act on it.

[17] Alexander and Ferzan (n 1 above) 242–44.

Second, the link between resoluteness and culpability remains unexplained. Aside from showing that the intention to commit a culpable act really does exist, the resoluteness with which it is held, which is what duration is supposed to demonstrate, at most only affects (negatively) the likelihood of abandonment. It does not affect the culpability of the intention itself.[18] Perhaps the idea is that the culpability of an intention should be discounted by the strength with which it is held, so that an intention held half-heartedly can only be half as culpable as an intention held resolutely. In any event, we leave it to those who find intentions to commit culpable acts to be themselves culpable acts to work this out.

iv Why Should Incomplete Attempts Merge with Completed Attempts or Successful Crimes?

If forming and maintaining an intention to commit a culpable act is itself a culpable act, then when the actor actually commits the intended culpable act and unleashes the risk beyond his control to recall (or so he believes), why has he not committed *two* crimes? If the risk is realised, why has he not committed both a successful crime and the inchoate crime of intending it? If the risk is not realised, why has he not committed both that inchoate crime and a completed attempt? Indeed, for reasons already mentioned, the culpability of the completed crime or attempt may be less than that of the incomplete attempt because the circumstances that the actor believes exist at the time he unleashes the perceived risk may make his act less culpable than the circumstances he envisioned would exist at the time the intent was formed. When Barb formed the intention to blow up the football stadium on Saturday, she may have thought the stadium would be full of spectators. When on Saturday she detonates the bomb, or tries to, she may realise that there is no home game that day and that the stadium is empty. The only damage the bomb will cause is to the stadium itself. Barb's final act is culpable, but it is much less culpable than she believed it would be when she formed the intention. Had she been arrested earlier, and if incomplete attempts are culpable, then she would have been more culpable than she was when her intended act was executed. Why then should she not be guilty of *two* culpable acts?

No one to our knowledge has proposed making an incomplete attempt that then is followed by a completed attempt or successful crime a separate crime from the latter crimes. It is assumed that the incomplete attempt merges with the crime or the completed attempt. If, however, the incomplete attempt is *more* culpable than the completed attempt or the crime attempted – and remember, for us, results do not affect desert, so completed attempts are all that matter and deserve the same punishments as the crimes they attempt – then any merger would have to go in the opposite direction.

[18] Thus, the duration with which an intention is held is unlike the quality of the deliberation leading up to forming the intention, which *can* affect culpability. See ibid 166–68.

In any event, we are not going to try to resolve this problem. We leave that to the proponents of deeming incomplete attempts to be culpable.

v The Revocability of Intentions

There is a final problem with deeming intentions to be culpable and punishable, and this concern is decisive for us. This is the problem that intentions are open to reconsideration and thus revocable. On the one hand, if it is not necessarily rational to reconsider one's intention,[19] the decision to do wrong may be the point at which the balance of reasons has shifted for the actor, and he has committed the culpable – unreasonably dangerous – act. The formation of the intention might then be analogous to the lighting of a long fuse where, although the actor may still exert control over whether the harm does materialise, the risk to the victim has nonetheless increased. One might thus argue that from the actor's perspective, the risk to the victim has increased because, even from the actor's perspective, the actor's balance of reasons has shifted. Thus, if this risk is being imposed for insufficient reasons, the actor has committed a culpable act in forming the intention itself.

However, when one is planning to commit a crime, it will *always* be rational to reconsider.[20] Indeed, many intentions are formed with the proviso that there can always be later reconsideration. Although intentions may serve to guide our future decisions, they are not irreversible, nor may they be carried out without any further effort on our part. The risk from the actor's point of view – objectively risk is always zero or one – may have increased, because the actor believes he will act as he now intends; but the actor still remains in total control of whether this risk will be unleashed, and he knows this.

Now, it may be said that there is a distinct difference between rationality and culpability. After all, an individual who has lit a fuse will also be under rational pressure to stomp out the fuse, so the pressure to reconsider cannot itself suffice to make the act of forming the intention nonculpable. Even if the actor may be able to change his mind and 'revoke' his intention, how does any irrationality in not reconsidering render the initial choice less culpable?

Unlike a lit fuse, however, which the actor may find himself unable to put out even if he now wishes to do so, the actor who only intends to unleash risk in the future knows that he is still in control of his actions. And, indeed, just as crucially, through the exercise of reason and will alone, he may 'stop' the harm from occurring. The common law's focus on *locus penitentiae* is best thought of not as an opportunity to abandon or renounce but as an opportunity to continue deliberating and change one's mind. Just as the criminal law seeks to influence the reasons for which one acts, the criminal law should allow room for deliberation, even including room for the formation and

[19] See Bratman (n 16 above) 64.

[20] ibid 67.

renunciation of an intention. The actor may still deliberate and think the better of his plan.[21]

Moreover, often when actors intend an act that may in some circumstances be culpable, actors will not have considered whether they will really go through with it in those circumstances. Or they may have considered it, believing that they will, but in fact they will not. Actors cannot know until they actually commit the act in the culpability-creating circumstances (or fail to commit it).

In our view, even if there is rational pressure to stick with one's intention – pressure that in some way increases the risk of harm – there is also rational pressure to abandon one's criminal plan, pressure that decreases the risk of harm. Hence, rationality cuts in both directions and cannot therefore point to an increase in risk. In short, an actor cannot regard his future acts as properly subject to a risk assessment; for he cannot regard himself, even given his intention, as a force beyond recall. One may know that forming the intention, or buying the gun, does in some sense make one 'more committed' to the crime, but one also knows that one can *and should* think the better of one's plan, and this influence serves as an important counterweight. Intentions are guides to future actions that do not prevent our later reconsideration. It follows that an actor has committed a culpable act only at the point where the actor has truly relinquished control, not at the point at which he forms the intention to unleash a risk in the future.

IV INCHOATE CRIMES AND DANGEROUSNESS

Up to this point we have been considering whether true inchoate crimes, of which incomplete attempts are the dominant paradigm, are culpable, and if so, how their culpability is to be gauged. We have put aside incomplete attempts that culpably unleash beyond the actor's control ancillary risks, such as that of the accidental discharging of the intended murder weapon, the possibility of an auto accident, or the creation of fear. We have concentrated on the act that is the object of the attempter's conduct, the intended killing or theft or fast driving. We have asked whether intending that conduct, and perhaps taking steps towards executing that intention, is itself culpable conduct, and if so, how culpable.

Suppose, however, that the reason we might wish to punish incomplete attempts and other true inchoate crimes is not a retributive one based on the actor's culpability, but is rather a preventive one based on the actor's dangerousness. Is that a better reason than the retributive one, given all the problems with assessing the culpability, if there be culpability, of incomplete attempts?

The problems with the preventive rationale for inchoate crimes are these. First, there is the general problem with justifying preemptive incursions on life,

[21] See RA Duff, *Answering for Crime: Responsibility and Liability in the Criminal Law* (Oxford, Hart Publishing, 2007) 104.

limb, and liberty. We do, of course, believe some such incursions are justified. Self-defence is always a preemptive action, one that to be truly defensive, as opposed to retaliatory, must occur before the anticipated act to which it is a defence. Restraining orders, anti-stalking laws, restrictions on sex offenders, and even laws restricting the possession of guns and other potential weapons are all examples of actions that preemptively restrict liberties in order to avert future criminal acts. They are preventive responses to dangerousness rather than retributive responses to culpability.

Assuming that such preemptive restrictions are justifiable, however, does not by itself eliminate the worry about inchoate crimes, for inchoate crimes as a category are both under and over-inclusive with respect to dangerousness. Someone who has never formed a culpable intention may be highly likely to do so in the future. On the other hand, some who form culpable intentions may not be dangerous at all. (Consider Charlie, locked in a cell for life, who believes that by committing certain mental acts he can kill the president, or that he can do so by sticking pins in an effigy; when he performs those acts he is acting culpably, but he is not and can never be dangerous.)

Still, what do we do with someone who we know now possesses an intention to commit an act that we believe might be very culpable if committed? If we catch Frankie lying in wait for Johnny with her .44, intending to shoot him on sight, we cannot just let her go, or so it seems. Even if we could punish her for her culpability in consciously risking an accidental discharge of her gun, a traffic accident en route to Johnny's house, or causing fear, her culpability and her consequent justly deserved punishment will not be sufficient to allay our fear that she will shoot Johnny once her punishment is served. Her intent to kill Johnny, unless it is renounced forever, makes her a danger to be left at liberty.

Our conclusion is that we should think of inchoate crimes such as incomplete attempts as falling into the category of dangers that might warrant preemptive restrictions of liberty. Our response to inchoate crimes should be governed by the same norms that govern all preemptive responses to predicted dangerousness. It should not be governed by retributivism, for it does not appear to be a response to a culpable act.

6

Risks, Culpability and Criminal Liability

RA DUFF

I INTRODUCTION: INCHOATE OFFENCES IN THE CRIMINAL LAW

OUR PRACTICAL LIVES are filled with enterprises: activities large or small, long or short, major or minor, structured by their orientation to an intended goal, analysable into indefinitely large sets of specific actions. My current enterprises include writing this chapter – today's part in that enterprise being the writing of this first section; making dinner for friends this evening, which involves planning the menu and shopping this morning; going to the gym – which I do every weekday; selling my house – for which there is nothing that I need do today. An enterprise is defined initially by its relationship to its intended goal (a goal that might itself be a final end or a means to some further goal, or a constituent of a larger goal): writing this chapter, giving a dinner party, getting fit, selling my house, are the ends for whose sake I act; they define my current enterprises. However, enterprises can also be described in different terms, including some that the agent would not herself use. Two ways in which that can happen are of interest here. First, the very end in terms of which I define my enterprise might be re-described through the describer's normative perspective: writing this chapter might be re-described as indulging in a pointless intellectual game; giving this dinner party as murdering animals; going to the gym as narcissistic posturing; selling my house as alienating my family's heritage. Second, the enterprise can also be described in terms of some of its actual or likely side effects (effects other than those directly intended, some known to the agent, some not): in writing this chapter I am neglecting my students; as a consequence of making this dinner for my friends I will go overdrawn at the bank; given my weak heart, going to the gym as I do endangers my health; selling my house will deprive the relatives who have been living with me of their home.

Some of our enterprises are premeditated and planned: we can trace their history back to the time when the agent first contemplated them, explored the means by which they might be undertaken, formed the intention to undertake them, and made plans for them. Some involve preparation: to write this chapter I must clear my diary of other commitments, read and think about some of the relevant literature, ensure that my (unreliable) computer is working – not to mention the displacement activities I must go through before I begin writing. The distinctions in play here – between (mere) contemplation and intention, between (mere) preparation and the execution of the plan – are not sharp. It might be unclear whether an agent yet intends to Φ, or is still just contemplating it; whether what he is doing is planning how to carry out the intention he has formed, or exploring how he could carry it out were he to form it. This might be not merely unclear to observers, for epistemic reasons having to do with their access to the agent's practical reasoning, but genuinely indeterminate (and therefore uncertain even for the agent herself): sometimes it is only in virtue of what happens later (that an enterprise is firmly started or carried through) that what came earlier can be described as intention formation or as planning. Sometimes there is no prior stage of deliberation, decision and planning. Some enterprises are spontaneous: I meet a friend in the street, she says 'Let's go for a coffee', and I at once say 'Yes', as I begin to walk with her to our regular cafe. Some are habitual: I go to the same cafe every day for coffee at the same time, without any need to deliberate or decide. Indeed, some are habitual by design and by self-training: I go to the gym every morning that I can, at the same time, and (given my weakness of will) it is crucial to my going that I do *not* deliberate each day about whether to go (since then I too often wouldn't go); I have schooled myself to treat it as a given that I go at that time every day – though I must sometimes resist the temptation not to go.

Our descriptions of our enterprises often make clear what counts as completion: I finish this chapter (although even that is susceptible to different interpretations, as authors and editors know all too well), I sell my house, I give the dinner party, I complete my exercise routine at the gym. Sometimes nothing (except perhaps death) counts as completion: I engage in some ongoing activity (exploring the problem of outcome luck; keeping fit) that has no determinate end point – though it has internal criteria of successful engagement. However, we can also describe enterprises in ways that prescind from their success or failure, most obviously by talking of what the person is trying to do. I am trying to write this section, to prepare dinner, to get fit, to sell my house. Such descriptions do not pick out a particular activity, or particular segment of the activity: they rather set my more specific actions in a purposive context that gives them their point – and sometimes signal the difficulty of the enterprise, or its doubtful success.[1]

Sometimes our enterprises fall under descriptions that bring them within the scope of the criminal law. This might be in virtue of the end at which they are aimed. My goal is to rob this bank, or to kill this person – probably not as a

[1] See further P Heath, 'Trying and Attempting' (1971) 45 *Proceedings of the Aristotelian Society* (supp vol) 193; P Winch, 'Trying' in his *Ethics and Action* (London, Routledge, 1972) 171; RA Duff, *Criminal Attempts* (Oxford, Oxford University Press, 1996) ch 10.

final end, but as a subordinate end, which I pursue as a means to further ends. Or it might be in virtue of some side effect of my pursuit of that end. My goal is to get home, after a few drinks, in time for dinner; in my pursuit of that goal, I drive with an excess of alcohol in my blood, and in a way that creates an obvious and unjustified risk of serious harm to persons or to property. In asking when an enterprise should bring the agent within the reach of the criminal law, we then face three familiar questions.

First, what should count in law as the completion of a criminal enterprise? In our extra-legal discourse, an enterprise's completion is its successful completion, which often involves the actual occurrence of intended results in the world. I might describe my current enterprise as 'trying to sell my house', and the enterprise as thus described is completed in the attempt, even if it is unsuccessful – even if I don't manage to sell it. But what I count as success in my enterprise is actually selling the house, so that the basic enterprise is really that of selling the house. Analogously, when we describe an enterprise in terms of its predicted or predictable side effects, we distinguish the case in which those effects occur from that in which they do not: we might describe my drive home as 'dangerous driving', or as 'drunken driving'; but if I have an accident and cause damage, we will apply descriptions that incorporate the damage I cause – we will say that I killed someone, or destroyed someone's garden wall by driving carelessly. In other cases, the actual occurrence of further effects in the world does not seem so crucial to the completion or success of the enterprise, and is therefore not so salient in our description. If I am grappling with the problem of outcome luck, I would of course like to get clearer about it (if not actually to solve it, whatever might count as 'solving'), but that does not mean that the enterprise is radically incomplete or a total failure if I end more uncertain than I began. If I am quarrelling with my partner, it might not be clear what would count as 'success', and whether the quarrel is carried through does not depend on whether it has any specific further effect (although it matters that I engage with the world – that my partner hears and responds to what I say in the appropriate spirit). But what of the criminal law: should it describe complete criminal enterprises in terms of their actual effects, or should it prescind from such effects – from the actual occurrence of intended results, and of side effects?

Second, what should the law count as the beginning of a criminal enterprise? How early in what will (or might) become, if completed, a criminal enterprise should the agent become criminally liable? Our extra-legal discourse does not generally provide sharp starting points, because it does not need to: it might not be clear, because it does not need to be clear, just when I began writing this chapter, selling my house, making dinner, or robbing this bank or killing this person. The criminal law, however, needs to specify with tolerable certainty and clarity when I become liable to conviction and punishment.

Third, I distinguished above between two kinds of outcome of an enterprise: the intended results, which constitute the conditions for its success or failure; and the side effects that will or might ensue in the course of the enterprise, or if it is carried through to completion. Should the criminal law draw any distinction between intended outcomes and side effects?

Our existing laws do not offer clear general answers to any of these questions, although certain rough patterns can be identified.

First, they sometimes count a criminal enterprise as complete only if the intended effects, or the relevant side effects, actually ensue. More precisely, they sometimes describe criminal enterprises in terms that include such effects, and distinguish, either as non-criminal or as not so seriously criminal, incomplete versions of those enterprises. Homicide involves the actual death of a human being, whether the homicide is murder or some lesser offence; the familiar *mala in se* are typically specified in this way. They also typically criminalise conduct falling short of completion as thus defined: in particular, for present purposes, they criminalise what we can call complete attempts, as well as at least some complete endangerments – an attempt or endangerment counting as 'complete' when the agent has acted in a way that (as far as she knows) will or might cause the relevant result without further action on her part, and will or might have put the occurrence or non-occurrence of that result beyond her own control. Thus we have a general offence of attempt, which certainly covers such 'last act' attempts; some codes have general offences of endangerment;[2] others have specific endangerment offences covering particular kinds of risk to particular interests.[3] Sometimes, however, the law defines criminal offences 'in the inchoate mode': the result that would in the agent's eyes render the enterprise a success, and looks like the mischief at which the law is aimed, need not ensue for the complete offence to be committed. This is true of bribery and fraud in English law.[4] The offence under section 2 of the Fraud Act 2006, for instance, requires only that the defendant made a false representation with the intention of causing loss or gain: he need not have deceived anyone, or caused the intended loss or gain. Similarly, I commit an offence under section 1(2) of the Bribery Act 2010 if I offer another person 'a financial or other advantage', intending the advantage 'to induce [the] person to perform improperly a relevant function or activity': the offence is completed even if the person does not accept the offer, or improperly perform any function. If the mischief at which the law is aimed is, respectively, depriving others of their property by fraud, or securing the improper performance of someone's function, the offence as defined by the law is completed even if the mischief does not ensue.[5] Similarly with side effects: sometimes the law defines offences in terms of actual harm, or distinguishes between (mere) risk creation that in fact does not cause the relevant harm, and

[2] See, eg Model Penal Code s 211.2.

[3] See generally RA Duff, *Answering for Crime* (Oxford, Hart Publishing, 2007) ch 7.

[4] See AJ Ashworth, 'The Criminal Law's Ambivalence about Outcomes' in M Kramer, R Cruft, M Reiff (eds), *Crime, Punishment and Responsibility* (Oxford, Oxford University Press, 2011).

[5] One could of course suggest that the mischief lies in the very attempt to deceive or to bribe, since that will undermine trust in our essential social institutions. I cannot pursue this issue here, but it reminds us that it can be very hard to determine what mischief a statute is or would rationally be aimed against.

risk creation that causes it; but sometimes it defines the relevant offence 'in the inchoate mode', criminalising simply the creation of a risk whether or not the relevant harm is actually caused.[6]

Second, as to the starting points for criminal liability, our laws do typically criminalise conduct that falls well short of a complete attempt, especially when the enterprise is intended to produce a criminal result. Our general attempt laws might require the agent to have come close to completing the attempt and thus (absent impossibilities) to completing the crime, as when they require some 'more than merely preparatory act', or that the agent have 'embarked on the [crime] itself';[7] or they might require something well beyond the initial stages of the enterprise, such as a 'substantial step' towards its completion:[8] but although they thus require much more than a 'first step' in (what would become if carried through) a criminal enterprise, they do not require as much as the 'last step'. (General endangerment offences are, however, more like 'last act' offences: for if my conduct is to endanger others, it must actually create a risk that would, if realised, harm them.) But other, specific offences extend liability further back than this.[9] Without examining the whole range of 'precursor' offences,[10] we can take particular note of offences of possession – some of which involve possession with intent to commit a further offence, whilst others involve nothing more than possession:[11] whether the mischief consists in the risk of harm that might occur without further human agency, or in the crimes that the possessor might go on to cause, or those that others might be enabled, tempted or provoked to commit, merely possessing something falls a long way short of attempting to commit the substantive crime to which such possession might lead. Possession offences that do not require an intention to commit some further, substantive criminal wrong are also hard to see as parts of what could count as a criminal enterprise. When an item is possessed with criminal intent, as with other preliminary steps towards a planned criminal goal, we can see possession as part of a criminal enterprise, since that is what it is intended to become. Absent such an intention, however, the most we can say is that it is a part of an enterprise that might become or might lead to a criminal action – depending on how things (some beyond the agent's control) turn out; indeed, even that might be saying too much, since my possession of X need not be part of any purposive scheme.

Third, our criminal laws seem, at first glance, to attach weight to the distinction between intended goals and side effects. For a range of familiar complete

[6] A range of health and safety regulations define offences in the inchoate mode. The offence of 'careless driving' is also a good example: until 2006 this was an inchoate-mode offence, but s 20 of the Road Safety Act 2006 introduced a new offence of causing death by careless driving.

[7] Criminal Attempts Act 1981 s 1(1), as interpreted in *Gullefer* [1990] 1 WLR 1063.

[8] See Model Penal Code s 5.01(1)(c): a substantial step is one that corroborates the agent's criminal intent.

[9] As do such general offences as solicitation, incitement and conspiracy.

[10] See D Husak, 'The Nature and Justifiability of Nonconsummate Offenses' (1995) 37 *Arizona Law Review* 151; *Criminal Attempts* (n 1 above) ch 5.

[11] See generally MD Dubber, 'Policing Possession: The War on Crime and the End of Criminal Law' (2001) 91 *Journal of Criminal Law and Criminology* 829.

offences, liability can be for intended effects or for side effects: I am as guilty of murder if I knowingly cause someone's death as I am if I kill my victim with intent; I am as guilty of criminal damage if I knowingly or recklessly damage another's property as I am if I damage it with intent; and so on. But a number of offences require a further intention with which the criminal action is done:[12] theft is an obvious example. More obviously, even when recklessness suffices for a consummate offence (when the result that renders the action criminal need only be a side effect), criminal attempts require an intention to commit the offence.[13] However, whilst it follows that recklessness cannot suffice for a criminal attempt,[14] it does not follow that I cannot be guilty of a criminal 'attempt' to bring about what would, if it ensued, be a side effect of my action: for given the notorious controversy (and judicial unclarity) over the legal meaning of 'intention', and given the prevalence of the view that intention should be taken to include certain foresight, I might be judged to have 'intended' an effect which was no part of my aim, but whose occurrence I thought to be practically certain (if I achieved my aim).[15] So whilst the law does distinguish 'intended' results from side effects, it is prone to count some side effects, those that the agent foresees as certain, as intended.

So much for what the law is: but what *should* it be? The literature abounds with answers to that normative question; my focus is on the radical answer that Alexander and Ferzan offer in their book, and in their contribution to this volume.[16] I will argue that, although their account begins from premises that I might share, it ends with a position that is at best under-supported and at worst untenable.

II UNLEASHING RISK

Alexander and Ferzan (to whom for brevity's sake I will hereafter refer as Alexerzan) offer a seemingly simple view. It can be summarised in five propositions.

First, punishment (as distinct from other kinds of pre-emptive measure that we might take in order to avert future harm) must be justified in retributive terms of penal desert, which is itself determined by culpability: an agent deserves punishment only if he is culpable (only for that for which he is culpa-

[12] See generally J Horder, 'Crimes of Ulterior Intent' in AP Simester and ATH Smith (eds), *Harm and Culpability* (Oxford, Oxford University Press, 1996) 153.

[13] See, eg Criminal Attempts Act 1981 s 1(1); Model Penal Code §5.01.

[14] At least as to consequential aspects of the complete crime: as to circumstantial aspects, whatever *mens rea* is required for the complete offence might suffice.

[15] This is not the place to rehearse the long and messy controversies about the meaning of 'intention'.

[16] L Alexander, KK Ferzan (with S Morse), *Crime and Culpability: A Theory of Criminal Law* (Cambridge, Cambridge University Press, 2009) [hereafter *Crime*]; L Alexander, KK Ferzan, 'Risk and Inchoate Crimes: Retribution or Prevention', ch 5 of this volume [hereafter *Risk*].

ble), and the severity of his deserved punishment is determined by the extent or seriousness of his culpability. So far there is nothing from which I need dissent, and nothing that need raise any eyebrows, especially if we read this as a version of so-called 'negative retributivism', forbidding punishment that exceeds what is deserved, but without implying that we should punish to the extent that it is deserved and for no other reason than that it is deserved, thus leaving open the possibility that desert and the prospect of beneficial consequences are jointly necessary for justified punishment.[17] As I would put it, punishment communicates a censorial message, which must be deserved if the punishment is to be just; only the blameworthy, the culpable, deserve censure, and they deserve only such censure as is proportionate to their culpability. A lot depends, however, on how we should understand culpability – on what we can properly be blamed for.

Second, Alexerzan deny that the distinction between ends and side effects is intrinsically significant for culpability: I am as culpable for acting in a way that I am confident will bring a specified harm about as I am for acting with the intention of causing that harm. I do not share this view: I have argued that the distinction between an attack (action intended to harm) and endangerment (action creating a risk of harm as a side effect) is morally, and should be legally, significant, even when the agent of the endangering action is sure that it will cause harm.[18] I'll say a little more about this later, but this view of Alexerzan's is neither radical nor controversial; it is shared by many criminal law theorists and moral philosophers.

Third, they deny that results, the actual outcomes of actions as would-be interventions in the world, can affect culpability: since causation by itself, the mere fact that my action causes harm, cannot ground penal desert, those who would penally distinguish failed attempts from completed crimes must claim that 'culpability plus causation has some moral magic' which increases penal desert over culpability by itself; but they 'do not see how causation suddenly gets this moral power'.[19] This view too is not radical among theorists, though if implemented it would of course make significant differences to our existing criminal laws: many would agree that results should not affect criminal liability because they cannot affect culpability or desert; and they would agree because they agree that culpability is determined by choice (not, they might add, by matters of chance). It is again a view from which I dissent, largely because I take a different view of blame.[20] On my view to blame someone is to say, in critical tones, 'Look what you have done': we blame people for what they do (and for other things too – but that need not detain us here); and what they do depends

[17] Alexerzan prefer a stronger version of retributivism (*Crime* (n 16 above) 7–10), but this need not concern us here.

[18] See *Answering for Crime* (n 3 above) 147–58. For criticisms by Alexerzan, see KK Ferzan, 'The Structure of Criminal Law' (2009) 28 *Criminal Justice Ethics* 223; L Alexander, 'Duff on Attempts' in *Crime, Punishment and Responsibility* (n 4 above).

[19] *Crime* (n 16 above), 173.

[20] See *Criminal Attempts* (n 1 above) ch 12.

not just on what they choose or try to do, or believe they are doing, but on what they actually bring about in the world. Someone who succeeds in harming another is to blame for that harm, and a key aim of her conviction and punishment should be to bring her to face up to what she has done and its implications. One who tries but fails to harm another is still of course to blame for that attempt: but he is to blame for, he must face up to and try to make amends for, something different from and less than the one who succeeds.

The combination of these three propositions is not itself what makes the Alexerzan view so striking: what is striking is the effect of combining these three with two other propositions.

Fourth, the culpability of a choice, and thus of its agent, depends solely on whether, and the extent to which, the chosen action, as seen through the agent's eyes, endangers another's interests (interests that the law protects); and on whether, and the extent to which, the agent is unjustified in taking that risk – which depends on an objective or interpersonal assessment of the reasons for and against taking it. I am blameworthy, deserving of punishment, just insofar as I culpably unleash an unjustified risk to a legally protected interest; I unleash a risk just so long as that is what I take myself to be doing. This goes beyond the claim that penal desert is determined by choice, since that claim is consistent with a more familiar conception of the proper content of the criminal law's special part: that it captures a range of different wrongs, described in the relatively rich language of ordinary penal codes. Alexerzan offer a radically simplified view of criminal wrongdoing and liability: to do criminal wrong is to unjustifiably endanger (unleash risks upon) others; I incur liability if I do such wrong recklessly. Nothing less than this should suffice, since negligence does not constitute culpability; nothing more than this is necessary, since intention and foresight – as far as culpability is concerned – are also matters of consciously unleashing risk. Culpability consists 'in the insufficient concern the actor displays for the legally protected interests of others',[21] which is displayed in (what he takes to be) the unleashing of a risk that it is now (as far as he believes) 'beyond his ability to alter'.[22] I cannot discuss this view here,[23] but turn instead to the fifth proposition, which will be the main focus of the rest of this chapter.

As noted above, our existing criminal laws attach liability to a wide range of actions that fall far short of satisfying a traditional 'last act' criterion: I can become criminally liable even when whether the relevant criminal harm eventuates depends on further actions that I could refrain from undertaking. This is true of the general law of attempts: even if what is required is that the agent has 'embarked on the [crime] itself', or she be 'on the job',[24] she is guilty of an

[21] *Crime* (n 16 above) 24.

[22] *Risk* (n 16 above) 103.

[23] Save to say that, while it is true that both the person intent on murder and the person who consciously takes a risk of causing death that he should not take show 'insufficient concern' for the interests of those who might be killed, it is true only in the (somewhat misleading) way in which it is true that both a poison and a deep-fried Mars Bar are 'insufficiently nutritious'.

[24] *Gullefer* [1990] 1 WLR 1063 (see at n 7 above); *Osborn* [1919] 84 JP 63.

attempt before she has done all that she needs to do to complete the crime. It is also (although less straightforwardly) true of that range of precursor offences of which possession offences are paradigm examples. For Alexerzan, however, only last acts merit criminal liability: only when 'the actor engages in the act that unleashes a risk of harm that he believes he can no longer control (through exercise of reason and will alone)' does he 'perform[] a culpable action'.[25] We should note two interpretive points about this specification.

First, I 'unleash' a criminal risk if and only if I act in a way that I believe creates a direct risk to a legally protected interest; a risk is 'direct' when the occurrence of the relevant harm would not depend on my further voluntary acts. What counts is the action as seen through the lens of the agent's own beliefs: objectively, Alexerzan insist,[26] there is no such thing as risk, since an action either will cause harm or will not; what renders me culpable is acting in a way that, as I think, unleashes a risk.

Second, there are cases, which Alexerzan call 'lit fuse' cases[27], in which the agent has initiated a process (lit a fuse) that (if the world is as he believes) will or might cause the relevant harm (detonate the death-causing bomb) without further action on his part, but that he could interrupt so as to prevent that harm (he could extinguish the fuse). It might now seem that these should count as incomplete and therefore non-criminal attempts, but that is not true, at least for rational agents – which is why 'through exercise of reason and will alone' matters. In a standard incomplete attempt, there is more for me to do as the agent: I must pull the trigger, and whether I pull it or not depends wholly on my 'reason and will' – on whether I decide to pull it or not to; for even if, once I embark on the shooting, no further decision to pull the trigger is required, it is normally within my rational power to decide not to pull it and thus not to pull it. In a lit fuse case, by contrast, I might believe that I can yet intervene to extinguish the fuse, but doing so does not depend *entirely* on my reason and will: for I could decide to extinguish it, but find that for any of a variety of reasons I cannot do so. It is true that, by the Alexerzan test, I am less culpable than I am in a case in which I do not think I can intervene, just because to the extent that (I believe) I can intervene, the risk that (I believe) I create is lower: but I have nonetheless unleashed what might, for all I know, be an irrevocable risk.[28] In what follows, I will use the idea of unleashing a risk to capture this idea of unleashing a risk that is, for all I know, irrevocable.

This account raises two questions, which occupy the following two sections. First, how radical are its implications for the scope of criminal law: would it significantly narrow, or extend, the substantive criminal law? Second, is it

[25] *Crime* (n 16 above) 197.

[26] ibid 27–31.

[27] ibid 220–21; *Risk* (n 16 above) 106.

[28] However, given Alexerzan's robust subjectivism, if the agent stupidly believes that he certainly can intervene to prevent the risk being actualised, the 'lit fuse' attempt must count as incomplete, and therefore non-criminal.

normatively tenable: does it express a plausible conception of the proper grounds, structure and scope of criminal liability?

III A RADICALLY NARROWED CRIMINAL LAW?

Alexerzan's view has radical, simplifying implications for the structure of the special part of the criminal law, which defines particular criminal offences; these are not our concern here.[29] It also seems at first glance to have radical implications for the scope of the criminal law: for if liability is to require the irrevocable unleashing of a risk, then only completed attempts, and completed endangerments in which whether the harm occurs does not depend on any further, voluntary actions by the agent, will be criminal. So long as I still have more to do to complete my attempt, even if that 'more' is simply moving my finger on the trigger of the loaded gun I aim at my victim, I am not criminally liable; so long as my action poses no direct threat to others' interests, I am not yet criminally liable, even if it is vastly likely that I will soon pose such a threat if I continue, as when I get into my car with my capacities seriously impaired by alcohol and turn on the ignition. On closer inspection, however, we can see that it does not have such drastically narrowing implications; indeed, it could in principle extend the scope of the criminal law quite radically, albeit with some lightening of its penal severity.

Consider first intended crimes, and the early steps that might be taken in the enterprises that are to lead to them. The law of attempts has not traditionally captured the 'first steps' in a criminal enterprise, but many such steps are in principle criminalisable by the Alexerzan test. If I start to drive to the place where I intend to murder *V*,[30] I unleash a risk of harm (driving always creates a risk). Since my reasons for driving are bad reasons, which cannot justify that risk, I unleash an irrevocable and unjustified risk of harm: I have acted culpably, and am in principle eligible for criminal liability – although not for attempted murder, or for endangering *V*'s life, but only for creating this relatively modest risk to other road users. The same is true of other preparations that I might make, including the acquisition or possession of items to be used in a crime: however securely I think I am keeping them, accidents can happen, others can take advantage of them – and harm can then ensue (there is also the risk of creating anxiety if my intentions become known). The intended murder weapon, the forged financial statement with which I intend to defraud, the information about bomb-making that I intend to use: all are dangerous in ways I cannot completely control, and my bad reasons for possessing such items cannot justify creating those risks.

[29] Some of those implications are discussed in Alexander and Ferzan, 'Beyond the Special Part' in RA Duff and SP Green (eds), *Philosophical Foundations of Criminal Law* (Oxford, Oxford University Press, 2011).

[30] *Risk* (n 16 above) 107.

Cases of endangerment are not quite so straightforward, since the agent may have reasons for engaging in the risk-creating activity that can go at least some way towards justifying the risk, and are not clearly (as the reasons that inform criminal intentions are clearly) inadequate to justify any risk at all. Nonetheless, I can culpably unleash risk well before what might look like a 'last act' endangerment. If my car has defective tyres, and I know that to drive it with those tyres would endanger others (a risk that, given the relatively modest cost of new tyres, I would not be justified in taking), but yet I fail to change them, it might seem that I unleash no risk until I actually drive the car: but that is not so. Cars can be stolen, or taken without their owner's consent: in keeping my car with unsafe tyres, I unleash the risk that someone will take it and drive it to the danger of others. The same is true of such other dangerous items as firearms, explosives, and various kinds of drug: however securely I try to keep them, there is a risk that things will go wrong, or that others will steal them and use them to unleash risks. I might have non-criminal reasons for what I do: for keeping the potentially dangerous items, for not taking more stringent precautions against their misuse, or for not changing my tyres. Most obviously, I might want to avoid (or postpone) the expense of time or money that more stringent precautions would involve, without having to give up items that I want to keep; and avoiding expense is not in itself a reason that lacks all justificatory power (in the way that a criminal intention lacks justificatory power). However, my reasons might be insufficient to justify the risk I unleash: in which case, again, I am in principle eligible for criminal liability. If the risk is small, and there is some (although insufficient) reason to take it, my culpability will be relatively slight: but it is enough to bring me, in principle, within reach of the criminal law.[31]

An Alexerzan code would not include a category of incomplete attempts as such: but it could find room for a range of lesser offences of risk-unleashing that are, taken together, not notably narrower in scope than our current laws of inchoate and precursor crimes. Those who commit such crimes might be liable to lighter punishments (and less condemnatory verdicts) than are those whom our current laws will convict of incomplete attempts; but they can still face criminal liability.

Two general questions now arise. One is extensional: should we aspire to a criminal law with the scope that an Alexerzanian criminal law would have, and imposing punishments of the kind of severity that their criminal law would impose? The other is intensional: even if we should aspire to a criminal law of roughly that scope and severity, do they provide a helpful, illuminating account of the grounds of criminal liability and of the logic of criminal offences? I will focus primarily on the second question, in answer to which there are two possible lines of defence for Alexerzan's account. They could argue that it accurately reflects our rational moral criteria of culpability; or that it maps the ways in

[31] For the risk need not be 'substantial' independently of its unjustifiability (*Risk* (n 16 above) 104; see *Crime* (n 16 above) 25–27).

which the criteria of criminal liability should diverge from those of moral culpability (although if the law is still to be retributively just, and punish only the deserving, any divergence will need to narrow, rather than extend, the bounds of liability). I will focus initially on the first line of defence, and argue that moral culpability is certainly not limited to risk-unleashing.

IV MORAL CULPABILITY WITHOUT UNLEASHING RISK

Though Alexerzan deny any intrinsic significance to the distinction between intended results and foreseen side effects, I will treat them separately here, since the logic of culpability is, I will argue different in the two cases. I will begin with cases in which the agent has embarked on an intended criminal enterprise: that is, she is acting now with the intention of committing a future wrong; her immediate activities are intended to contribute to that further end.

To establish that one can be morally culpable without (yet) irrevocably unleashing risk, it is not enough to show that one can properly be the subject of adverse moral judgement before unleashing a risk.[32] We can note the defective character trait that Jim displays in planning to defraud Jane, we can comment on the moral ugliness of his hopes and desires; but not all adverse moral comment constitutes blame, and not all moral defects can be called blameworthy. An obvious reason for denying that Jim's hopes or desires make him blameworthy is that they are things that happen to him, outwith his control, rather than things that he voluntarily does: 'I can't help what I want (hope)' implies 'So you can't blame me for wanting (hoping that) Φ'. That move is too quick, but need not distract us here: for when an agent embarks on a criminal enterprise, when Jim begins to plan Jane's death, he is certainly both active and in control; intending and planning, even when they do not involve overt action, are actions that the agent initiates and controls.[33] Why then should they not be culpable?

Alexerzan offer five reasons, the fifth of which they think is 'decisive'.[34] I'll therefore focus on the fifth, but should comment briefly on the other four. First, however, we should notice the weakness of a key move they make, in arguing that in incomplete attempts (and so, a fortiori, in any enterprise that has not yet even become an incomplete attempt) 'the element . . . that does the inculpatory work is the intent to commit the crime'.[35] Now it is true that, absent the intention, there may be nothing culpable in what the agent does; but it is also true that what he is culpable or blamed for is not just the intention, but the actions that he undertakes in order to carry that intention out. Action does not serve merely to confirm the intention, or indicate the agent's dangerousness; it consti-

[32] *Risk* (n 16 above) 110.
[33] ibid 108.
[34] ibid 118.
[35] ibid 110

tutes the wrong as a more substantial wrong.[36] In Alexerzan's example,[37] Dan (who has brought his specially purchased jackhammer to the place where he intends to use it to murder Victor) and Dana (who sees the jackhammer and its potential and forms the intention to use it to murder Victor) do intend to kill Victor '*in exactly the same circumstances*'[38] – if we treat those circumstances as if they had come into being independently of either agent. However, since they are circumstances (the presence of the jackhammer) created by Dan precisely in order to kill Victor, Dan's criminal enterprise has taken on (he has given it) a more substantial, concrete existence than has Dana's.

The first problem Alexerzan note is the difficulty of distinguishing intention from desire, or fantasy. There is indeed a difficulty here, and it is (as noted above) more than epistemic: it might be genuinely indeterminate, and not just hard to determine, whether I intend to *Φ* or am merely considering *Φ*-ing or fantasising about it. But they presumably would not deny that it is sometimes determinate and determinable that an agent intends to commit a wrong; and it is with the culpability of such agents that we are concerned.

A second (in their eyes larger) worry concerns the conditionality of intentions.[39] Some of the conditions are explicit: in forming or declaring my intentions I would say 'I intend to *Φ* if C'.[40] Others are implicit: I say baldly 'I intend to *Φ*', but if asked 'What, even if not-C?', I'll reply 'Of course not'.[41] Some conditions concern whether I have reason to *Φ* at all: I intend to go for a picnic if the weather is fine; if it is raining, I will not have (good enough) reason to go for a picnic. Other conditions concern my chances of success in *Φ*-ing – and so, of course, my reasons for embarking on the endeavour to *Φ*: I intend to kill Jones if he walks by; that he does not walk by does not negate or undermine my reason for killing him, but undermines my ability to do so (as distinct from the case in which his walking by gives me reason to kill him, for instance because he would then be invading my territory). In the former case my intention is non-culpable if the conditions are such that, were they satisfied, the intended action would be permissible: I intend to take Jim's car, on condition that he agrees to my request to borrow it. Otherwise, we can say in both kinds of case that the agent is at fault, culpable, in forming a morally illegitimate intention, although the depth of his culpability will depend on how far he has gone in giving that intention concrete actualisation in the world, and that is quite likely to depend partly on how likely he thinks it is that the conditions will be satisfied, and how soon. It is hard to know just what we should say about Roger, who according to Alexerzan intends to steal the Mona Lisa if it is in the Metropolitan Museum

[36] See further *Criminal Attempts* (n 1 above) 63–64, 310–26, 386–89.

[37] *Risk* (n 16 above) 108.

[38] ibid 109.

[39] See generally JPW Cartwright, 'Conditional Intention' (1990) 60 *Philosophical Studies* 233; K Campbell, 'Conditional Intention' (1982) 2 *Legal Studies* 77.

[40] Or 'so long as C', or 'unless not-C', depending on how confident I am that the condition will be fulfilled.

[41] This differs from the case in which I intend to *Φ*, but change my mind when I realise that not-C.

and unguarded, and enters the museum with that intent,[42] without learning more than Alexerzan tell us. Does he go to the museum in order to steal the Mona Lisa if it is there and unguarded; or does he go there anyway, but will seize the chance if it presents itself? Has he made any preparations for this proposed theft? What does he think the chances are that it will be there, and unguarded? Insofar as his intention to steal is not given concrete actualisation, as the meaning or pattern of his actions, its culpability is (like its existence) aetiolated; but I see nothing problematic in saying that he is culpable for forming, maintaining and acting on a wrongful intention.[43]

A third problem concerns 'the duration and renunciation of intentions'.[44] I will deal with renunciation shortly, since it bears on the 'decisive' problem – the revocability of intention. As for duration, it is hard to see how the mere fact of duration can affect culpability (unless we are misled by an equivocation on 'for' into thinking that to be culpable for longer is to be culpable for more and therefore more culpable). Other factors that bear on the extent to which the intention has been given concrete form in the agent's actions are significant for that reason, and might be contingently correlated with duration (though imperfectly so); but duration by itself is immaterial.

A fourth problem is why the person who completes a crime should not be guilty of two offences – the incomplete attempt and the completed crime.[45] Of course, we are not committed to counting moral offences in the way that we are committed to counting criminal offences, but the answer seems simple: to blame a person for an incomplete attempt, or for an action of preparation or planning, is as it were to blame her incompletely for the enterprise she does not complete: had it been completed, she would have been to blame for Φ-ing; if it has not been completed, she merits an aetiolated version of that blame for trying or preparing to Φ. If, after we have criticised the person for the planning, preparation or incomplete attempt, she goes on to commit the full wrong, our blame is no longer aetiolated: but it is directed throughout at the wrongful enterprise in which she is engaged; there is one wrong in play, not two (or 20, or an infinite number).

What then of the 'decisive' problem – that intentions are revocable and that an agent who has not yet completed his attempt can still abandon it? Why should that incline us not to hold the agent culpable before the attempt is complete or if he is prevented from completing it? At some points,[46] Alexerzan appear to suggest that what matters is the likelihood that the agent will not go through, or would not have gone through, with the attempt, but that does not give us reason to exempt all incomplete attempts from blame. What matters

[42] *Risk* (n 16 above) 111–12.

[43] Matters might be more complicated if his professed intention was so utterly unrealistic that it failed really to engage with the world: see *Criminal Attempts* (n 1 above) 219–33.

[44] *Risk* (n 16 above) 115.

[45] ibid 117–18.

[46] ibid 119.

must rather be the logical possibility that the agent will abandon the attempt – a possibility that always exists until the attempt is completed, even if we are, with good reason, empirically certain that the agent will not abandon or would not have abandoned the attempt; and that matters, presumably, because were he to abandon the attempt, that would make a significant difference to his culpability.

This is not the place for a detailed discussion of the significance of abandonment either for moral judgment or for the criminal law; all we need note here is that even fully voluntary abandonment for the appropriate moral reasons does not render the agent's pre-abandonment conduct non-culpable. Suppose that Jim embarks on a serious attempt to harm me, perhaps to defraud me of my savings, but comes to his moral senses before the attempt is completed, and abandons it; suppose too that his actions create no risk that is independent of his completion of the attempt (and that I do not find out about it until later). If I challenge him about what he was doing and was going to do, he might reply, defensively, 'But at least I abandoned it off my own bat', and that should indeed make *some* difference to my moral response. However, if Alexerzan are right, it should make *all* the difference: Jim's defence should not be such a concessive 'But at least . . .' (which speaks of mitigation rather than complete exculpation); it should instead be 'You have nothing to blame me for because I abandoned the enterprise' – in which case Jim also has nothing to blame himself for. That seems implausible: surely Jim's abandonment cannot make it as if he had never embarked on the enterprise in the first place. True, I cannot justly blame him for defrauding me, or even for a complete attempt to defraud me, since it is unjust to blame a person for something he has not done. But I can blame him, and he should feel guilty, for what he has done – for the steps he took towards defrauding me.

To blame someone is to hold her culpably responsible for acting as she had conclusive moral reason not to act. Now assuming that it would have been wrong for Jim to defraud me, he had conclusive moral reason not to defraud me, and it follows that he also had conclusive moral reason not to form the intention, to plan, to prepare to defraud me, or to take the first and subsequent steps in the enterprise of defrauding me.[47] Jim has therefore acted as he had conclusive moral reason not to act – something that his abandonment cannot negate; and he is therefore blameworthy for doing so. It is true that the wrongness of what he has done depends on the wrongness of the fraud that he does not in the end commit: it is because it would have been wrong to defraud me that it was wrong to intend, prepare and begin to defraud me, and those preparatory activities are wrong because of their connection to actually defrauding me. However, that is not to say (which I take to be the Alexerzan view) that they are culpable because and only because they unleash a risk that Jim will actually

[47] I leave aside, as not relevant here, unusual cases (of which it used to be argued that nuclear deterrence was one) in which it might be legitimate to form an intention that it would be irrational and wrong to carry out.

defraud me (or that someone else will take advantage of his preparations and defraud me). What makes it wrong to intend, plan and prepare to Φ, and wrong in a way that merely contemplating and thinking about Φ-ing are not wrong (though they can also be wrong) is indeed that intending, planning and preparing to Φ are directed towards Φ-ing, and (as a matter of logic rather than merely of contingent fact) typically lead to Φ-ing: but that is not to say that their wrongness consists simply in the fact that they make it more likely that the agent (or someone) will Φ. Jim's actions are culpable because it is wrong to connect oneself as an agent to the commission of a wrong.[48]

If Jim, who voluntarily abandons his immoral enterprise, is still culpable for what he has done, so a fortiori is someone whose enterprise is aborted or interrupted before she completes it. Suppose that Ian is detected before he completes the fraud, and I castigate him for what he has done and was trying to do: should my blame be qualified or mitigated by his plea 'But I still had time to abandon the enterprise'? Of course, if he can persuade me that he would have abandoned it, or even that there was a good chance that he would abandon it voluntarily, his position is more like Jim's (although we are at best in the realm of good intentions, or of good character, rather than of right actions): but if all he can appeal to is the logical possibility of abandonment, the bare space for a *locus poenitentiae* of which he has given me no reason to believe he would have taken advantage, why should I modify my judgment of his culpability? I should not blame him as I would have done had he completed the attempt to defraud me, or had he actually defrauded me; but that is simply because I should not blame him for what he has not done.

Do I blame Jim for trying to defraud me (as something distinct from, and more culpable than, intending, planning and preparing to defraud me)? Our moral judgements and responses do not need to be categorised in the way that a criminal court's verdicts must be: we do not need to decide definitively whether or when Jim's activity should count, for instance, as mere preparation or as attempt; I can criticise Jim for embarking on his fraudulent enterprise, and do not have to decide whether what I am criticising him for yet constitutes an attempt. But for what it is worth, it would be natural to describe Jim as attempting to defraud me well before a 'last act', and even if he abandoned the attempt voluntarily: he was trying to defraud me, but then came to his moral senses and abandoned the attempt.[49]

Are matters any different when we turn from intended results to foreseen side effects (as I would put it, from attacks to endangerments)? We must here consider cases in which what the agent has so far done does not create a direct risk

[48] See also G Yaffe, *Attempts in the Philosophy of Action and the Criminal Law* (Oxford, Oxford University Press, 2010) 21–46: what he says about attempts applies to preparatory conduct more generally.

[49] Perhaps it is significant that the continuous 'was trying' comes more naturally to the lips than the more definitive aorist 'tried': 'he tried' implies either a completed attempt or one that was frustrated.

to others; indeed (since as I use 'direct', a risk is direct when its actualisation does not depend on any further actions by the agent who creates it), we should also consider cases in which the actualisation of the risk will depend on the voluntary actions of others.

We can deal quickly with one kind of 'incomplete endangerment' case: that in which the agent has not yet unleashed a risk, but is embarked on an enterprise that will unleash a risk if she completes it or continues it *as she now intends*. Dave, for instance, intends to go to the pub for several hours, to drink his usual six pints of beer, and then to drive home. As he leaves the pub after his sixth pint and walks towards the car park, he has not yet unleashed a risk; and – since he is a practised drinker – he is still perfectly capable of changing his mind and taking a taxi home. However, if he continues to carry out his intention to drive home (an intention he has already begun to carry out) he will inevitably, given how much he has drunk and its effect on his driving abilities, endanger others; he is thus at least preparing to commit, and will at some point be attempting to commit, a wrong of endangering others.[50] His position is thus the same as that of someone who has embarked on a wrongful enterprise, who intends to commit and has taken steps towards committing a wrong: the only difference between him and a case like Jim's is that his wrong is one of endangerment rather than attack.

Consider next a case in which whether the risk is actualised depends on the future actions of other (sane, adult) people. It matters whether those actions would be reasonable. Suppose first that they would be reasonable – perhaps reasonable responses to what I do: if I drive at high speed down a busy road, some of the risks I create will be actualised by the reasonable evasive actions taken by others. In that case I effectively force others to take such dangerous evasive actions, and am culpably responsible for the risks those actions involve. But suppose instead that their actions would be unreasonable: I leave my gun and ammunition in full view in my car, knowing that someone might steal them and use them harmfully. Everything now depends on what responsibilities I have to take precautions not only against directly causing harm myself, but against harms that my actions might enable others to cause. I certainly have some such responsibility: the victim of a shooting will rightly be unimpressed by my claim that, since I did not myself shoot her or instigate her shooting, I am entirely non-culpable in the matter, if the shooter was only able to shoot her because I left a loaded gun in full view in my unlocked car. My culpable responsibility for danger that ensues only via the unreasonable actions of others is no doubt less than it would have been had I directly caused, or encouraged or deliberately assisted others to cause, that danger; but their intervening agency does not by itself enable me to deny all culpable responsibility. However, the mere fact that (as I realise) my actions might make it easier for others to do harm does not by

[50] It is not his purpose to endanger others, but he acts with intent to endanger them: he acts with an intent such that he will necessarily endanger others if he carries it out; see *Criminal Attempts* (n 1 above) 22–29.

itself suffice to make me culpably responsible for 'unleashing' that risk. This is not because, as Alexerzan would say, I might have reasons for what I do that justify unleashing that risk. Such a justification would avert culpability, but presupposes responsibility: to justify unleashing a risk is to accept that I am (retrospectively) responsible for its creation, which presupposes that I had a (prospective) responsibility to attend to such risks as sources of reasons for action. Sometimes, however, I may deny such a prospective responsibility. As an ironmonger, I realise that those to whom I sell tools might use them for nefarious ends: but, I argue, I have no responsibility to attend to that chance in deciding what to sell to whom. I trade legitimately in items whose primary use is legitimate: it is not my business if customers choose to misuse them. Such a claim must be rebutted if we are to hold such a shopkeeper responsible for unleashing a risk of harm.[51]

The trickier case is that in which not only the prospective harm, but even the direct risk of that harm, depend on future actions of mine that I do not (yet) intend to perform, but which I might perform. It may be tempting to take a robustly Kantian line here: if I am a responsible agent, and do not yet intend a harmful action, there is nothing for which I yet can be blamed. I am entitled to the presumption that I will not form a dangerous intention – not just because I am entitled to a moral presumption of innocence, but because I am entitled to treat myself as a rational agent, and not pre-empt my future choices by assuming that they might be wrongful choices against which I must now take precautions. But can we really take that line? I know I am weak-willed in some matters: perhaps I find it hard to resist the temptation to drive home after drinking too much, if I have the chance to do so. If I drive my car to the pub, intending to take a taxi home and collect my car the next day, but knowing that I am likely to give in to the temptation to drive home after several drinks, can I really rebut a charge of recklessness by saying that it is still within my power to carry through my intention not to drive home; or could others criticise me for trusting myself although I know that I cannot be trusted in this matter? To take precautions against my own expected weakness of will would indeed be not to treat myself as a fully rational agent (for weakness of will is irrational): but since I am not a fully rational agent in this respect, and since my failures of rationality will be dangerous to others, perhaps I should treat myself realistically rather than idealistically.

In endangerment cases, when I do not intend the future action that will endanger others, there is thus more plausibility to a claim that I deserve blame only when I irrevocably unleash a risk on the world: for the creation of such risk is central to wrongs of endangerment. Even here, however, things are not straightforward: there are normative questions about how far I am culpable for acting in ways that might enable others to unleash risks, and about whether I have a responsibility to take precautions against my own predictable irrationality.

[51] See further *Answering for Crime* (n 3 above) 30–36. My concern here is with our moral responsibilities: I comment on legal responsibility in s V below.

V CRIMINAL LIABILITY AND MORAL CULPABILITY

We can, I have argued so far, be morally culpable for actions that fall far short of irrevocably unleashing a risk. Alexerzan could still argue, however, that criminal liability, or the kind of culpability that merits criminal punishment, should be narrower than moral culpability: that I should be criminally culpable, in the eyes of the law, only once I have irrevocably unleashed a risk to the protected interests of others. We should again treat the two kinds of unleashing, attacks and endangerments, separately.

Consider first the case of intended criminal wrongdoing. Here we must consider again the significance of the *locus poenitentiae*. Even if we should not always treat ourselves as purely rational beings who can be expected to refrain from wrongdoing and to resist temptations to do wrong, it is important that we treat each other as responsible moral agents who are within the reach of reason, and who could in principle be persuaded by moral appeals to refrain from wrongdoing – as beings, that is, who could, even at the last moment, see the light and refrain from wrongdoing. The law of what aspires to be a liberal republic of citizens should treat its citizens in the same light – as responsible agents who, albeit fallible in various familiar ways, are within the reach of the kinds of moral reason on which the criminal law rests and to which it appeals; and as agents who could, even at the last minute or after a career of crime, see the error of their ways.[52] The fact that someone who has yet to complete her criminal attempt still has some *locus poenitentiae*, that her intention is revocable, is therefore significant: we, and the law, must not assume in advance that she will not avail herself of that *locus* to repent and abandon her criminal enterprise. But what implications does this have for criminal liability?

Suppose first that what frustrates the completion of the attempt is not the law (the police intervening to arrest the intending criminal) but some independent factor. This case should be treated in a way analogous to the moral case in which Jim's fraudulent attempt is frustrated: the agent has done wrong, in embarking on a criminal enterprise, and that wrongdoing is not negated by the fact that he could still have abandoned the attempt. He is not condemned for what he has not done – for a complete attempt or a completed crime; he is justly condemned for what he has done – for the significant steps he has taken towards a criminal goal. We thus have some reason to criminalise even the early stages of a criminal enterprise (although we also have reasons, to do with individual privacy and freedom, on the other side).

But suppose, second, that what frustrates the completion of the attempt is the law: that the police intervene to arrest the would-be criminal. Now we should see a significant disanalogy between this case and the moral case. If I morally

[52] This thought has particular importance (and is also particularly challenging) in the context of punishment, as the thought that we must never suppose anyone, however grave and persistent their crimes, to be beyond redemption.

castigate the as yet incomplete attempter, I do not deprive him of a *locus poenitentiae*; I might indeed hope that my moral criticism will induce him to avail himself of that *locus*, and abandon his wrongful enterprise. Moral blame for the as yet incomplete attempter is fully consistent with leaving him the *locus poenitentiae* that he always had. But when the police intervene, they deprive the arrested person of a *locus poenitentiae*: he no longer has the chance to repent and to abandon the enterprise for himself. That is the moral cost of allowing police intervention before the last act, as is allowed by any definition of criminal attempts broader than a last act test; and of any law that allows police intervention before the completion of a criminal enterprise – of all those kinds of precursor offence that we noted earlier. This is not yet to say that we must follow Alexerzan, and allow criminal liability only once the last act has been committed and a risk irrevocably unleashed. Outside the law, we can be morally justified in intervening forcibly before the completion of an attack so as to prevent the attacker from carrying it through, even though in doing so we deprive the attacker of a morally valuable *locus poenitentiae*; the same is true within the law. For, first, the intending criminal has done and is doing culpable wrong. Second, we owe it to the intended victims, and the law owes it to all of us, to defend them against such an attack: nor can the attacker complain that he has been unjustly treated, since at the moment of forcible intervention he is engaged, without evidence of an intention not to complete it, in a wrongful attack. We should regret depriving the attacker of a *locus poenitentiae*, but he cannot complain about it, since it was his own wrongful attack that gave us such good reason to do so. The most we can say is that in the criminal case we have *some* reason to hold back that we do not have in the moral case: that reason is not strong enough to justify a 'last act' criterion for attempts, given the demand to protect potential victims; but it is reason to confine the law of attempts within quite narrow bounds.[53]

Suppose, finally, that what prevents completion is the agent's voluntary abandonment of her enterprise: not because she decides to postpone it to a more favourable occasion or because she realises that there is a possibility of getting caught, but for the kind of moral reason that underpins the law's definition of her intended enterprise as a crime. Her abandonment should make a difference to her legal fate – not just because it is a good to balance against the evil created by the attempt, but because it alters our understanding of the attempt: even if the agent was wholeheartedly committed to the enterprise before she abandoned it,[54] her change of heart puts that enterprise in a new light. Her case is analogous to, although luckier than, that of someone who repents his crime the

[53] Could we not allow police intervention to prevent the completion of the crime without imposing criminal liability, because he has not yet spurned his last chance to withdraw? In theory we could, but that would put the police in an invidious position of having to choose between prevention and prosecution.

[54] It might be tempting to think it a matter of logic that one who voluntarily abandons her enterprise was not *wholeheartedly* committed to it; but a sufficiently dramatic, Damascene, change of heart could dissuade a genuinely wholehearted wrongdoer from continuing.

moment it has been committed – as soon as he realises what he has done. Even those who think that repentance should not generally secure any mitigation of sentence might think that some mitigation is appropriate in this case, when the repentance is so closely connected to the commission of the crime that it casts both the crime itself and its perpetrator in a new light;[55] so much more so in this case when, luckily for both victim and offender, the agent can prevent the completion of the crime rather than merely repenting it. She has still done wrong, however, as we saw in the last section, and is surely thus still eligible for conviction and punishment; her abandonment makes mitigation, rather than a full defence, appropriate.[56]

What then of cases of endangerment? The tricky cases, as we saw, are those in which the actualisation of any direct risk depends on the voluntary actions of others; and those in which the actualisation of a direct risk depends on further, not currently intended, actions by the agent himself. In both cases, we must decide what kinds of responsibility the criminal law should recognise; only then can we determine whether the agent is criminally culpable.

When the actualisation of the risk depends on the actions of others, the question concerns the extent to which and the ways in which the criminal law should enforce a prospective legal responsibility not just to avoid directly causing harm ourselves, or deliberately encouraging or helping others to cause harm, but also to avoid enabling others to cause harm. Offences of aiding and abetting raise this question directly, as do recent criminal statutes which quite radically expand citizens' responsibilities to attend to the ways in which their conduct might connect, through others' criminal actions, to some criminal mischief.[57] No general a priori answer to this question is possible. It is in the end a matter for political theory to provide an account of our civic responsibilities as members of a polity – and of when those responsibilities should be recognised and enforced by the criminal law. Only when we have a clearer account of that matter can we decide whether people who realise that their action might facilitate the commission of crimes by others should count as unleashing a criminal risk: for if it is not their prospective responsibility to attend to what others might do, they cannot be held retrospectively responsible for unleashing the risk that those others might do it.

Similarly, when the actualisation depends on the agent's own future and not yet intended actions, we must ask what kind of responsibility (if any) I should have as a citizen to guard against my own possible future wrongdoing: how far do I owe it to my fellow citizens not to trust myself to refrain from forming and

[55] See my 'The Intrusion of Mercy' (2007) 4 *Ohio State Journal of Criminal Law* 361, 384.

[56] Contrast my (as I now see it) misguided view in *Criminal Attempts* (n 1 above) 395–97.

[57] See, eg Proceeds of Crime Act 2002 s 328 (but the law exempts those professionally engaged in litigation from the responsibility to attend to whether their actions might facilitate the acquisition, use or control of criminal property); also Terrorism Act 2000 ss 57–58, on possessing items that might be of use to, or arouse suspicion of, terrorist purposes. See more generally RA Duff, 'Can I Help You? Accessorial Liability and the Intention to Assist' (1990) 10 *Legal Studies* 165.

acting on wrongful intentions when I know that I am empirically not trustworthy? Only when we have a clearer idea on this issue, and of the kinds of situation (if any) in which, given the risk involved, I should be required not to trust myself, can we decide whether I should count as having unleashed a risk that I might act wrongfully.

In both cases, accordingly, the question is not so much whether the agent should be held liable before he has irrevocably unleashed a risk: it is when he should count as unleashing the risk – which depends on an account of his prospective responsibilities.

I conclude, therefore, that neither moral nor legal principle can justify Alexerzan's view: quite apart from the point that judgments about whether an agent has irrevocably unleashed a risk must often depend on prior normative judgments about her prospective responsibilities, we have good reason to count intending criminals as criminally culpable and liable before they irrevocably unleash a risk of harm to others' protected interests.

7

*Preventive Detention at the Margins of Autonomy**

JOHN STANTON-IFE

I INTRODUCTION

HAVE WE CREATED a crime of antisocial mental disorder? Brenda Hale poses this question only to leave it hanging without a final response.[1] It does not take a senior legal academic like Hale who also doubles up for good measure as Baroness Hale, a senior member of the judiciary, to know that the literal answer is no. One will look in vain for 'antisocial mental disorder' in any authoritative list of criminal offences. No crime goes by that name. Mentally disordered persons, like persons in general, can of course find themselves on the wrong side of the criminal law, accused of the standard crimes of grievous bodily harm, theft, murder, rape, criminal damage and so on. However, true as that is it is plainly not what the question is getting at. It will not be answered by pointing out that separately identified crimes can be committed by various categories of sometimes overlapping persons, adult men, adult women, teenagers *and* mentally disordered people. The law allows for the compulsory detention under certain circumstances of mentally disordered persons, most notably under the Mental Health Act 1983. However, that is the stuff of the civil law. Detention in that context needs no arrest, there will have been no question of a bail application, no trial, no conviction and no sentence.[2] Hale's question, however, is clearly not to be taken literally and immediately after asking it she adds, *if* we have created such a crime, perhaps we should admit it.[3] Any 'crime' here then is covert, something we keep quiet about, something that is criminal in a *non-formal* sense that nonetheless ought to concern us.

* I am grateful to Bob Sullivan and Ian Dennis for their encouragement, to Larry Alexander and Antony Duff for stimulating comments and to Grant Lamond and Bob Sullivan (again) for very helpful written feedback on a draft.

[1] Brenda Hale, *Mental Health Law*, 5th edn (London, Sweet and Maxwell, 2010) 70.

[2] My concern in this chapter is restricted to the detention of mentally disordered persons for reasons unconnected with any formal charge, conviction or sentence for any criminal offence. I do not consider 'imprisonment for public protection' under the Criminal Justice Act 2003. See the chapters by Lucia Zedner, Peter Ramsay and Martin Wasik in this volume.

[3] Hale (n 1 above) 70.

However, in what sense exactly could the civil detention of the mentally disordered under the Mental Health Act be thought criminal? To what exactly might we need to admit? The answer, should this line of thought be ultimately vindicated, is I imagine that such detention shares many of the features and consequences of overtly labelled criminal behaviour without also sharing the procedures safeguarding the interests of defendants upon which the criminal justice system insists. In other words, the civil law is encroaching on territory which, if properly occupied by the law at all, ought to be occupied by the criminal law. For the criminal procedures in question, especially where the defendant does not plead guilty, are *very* demanding. Take Blackstone's famous slogan: It is better that 10 guilty persons escape than one innocent suffer. Even if not everything about that saying sounds quite the right note – why the precise ratio of 10:1? – it stands for the conviction that it is especially abhorrent to deprive the innocent of their liberty or visit upon them the other incidents of punishment and hard treatment.[4] So abhorrent is it that we must have no illusion that the cost of its avoidance is high. Indeed, it is so high that we may sometimes have to put up with *guilty* people going free. At certain points this is exactly the stance the criminal justice system adopts. The most obvious example is the ordinary burden of proof in a criminal case: proof beyond a reasonable doubt. Where juries think it more likely than not a defendant is guilty as charged – even a lot more likely than not – they are still required to acquit. Guilt must not only exist, it must be strongly demonstrated, an elaborate, expensive and time-consuming aspect of a trial process that must be set in place as a condition for the imposition of punishment and stigma on defendants who enter 'not guilty' pleas. Of course if the criminal justice system insists on toleration of the continued liberty of people who are, more likely than not, already thought to be guilty of serious criminal offences, then it seems only reasonable to insist on the liberty of those whose offences are suspected to lie in the future.

In short, what might be thought 'criminal' about the civil detention of the mentally disordered is that the suffering usually consequential upon a criminal conviction of which Blackstone spoke – the forced deprivation of freedom and the resultant stigma – can be secured without these demanding procedures mandated by the (real) criminal justice system. As Andrew Ashworth and Lucia Zedner put it there is

> an important concomitant of the decision to criminalize: if the state decides to create a crime of X-ing, all those persons accused of X-ing are entitled to a criminal trial that observes those additional safeguards, in view of the public censure and liability to punishment that follow conviction in such a trial.[5]

[4] For discussion, see Jeffrey Reiman and Ernest van den Haag, 'On the Common Saying that it is Better that Ten Guilty Persons Escape than that One Innocent Suffer: *Pro* and *Con*' in Ellen Frankel Paul, Fred D Millar, Jr and Jeffrey Paul (eds), *Crime, Culpability and Remedy* (Oxford, Blackwell, 1990) 226–48.

[5] Andrew Ashworth and Lucia Zedner, 'Just Prevention: Preventive Rationales and the Limits of the Criminal Law' in RA Duff and Stuart P Green (eds), *Philosophical Foundations of Criminal Law* (Oxford, Oxford University Press, 2011) 279–303, 294.

Hale's question asks if there has been a covert act of criminalisation by virtue of the Mental Health Act that has got under the radar of the procedural protections of the criminal justice system. Are mentally disordered people subject to the potential burdens of the criminal justice system without the protections?

In the first part of what follows I consider this question. In the second, rather different part, for reasons I will explain, my main aim is to come to a provisional understanding of what the difference is between having autonomy in a small degree and not having autonomy at all. In the first part I take the Anti-Social Behaviour Order (ASBO) as a case in which the charge of a subversion of the criminal law on the part of the civil law can be made to stick, and will then ask if the same can be said of the civil detention of the mentally disordered under the Mental Health Act. I argue that there is a significant difference between the two cases. The former culminates in what is clearly criminal punishment, while the latter does not. There are also other rather delicate issues, particularly the aim of meeting the therapeutic needs of mentally disordered persons that make the civil detention context different from that of the ASBO. Civil detention is not subversive criminalisation in the sense that the ASBO is. However, nevertheless there is serious cause for concern over whether preventive action on the part of the state with deprivation of liberty as its consequence is being undertaken without an adequate set of safeguards for the detainee. Two special problems with civil detention are the potential for serious violation of the autonomy of mentally disordered persons and for unjust discrimination against them. As for the second part of the chapter, it is commonly said that the Mental Health Act fails to respect the autonomy of mentally disordered persons. I focus on a form of justification which, if successful, could partially justify the practice of civil detention in the light of the twin dangers of autonomy-violation and unjust discrimination. I refer to this form of justification as the 'diminished-autonomy justification'. However, it is far from clear how we are to understand autonomy in small degrees or, to put it another way, autonomy immediately beyond the threshold at which one begins to have it. The leading works of liberal theory do not specifically take up the question of the relationship between autonomy and mental disorder.[6] I consider two different kinds of account of minimal autonomy, one of which focuses simply on 'autonomous action', the other on autonomous action in the light of broader considerations of an autonomous life. There is reason, I suggest, for preferring the second kind of account. I conclude that the diminished autonomy justification can partially justify certain aspects of the civil detention of the mentally disordered, at least in principle, but it fails to justify all cases in which such detention threatens the autonomy of mentally disordered persons and unjustly discriminates against them. Finally I state my belief that much more thinking is needed if we are to come to a satisfactory understanding of what minimal

[6] For example John Rawls, *A Theory of Justice* (Oxford, Oxford University Press, 1972); Joseph Raz, *The Morality of Freedom* (Oxford, Oxford University Press, 1986).

autonomy is. Although it goes too far to claim that the Mental Health Act involves a subversion of the criminal law, such a claim is not outlandish. The Act comes dangerously close to just that: close enough to require strong protection for mentally disordered persons, far stronger than they are currently getting.

II CIVIL DETENTION OF THE MENTALLY DISORDERED AND THE SUBVERSION OF THE CRIMINAL LAW

There are plainly a number of ways in which the operation of the Mental Health Act must make mentally disordered persons feel as if they are being processed through the criminal justice system. Under section 136 of the Act, for example, if a police officer finds 'a person who appears to him to be suffering from a mental disorder and to be in immediate need of care and control' in a public place, that person can be removed to 'a place of safety,' for 72 hours and in order to be professionally examined. The Code of Practice to the Mental Health Act suggests that a police station should only exceptionally be used as a place of safety under section 136,[7] but a recent study found 11,500 people on average per year were being detained under the section in police custody, while 5,900 were being detained in hospital.[8] The remedy here, of course, might be that redoubled efforts and additional resources are necessary genuinely to comply with the Code of Practice. However, is it helpful or accurate to take civil detention quite generally as in any way constituting a parallel (and illegitimate) criminal justice system? Practitioners and lay persons of various stripes can sometimes show impatience with what they take to be the academic predisposition to see sinister forces at work, 'state control', when all they themselves see is a series of often admittedly imperfect attempts to cope conscientiously and humanely with what are intractable and sometimes poignant aspects of human existence. How far should we see in the Mental Health Act a subversion of the criminal law?

A full blown analysis of the complex and recently substantially amended wording of the Mental Health Act is beyond the scope of the current chapter.[9] However, if we focus on what is colloquially known as 'sectioning' under section 3 of the Act, do we see anything we might want to chalk up as part and parcel of such an illegitimate, parallel criminal justice system? Under section 3 of the Act, admission for treatment in hospital can be made on the basis that a person is suffering from a mental disorder, that the nature of, or degree of, the person's mental disorder makes medical treatment in hospital appropriate, that

[7] Department of Health, *Mental Health Act Code of Practice* (2008) 10.21.

[8] Andrew Cole, 'Overuse of Police Cells for Detaining People with Mental Health Problems "Intolerable"' (2008) 337 *British Medical Journal* 1636; discussed in Emily Jackson, *Medical Law: Text, Cases and Materials*, 2nd edn (Oxford, Oxford University Press, 2010) 308–09.

[9] For a good introduction see Jackson (n 8 above) 284–348. For a comprehensive treatment, see Lawrence Gostin, Peter Bartlett, Phil Fennell, Jean McHale and Ronnie Mackay (eds), *Principles of Mental Health Law and Policy* (Oxford, Oxford University Press, 2010).

the treatment is necessary for his or her health or safety or for the protection of other persons, that the treatment cannot be provided unless the person is detained under this section and that appropriate medical treatment is available. There are further conditions relating to the necessity of written recommendations on the part of two registered medical practitioners, including certain obligations to give reasons. Admission for treatment under section 3 allows detention of the individual for up to six months and annually thereafter. The length of detention can be indefinite, subject to regular review. One kind of mental disorder, namely learning disability, although initially excluded, can become a relevant mental disorder for the purposes of a section 3 admission provided the learning difficulty in question is 'associated with abnormally aggressive or seriously irresponsible conduct' on the part of the learning disabled person. In order to consider how far this section and the Act in general constitute a subversion of the criminal law, let us briefly consider a different example of something that has been thought by some to be subversive of the criminal law, namely the ASBO.[10]

Hale's question related to the potential criminal nature of 'antisocial mental disorder'. ASBOs focus more generally on anti-social behaviour. They are made when it is the view of a civil, not criminal, court that the defendant (who of course need not be mentally disordered) has acted in an anti-social manner and that instituting an order is necessary to protect relevant persons from further anti-social acts by that person. On one important issue, it is clear that the ASBO cannot fairly be accused of any subversion of the criminal law, *viz* on the question of the appropriate standard of proof needed to satisfy the civil court that the defendant has acted in an anti-social manner. The House of Lords has made clear that the standard is essentially the criminal standard of proof beyond a reasonable doubt, not the civil standard of a balance of probabilities. The court must be 'sure' that the defendant has acted anti-socially.[11] Beyond that one issue, civil rules of evidence apply. There are a series of objections pertinent to the question of the civil-criminal divide.[12] One relates to the potentially severe punishment of infringing the ASBO, another to how the proscribed behaviour that may trigger the punishment is identified. Breach of the ASBO is explicitly styled as a criminal offence, for which a punishment of up to five years in prison can be imposed. That is a maximum sentence higher than that available for any of assault, affray or assaulting a police officer.[13] Moreover, the sentence if and when imposed is for 'doing anything which [one] is prohibited from doing by an anti-social behaviour order'. This could include the offences we have just mentioned of assault and so on whose maximum sentence is less than five years, as

[10] Crime and Disorder Act 1998. Ashworth and Zedner (n 5 above) 298–302.

[11] The high standard of proof does not, however, apply to the question of whether the order is necessary to protect relevant persons from further anti-social acts by the defendant. *Clingham v Royal Borough of Kensington and Chelsea; R (on behalf of McCann) v Crown Court of Manchester* [2003] 1 AC 787.

[12] See Ashworth and Zedner (n 5 above) 293–303.

[13] ibid 299.

well as a vast range of behaviour not otherwise criminal, such as being in possession of birdfeed in a specified area and/or 'engaging in behaviour calculated to cause birds to flock [to the area in question]'.[14] The behaviour that can land one in prison is not identified by Parliament. It is picked out by 'relevant authorities' such as local councils or the police and approved by the civil courts.[15] It is clear that the relevant authorities and civil courts have a wide and open sea from which to fish for the subject matter of any prohibition. However, it is far from clear that any systemic examination – or indeed any examination – is made of the standard issues of legitimate criminalisation: is the behaviour to be proscribed harmful and/or wrongful? If there is harm is it a rather remote harm? If the behaviour is wrongful is it really desirable to use coercion to discourage it? And so on. As already mentioned, the 'criminalised' behaviour could involve behaviour already independently and formally criminal or behaviour not independently criminalised at all. It can also include, as Ashworth and Zedner point out, behaviour that Parliament has clearly decided is *not* criminal, however often it is engaged in:

> When in 1982 Parliament abolished imprisonment for the offences of begging and soliciting for prostitution, it was clearly conscious of the fact that some people commit these offences repeatedly; evidently it took the decision that, no matter how often the offences are repeated, the offender should not be liable to imprisonment. Yet this democratic decision can now be undermined by a court if it decides to insert into an ASBO a prohibition on begging or on soliciting, breach of which provision may result in imprisonment for up to five years. This shows the tremendous power – and the subversive power – of the ASBO as currently constituted.[16]

In short ASBOs can culminate in lengthy incarceration; while the 'drafting' of the triggering 'offences' lies outside Parliament and the criminal courts. They float free of the standards of criminal procedure, except in relation to proving in a civil court that some anti-social behaviour has been engaged in by the defendant, behaviour which in any case can be much narrower in scope than the content of the behaviour then to be proscribed by the order itself. Ashworth and Zedner are, I believe, correct to conclude that the ASBO amounts to a subversion of the criminal justice system.

Can the same be said of the civil detention of the mentally disordered under the Mental Health Act? One might begin consideration of this question by making the obvious point that there is no necessity that the state should seek to perform its function of preventing harms befalling its citizens exclusively through the criminal law. Many other areas of law, such as health and safety legislation and the provision of the National Health Service, also have this aim. Moreover, one cannot automatically insist that there must be an exception to this simple proposition where part of the means adopted for preventing harm to

[14] Warwickshire Police, 'List of ASBOS and CRASBOS', available at www.warwickshire.police.uk/currentIssues/WPASBOs/WarwickD/Alan.

[15] Crime and Disorder Act 1998.

[16] Ashworth and Zedner (n 5 above) 299.

citizens involves the compulsory deprivation of liberty of other persons, as the example of quarantine in specific circumstances shows.[17] Perhaps the conclusion will need to be that the deprivation of liberty involved in the compulsory detention of the mentally disordered is akin to the compulsory quarantining of persons with severe infectious diseases, the detention in both cases regrettable but in both cases necessary. What, though, of the two features we have just highlighted as illegitimate in relation to the ASBO, the way in which the proscribed behaviour is identified and the nature and degree of punishment it can lead to?

As for the first point, it cannot be said that the compulsory detention in hospital of a mentally disordered person because necessary 'for the health or safety of the patient or the protection of other persons' is subject to clear limits or rigorous scrutiny. Neither are those involved in making such applications and decisions – be they nearest relatives, authorised mental health professionals (often social workers) and doctors – particularly fitted for making those sorts of judgement, if conceived of as judgements about criminalisation. Of course, criminal standards of proof do not apply. Most of the indicators are that both forms of necessity, related respectively to protection of the patient and protection of others, can be interpreted widely. Hale observes that the idea of necessity for the health or safety of the patient or for the protection of other persons cannot be construed so strongly as to mean the patient is *dangerous* to him- or herself or *dangerous* to others. Had the drafters intended to use that term in section 3 they would have done so, as they did elsewhere in the Act.[18] The wording of section 3 appears to support the claim that protection of property without more cannot be said to be 'for the health or safety of the patient or the protection of other persons' and that at least seems significantly to narrow down the potential behaviour capable of triggering detention by way of comparison with the ASBO. The Code of Practice, however, states that harm to other people includes psychological as well as physical harm.[19] That harm in this context can be psychological is entirely plausible in principle, but the scope for identifying psychological harm to husbands, wives, partners, children, carers, as well as close friends and neighbours is very wide. It may even render less significant the line in the sand we just drew at the point of mere damage to property. Damage, for example, to a neighbour's property or the risk of it is likely in the nature of things to cause the neighbour psychological or emotional anguish, and the concern is that not especially severe anguish will be enough for the requisite extra element beyond the damage to property. To engage a criterion of 'necessity' in a statute can at first sight give the impression that a robust

[17] On various aspects of quarantine see two papers in Peter A Singer and AM Viens (eds), *The Cambridge Textbook of Bioethics* (Cambridge, Cambridge University Press, 2008). The papers in question are Harvey Kayman, Howard Radest and Sally Webb, 'Emergency and Disaster Scenarios' 281–88 and Jay A Jacobsen, 'Infectious Diseases Ethics' 481–86.

[18] A nearest relative can be prevented from discharging a patient by virtue of s 25 of the Act if the patient is likely to 'act in a manner dangerous to other persons or to himself'. See further, Hale (n 1 above) 58.

[19] Department of Health, 'Mental Health Act Code of Practice' (2008) 4.8.

criterion is in place. However, at least since Aristotle it has been clear on deeper examination that it can carry a considerable range of meaning and many degrees of seriousness.[20]

A great deal more could be said about the idea of protection under section 3, but let us move to a consideration of the end result of the process, that is, to the deprivation of liberty of the mentally disordered person itself. As we have seen in the case of the ASBO, up to five years imprisonment lies in wait for someone who violates the terms of the order in question and in the case of civil detention the detention can, subject to regular review, be indefinite. It would seem, however, that there is a significant difference between any deprivation of liberty in the case of the ASBO and in that of civil detention. For the former culminates in punishment and the latter does not. One might immediately counter that being imprisoned on the one hand and being compulsorily detained for prolonged periods in hospital on the other may not strike the detainee as significantly different and I will come to that point below. First we should spell out in more detail the suggestion that the liberty deprivation in the case of the ASBO is punitive in a way it is not in the case of civil detention. Richard Lippke helpfully distinguishes between material and symbolic dimensions of imprisonment.[21] Material dimensions of imprisonment relate to the living conditions of prisoners, to the restrictions imposed on them, while symbolic dimensions, as the name implies, relate to what the imprisonment symbolises, what messages it communicates both to the public at large and to the prisoner. Lippke lists six kinds of material deprivation:

(1) Restrictions on freedom of movement.
(2) Low levels of comfort and amenity.
(3) Idleness, especially a paucity of opportunities for paid labour.
(4) Relative isolation from family members, friends, and the larger community.
(5) Significant diminution of autonomy especially insofar as prisons subject their inhabitants to a degree of bureaucratic control which might be categorised as the 'subservience of youth'.
(6) Diminishment of privacy.[22]

[20] 'We call NECESSARY', said Aristotle, '(a) that without which . . . it is not possible to live, as for instance breathing and nourishment are necessary for an animal, because it is incapable of existing without them; and (b) anything without which it is not possible for good to exist or come to be, or for bad to be discarded or got rid of, as for instance drinking medicine is necessary so as not to be ill, and sailing to Aegina so as to get money.' *Metahphysics V*, 1015a20. Aristotle's understanding covers everything from what is necessary to save someone from starving to death to the necessary means for collecting money from a debtor. In the Mental Health Act, the necessity does of course have to be for 'health or safety', but this can stretch all the way from saving a life to preventing anguish at the threat to one's property. In the case of the ASBO, Asworth and Zedner suggest the requirement that the prohibitions in an ASBO be 'necessary' for the protection of others from anti-social behaviour has not been 'enforced rigorously.' Above n 5 298.

[21] Richard L Lippke, 'No Easy Way Out: Dangerous Offenders and Preventive Detention' (2008) 27 *Law and Philosophy* (2008) 383–414, 408. See also his *Rethinking Imprisonment* (Oxford, Oxford University Press, 2007).

[22] ibid.

Now, all six of these are likely to apply very significantly to the compulsorily detained mentally disordered patient just as they do to the imprisoned offender.

It is true that the therapeutic environment for a patient detained under the Mental Health Act can be good and the relationship between staff and patients very different from that between warder and prisoner. However, even where the former relationships are not good, there remains a highly significant difference between the cases of imprisonment and civil detention. The major difference seems to lie in the *symbolic* aspects of imprisonment. The criminal conviction communicates censure to the convicted offender and the public for the offender's past conduct and imprisonment based on it amplifies and reinforces the messages.[23] In the case of the ASBO this feature remains in place; imprisonment implies and communicates censure, notwithstanding the fact that the ordinary safeguards of criminal procedure have been bypassed. In the case of civil detention there has by contrast been no conviction and so no similar communication. It is not, in short, punishment. One might also add that in the case of punishment most of the material deprivations are intended, ie the conditions are meant to amount to material deprivation whereas in the case of civil detention the material deprivation is a foreseen consequence (and not a desired one) – it is a side effect of the need to provide the type of treatment and protection that the mentally disordered are thought to need. If all of this is right, there would appear strong reason to answer Hale's question in the negative. Not only is civil detention not literally criminal, it is also not conceived in a helpful way as metaphorically criminal since the essential elements of censure and punishment are missing.

One might respond that this conclusion is too quick. As touched on above, if a detainee is insensitive to the symbolic features of situations, the detainee may see little or no difference between civil detention and imprisonment. Also, is the distinction between material and symbolic aspects of imprisonment not more fluid than the above argument assumes? Lippke himself sees standard forms of imprisonment as communicating that the individuals subject to them have 'engaged in serious wrongs [that are] sufficient to merit their being excluded from civil society for some period of time.'[24] What merits the exclusion is the finding of wrongdoing; the wrongdoing and the exclusion are internally related. So far that tells against any equivalence between the case of the ASBO and that of civil confinement. However, he also adds that the communicative message in imprisonment may vary with the kinds of deprivation imposed: 'Supermax confinement', he suggests, 'with its extreme diminishment of the agency of inmates, arguably conveys the message that its inhabitants are little better than wild beasts of prey, who must be tightly controlled and watched over.'[25] Now Lippke

[23] On the communicative aspect of criminal law, see RA Duff, *Punishment, Communication and Community* (Oxford, Oxford University Press, 2001).

[24] Lippke (n 21 above) 409.

[25] ibid.

does not himself mean to imply that the element of censure for wrongdoing drops out of the picture in the case of Supermax confinement; he means to say as I understand him that the condemnatory message can be ratcheted up by such confinement in order to communicate (he thinks this degrading and inhumane) that Supermax detainees deserve such near bestial treatment. At this point our imaginary responder may intervene in order to claim that civil confinement effectively communicates the message that we are dealing with near animals quite independently of the censuring function of the criminal law: the mentally disordered need to be confined, because, animal-like, they need to be incarcerated, controlled and manipulated, not reasoned or engaged with: that is the message. In many ways, the suggestion concludes, it is like the most extreme sort of imprisonment of which Lippke speaks, despite the absence in the case of civil confinement of official censure. Even if it is unlike less serious post-conviction symbolic communication, it is like the more serious post-conviction communications. Hence we can equate civil confinement with criminal punishment symbolically as well as materially.

In my view this response is not satisfactory. For one thing, one must not forget the therapeutic dimension of civil confinement that is also insisted upon in section 3 and elsewhere in the Mental Health Act. On one influential view of psychotherapy, the 'central aim . . . is that of enlarging people's ability to live their lives by choice'.[26] The aim of psychotherapy on this view is essentially the enhancement of autonomy where possible. In the words of the Consultant Psychotherapist, Anthony Ryle:

> While the removal of symptoms is a worthwhile act, and is sometimes all the patient requests, the nature of psychologically derived symptoms is such that wider aims are nearly always implied. These aims are achieved by enabling patients to acquire a more accurate and fuller experience in place of muted, denied or distorted experience and by reducing those aspects of life that are lived by compulsion or evasion, and extending those that are lived by desire and intention.

Now Ryle speaks of what the patient 'requests'. Section 3, however, licenses compulsory detention, so consent or rather a lack of it will block neither detention nor (an attempt at) treatment, an issue to which we will return when considering the legitimate scope of civil detention. However, as far as the current issue is concerned, it is implausible to suggest that the symbolic message of civil confinement is essentially the near bestial one described by Lippke in relation to Supermax confinement, notwithstanding the lack of official censure in the case of civil confinement. For while civil detention is coupled with the insistence that treatment be made available which, in aspiration at least, aims at autonomy improvement, the symbolic message cannot be understood by this route to be equivalent to the symbolic message of a criminal conviction.

[26] Anthony Ryle, quoted in Jeremy Holmes and Richard Lindley, *The Values of Psychotherapy*, revised edition (London, Kamac Books, 1998) 43.

But might the responder not say, less elaborately, that detention under the Mental Health Act is practically equivalent to imprisonment following a standard criminal law conviction in virtue of the fact that being 'sectioned' is stigmatic? One can only speculate as to how far detention under the Mental Health Act is stigmatic, although it is widely accepted that it is.[27] The reason, so this more simple response runs, that we need a complex criminal procedure safeguarding the rights of accused persons in criminal trials is precisely that conviction of a criminal offence is stigmatic. The source of the stigma is relatively unimportant, whether funnelled through a state act of censure or blame or based on the unmediated attitudes of some of the detainee's fellow citizens. So the response concludes. However, the idea of stigma is itself ambiguous. It can be, as I have argued elsewhere, psychological on the one hand and normative on the other.[28] Stigma is imposed in the normative sense where there is a sound reason for A to stigmatise B or for B to feel stigmatised and it is imposed in the psychological sense where it is in fact projected by A and felt by B or simply felt by B, whether or not there is any sound reason for its imposition. Historically, many have been stigmatised in the psychological sense, for say disease and misfortune, without any normative justification, while many have not been stigmatised in the psychological sense when they should have been, say for an act of racist murder or for institutions such as slave-owning. Now the stigma that attaches to sectioning is obviously of the psychological variety. It is projected and felt without there being sound reason for either. The censure of a criminal trial by contrast is at least claimed to be normatively stigmatising or blaming, whether or not it always succeeds in being so. This, I believe, makes the symbolic message of a criminal conviction different from the symbolic significance of civil detention. However, it is true that psychological stigma can be terrible for people subject to it and this fact should ground state obligations to take steps where possible to counter it, through education for example. However, although that is not enough to equate symbolically the stigma that follows civil detention, where the stigma is psychological and not aimed at, with the stigma or blame involved in the censure of a criminal conviction, where it is aimed at and is claimed to be normative, it would be wrong to rest matters there. For there still remains the sense that the bad effects of (misguided) public stigma on mentally disordered people have not yet been given their due. For this public stigma, however misguided and unsought for by the state, does seem to furnish a good reason for the state to be especially careful about imposing the conditions that give rise to the stigma. What this shows, I think, is that we need to be careful about falling too readily into compartmentalised thinking. Civil detention as I have suggested is neither literally criminal nor, in the sense of the ASBO, a subversion of the criminal law, but it has features that render it uncomfortably close to being so. This is likely to imply that the level of procedural

[27] *cf* Hale (n 1 above) 143: '[T]here is certainly a stigma in being "sectioned".'

[28] John Stanton-Ife, 'Strict Liability: Stigma and Regret' (2007) *Oxford Journal of Legal Studies* 1–23, 6–8.

protection should be, if not as great as in the case of crimes proper, not very far short.[29]

The upshot, I believe, is that, unlike the ASBO, the Mental Health Act does not create a subversive crime of anti-social mental disorder. While I readily agree that the material aspects of civil detention can be as bad as the material aspects of imprisonment, the symbolism of the latter is constituted by a highly significant element – the communication of censure – that is lacking in the former. However, there is still cause for serious concern about the Mental Health Act. That is what this *gestalt* exercise in seeing the Mental Health Act as criminal in nature has revealed.

III THREE ISSUES: AUTONOMY, UNJUST DISCRIMINATION AND THE RIGHT TO BE IRRATIONAL

Thus far I have not tried to address the question of when the compulsory civil detention of the mentally disordered can be legitimate. I have, to be sure, assumed that the practice is not always illegitimate. I have assumed that there can be cases in which such detention with treatment is appropriate, but have not tried to say anything about the scope of such legitimate treatment. However, is even that relatively modest conclusion justified? We have seen that there is much cause for concern in the wording of section 3 of the Mental Health Act, which we briefly examined earlier. First, there is a concern that it violates the *autonomy* of mentally disordered persons, in riding roughshod over any consent (or withholding of consent) on their part and also in detaining them in a way that is, as we have seen, materially akin (if not symbolically so) to imprisonment after a criminal conviction. Such detention involves the denial of autonomy in multiple ways.

Second, civil confinement appears to discriminate against mentally disordered persons on the basis that they are mentally disordered. Of course there is no denying that some mentally disordered persons can be a danger to themselves or others for significant lengths of time. We have seen that section 3 does not require as a condition of detention that mentally disordered people be thought dangerous, instead detention must be thought necessary for the protection of others or for the health or safety of mentally disordered people themselves. However, non-mentally disordered persons may similarly need their health or safety protected and may be the same sort of threat to the interests of others. However, in their case they may not be detained compulsorily. Surely, one might insist, these cases should stand or fall together? If it is legitimate to detain a mentally disordered person because he or she might (in the relevant sense) threaten others or their interests, then it should be similarly legitimate to detain a non-mentally disordered person if they pose the same threat. Alternatively, if we can't stomach the detention of the non-mentally disordered

[29] See generally, Larry Alexander, 'Scalar Properties, Binary Judgments' (2008) 25 (2) *Journal of Applied Philosophy* 85–104.

in these cases, then we should similarly refuse to do so in relation to the mentally disordered. The same also goes for detention for the health or safety respectively of mentally disordered and non-mentally disordered persons.

This brings us to a third point. As far as the non-mentally disordered are concerned, it has long been accepted in medical law that they have a right to choose irrationally. In the words of Butler-Sloss LJ:

> A man or woman of full age and sound understanding may choose to reject medical advice and medical or surgical treatment either partially or in its entirety. A decision to refuse medical treatment by a patient capable of making the decision does not have to be sensible, rational or well-considered.[30]

If the fact that a person of sound understanding makes a stupid, irrational and poorly considered decision does not count against its validity, why does the stupid, irrational and poorly considered decision of a mentally disordered person who does not wish to be treated in hospital count by contrast against its validity?

In due course I will attempt to say something about these three related issues, of autonomy, unjust discrimination and the putative right to be irrational, and their relevance for the legitimacy or otherwise of civil detention. However, before doing so I will try to get as clear as possible about the often invoked notion of autonomy and in particular the question of what the minimal conditions are for the possession of autonomy.

A The Diminished Autonomy Justification

I propose to launch a discussion of the minimum conditions of autonomy with a kind of justification that might to some limited extent be able to justify the practice of civil detention. According to Antony Duff:

> The preventive detention of the mentally disordered can be consistent with the demands of justice and autonomy – given a suitably restrictive definition of the kinds of disorder which could justify it. We can define mental disorder as a condition involving a serious impairment of the agent's capacities for rational thought or action, and thus for their capacity for rational self determination. The mentally disordered are less than normally autonomous; in severe cases, they are not autonomous agents at all. The requirement that a state respect its citizens autonomy, whilst it requires respect for such autonomy as disordered agents do retain, and efforts to restore them to full autonomy, does not preclude their detention, to prevent serious harms which they would otherwise be likely to cause (because of their disorder) to themselves or others.[31]

I will label this 'the diminished autonomy justification'. There will be no violation of autonomy, it says, if there is no autonomy or insufficient autonomy to

[30] *Re T (Adult: Refusal of Treatment)* [1993] Fam 95.

[31] RA Duff, 'Dangerousness and Citizenship' in Andrew Ashworth and Martin Wasik (eds), *Fundamentals of Sentencing Theory: Essays in Honor of Andrew von Hirsch* (Oxford, Clarendon Press, 1998) 112–55, 149.

violate in relation to a specific decision or person. It is worded so that it can only be seen as a necessary condition for the legitimate detention of the mentally disordered persons in question. For there to be sufficient justification for such detention, it is most likely that other conditions need to be satisfied, for example that the detention should be in the best interests of the person detained or of third parties. It is worth repeating that justifying *some* instances of the civil confinement of mentally disordered persons is the best it can potentially do. The decisions of mentally disordered persons who *do* have sufficient autonomy will not be included under the justification and would accordingly be entitled to respect for that autonomy in the same way as would someone with no mental disorder. I believe this form of (partial) justification is essentially correct. However, if it is, enormous strain is placed on the idea of who has autonomy and who has not, or on who has enough autonomy and who has not. What is it to have enough autonomy? Let us now look in some detail at that idea.

B Two Conceptions of Minimal Autonomy

When does someone cease to be in a position to make an autonomous decision? Broadly speaking, I will consider two possible understandings. Both see autonomy as a scalar concept, ie both understand autonomy as coming in degrees. However, where does one draw the line or set the threshold above which what we have is autonomy (at least to a minimal degree) and below which what we have is no longer autonomy at all? The first understanding is that of Tom Beauchamp,[32] one half of the Beauchamp and Childress pair, whose medical ethics textbook is the most influential one of the last three decades or so, and second that of Joseph Raz, one of the best known accounts of autonomy in the literature of political philosophy.[33] Examination of Raz's view turns up two different possible views in turn, as we will see.

i Beauchamp on Minimal Autonomy

Beauchamp suggests autonomous action should be analysed in terms of normal choosers who act:

(a) intentionally;
(b) with understanding; and
(c) without controlling factors.[34]

[32] Tom L Beauchamp, 'Who Deserves Autonomy, and Whose Autonomy Deserves Respect?' in James Stacey Taylor (ed), *Personal Autonomy* (Cambridge, Cambridge University Press, 2005) 330. Essentially the same account is given in Tom L Beauchamp and James F Childress, *Principles of Biomedical Ethics*, 6th edn (Oxford, Oxford University Press, 2009) 99–148.
[33] Raz (n 6 above).
[34] Beauchamp (n 32 above) 314.

Beauchamp is keen to stress a theory of autonomy should focus on autonomous *action*, rather than on traits of the autonomous *person*. Those we think of as autonomous persons, he says, sometimes fail to act autonomously. That could be because of temporary constraints caused by illness or depression, circumstantial ignorance, coercion, or other conditions that restrict options. Conversely, in his view, some persons we think of as generally incapable of autonomous decision-making make some autonomous choices. For example, some patients in institutions for the mentally disordered who are unable to care for themselves and are considered legally incompetent nonetheless make autonomous choices such as ringing for a nurse, stating preferences for meals and making telephone calls to friends. Such persons act autonomously, he says, even if they fail to possess what we usually think of as critical conditions of the autonomous person.

What Beauchamp is keenest of all to stress is what he takes to be a constraint on any account of autonomy worth its salt. In his words:

> [My] theory of autonomy presumes the cardinal moral importance of protecting, under the principle of respect for autonomy, everyday choices. A critical test of the adequacy of any theory of autonomy, then, is whether it coheres with the moral requirement that we respect everyday choices such as opening bank accounts, purchasing goods in stores, and authorizing an automobile to be repaired.[35]

Mainly so that Beauchamp's account of autonomy can pass his self-imposed test of coherence with everyday choices, he takes it to be a minimal one. However, is it too minimal? One might ask if certain non-human animals can meet the test as he conceives it. Take dogs as an example. As far as the first criterion is concerned, dogs can act intentionally or purposefully – they do so all the time. As for the second, their activities presumably require understanding of a certain sort – Beauchamp says that his understanding criterion is a matter of degree and one must not put heavy demands on it. Third, one can apply the 'controlling influences' test on dogs, certainly the *external* controlling influence test which Beauchamp emphasises. To illustrate this, imagine two dogs at one time swimming in the river. One jumped in the water because it loves to swim. The other is scared of the water and is only in the river because some nasty boys threw it in. Dog 1 is acting purposefully, with implicit understanding and without controlling influence; Dog 2 is also acting purposefully, albeit with a different purpose from Dog 1 (get out quick!) and is *not* acting without controlling influence, having been unceremoniously dumped in the water. Should we conclude Dog 1 acts autonomously and Dog 2 does not? However, would not any conclusion other than one affirming that *neither* dog is acting autonomously be unacceptable? Or does the seemingly counterintuitive conclusion that dogs often act autonomously become more easily acceptable if we stress that they only have autonomy to a small degree?[36]

[35] ibid 313.

[36] *cf* Mark Rowland, *Animals Like Us* (London, Verso, 2002) 22–23, on the claim that some non-human animals can be autonomous.

Beauchamp indeed seems willing to embrace the implication that many acts of non-human animals are autonomous on his account, or at least he seems not to be put off by it. The key for him is to maintain his insistence that everyday human choices be counted as autonomous.[37] Beauchamp's concern seems indeed to be important. There is often reason to be sensitive to the sorts of choices he has in mind – ringing for a nurse, meal preferences – but one might wonder if the respect in question is necessarily based on the autonomy of the chooser, as opposed to something else. In cases in which a small number of choices of the sort Beauchamp has in mind are the only ones of which a patient is capable, it may indeed often be in a patient's best interest that his or her ringing for a nurse or expression of a preference for one kind of food over another be acceded to, to avoid the patient becoming distressed and so on. However, doing X because it is in a patient's best interest is different from doing X to respect a patient's autonomy. We will come back to this issue when we get to the second kind of minimal autonomy account in due course.

Whether or not Beauchamp has in mind a view of choice and decision of the sort, his view of autonomous choice and decision-making seems congenial to the Thomas Hobbes school of thought and the tradition following him. In Hobbes we see just such a continuity between human choices and decisions and those of some non-human animals that we appear to see in Beauchamp. Hobbes claimed that it is appetites or desires that determine the will. Someone's appetites can of course conflict with one another and in such a case Hobbes thought that it is the 'last appetite' that determines the will:

> Will therefore is the last appetite in deliberating. And though we say in common discourse, a man had a will once to do a thing, that nevertheless he forbare to do; yet that is properly but an inclination, which makes no action voluntary; because the action depends not of it, but of the last inclination, or appetite.[38]

According to this account, then, there is no radical discontinuity between decisions of humans with very severe learning disability or some non-human animals, on the one hand, and the ordinary human being free of such severe learning disability on the other. It is not, however, that Hobbes himself thought there was nothing distinctive about human decision-making. He did believe that ordinary humans are distinctive in their use of language. While human rationality is not a special faculty in the human mind, humans have a special ability to develop and use a particular physical tool, which is how he conceives language.[39] After examining the Hobbes view in detail, Thomas Pink concludes: 'By language humans can use words to express their thought – which otherwise are just

[37] Beauchamp (n 32 above) 322.

[38] Hobbes, *Leviathan* Part I: 'Of Man'. Chapter VI in DD Raphael, *British Moralists 1650–1800 I: Hobbes-Gay* (Indianapolis, Hackett, 1991) 27.

[39] See Thomas Pink, 'Suarez, Hobbes and the Scholastic Tradition in Action Theory' in Thomas Pink and MWF Stone (eds), *The Will and Human Action: From Antiquity to the Present Day* (London, Routledge, 2004) 127–53, 144.

like animal thoughts, occurring within a wholly corporeal imagination.'[40] Of course some adult human beings, such as certain persons with severe mental disorder, lack language. However, this fact is easily accounted for on the Hobbes account since language is conceived as a physical tool one may or may not have overlying one's decisional capacity. Similarly, the possibility entertained by some today, if not in Hobbes's day, that some non-human animals may have rudimentary language would be easily assimilable to the view.[41] If this view or some suitably developed and qualified version of it carries conviction, the Beauchamp view may use it in its support. Ringing for a nurse or choosing peas over beans, even for those capable of nothing more sophisticated, are fully continuous with the decisions of those capable of much more, getting married, signing a contract that binds one for many years and so on. The key difference is one of degree only. In such cases there is autonomy to respect, even if not much of it.

ii Raz on Minimal Autonomy

Let us now turn to the second kind of view of minimal autonomy, a view that sets the bar for autonomous choice above the last-appetite or last-desire view we see in Hobbes. This is Raz's view as originally developed in *The Morality of Freedom*. We have seen that Beauchamp's emphasis was on autonomous action, rather than on traits of the autonomous person. The centrepiece of the Razian notion of autonomy is the idea of part authorship of a life. This involves a rather different emphasis. While, especially in the context of the current chapter, the focus should remain on individual decisions, what is especially important here are the decisions of people who are authors, or part authors of their own lives:

> An autonomous person is part author of his own life. His life is, in part, of his own making. The autonomous person's life is marked not only by what it is but also by what it might have been and by the way it became what it is. A person is autonomous only if he has a variety of acceptable options to choose from, and his life became as it is through his choice of some of these options. A person who has never had any significant choice, or was not aware of it, or never exercised choice in significant matters but simply drifted through life is not an autonomous person.[42]

Raz, by contrast with Beauchamp, focuses on traits of the autonomous person rather than on autonomous action. In the light of the guiding idea of part authorship of a life, he claims that a state should furnish for all the ability to choose between an adequate range of valuable options and to do so independently. There is potentially a lot to unpack here, but I will pick out two features, the idea of choice and the idea of options. Broadly speaking, the idea of choice

[40] ibid.

[41] Paola Cavalieri and Peter Singer, 'The Great Ape Project' in Helga Kuhse (ed), *Peter Singer: Unsanctifying Human Life* (Oxford, Blackwell, 2002) 128–41, 138 *et seq*.

[42] Raz (n 5 above) 204.

focuses on features internal to the individual him or herself, the idea of options on features external to the individual.

First, we will look at the idea of options. Raz's well known slogan refers to an adequate range of valuable options. There are various conditions he lays down on what should be seen as an adequacy of options.[43] One is that all one's decisions had better not be trivial. This he illustrates with his example of the man in the pit, an unfortunate who has fallen into a pit miles from anywhere from which he cannot escape.[44] There is sufficient vegetation in the pit to keep him alive, but his only choices are of the order of: do I scratch my nose or not, do I eat now or in 20 minutes' time. If these are the only options open to him, he does not have the adequacy of valuable options required for autonomy. The point here has not to do with any condition internal to the person in question, but to do with the options external to the person. The man in the pit is not in any way mentally or physically disordered. Beauchamp, as we saw, thought it a condition of adequacy on an account of autonomy that we should count ordinary choices as autonomous, ringing for a nurse, stating preferences for meals and making telephone calls to friends were three of his examples. On Raz's account, I think that the third one of these, making calls to a friend, may well in certain circumstances count as autonomous, but the first two, without more, would not. For if none of a person's choices went beyond the order of ringing for a nurse or choice of peas or beans for supper, the person is not choosing as someone living an autonomous, (partially) self-authored life.

The second point moves focus to choice and choosing, rather than on the options from which choices are made. An autonomous choice, according to Raz and others, involves reflective endorsement. I may have a desire or passion that just springs up in me and presumably in the Hobbesian vein I may have conflicting desires and passions which vary in strength and intensity. It is only if I am capable of standing back from these desires and either endorsing or refraining from endorsing them critically, at least some of the time, that they are my autonomous choices. More specifically at the time of *The Morality of Freedom*, Raz followed Harry Frankfurt in seeing autonomous choices as those with which one *identifies*. 'To be autonomous', in Raz's words, 'one must identify with one's choices, and must be loyal to them'.[45] This view plainly marks a difference in kind between the ordinary canine choices we mentioned earlier and ordinary human choices, as Beauchamp's view and the Hobbesian view appeared not to do. It also opens up the possibility that some human choices will fall below the posited autonomy threshold. This, as we have seen, is exactly the result Beauchamp wished to avoid. However, as already noted, to say such choices are not autonomous choices is not yet to say anything practical about how they should be treated or respected. There may be reasons based on some-

[43] ibid 369–78.
[44] ibid 373–74.
[45] ibid 382.

thing other than autonomy to respect such choices, based for example on what might be in the best interests of the chooser.

While Raz took the question of whether or not an individual could be said to identify with his or her choices as a key issue in accounting for autonomous choices in *The Morality of Freedom*, I doubt whether he would hold exactly the same view today. For in the years since the publication of that work he has been critical of Frankfurt's notion of identification, albeit not explicitly in relation to the idea of autonomy, but in relation to the related idea of the active and passive in the human life, of when we can say desires, intentions and emotions are our own desires and so on.[46] The central idea in the new account is *responsiveness to reason*.[47] This involves an interweaving of subjective and objective elements, a point which will require some explanation. It will also point towards a new way of fixing a threshold between autonomy and non-autonomy. If being active is a matter of responsiveness to reason, does Raz mean this objectively or subjectively? Does he mean that it is whether people *believe* themselves responsive to reason that matters, or whether they are responsive to reason, whether or not they believe themselves so? The answer is 'both' and 'it depends'. According to what Raz calls the 'core account' of the active, it is the former that matters:

> . . . we are ourselves so long as, *as we see it*, we are responsive to reason. What counts, however, is not the justification or rationality of our view, but the view itself. We are ourselves and we lead our own life so long as *we see ourselves* as rational agents, so long as we conduct our life under the semblance of rationality.[48]

Here the subjective is primary. It is clear that we cannot, Raz thinks, interpret the relevant idea of responsiveness to reason so that every time we are not entirely rational about some matter, that suggests we are not active, not living our own lives. For one thing, while people in general want to be rational, they may yet want to be irrational once in a while.[49] Moreover, it is common to have certain beliefs that are induced by self-deception or wishful thinking 'or other forms of irrationality which we do not recognize as such'.[50] Many ordinary people are prone to flattery for example. However, these beliefs are not inconsistent with our leading our own lives. Beliefs characterised by self-deception and wishful thinking will often remain active because they appear to us rational. In fact their ability to deceive us depends on their appearance *qua* rational, on their semblance of rationality.

[46] Joseph Raz, 'When we are Ourselves' in his *Engaging Reason: on the Theory of Value and Action* (Oxford, Oxford University Press, 1999) 5–21. Raz raises a number of objections to Frankfurt's view. One is the following. Many people disapprove of certain aspects of themselves. On Frankfurt's account, these aspects cannot be truly theirs. I might be a jealous person. I might dislike this aspect of myself, not wish it to move me to action or to lead me to entertain jealous thoughts or emotions. But it is truly me: that's the problem! It would be self-deceptive of me to think otherwise, 18.

[47] ibid 15.

[48] ibid 19. Emphasis added.

[49] ibid.

[50] ibid 16.

In making these points, I understand Raz to have in mind ordinary people leading ordinary, everyday lives. Perfectly ordinary people will standardly admit to some measure of irrationality in their lives and this fact needs to be accommodated in an account of the active life in general. I said that Raz's claim that being active is a matter of responsiveness to reason is to be understood *both* objectively and subjectively? We have just seen the way in which it is to be understood subjectively. However, *seeing oneself* as responsive to reason is not always sufficient for living one's own life in the way just described. This brings us to the way in which Raz's claim is to be understood objectively. The processes which govern the mental lives of the ordinary people just mentioned – the beliefs they form, the moods they get in, the desires they have and the emotions they feel – are generally functioning properly. However, of course other people's mental processes are not functioning properly, notably and to varying extents persons with mental disorders. In the case of some persons with a mental disorder, the fact that they may *see* themselves as rational does not have the significance we noted it had for ordinary persons in the previous paragraph. Take the case of serious paranoia and delusion. Daniel McNaughton had such paranoid delusions; and famously his fatal shooting in Victorian times of Sir Robert Peel's Private Secretary led to the formulation of the rules on insanity named after him. After the shooting McNaughton himself explained:

> The Tories in my native city have compelled me to do this. They follow and persecute me wherever I go, and have entirely destroyed my peace of mind. They followed me to France, into Scotland, and all over England; in fact, they follow me wherever I go. I can get no rest [from] them night or day. I cannot sleep at night in consequence of the course they pursue towards me. I believe they have driven me into a consumption. I am sure I shall never be the man I formerly was. I used to have good health and strength, but I have not now. They have accused me of crimes of which I am not guilty; they do everything in their power to harass and persecute me; in fact, they wish to murder me. It can be proved by evidence.[51]

McNaughton appeared to believe he was guided by reason. He regularly used locutions like 'in fact' and talked of what can be established with 'evidence', and put his suffering down to the actions of others, not the malfunctioning of his own mind. He had entered a parallel universe. His mental functioning was not sensitive to facts or to the evidence. It was not that the reasons he cited for his actions were not intelligible. If the Tories had really been deploying many of their number to follow him obsessively over a long period of time and were really trying to persecute, harass, frame and murder him he would have had excellent reason to take self protective measures. But he was suffering paranoid delusions.

Even if McNaughton's actions seemed to him rational, they clearly cannot be taken to be so. Raz himself gives the example of a demented person 'whose

[51] Quoted in Henry R Rollin, 'McNaughton's Madness' in Donald J West and Alexander Walk, *Daniel McNaughton: His Trial and the Aftermath* (Ashford, Kent, Gaskell Books,1977) 91–99, 92.

memory is confined to a few minutes, and who, being unaware of his dementia, thinks he is generally reacting reasonably to situations he is in'.[52] Again, that he believes himself responsive to reason does not establish that he is so. To repeat, it is here that Raz's account is primarily objective. 'Having a unified personality', he says, 'and being in general rational are presuppositions of being oneself, and being able to lead one's own life'.[53] Presumably, one can lack rationality in significant pockets of one's life and still count on this view as generally rational, but plainly much more would need to be said on how the notion of being in general rational is to be understood. This, then, suggests a different understanding of a threshold between the autonomous and the non-autonomous.

Being active and being oneself, ideas we are taking as essential components of autonomy, is a matter of being properly responsive to reason. For those who are generally rational and whose personalities are sufficiently unified, the main thought is a subjective one: do they think themselves generally rational, are they acting under the semblance of rationality? For those who are not generally rational and whose personalities are insufficiently unified, the main thought is an objective one. They will not be properly responsive to reason even if they believe themselves to be so. So the threshold above which we have at least minimal autonomy and below which we do not have autonomy at all will be marked at least in part by the idea of proper responsiveness to reason.

C The Diminished Autonomy Justification Again

I have canvassed some different ways of understanding what minimal autonomy is. All agree that autonomy is a matter of degree, but differ as to where one draws the line between minimal autonomy and no autonomy. The first, Beauchamp's view, posits a very undemanding threshold. Any sentient animal with the capacity to form intentions with minimal understanding and free of controlling factors lies above the threshold for autonomy. I then considered what turned out to be two different views of minimal autonomy from Raz. In both cases autonomy focuses initially on the autonomous life, on part-authorship of the life. The first view, inspired by Frankfurt, took autonomy to require reflective endorsement. Having a set of desires and passions which lead one to various decisions is not enough: one must also be able to step back and endorse or refrain from endorsing the desires and passions. As I observed, it is unlikely Raz would still hold that view in the light of his subsequent criticism of Frankfurt. This brought us to the second Razian view of minimal autonomy. In order to be autonomous on this view one must, I take it, be able to do what Beauchamp required – to act intentionally, with sufficient understanding and without controlling factors – and one must in Raz's well known phrase be able

[52] Raz (n 46 above) 16.
[53] ibid.

to choose between an adequate range of valuable options, but in such a way that one is at a minimum responsive to reason, not simply buffeted by one's Hobbesian desires and passions. An ordinary person who is not rational in all regards (say, a little prone to flattery) is nevertheless properly responsive to reason since his or her personality is sufficiently unified and the person is generally rational (the objective aspect) and sees his or herself as rational (the subjective aspect). The McNaughton and dementia examples also showed that one may not be properly responsive to reason notwithstanding the fact that one sees oneself as such. For what it is worth, however, I tend towards the third – responsiveness to reason – account, it would be much too large a job to attempt to adjudicate here between these views in any satisfactory fashion. I will content myself with one simple point. The Beauchamp view appears not to give any sort of account of why autonomy, so minimally conceived as intentional and unhindered choice, is not just valuable but is the special value that has gained such prominence in contemporary culture.[54] By contrast the Razian view, especially the latter variant, in stressing the link between choice and part authorship of one's own life, does seem to focus on something truly important, that people live *their* lives, that they are at least in part the authors of those lives.

In the terms therefore of what we called the diminished autonomy justification, if someone is below a threshold marked in the way just described by responsiveness to reason, the requirement that the state must respect its citizens' autonomy does not preclude their detention, provided all other relevant principles are adhered to. This would, on being fully worked out, give some limited support to the civil confinement of mentally disordered persons under the Mental Health Act. Obviously if there is a threshold of minimal autonomy as we have suggested there is, one can either fall below it or above it. That of course implies that there is also an autonomy-based objection to the detention of mentally disordered persons above or far enough above the threshold of autonomy, and thus reveals the current practice of civil detention to be overbroad in terms of legitimacy. The alternative view of Beauchamp may or may not have different practical implications. Certainly it will be rarer on his view that any mentally disordered person has *no* autonomy, but the view might still be consistent with the diminished autonomy justification, if the emphasis were on the non-preclusion of detention in cases of *insufficient* autonomy.

D Unjust Discrimination and the Right to be Irrational

So much for cases in which the principle of autonomy can be said not to preclude legitimate detention. However, what of the two other related concerns we raised above prior to examining the notion of autonomy, viz. the unjust dis-

[54] *cf* Richard Dean, *The Value of Humanity in Kant's Moral Theory* (Oxford, Oxford University Press, 2006), 203–04.

crimination principle and the putative right to be irrational? Let us take the latter idea first. We cited above the well known judicial statement of Butler-Sloss LJ of the right on the part of persons of sound mind to be irrational in refusing medical treatment.[55] When juxtaposed with the compulsory detention of mentally disordered persons this is apt to sound a little puzzling. True the mentally disordered person is likely to be irrational more often than the person with sound mind, but if the latter is being just as irrational on this occasion in relation to this particular needed treatment, why in consistency should his or her refusal nonetheless be valid? The third of the views of autonomy canvassed above, based centrally on responsiveness to reason, does appear to give at least the beginnings of an answer to that question. For if the refuser of treatment is not responsive to reason in virtue of an insufficiently unified personality and a lack of rationality in all or significant segments of her life (Raz's objective aspect), her refusal cannot be said to be 'of herself' in the way that a similar refusal could be on the part of someone with an essentially unified personality, who is rational in general and who sees herself as rational (Raz's subjective aspect). The refusal emanates from the self in the latter case in a way it does not in the former.

What of the anti-discrimination principle? Does the Mental Health Act discriminate against mentally disordered persons unjustly, on the basis of nothing other than their mental disorder?[56] As we mentioned above, a mentally disordered person thought to pose some risk to others, which need not stretch to the belief that the person in question is a 'danger' to others, can be detained, when plainly this would be woefully inadequate as a ground for the detention of someone without a mental disorder thought to pose an identical risk. It is hard to see how one can avoid the charge of unjust discrimination here. Another much commented upon feature of the Act is that it allows detention of mentally disordered persons who *pass* the legal test for capacity to refuse treatment. Is this another clear case of unjust discrimination? Plainly, key work in the detention of such a person is again being done simply on the basis of the person's mental disorder. The non-mentally disordered person, competent to refuse, who refuses, cannot be compelled; the mentally disordered person, competent to refuse, who refuses, can. Is the remedy, at least in cases where the proposed detention relates to the health and safety of the mentally disordered person his or herself, to insist that if the person is competent to refuse, the refusal must be every bit as valid as in the case of persons free of any mental disorder? I think not. For that could lead to the potential abandonment in certain cases of the serious interests of some profoundly mentally disordered people. However, the culprit here is not the anti-discrimination principle, but something else, the legal test for competence, perhaps, or the lack of a further necessary criterion

[55] See n 30 above.

[56] For a forthright version of the claim that the Mental Health Act violates the anti-discrimination principle, see Tony Hope, *Medical Ethics: A Very Short Introduction* (Oxford, Oxford University Press, 2004) 77–85.

before detention is permissible. Briefly, the (abridged) legal understanding of competence is as follows:

> . . . a person is unable to make a decision for himself if he is unable –
>
> (a) to understand the information relevant to the decision,
> (b) to retain that information,
> (c) to use or weigh that information as part of the process of making the decision.[57]

This is primarily a cognitive set of considerations; and it can thus happen that a mentally disordered person is able to understand, retain, use and weigh information perfectly well and is thus legally competent on the current test. Indeed, mental disorders are often cognitive in nature but they can also be made up of volitional, evaluative and emotional failures as well or instead.[58] A woman, for example, may not wish to suffer the harm non-treatment would cause. She understands that non-treatment will cause that harm, but by reason of a phobia cannot bring herself to consent to the treatment. Raz's notion of responsiveness to reason was meant to apply to more than the cognitive aspects of a person's functioning, to his or her desires, emotions and moods as well. As he puts it, 'Our life is my own when it is under our control and that means when our various emotions, hopes, desires, intentions and action are guided by reason.'[59] The danger then is that if one were to combine the non-discrimination principle with a heavily cognitive test of competence, as that cited above appears on its face to be, one risks denying help to persons whose decisions are not their own in Raz's sense, but whose disorder is not impairing them in a relevant cognitive way, but rather in a volitional, emotional or evaluational way.[60] What is necessary appears to be an acknowledgement that mental disorder can interfere with one's decision making in many different ways. It may indeed interfere with one's ability to make decisions with understanding, but it may leave one's ability to do this intact while interfering with one's ability to make decisions that are truly those of 'oneself' in Raz's sense. The Scottish criterion for compulsory detention may be able to meet this desideratum, with its insistence that a condition of compulsion is that the person's judgment in relation to the decision to accept

[57] Mental Capacity Act 2005 s 3(1).

[58] On 'volitional disability' see Bernard Gert, Charles M Culver and K Danner Clouser, *Bioethics: A Systematic Approach*, 2nd edn (Oxford, Oxford University Press, 2006) 174–78. On various kinds of mental disorder beyond cognitive disorders, see Victor Tadros, *Criminal Responsibility*, (Oxford, Oxford University Press, 2005), especially his discussion of mental disorder and character change, 322–47. See also George Graham, *The Disordered Mind* (London, Routledge, 2010) and the discussion in Craig Edwards, 'Beyond Mental Competence' (2010) 27 (3) *Journal of Applied Philosophy* 273–89.

[59] Raz, 'Introduction' in his *Engaging Reason* (n 46 above) 1.

[60] Another solution would be to interpret the idea of 'weighing information' in the Mental Capacity Act so that it includes the dimensions other than the cognitive mentioned in the text. Bert, Clouser and Culver are highly critical of what seems the same idea, stretching what they call the 'Understand and Appreciate Definition', above n 58, 220–34. However, this does not seem like a stable solution anyway. For the problem is not an inability 'to make a decision', the problem is the *ability* to make a decision and its content.

treatment must be significantly impaired.[61] However, there is not space to explore that further here. The anti-discrimination principle is significantly compromised by the Mental Health Act. Often, as I've suggested, mentally disordered people are treated less well for no reason other than that they are mentally disordered. However, I have argued that mental disorder can find more routes than just one to interfere with one's ability to make decisions reflective of one's self and in various ways responsive to reason. In such cases overriding a decision made with understanding may not be unjustly discriminatory.

IV CONCLUSION

I began by taking seriously Brenda Hale's question of whether we have created a crime of anti-social mental disorder by stealth. Plainly, a literal answer in the affirmative was never on the cards and I also suggested that it goes too far to suggest there is a crime in a useful metaphorical sense. However, that is not to say there is no serious concern about the capacity of the Mental Health Act to subvert the criminal law. It can impose something whose nature is not far enough away from the hard treatment and stigma of a criminal conviction. Criminal lawyers are used to questioning the moral legitimacy of criminalising specified behaviour. There is a good case I believe for considering these principles not only in relation to cases in which there is no governmental intention to bypass the procedural requirements that accompany standard crimes, as well as to the sort of manoeuvres subversive of the criminal justice system witnessed, for example, in the ASBO, but also to cases where there is reason for saying that what is under scrutiny is neither literal criminalisation nor a subversion of criminal justice, but rather something uncomfortably close to the latter. The compulsory civil detention of mentally disordered persons, I have suggested, belongs in this final category.

The therapeutic element in civil detention coupled with the absence of the symbolic aspects of punishment were what prevented me from fully endorsing the suggestion that civil detention is as much of a subversion of the criminal law as the ASBO. However, as regards the former, therapeutic, consideration, beneficent as it sounds, the legitimacy of providing medical treatment depends on two necessary conditions, that the treatment is needed and that it is consented to. Consent is conspicuous by its absence from the conditions for compulsory civil detention of the mentally disordered. That absence compromises the legitimacy of the Mental Health Act at least in many cases. So much the worse for the legitimacy of the Mental Health Act I have suggested, at least in many cases. In other cases, the absence of consent cannot be thought of as decisive. The most important consideration is what mental disorder does to the person him or herself. Is he himself? Is she herself? Is a given aspect of his or her behaviour

[61] Mental Health (Care and Treatment) (Scotland) Act 2003 s 57.

or thinking responsive to reason? The mental disorder may not interfere at all with such selfhood or responsiveness to reason, in which case it is almost certainly discriminatory to treat mentally disordered people less favourably than other people. If mental disorder has interfered with selfhood or responsiveness to reason in this way, there may be little or no autonomy to speak of and so, as the diminished autonomy justification suggested, detention is not precluded by the principle of autonomy.[62] It may be precluded, however, by something else. Detention may not be in the best interests of the mentally disordered person in question for example.

The compulsory detention of persons at the margins of autonomy will remain one of the most disquieting aspects of the law. Mental disorder can severely interfere with one's selfhood and responsiveness to reason. In some cases compulsory detention may regrettably be necessary under certain conditions as a result. However, mental disorder is *itself* no reason for compulsory detention. Far too few obstacles currently stand in the way of its being in reality just that.

[62] If it is right, as I believe it is, to stress the capacity to respond to reason when accounting for minimal autonomy, perhaps it is unnecessary to invoke the value of autonomy at all. In the text we dealt with responsiveness to reason as no more than a necessary condition for minimal autonomy. Perhaps it would be clearer to drop talk of autonomy and stick simply to the notion of responsiveness to reason or perhaps something essential would be lost in taking such a step. However, I will not try to settle that issue here. It is interesting to note that Duff, in a recent paper on psychopathy, does not repeat his autonomy-based argument cited above (see text accompanying n 31), but takes the capacity to respond to reason as central. See Antony Duff, 'Psychopathy and Answerability' in Luca Malatesti and John McMillan, *Responsibility and Psychopathy: Interfacing Law, Psychiatry and Philosophy* (Oxford, Oxford University Press, 2010) 199–212.

8

Security, Risk and Preventive Orders

IAN DENNIS*

I INTRODUCTION

THIS CHAPTER DEALS with the use of civil preventive orders as a technique of promoting security against a risk of harm thought to be presented by the person subject to the order. There are definitional issues associated with the concept of 'civil preventive orders',[1] but for now we may refer to them broadly as civil legal orders, backed by coercive sanctions for breach of the order, which are directed to identified individuals relating to their future behaviour. The purpose of such orders is to regulate the person's behaviour and thereby to prevent the harm which the person is considered to be at risk of perpetrating. The orders may consist of positive obligations, such as to wear an electronic tag or to report to a police station, or negative obligations, such as to abstain from certain activities or to stay away from specified places, or a mixture of both.

While the idea of preventive orders has been known to the law for centuries,[2] it is only in recent years that they have become a controversial feature of the legal landscape. This is because the last Labour government expanded considerably the number of such orders enforceable by criminal penalties for breach. At this stage we should notice that civil preventive orders are of different types, depending on the nature of the coercive sanction which enforces them. There are now at least 17 civil preventive orders in existence, which may impose extensive restrictions on a person's freedom of action, where breach of the order constitutes a criminal offence.[3] Other types of civil preventive order are enforceable

* I am grateful to Jeremy Horder, Bob Sullivan and Lucia Zedner for helpful comments on an earlier draft. The usual disclaimer applies.

[1] For a valuable discussion see A Ashworth and L Zedner, 'Preventive Orders: A Problem of Undercriminalization?' in RA Duff, L Farmer, SE Marshall, M Renzo and V Tadros (eds), *The Boundaries of the Criminal Law* (Oxford, OUP, 2010) ch 3 (hereafter Ashworth and Zedner 2010).

[2] Namely, orders binding over a person to keep the peace and be of good behaviour which derive from the medieval jurisdiction of justices of the peace (Justices of the Peace Act 1361).

[3] The list includes anti-social behaviour orders (ASBOs), parenting orders (Crime and Disorder Act 1998 ss 1, 8, 8A); football spectator banning orders (Football Spectators Act 1989 s 14A); sexual offences prevention orders, foreign travel restriction orders, risk of sexual harm orders (Sexual Offences Act 2003 ss 104, 114, 123); travel restriction orders (Criminal Justice and Police Act 2001

by sanctions for civil contempt in the event of breach,[4] or by regulatory penalties.[5] Preventive orders can be used in widely varying contexts and in relation to an extensive range of behaviour that presents a risk of harm. The risks extend from the causing of harassment, alarm and distress in the case of anti-social behaviour orders (ASBOs) to the causing of death, serious injury and psychological trauma in cases of terrorism and violent and sexual offences.

Preventive orders differ considerably in terms of their conditions of availability, and I will say more about this later. However, they have a common structure, consisting of what Simester and von Hirsch describe as a 'two-step prohibition'.[6] The first step occurs when a person (whom we will call for convenience the defendant) engages in conduct which satisfies the conditions for the making of a preventive order. The second step is then the making of the order. The order is not itself a conviction for an offence. Where the order is to be backed by criminal penalties, the legislation creating the order will provide that breach of the terms of the order is an offence, and such an offence may carry a significant maximum penalty (five years on conviction on indictment is not uncommon).[7] This chapter is primarily concerned with preventive orders of this type, but I will make some reference to the use of civil sanctions for breach.

Most preventive orders are made by courts. However, non-derogating control orders for suspected terrorists are made by the Home Secretary,[8] and, as noted above, regulatory compliance orders can be made by a large number of government departments, local authorities and statutory regulators. As regards court orders, some preventive orders can only be made on conviction for an offence, when they are an adjunct to the sentence for the offence.[9] Others can only be

s 33); drinking banning orders (Violent Crime Reduction Act 2006 s 1); exclusion from licensed premises orders (Licensed Premises (Exclusion of Certain Persons) Act 1980 s 1; serious crime prevention orders (Serious Crime Act 2007 s 1); control orders (Prevention of Terrorism Act 2005 s 3); violent offender orders (Criminal Justice and Immigration Act 2008 s 98); restraining orders (Protection from Harassment Act 1997 s 5); non-molestation orders (Family Law Act 1996 s 42A); financial reporting orders (Serious Organised Crime and Police Act 2005 s 76); disqualification from being a company director (Company Directors Disqualification Act 1986 s 1); disqualification from driving (Powers of Criminal Courts (Sentencing) Act 2000 ss 146, 147). This list does not include a very large number of regulatory orders and notices that can be issued to individuals by Government departments, local authorities and statutory regulators, where breach of the order or notice is a summary offence. One example amongst many is the issue of a warning notice by an officer of a local authority to discontinue excessive noise from a dwelling at night (Noise Act 1996 s 3).

[4] Examples include anti-social behaviour injunctions (Housing Act 1996 s 153A) and public nuisance proceedings under the Local Government Act 1972 s 222.

[5] An example is the seizure of equipment used in the emission of excessive noise from a dwelling in breach of a notice issued under s 3 of the Noise Act 1996.

[6] AP Simester and Andrew von Hirsch, *Incivilities* (Oxford, Hart Publishing, 2006) ch 7.

[7] This is the maximum penalty for example for breach of ASBOs, control orders, travel restriction orders, serious crime prevention orders, sexual offences prevention orders and violent offender orders.

[8] Under the Prevention of Terrorism Act 2005 s 3. There is a right of appeal to the High Court against the making of such an order.

[9] For example, a travel restriction order imposed on a person convicted of a drug trafficking offence under the Criminal Justice and Police Act 2001 s 33. Other possibilities include financial reporting orders under the Serious Organised Crime and Police Act 2005 s 76, and disqualification from driving under the Powers of Criminal Courts (Sentencing) Act 2000 ss 146 and 147.

made on application to the court by specified persons or authorities, and will require evidence of conduct by the defendant to support the claim that the defendant is considered to present a risk of causing the relevant harm.[10] A third group, which comprises the majority of preventive orders listed in note 3 above, may be made either on conviction or on application.[11] The making of an order on application is generally regarded as a civil procedure, with an important consequence in terms of the applicable rules of evidence.

Breach of a preventive order may be specified to be a criminal offence, irrespective of whether the conduct constituting the breach amounts to a separate offence under the general criminal law. Preventive orders backed by criminal penalties which are made against individual citizens[12] thus exist in addition to the general criminal law applicable to all citizens. In this way such orders amount to a form of forward-looking individualised criminal law, and may in effect criminalise conduct that might not be criminal if engaged in by others. They are an indirect form of *ex ante* criminalisation.[13]

The proliferation of these orders has spawned a considerable body of literature.[14] Much of this is highly critical, particularly of control orders[15] and ASBOs,[16] the two types of preventive order which have tended to command the highest public profiles. However, it is not the purpose of this chapter to undertake a comprehensive review of the literature; nor is it feasible to analyse all the numerous preventive orders in detail. Instead, this chapter offers some discussion of three broad questions. The first question is why it has been thought necessary or desirable to supplement the general criminal law with individually-tailored preventive orders. If the general criminal law has a preventive aim, as Hart[17] and others[18]

[10] For example, violent offender orders under the Criminal Justice and Immigration Act 2008 s 101.

[11] This group includes ASBOs under the Crime and Disorder Act 1998 ss 1 and 1C; serious crime prevention orders under the Serious Crime Act 2007 ss 1 and 19; sexual offences prevention orders under the Sexual Offences Act 2003 s 104; football banning orders under the Football Spectators Act 1989 ss 14A and 14B, and drinking banning orders under the Violent Crime Reduction Act 2006 ss 3, 4 and 6.

[12] I use the term 'citizen' broadly to denote any person subject to the criminal jurisdiction of the state, irrespective of their citizenship status.

[13] Simester and von Hirsch (n 6 above) 178.

[14] Space does not permit a full bibliography. Leading contributions on preventive orders in general include ibid; Ashworth and Zedner (n 1 above); A Ashworth and L Zedner, 'Just Prevention: Preventive Rationales and the Limits of the Criminal Law' in RA Duff and SP Green (eds), *Philosophical Foundations of Criminal Law* (Oxford, OUP, 2011) ch 13 (hereafter Ashworth and Zedner 2011).

[15] For example, L Zedner, 'Preventive Justice or Pre-Punishment: The Case of Control Orders' (2007) *Current Legal Problems* 174. See also D Bonner, 'Checking the Executive? Detention Without Trial, Control Orders, Due Process and Human Rights' (2006) (12) *European Public Law* 45.

[16] See in particular A Ashworth, 'Social Control and Anti-Social Behaviour Order: The Subversion of Human Rights?' (2004) 120 *Law Quarterly Review* 263; P Ramsay, 'What is Anti-Social Behaviour?' (2004) *Criminal Law Review* 908; E Burney, *Making People Behave: Anti-Social Behaviour, Politics and Policy*, 2nd edn (Cullompton, Willan Publishing, 2009); S Hoffman and S Macdonald, 'Should ASBOs be Civilized?' (2010) *Criminal Law Review* 457.

[17] HLA Hart, *Punishment and Responsibility* (Oxford, Clarendon Press, 1968) 6.

[18] See for example A Ashworth, *Principles of Criminal Law*, 6th edn (Oxford, OUP, 2009) 16 ff; Ashworth and Zedner 2010 (n 1 above) 73ff.

have argued, what do preventive orders add to the deterrent force of the general law? The second question focuses on some key criticisms that have been made of preventive orders. It asks how persuasive these criticisms are, and what should we make of the point that only some of the orders, and not others, have attracted significant adverse comment? The third question is about the future of preventive orders. The Coalition Government has recently published reviews of control orders[19] and ASBOs,[20] which both seem likely to undergo substantial change in view of the difficulties associated with them. Does our discussion of their rationales and the criticisms of them lead to any useful conclusions about the proper design and use of preventive orders?

The discussion deals mainly with the two most controversial orders, namely ASBOs and control orders, but I will refer to a number of the others from time to time. The discussion has to take for granted common understandings of the key concepts of 'security',[21] 'risk'[22] and 'harm'.[23] I cannot pursue in this chapter the numerous issues concerning the scope and limits of these terms and their roles in theories of criminalisation and the justification of punishment. These issues are taken up by a number of other contributors to this volume.

II WHY HAVE PREVENTIVE ORDERS BECOME COMMON TECHNIQUES OF CRIME CONTROL?

In one sense there is an obvious answer to this question. It is widely accepted that the state has a primary duty to its citizens to safeguard their security and protect them from harm.[24] As Lord Hope put it in *R (McCann) v Manchester Crown Court*, the leading case on ASBOs, 'In a democratic society the protection of public order lies at the heart of good government'.[25] From the standpoint of citizens at risk of harm from the defendant, prevention is better than cure. Governments are likely to agree. As Poole has suggested in the context of counter-terrorism measures:

[19] Contained in the 'Review of Counter-Terrorism and Security Powers' (Cm 8004, TSO, 2011). See also the accompanying Report on the *Review* by Lord Macdonald of River Glaven QC (Cm 8003).

[20] 'More Effective Responses to Anti-Social Behaviour – A Consultation' (Home Office, 2011).

[21] See in particular V Tadros, 'Crimes and Security' (2008) 71 *Modern Law Review* 940; L Zedner, *Security* (London, Routledge, 2009) ch 1.

[22] See in particular RA Duff, *Answering for Crime* (Oxford, Hart Publishing, 2007) ch 7.

[23] The classic study of the harm principle is Joel Feinberg's four-volume treatise, *The Moral Limits of the Criminal Law,* comprising *Harm to Others* (Oxford, OUP, 1984), *Offense to Others* (Oxford, OUP, 1985), *Harm to Self* (Oxford, OUP, 1986), *Harmless Wrongdoing* (Oxford, OUP, 1988).

[24] Ashworth and Zedner 2011 (n 14) 279–82. For a thoughtful discussion of the correlative 'right to security' see L Lazarus, 'Mapping the Right to Security' in B Goold and L Lazarus, *Security and Human Rights* (Oxford, Hart Publishing, 2007) 325.

[25] *R (McCann) v Manchester Crown Court* [2003] 1 Cr App R 27 [41].

> Risk management . . . brings to the conduct of public administration a sense of 'strategy and control'. This illusion of mastery can provide a measure of security to a worried public and offers a useful legitimating device for the government (or other agency) deploying it.[26]

If then we were to conceive of punishment, a core identifying characteristic of the criminal law, as a 'cure' (in the sense of penalty) for a crime that has already been committed, prevention of the crime in the first place seems self-evidently preferable.[27] Interestingly this was the declared view of Blackstone. In the *Commentaries* he devoted a chapter to binding over orders. He described them as 'preventive justice' and contrasted them with the traditional concern of the criminal law with punishment for offences:

> . . . preventive justice is, upon every principle of reason, of humanity, and of sound policy, preferable in all respects to punishing justice; the execution of which, though necessary, and in its consequences a species of mercy to the commonwealth, is always attended with many harsh and disagreeable circumstances.
>
> This preventive justice consists in obliging these persons, whom there is a probable ground to suspect of future misbehaviour, to stipulate with and to give full assurance to the public, that such offence as is apprehended shall not happen, by finding pledges or securities for keeping the peace, or for their good behaviour.[28]

However, while we might accept that the state should have power to take some preventive measures in the interests of security,[29] an unqualified claim that the protection of 'security' can justify preventive measures against all 'risky' or 'dangerous' persons must surely be treated with extreme caution. Such a claim would seem seriously over-inclusive. A democratic polity which attaches a high value to the liberty of its citizens cannot permit the state to use the promotion of security as a comprehensive justification for whatever liberty-limiting measures it deems appropriate.[30] In addition to the threats to individual freedom that would be involved, there would be a serious concern about the width of the discretion that would be conferred on state agents. Preventive orders against individual citizens, used freely at the whim of the executive and without appropriate constraints, would carry numerous dangers of misuse. The way would be open to authoritarianism, arbitrariness, inequality, discrimination and oppression of unpopular

[26] T Poole, 'Courts and Conditions of Uncertainty in "Times of Crisis"' (2008) *Public Law* 234, 244.

[27] For this argument to carry weight, we should be satisfied that in the absence of preventive measures the crime is likely to occur, that the measure in question is likely to prevent it, and that no lesser liberty-limiting measure is likely to prevent it. Provided these conditions are satisfied then the worse the crime, and the more irremediable the harm it is likely to cause, the stronger is the argument for prevention rather than retribution or redress. See further ch 4 by Jeremy Horder in this volume.

[28] 4 Bl Comm, Ch XVIII, 251.

[29] Compulsory searching of airline passengers for potentially dangerous articles is an obvious example.

[30] As Zedner has pointed out in *Security* (London, Routledge, 2009) 12, the value of restraints on claims that can be made by reference to security is that otherwise 'in the name of security things that would ordinarily be politically untenable become thinkable'.

minorities. The argument for the use of preventive orders to promote security by supplementing the general criminal law therefore needs to be refined. [31]

I suggest the refinement can usefully start by asking why the general criminal law, which functions at least in part as a behaviour-influencing method of social control, is thought to be insufficient in some cases for the purpose of public protection. While there may be much disagreement about the justification and purpose of punishment of offenders, it is surely the case that a key objective of the criminal law as an institution is deterrence. When the law prohibits forms of conduct under threat of punishment it not only expresses condemnation of this conduct but aims to prevent crime by deterring rational self-interested actors from engaging in the conduct.

Moreover, it is worth reminding ourselves of the trite point that for many years the general criminal law has been concerned not only with prohibiting the causing of actual harm. Its reach has extended to numerous forms of conduct which create the *risk* of harm; there are many offences consisting of different types of risk-creation or endangerment. Offences of possession of an offensive weapon in a public place,[32] dangerous driving[33] and perjury[34] are just three well-known examples. In addition, the criminal law has a general prohibition on conduct preliminary to the commission of a substantive offence which amounts to an *attempt* to commit an offence,[35] and there are separate offences targeting the promotion of crime by others which prohibit acts of assistance or encouragement to them.[36] Given this range of prohibitions addressed to all citizens of the state, what is the justification for supplementing the deterrent force of the general criminal law with additional individualised deterrence?

It is helpful at this stage to distinguish between issues of substance and process. Let us consider first some points of substance. First, as noted earlier, some preventive orders may target conduct which does not otherwise constitute an offence. The conduct may well be remote from the commission of even an attempted offence. These preventive orders thus shift the focus of the law further back to stages before an attempt and address conduct which is merely preparatory for an offence, or which might simply provide an opportunity for an offence. In the case of ASBOs, examples of such conduct might include entering a local car park, or carrying a can of spray paint in public.[37] We would generally think of such conduct as innocuous in itself. When performed by the average

[31] The need for a justificatory framework for preventive measures is emphasised by Ashworth and Zedner 2010 (n 1 above) 71–73. On limiting principles see Ashworth and Zedner 2011 (n 14 above) 293 ff.

[32] Prevention of Crime Act 1953 s 1.

[33] Road Traffic Act 1988 s 2.

[34] Perjury Act 1911 s 1.

[35] Criminal Attempts Act 1981 s 1.

[36] See the Serious Crime Act 2007 pt 2.

[37] The last of these is an example given by Hooper LJ in *R v Boness* [2006] 1 Cr App R (S) 120 [35].

citizen it causes no harm and does not wrong anyone. However, the assumption underlying the use of preventive orders in these cases is that the conduct when performed by particular individuals may present an unacceptable risk of leading to further anti-social acts by the defendant which will cause or are likely to cause harassment alarm and distress to local residents. This is harm which Parliament has decreed to be a proper subject of criminal prohibition,[38] but the general criminal law may be perceived as too limited in its reach to provide adequate protection against it. Thus, the preventive order can be seen as addressing the *conditions* (in the form of the defendant's preliminary conduct) for the harm to occur rather than its more immediate causes. It aims to increase the preventive efficacy of the law by controlling the situations in which the harm is more likely to occur.

Are there any arguments from theory which might be deployed in support of the strategy of targeting such conduct remote from the harm in question? One argument might be that such conduct does in fact satisfy the harm principle when engaged in by the individual in question. We could consider Gardner and Shute's refinement of the harm principle:[39]

> It is no objection under the harm principle that a harmless action was criminalised, nor even that an action with no tendency to cause harm was criminalised. It is enough to meet the demands of the harm principle that, if the action were not criminalised, *that* would be harmful.

In this context we would not be using the formulation as a reason for prohibiting such conduct as part of the general criminal law. We would not be arguing that harm may ensue from others engaging in the conduct if it is not made criminal. We would not, in other words, be seeking to rely on a 'slippery slope' principle of criminalisation.[40] To take the ASBO examples mentioned above, an argument for general criminalisation would require us to ask whether it would be harmful to society not to criminalise the acts of entering a car park or carrying a can of paint in public. Would there be an increased risk of harm from these acts? Would, for example, people entering parks be likely to cause affrays or steal from cars, or would people be likely to make mistakes about other articles which they could legally carry in public? It seems plain that any such risks would be fanciful, or trivial at best. No harm is likely to result from such actions as people entering car parks, nor are people likely to make mistakes about the legality of other related actions. People generally know, for example, that while they may carry cans of paint in public, it is illegal to carry firearms or knives. A general prohibition could not therefore be justified by reference to this refinement of the harm principle.

[38] Public Order Act 1986 ss 4A and 5.

[39] J Gardner and S Shute, 'The Wrongness of Rape' in J Horder (ed), *Oxford Essays in Jurisprudence 4th Series* (Oxford, OUP, 2000) 193, 216.

[40] See J Rogers, 'Prosecutors, Courts and Conduct of the Accused Which Engages a Qualified Human Right' (2005) *Current Legal Problems* 101, 119.

However, we might claim that if a specific individual has demonstrated by prior conduct that there *is* an increased risk that he or she will cause harm under such conditions, the collective interest of the local community in security from harm from the individual will be undermined if the preventive order is not made. In other words, we might say that a form of harm occurs if this person may enter the car park or carry the paint can in public free of legal restraint. The welfare interest of the local community in freedom from harassment alarm and distress is set back. The concern would be that persons in the vicinity of the car park at the time should not feel harassed or alarmed or distressed about what might happen, or that local residents and others should not be similarly concerned about property being vandalised by graffiti.

A number of objections can be taken to an argument in this form. The first is that preventive orders which target conditions for causing harm take no account of the defendant's intentions. The defendant is prohibited from entering the car park or carrying a can of paint in public irrespective of whether he or she intends to cause any harm at the time. In this sense culpability as a requirement for making the order is immaterial. In contrast, the general law of attempt only penalises acts which are more than merely preparatory to the commission of a substantive offence, *and* only where the defendant intends to commit the offence. The individualised preventive order is therefore significantly wider in both respects. The second and related objection is that even if the defendant does intend to cause harm when entering the car park or carrying the paint, the preventive order provides no opportunity for a change of mind. There is no *locus poenitentiae*, no point where the defendant is permitted to think better of the proposed actions before the harm in question is done.

Third, building on these first two points, we now have to replay a familiar debate from the law of attempt. If we criminalise acts falling short of the complete substantive offence where do we stop? What are the proper limits of the law's power to interfere with a person's freedom of action? Defining the *actus reus* of an attempt is a problem that has bedevilled the criminal law for many years,[41] and numerous different tests have been suggested. The issue becomes even more acute in the case of preventive orders, which may have the effect of criminalising acts which are not necessarily preparation in any form for an offence. If we are to prohibit the defendant from entering the car park why should we not prevent him from leaving his house in the first place? Might not local residents suffer alarm and distress as soon as they see him emerge from his front door? If we are to prohibit the defendant from carrying a can of spray paint in public, why should we not prohibit him from buying or possessing spray paint in any circumstances? Targeting the conditions for harm to occur on the basis that not doing so is itself harmful creates a basis for intervention that has no clear principle of limitation compatible with the individual's freedom of

[41] RA Duff, *Criminal Attempts* (Oxford, OUP, 1996); CMV Clarkson, 'Attempt: The Conduct Requirement' (2009) 29 *Oxford Journal of Legal Studies* 25.

action. Indeed, the argument, if pressed to its logical conclusion, could entail restrictions on liberty amounting to virtual house arrest (as it has done in the case of control orders).

A similar conclusion could be reached using an alternative possibility for justifying preventive intervention against specific individuals which goes beyond the general criminal law. This is the 'precautionary principle'. As Zedner notes in chapter 10 of this volume, this principle was first developed in the context of environmental law, but has become a standard justifying principle for risk management in many spheres of government. Fisher explains it in these terms, 'where there is a threat to human health or environmental protection a lack of full scientific certainty should not be used as a reason to postpone measures that would prevent or minimise such a threat'.[42]

Human health and environmental protection are of course some distance from criminal justice in a state's responsibilities. They are hardly cognate concerns. And the uncertainty referred to in this statement of the precautionary principle is scientific uncertainty about cause and effect, not the uncertainty associated with the unpredictability of human wrongdoing. Preventive orders might be distinguished from the 'measures' referred to on either or both of these grounds. Nevertheless, as Fisher says, this is a public law principle.[43] It is capable of being generalised to legitimate regulatory action in many spheres of government. An argument might therefore be constructed that a person who can be shown to satisfy the conditions for a preventive order presents a sufficient risk to the security of others from harm to justify pre-emptive action by the state, despite the uncertainty whether the harm will in fact occur.[44] The precise preventive measures to be adopted would then depend on the nature, gravity and likelihood of the harm which the individual is thought to present a risk of causing. In an extreme case, such as the risk of a terrorist atrocity, imprisonment without trial or house arrest might be considered to be the only adequate preventive measures. This point is developed further below.

However, as with the harm principle discussed above, a number of objections present themselves. The risk assessment is likely to be objective; it does not necessarily require attention to the defendant's culpability. Of course, a proved intention to do harm is likely to increase the risk of the harm occurring, but the risk might be judged sufficient on the basis of the defendant's past conduct or current behaviour and associations, irrespective of his or her actual intentions when the order is made. Arguably, as a matter of principle, measures restricting

[42] E Fisher, *Risk Regulation and Administrative Constitutionalism* (Oxford, Hart Publishing, 2010) 40.

[43] ibid 41.

[44] In *A v Secretary of State for the Home Department* [2004] UKHL 56; [2005] 2 AC 68 Lord Bingham commented at [29]: 'Any prediction about the future behaviour of human beings (as opposed to the phases of the moon or high water at London Bridge) is necessarily problematical. Reasonable and informed minds may differ, and a judgment is not shown to be wrong or unreasonable because that which is thought likely to happen does not happen. It would have been irresponsible not to err, if at all, on the side of safety.'

a person's liberty, in ways not applicable to citizens generally, ought not to be imposed in the absence of evidence that the person intends to perpetrate the harms which the measures are intended to guard against.[45] Second, preventive measures targeted at the conditions in which the risk of harm is sufficiently present provide no opportunity for a change of intention. Failing to provide a *locus poenitentiae* is arguably failing to show the person the respect to which he or she should be entitled as a responsible citizen with the capacity to respond to the law's requirements by thinking better about their intended behaviour.[46] Third, risk assessements of future offending behaviour are notoriously problematic. I will not develop the point here, since it is the subject of the chapter by Lucia Zedner in this volume.[47] As she rightly concludes, '. . . [it is] worryingly clear that risk tools, risk data, and their interpretation are so contested as to render judgments based upon them a source of concern'.[48]

A second way in which the general criminal law may be considered inadequate to protect the security of the community is where a prosecution for a specific offence or offences may give an incomplete picture of the aggregate *impact* of the defendant's behaviour. This is another of the justifying arguments for ASBOs.[49] It was expressed in *R (McCann) v Manchester Crown Court* by Lord Hope in the following terms:

> . . . there are some individuals for whom respect for the law and for the rights of others has no meaning. Taken one by one, their criminal or sub-criminal acts may seem to be, and indeed often are, relatively trivial. But, taken together, the frequency and scale of their destructive and offensive conduct presents a quite different picture. So does the aggression and intimidation with which their acts are perpetrated. The social disruption which their behaviour creates is unacceptable. So too is the apparent inability of the criminal law to restrain their activities. This provides the background to the enactment of s. 1 of the Crime and Disorder Act 1998 with which your Lordships are concerned . . .[50]

From this standpoint a preventive order which addresses the defendant's conduct as a whole and which is backed up by a substantial penalty for breach is a justifiable supplement to the general criminal law's focus on individual offences. There is a parallel here with an argument that has sometimes been used to justify liability for the inchoate offence of conspiracy. It can be maintained that charging a person with being party to an agreement to pursue a systematic

[45] Or at least that the harm in question is almost certain to occur in the absence of such measures; for example, we might wish to justify quarantine for persons suffering from certain highly infectious or contagious diseases on this basis.

[46] RA Duff, *Criminal Attempts* (Oxford, OUP, 1996) 387–89.

[47] See also ch 11 in this volume by Martin Wasik, discussing the test of 'dangerousness' for the purposes of the statutory provisions for sentencing dangerous offenders.

[48] Andrew Ashworth has concluded after a review of the debate on the difficulty of predicting dangerousness that there is at best a 50% success rate, so that there is at least one false positive for every true positive: *Sentencing and Criminal Justice*, 4th edn (Cambridge, CUP, 2005) 215–16.

[49] Ashworth and Zedner 2010 (n 1 above) 66.

[50] *R (McCann) v Manchester Crown Court* [2003] 1 Cr App R 27 [42].

course of conduct involving the commission of many offences may give a more complete picture of the offending than charging a succession of separate offences. The attraction of this possibility for prosecutors is almost certainly part of the explanation for the continued survival of the common law offence of conspiracy to defraud.[51] The parallel is not of course exact since the acts which are relied on to support an application for an ASBO may not be offences at all, but the underlying idea is the same.

A third point of substance concerns the point made above concerning the use of preventive orders as a means of *incapacitation* of the defendant. These are cases where the risk of harm from the defendant is perceived to be high, both in terms of its likelihood of occurrence and its severity if it does occur, but there is no or insufficient disclosable evidence to prosecute the defendant for a substantive offence or an attempt. This risk assessment may be coupled with a perception that neither the deterrents offered by the general criminal law nor a deterrent preventive order addressing the conditions for causing harm is likely to be effective. An order incapacitating the defendant from causing harm may then be seen as the only solution. This has been the Government's strategy in relation to suspected terrorists. As is well known, after 9/11 the Government introduced detention without trial for foreign suspected international terrorists.[52] Subsequently in the 'Belmarsh' case the House of Lords ruled the power to be unlawful because it was disproportionate and discriminatory.[53] The Government then fell back on a form of house arrest represented by a 'control order'. Through a battery of restrictions, including a home curfew of up to 16 hours a day, control orders are designed to make it as physically difficult as possible for a defendant to engage in terrorist activities. We will return to the objections to control orders, and their future after the recent government review, later in this chapter. However, it is worth noting at this stage the important point that incapacitating the defendant by house arrest makes the process of gathering evidence against him of participating in terrorist offences more difficult, if not impossible.[54] In that sense house arrest is an inferior alternative to intensive surveillance.

A fourth point concerns preventive orders as an adjunct to sentencing powers on conviction for an offence. There may be a perception that the defendant is unlikely to be deterred by the punishment for the offence from a repetition of the type of conduct in question. In such cases an individualised prohibition, targeted at the circumstances in which the conduct is likely to occur, may do three things. It may encourage the defendant to pay more attention to the law's requirements by providing an additional reason for not engaging in a repetition

[51] See the discussion of conspiracy to defraud in Smith and Hogan, *Criminal Law*, 12th edn (Oxford, OUP, 2008) 419–29.

[52] Anti-terrorism Crime and Security Act 2001 pt 4.

[53] *A v Secretary of State for the Home Department* [2004] UKHL 56; [2005] 2 AC 68.

[54] The point is well made by Lord Macdonald of River Glaven QC in the report referred to in n 19 above.

of the offence. It thus reinforces the specific deterrent effect of the punishment for the offence. Second, it may help the defendant not to repeat the offence by spelling out in detail the specific acts that the defendant should not do. Third, it may decrease the likelihood of the offence by restricting the defendant's opportunities to commit it. Sexual offence prevention orders, which, for example, prohibit the defendant from loitering in the vicinity of schools, or restrict the defendant's use of the internet,[55] are founded on this rationale. Again, such orders tend to address the conditions in which the harm may occur, and thereby aim to reduce the likelihood of its occurrence. We should note also the importance of the power of arrest in this context. Since breach of the order is an offence, for which the defendant may be arrested,[56] the police will be able to intervene at a preliminary stage, perhaps well before the defendant has reached the stage of an attempt, let alone the complete offence.

Turning to matters of process, several commentators have noted that civil preventive orders (those made on application to the court rather than on conviction) are not subject to the due process safeguards of the criminal law.[57] Because the applications do not involve the determination of a criminal charge, the fair trial rights under article 6(2) and (3) of the European Convention on Human Rights (ECHR) are not engaged. Nor do the strict rules of criminal evidence apply. This means that in particular hearsay evidence will be generally admissible to prove the matters of fact forming the qualifying conditions for the order. The point has been seen as critically important where the witnesses to those facts are too frightened as a result of intimidation or fear of reprisals to give oral testimony of the facts. A related point is that where witnesses are frightened it may be difficult for the police to assemble sufficient evidence on sufficient charges to convey the persistence and scale of the defendant's conduct; both points help to account for the creation of ASBOs as civil orders made on application to a magistrates' court.

However, it is important to note that applications for preventive orders backed by criminal sanctions for breach are not wholly governed by the rules of civil process. They are legal hybrids or crossovers, and the courts have recognised this by inventing a form of hybrid process. While the rules of *admissibility* of evidence are those applicable to civil litigation, the rules on *burden and standard of proof* are in effect those of the criminal process. So it has been held that in applications for ASBOS, allegations of criminal or quasi-criminal conduct which, if proved, would have serious consequences for the defendant, must be proved to the criminal standard of beyond reasonable doubt.[58] Similarly, a court hearing an application for a football banning order, which requires proof that the defendant has caused or contributed to any violence or disorder in the

[55] See I Walden and M Wasik, 'The Internet: Access Controlled!' (2011) *Criminal Law Review* 377.

[56] Police and Criminal Evidence Act 1984 s 24.

[57] See, for example, Simester and von Hirsch (n 6 above) 175; Ashworth and Zedner 2010 (n 1 above) 67.

[58] *R (McCann) v Manchester Crown Court* [2003] 1 Cr App R 27 [37], [82].

United Kingdom or elsewhere, should apply 'an exacting standard [of proof] that will, in practice, be hard to distinguish from the criminal standard'.[59]

III CRITICISMS OF PREVENTIVE ORDERS

A Process Issues

Let us continue with the issue of process just mentioned. Critics have argued that it is unfair that characterising preventive orders as civil orders results in the avoidance of the due process safeguards of the criminal law. Ashworth, for example, objects to ASBOs on a number of grounds; one of his principal concerns is the use of civil orders to bypass the protections given to defendants in the criminal process by article 6(2) and (3) of the ECHR.[60] Simester and von Hirsch make a similar point, arguing that the criminal proof rules ought to apply where the consequences for the defendant, in terms of substantial curtailment of liberty, are comparable in their impact to a criminal sanction for an offence.[61]

These objections are well made, but they are persuasive only up to a point. The differences between civil and criminal evidence rules can be overstated in this context. This is because of two factors which reduce the impact of the formal differences. The first is that, as noted above, the courts have blurred the distinction between civil and criminal process by devising a hybrid procedure whereby the rule to be applied to the standard of proof is the criminal and not the civil rule. Where this applies, as in the case of ASBOs, the factual allegations which constitute one of the grounds for making the order must be proved beyond reasonable doubt, or in other words so that the court is sure that they are made out. The criminal standard of proof is one of the major safeguards against epistemic error in criminal proceedings and consequent miscarriage of justice.[62] Its adoption for applications for preventive orders thus represents an important protection against their unfair use, a protection which helps to legitimise their availability.

Second, although the rules of admissibility of evidence are the less stringent rules of civil process, this is not such a disadvantage to defendants as it used to be. This is because recent reforms to the law of criminal evidence, carried out in the name of 'rebalancing' the system, have relaxed the strictness of the former law and made it less favourable to defendants.[63] Evidence that a few years ago

[59] *Gough v Chief Constable of Derbyshire* [2002] 2 All ER 985 [90].

[60] AJ Ashworth, 'Social Control and "Anti-Social Behaviour": The Subversion of Human Rights?' (2004) 120 *LQR* 263.

[61] See n 2 179.

[62] I Dennis, *The Law of Evidence*, 4th edn (London, Sweet & Maxwell, 2010) 455–57.

[63] This is not to say that the reforms are not controversial in this respect. However, the introduction of special measures for vulnerable and intimidated witnesses was widely welcomed, and the changes to the hearsay rule largely followed recommendations of the Law Commission in a lengthy report (Law Com No 245, 1997) following extensive public consultation.

would have been excluded or unavailable is now more likely to be admitted for the prosecution. This is important in relation to frightened and intimidated witnesses. Hearsay evidence from such witnesses is now more easily admissible, thanks to the enlarged exceptions to the hearsay rule in the Criminal Justice Act 2003, particularly section 116 and the new general discretion to admit hearsay in the 'interests of justice'.[64] Special measures protections for vulnerable and intimidated witnesses were introduced for criminal proceedings in 1999,[65] and have now been extended to applications for ASBOs.[66] Special measures are supplemented by the availability of statutory orders for witnesses to give evidence anonymously.[67] In these ways the rules of criminal evidence present fewer barriers to proof of facts from frightened witnesses than they used to. However, there does remain a major issue whether the use of hearsay and anonymous evidence in criminal proceedings is limited by a rule derived from the jurisprudence of the European Court of Human Rights that it must not be the 'sole or decisive' evidence.[68] The Supreme Court has rejected the rule, but we still await the Strasbourg reaction to that rejection.

One issue of due process which has presented great difficulty is the question of disclosure. This has been a particular problem for control orders. The process of making and reviewing control orders does not involve the determination of a criminal charge, since the purpose of a control order is preventive and not punitive.[69] This means that the defence rights under article 6(2) and (3) of the ECHR are not engaged. However, it has been held that at common law and under article 6(1) the defendant has a right to a fair hearing which includes a right to be aware of the case he or she has to meet.[70] Consequently, an issue arises about the content of a fair procedure for this purpose, and in particular how far the Home Secretary must disclose to the defendant the reasons for suspecting him of involvement in terrorism-related activity. If the defendant does not know the reasons – that is, the case against him – he plainly faces a major handicap in challenging it. The problem of course is that the Home Secretary may not wish to make full disclosure if that would tend to reveal sensitive information such as surveillance techniques, or the use of undercover agents, or information received from foreign intelligence agencies.

The procedure devised to resolve this dilemma creates a distinction between 'open' and 'closed' material. Open material can be disclosed to the defendant and his lawyers and examined in open court. Closed material may not be dis-

[64] Criminal Justice Act 2003 s 114(1)(d), discussed by Dennis (n 62 above) 765–71.

[65] Youth Justice and Criminal Evidence Act 1999 ss 16–33; Dennis (n 62 above) 641–55.

[66] Serious Organised Crime and Police Act 2005 inserting s 11 into the Crime and Disorder Act 1998. This development represents a further hybridisation of process in ASBO applications.

[67] Coroners and Justice Act 2009 pt 3 ch 2; Dennis (n 62 above) 655–60.

[68] See *R v Horncastle* [2009] UKSC 14, discussing *Al-Khawaja and Tahery v UK* (2009) 49 EHRR 1. See further Dennis (n 62 above) 773–82.

[69] *Secretary of State for the Home Department v MB* [2007] UKHL 46; [2008] 1 All ER 657.

[70] ibid, as explained in *Secretary of State for the Home Department v AF (No 3)* [2009] UKHL 28; [2009] 3 All ER 643.

closed to the defendant or his lawyers and will be examined by the court in closed session in the absence of the defendant and his lawyers. The defendant's interests are safeguarded by the appointment of special security-cleared counsel to examine the material on his behalf. The counsel can consult with the defendant and his lawyers before counsel sees the closed material but may not do so afterwards.

The use of this procedure was challenged in the House of Lords in *Secretary of State for the Home Department v AF (No 3)*.[71] Following the earlier decision of the European Court of Human Rights in *A v United Kingdom*,[72] the House of Lords held that a controlled person had to be given sufficient information about the allegations against him to enable him to give effective instructions in relation to the allegations. This was regarded in effect as a core principle – a minimum and non-negotiable requirement of natural justice. The House went on to say that if this requirement is satisfied the defendant does not necessarily have to be provided with the details or the sources of the evidence which form the basis of the allegations. However, where the open material consisted only of general allegations and the case against him rested solely or decisively on closed material, the requirement of a fair trial could not be satisfied however strong the closed material might be. The use of special counsel was not regarded as an adequate counter-balancing measure for non-disclosure, given that counsel could not take further instructions from the defendant after viewing the closed material.

This was a strong decision, emphasising the importance of the defendant's right to know the case against him as a process right, irrespective of the strength of the case against him. The Home Secretary argued that disclosure was unnecessary where it could not affect the result because the case on the closed material was overwhelming. The House of Lords firmly rejected this, partly because 'you can never know for sure', partly because justice had to be seen to be done, in order to maintain public confidence in the law (especially in the relevant community from which the defendant came), and partly as a matter of principle founded on respect for the rule of law. Accordingly the decision placed a question mark over the validity of all control orders where a significant part of the case against the defendant resides in closed material.

B Substantive Issues

We have noted already a number of objections that can be made against the use of preventive orders as a supplement to the general criminal law. We can now

[71] *Secretary of State for the Home Department v AF (No 3)* [2009] UKHL 28; [2009] 3 All ER 643.

[72] *A v United Kingdom* (2009) 49 EHRR 29. This case concerned not control orders but certification and detention of the applicant as a suspected international terrorist under (the now repealed) part 4 of the Anti-terrorism Crime and Security Act 2001. However, the same point arose as to the compatibility of the disclosure procedure with the rights of the defendant under the ECHR to challenge the legality of the executive action against him.

turn to a number of other concerns which critics have raised about the criminalisation of conduct which is the subject of a preventive order. Simester and von Hirsch have argued that the orders bypass a number of constraints imposed by the general criminal law on the state's use of moral censure of its citizens.[73] First, they note that the orders involve individual criminalisation imposed by a judicial officer, not a representative authority such as Parliament. This is said to be objectionable on rule-of-law grounds; it delegates too much discretion to administrative officials and magistrates to affect significantly the personal freedoms of citizens, and does this in the absence of an adequate regulatory framework for the exercise of the power.

As with the due process objection, there is force in this point about the danger of uncontrolled lawmaking discretion, but how much force is debatable. If one looks, for example, at the conditions for the imposition of an ASBO, we find two. The first is that the applicant for an ASBO must prove (to the criminal standard) that the defendant has acted 'in an anti-social manner, that is to say, in a manner that caused or was likely to cause harassment alarm or distress to one or more persons not of the same household as himself'.[74] The second is that [the order] 'is necessary to protect relevant persons from further anti-social acts by him'.[75]

In applying these conditions the courts have inserted a threshold seriousness limitation: 'the power is not meant to be used in cases of minor unacceptable behaviour but in cases which satisfy the threshold of persistent and serious anti-social behaviour'.[76] They have also stressed that the order must be *necessary* to prevent further anti-social behaviour,[77] and that the judgment of necessity must be founded on relevant supporting facts. A conviction for an offence without more, even an offence of robbery, may not be enough to show that the ASBO is necessary.[78] Such statements might suggest that the courts, or at least the higher courts, exercise the power to make a preventive order with a considerable degree of caution, and moreover that they are prepared to provide additional elements to the incomplete regulatory framework that Parliament enacted.

A second criticism is that criminalisation via a preventive order is, unlike the *general* criminal law, targeted at particular individuals. In this way it violates the principle of equality before the law; there is in effect one rule for the defendant and another for everyone else.[79] Furthermore, such orders may be perceived as discriminatory if the targeted individuals belong to unpopular minority groups. This argument is superficially attractive, but it needs scrutiny. The initial prem-

[73] Simester and von Hirsch (n 6 above) 179–81. I accept that the imposition of a preventive order, or at least of most preventive orders, will have a stigmatising effect on the defendant, albeit not perhaps as great as that involved in conviction for an offence.

[74] Crime and Disorder Act 1998 s 1(1)(a).

[75] ibid s 1(1)(b).

[76] *R (McCann) v Manchester Crown Court* [2003] 1 Cr App R 27 [25] (Lord Steyn).

[77] *R v Boness* [2006] 1 Cr App R (S) 120.

[78] *R v Wadmore* [2006] 2 Cr App R (S) 110.

[79] See Simester and von Hirsch (n 6 above) 181.

ise is at least debatable. Preventive orders *are* akin to the general criminal law in the sense that they represent a legal resource available for use against any citizen who meets the qualifying conditions. It is not the case that they may be used only against specified groups such as the residents of a particular housing estate, or Muslims, or persons with shaven heads and tattoos. It might be said therefore that a preventive order can only be 'earned' by the defendant's relevant conduct, not by virtue of his identity or membership of a particular target group. Similarly, a prosecution and punishment for an offence can only be 'earned' by criminal behaviour. I use the term 'earned' advisedly because it helps to explain why in some circles possession of an ASBO is said to be a mark of street credibility; it amounts to official certification that the defendant's conduct marks him or her out as dangerous.

It is of course true that the effect of a prohibition may be to prevent the defendant from doing things that may be done freely by others, and in that sense there is a formal inequality. However, the force of the point is lessened by the justification that the prohibition is founded on a judgment that the defendant's previous conduct presents a risk of harm that is not apparent from the conduct of others. The defendant is not therefore being treated unequally in the sense of being singled out without legal justification, although of course there may be dispute whether this kind of justification should be acceptable. At the same time I would not wish to deny that preventive orders are capable, like all legal powers, of being used in practice in a discriminatory way.[80] This is why ongoing empirical research into their use is essential to inform debate as to whether the legal frameworks and the conditions for their application are satisfactory.[81]

Simester and von Hirsch reinforce their complaint of inequality with a further point that individual prohibitions are not always targeted at conduct that constitutes a 'wrong'. In relation to ASBOs, for example, they comment that:

> the definition of qualifying 'anti-social' behaviour is expressed purely in terms of the reactions of the audience: conduct done 'in a manner that caused or was likely to cause harassment, alarm or distress to one or more persons not of the same household'. As such, it exposes D to the risk that his unconventional behaviour, which wrongs no one, may lead to a personal order purely because it causes, or is likely to cause, distress or alarm in others – whether or not that distress is appropriate or justified.[82]

The authors appear to have in mind the idea of 'wrong' as a violation of a legal right, although this is not entirely clear since in the following paragraph they refer to a wrong in the civil law context as a violation of P's rights *or* a failure by D to perform as promised. The use of the alternative here raises the question

[80] There is an obvious analogy with 'stop and search' powers, which also have a partly preventive rationale, and which research suggests have been used disproportionately against members of certain ethnic minorities; see A Sanders, R Young and M Burton, *Criminal Justice*, 4th edn (Oxford, OUP, 2010) ch 2.

[81] See, for example, L Koffman, 'The Use of Anti-Social Behaviour Orders: An Empirical Study of a New Deal for Communities Area' (2006) *Criminal Law Review* 593.

[82] Simester and von Hirsch (n 6 above) 185.

whether a moral wrong is sufficient. However, the import of the quoted passage seems to be that there should be no legal right not to suffer harassment alarm or distress without appropriate justification. This much can be conceded, and is recognised in section 1(5) of the Crime and Disorder Act 1998 which disqualifies from consideration any act of the defendant which he or she shows was reasonable in the circumstances. Although the reverse onus in this provision is objectionable in principle,[83] the objective limitation on the scope of the power to make a preventive order is welcome. As the authors note, this still leaves open the possibility that an ASBO might be made against a person whose conduct is unreasonable and distressing, but which is not a 'wrong' against anyone. The example is given of a woman who repeatedly attempted suicide by throwing herself into a river. It is suggested that this kind of self-regarding conduct should not be regarded as coming within the concept of 'anti-social' behaviour; it does not attack or endanger the objective security of others, or display an attitude of contempt for their welfare. An ASBO should not be made in these circumstances.[84]

A final point of substance concerns the failure of the empowering legislation to incorporate a requirement of proportionality, both in the making of the initial order and in relation to sentencing for breach of the order. This has been partly answered by the ruling of the Court of Appeal in *R v Stevens*,[85] to the effect that the sentence for breach of the order must be proportionate to the seriousness of the breach. If the conduct which constitutes the breach also constitutes a separate offence, the maximum for that offence will be relevant to the judgment of proportionality. However, the Court also confirmed that breach of the order is an offence in its own right, therefore it is not wrong in principle for a sentencer to give a custodial sentence even where an offence constituted by the breach (eg public drunkenness) would be punishable only with a fine.

IV REVIEWING PREVENTIVE ORDERS: WHERE DO WE GO FROM HERE?

As noted above, the Government has recently reviewed control orders and ASBOs, the two most high-profile and controversial civil preventive orders. I will deal first with the review of control orders, a review which formed part of a larger review of counter-terrorism and security powers.[86] Control orders have

[83] See I Dennis, 'Reverse Onuses and the Presumption of Innocence: In Search of Principle' (2005) *Criminal Law Review* 901; A Ashworth, 'Four Threats to the Presumption of Innocence' (2006) 10 *International Journal of Evidence and Proof* 241.

[84] The issues presented by mentally disordered defendants in this context, whose behaviour may well cause neighbours alarm and distress, are complex and will have to be left for another occasion.

[85] *R v Stevens* [2006] 2 Cr App R (S) 68. See further the Definitive Guideline issued by the Sentencing Guidelines Council, 'Breach of an Anti-Social Behaviour Order' (Sentencing Guidelines Council, 2008).

[86] 'Review of Counter-Terrorism and Security Powers' (Cm 8004, TSO, 2011). See also the accompanying Report on the Review by Lord Macdonald of River Glaven QC (Cm 8003).

been a key element of counter-terrorism strategy since 2005, although in purely numerical terms very few orders have been made. In total, 48 orders had been made up to the end of 2010, of which 28 were against foreign nationals and 20 against UK citizens. At the end of 2010, eight orders were still in force, all against UK citizens. The 'success' of control orders is hard to measure: the review noted that seven controlees absconded in 2006–07, which it acknowledged meant that the regime had not been fully effective in containing suspected terrorists. Nevertheless, the review maintained that the control order regime had had success in mitigating risk, and that there is a continuing need to control the activities of 'terrorists' [sic] who can neither be successfully prosecuted nor deported. Accordingly it is proposed to retain this form of preventive order, albeit with 'more precisely focused and targeted restrictions, supported by increased covert investigative resources'.[87] This, it is said, will still mitigate risk while increasing civil liberties.

This strategy received the endorsement of Lord Macdonald, the former Director of Public Prosecutions (DPP), who was commissioned to report on the review's process and outcomes. However, Lord Macdonald's report contained a strong warning that any replacement for control orders should not repeat the mistake of 'warehousing' suspected terrorists, with such tight restrictions on their movements and associations that the gathering of evidence against them becomes difficult or even impossible. His message was simple and powerful: if prosecution, conviction and imprisonment of terrorists remains the principal goal of public policy, as the review suggested, then measures taken in the interests of public safety, against suspects who cannot currently be successfully prosecuted, should be designed to further that goal and not frustrate it. Accordingly, he proposed that restrictions would require authorisation by a court (as recommended by the Review), and authorisation should be given only where the Home Secretary has reasonable ground to believe that a named individual is engaged in terrorist activity, and in the view of the DPP a criminal investigation into that individual is justified. The restrictions imposed, which 'would be closer in character to bail conditions', would be linked to the needs of the investigation and permit the individual to continue a typical pattern of life as far as compatible with public safety.

How, precisely, control orders will change remains to be seen. If the proposals of the review and of Lord Macdonald are followed through it seems likely that the most intrusive and restrictive features of control orders will be dropped. There will be an end to the forced relocation of controlees,[88] and to lengthy curfews. Greater freedom of communication and association will be permitted, with only limited restrictions on, for example, use of the internet. Orders will be time-limited to two years, and the police will be under a duty to keep the person's conduct under continual review with a view to bringing a prosecution

[87] 'Review of Counter-Terrorism and Security Powers' (Cm 8004, TSO, 2011) para 20.

[88] The Supreme Court had already dealt a heavy blow to this feature in *Secretary of State for the Home Department v AP* [2010] UKSC 24; [2010] 4 All ER 245.

if and when possible. Whether these or similar adjustments would be enough to satisfy the critics is doubtful. While noting some of the criticisms of principle discussed above, the review did not seriously engage with them, essentially accepting the risk-based justification for this form of preventive order. A striking omission from the review is any attempt to compute the cost of the very extensive litigation to which control orders have given rise. Given the small number of orders made, it would be instructive to know the average direct and indirect cost of each one to the public purse.

We can now turn to ASBOs. It is useful to look first at the statistics on the use of ASBOs and their breach. In 2010 the Ministry of Justice published figures covering ASBOs during the period from 1 April 1999 to 31 December 2008.[89] The total number issued was 17,000, with a high point of 4,122 in 2005, since when the annual figure has been declining. More ASBOs are issued following conviction for an offence than following an application – almost two thirds following conviction in 2008. As regards breach, more than half (55 per cent) have been breached at least once. If an ASBO is breached, it is breached an average of 4.2 times. There is a striking difference in rates of breach according to the age of the defendant. 65 per cent of child defendants aged between 10 and 17 breached their ASBOs, compared with 49 per cent of adult defendants.

If the object of an ASBO is to promote security and prevent harm,[90] these figures are not encouraging, particularly in relation to children. In crude terms ASBOs fail in two out of three cases involving children.[91] Perhaps this is not surprising. ASBOs, like all the preventive orders, address defendants as rational self-interested actors. They seek to deter them from the prohibited conduct by threats of penalties for breach. However, this is a problematic strategy in relation to children. The behaviour of many children is impulsive, heedless of consequence and heavily influenced by peer pressure and their home environment. If this is allied to rebelliousness, defiance of authority and any status attached to being considered dangerous, a deterrent strategy devised for risk-averse adults is quite likely to fail. The psychology of the law in this respect is plainly deficient.

The Home Office review of ASBOs is part of a wider review of the 'toolkit' available to the police and other agencies to deal with anti-social behaviour in general.[92] This review is even more pragmatic than the review of control orders. It does not engage with the concept of anti-social behaviour, preferring to

[89] 'Statistical Notice: Anti-Social Behaviour Order (ASBO) Statistics England and Wales 2008', available at http://rds.homeoffice.gov.uk/rds/antisocial1.html.

[90] That is, harm in the statutory form of harassment alarm and distress. I cannot pursue in this chapter the question whether these matters are properly regarded as 'harm' for the purposes of criminalisation debates.

[91] The claim that a high rate of breach signifies failure of the preventive strategy might be contested on the basis that breach may allow for interventions which prevent more serious harm from occurring. This can be conceded, although the point is necessarily speculative.

[92] 'More Effective Responses to Anti-Social Behaviour – A Consultation' (Home Office, 2011).

accept the statutory definition[93] and describing such behaviour in general terms as 'covering a broad range of crime, disorder and nuisance'. It does not address the criticisms of principle discussed above, nor does it consider the principles developed by the courts for the use of ASBOs or for sentencing for breach of them. Its focus is squarely on the legal remedies against anti-social behaviour as a widely-defined social problem. It therefore accepts a need for preventive measures against the risk of further harm, noting that ASBOs were intended to provide an alternative to prosecution where it was difficult to prove the commission of an offence, and a means of addressing the cumulative impact of an individual's ongoing behaviour.

Within its limited focus, this review then takes a more radical line than the review of control orders. It finds that there are too many 'tools', that some (including the ASBO) are bureaucratic, slow and expensive, and that the high rate of breach is suggestive of failure of their preventive function. Accordingly, it proposes to reduce the number of tools and to simplify their operation.

As noted above, most ASBOs are in practice made on conviction for an offence (this is the 'criminal' ASBO or CRASBO). Such an order is an adjunct to the sentence for the offence, and aims to give the offender detailed instructions as to acts to be avoided in future. The review proposes to retain this form of civil preventive order, but to relabel it as a 'Criminal Behaviour Order'. It should be available to the court on the same basis as at present (ie when the test in s 1 of the Crime and Disorder Act 1998 is satisfied), but with the difference that the court would be able to impose positive requirements on an offender as well as prohibitions. Positive obligations could require the offender to take action to address underlying causes of their behaviour. This is sensible, provided the obligations imposed are proportionate to the risk presented by the behaviour in question.

In relation to the non-criminal ASBO the review has a stronger proposal. This is to keep the concept of a civil preventive order, but to abolish the criminal sanction for breach. The ASBO would become a wholly civil order instead of the current hybrid.[94] It would be known as a 'Crime Prevention Injunction' (CPI), and would replace, in addition to the ASBO, a number of other current orders, namely anti-social behaviour injunctions, intervention orders and individual support orders. Like the proposed Criminal Behaviour Order, a CPI would be able to include positive requirements as well as prohibitions. The review anticipates that breach of a CPI would usually incur liability for a civil contempt, but would not result in a criminal conviction. In accordance with the usual rule,[95] a civil contempt would need to be proved beyond reasonable doubt. At the time of writing the review is out to consultation, so it remains to be seen whether this recommendation is taken further. There is certainly much to be

[93] Crime and Disorder Act 1998 s 1.

[94] A cogent case for this development was made by S Hoffman and S Macdonald, 'Should ASBOs be Civilized?' (2010) *Criminal Law Review* 457.

[95] *Re Bramblevale Ltd* [1970] Ch 128.

said for it as a reform measure, particularly if jurisdiction over CPIs for children is to be given to the Youth Court, which has the appropriate level of expertise in dealing with child offenders.

V CONCLUSION

This chapter has discussed the use of civil preventive orders as a technique of safeguarding security against perceived risks of harm arising from the conduct of certain dangerous or anti-social individuals. Its focus has been primarily on control orders and ASBOs, because these are the subjects of most of the critical literature on preventive orders. We have examined the arguments used to justify the orders and the main criticisms of principle levelled at the orders. While the criticisms have been well made and have an undoubted degree of cogency, they are not always compelling, particularly in the light of the handling by the courts of both types of order. The critics might of course claim that the courts have simply made bad law a bit less bad, and that it remains objectionable in principle. However, I suggest that the judicial modifications to the original schemes for control orders and ASBOs are significant and have been very largely accepted by government. The recent reviews suggest that, despite its difficulties, the precautionary principle will continue to form the basis of government policy, and so we may expect both types of order to survive, albeit perhaps in a less restrictive and punitive form.

It remains to note that there are numerous other types of preventive order which have not attracted anything like the same degree of criticism despite sharing many of the characteristics of control orders and ASBOs. Why might this be so? Space does not permit an extended discussion, but I will close with a few brief reflections. One group of preventive orders consists of disqualifications from certain activities which may be made on conviction for certain offences. Disqualification from driving is a well-known sanction for drink-driving, and in addition courts have general powers under sections 146 and 147 of the Powers of Criminal Courts (Sentencing) Act 2000 to disqualify on conviction for offences not necessarily connected with the driving of motor-vehicles. Prohibitions from driving for a given period in these circumstances seem to have been generally accepted. Certainly the possibility of receiving such an order has undoubtedly changed the behaviour of many drivers. Such acceptance might be rationalised on the basis that the central cases of disqualification are for driving-related offences and so the order is in effect an element of a justly deserved penalty for abusing the privilege of driving and placing the lives of other road users at serious risk.

Similarly offences connected with the formation or management of companies may result in the disqualification of the defendant from being a company director. Acting in breach of the disqualification order is an either way offence. The order may again be acceptable as a deserved penalty for abuse of a privilege, coupled with a perception that fraud and related offences in the management of companies present serious risks to the interests of creditors, shareholders and employees.

Orders which bar persons from working with children and vulnerable adults where a person has engaged in 'relevant conduct' represent a distinct category of preventive order. This category includes the three types of order which can be made under the Sexual Offences Act 2003, namely sexual offences prevention orders, foreign travel orders and risk of sexual harm orders.[96] All these orders aim to reduce the risk of sexual abuse of potential victims by targeting opportunities for the abuse to occur. Like ASBOs, they may considerably restrict the freedom of the defendants to use public space and meet with other persons, but unlike ASBOs they do not seem to have attracted the same degree of adverse comment. This may be because they are frequently aimed at child abusers, or users of child pornography, and the protection of children at serious risk from paedophiles is of course regarded as a major social priority. The far greater degree of harm involved provides a persuasive reason for regarding such orders differently from ASBOs. Control orders, by contrast, also concern very serious harm, but the restrictions on liberty imposed by the sex offence orders are much less severe, which again provides a reason for treating them as less objectionable. However, we should bear in mind in any debate about preventive orders that the more serious and stigmatic the behaviour in question, the more essential it is to ensure that appropriate tests of necessity and proportionality are rigorously applied to the preventive measures sought.

[96] For discussion see S Shute, 'The Sexual Offences Act 2003: New Civil Preventative Orders' (2004) *Criminal Law Review* 417.

9

Imprisonment under the Precautionary Principle

PETER RAMSAY*

IMPRISONMENT FOR PUBLIC Protection (IPP) was a penal regime enacted under the government of New Labour in 2003 and repealed within a decade. IPP subjected offenders who were assessed as dangerous to indeterminate sentences that ended only when the parole board assessed them as safe to release. From a practical point of view, the implementation of this regime left a lot to be desired. By 2011, IPP sentences were being handed down at the rate of 800 a year, more than 6,500 offenders were in prison under their terms, and the Ministry of Justice calculated that these offenders would comprise more than 10 per cent of the prison population by 2015.[1] The numbers of offenders involved represented a huge short-term and long-term financial burden for a cash-strapped prison system. Moreover, the capacity of the prison service to provide IPP prisoners with opportunities to show that they were safe to release was overwhelmed, leading to embarrassing legal challenges.[2]

At the time of writing, the Coalition Government has put proposals to abolish IPP to Parliament.[3] The Ministry of Justice plan is to replace IPP with a combination of extended determinate sentences for dangerous offenders and a mandatory life sentence for a smaller group of very serious offenders. The substitute sentences share some of the characteristics of IPP, although their effect will be less dramatic.

Here I want to explore two of the key characteristics of IPP: the presumption of dangerousness maintained against the sentenced offender and punishment for the wrong of dangerousness. Both these features are retained in the proposed

* I am particularly grateful to Jill Peay and Suke Wolton for their comments on a draft, to John Stanton-Ife for his comments on my presentation of the argument at the University College London seminar, and to Timothy Bradshaw for pointing out an error in my understanding of Christian doctrine. The opinions and remaining errors are my own.

[1] Ken Clarke, Minister of Justice, HC Deb 1 Nov 2011 c787.

[2] *R(Wells) v Parole Board; R (Walker) v Secretary of State for the Home Department* [2008] 1 All ER 138; *James, Lee and Wells v Secretary of State for Justice* [2010] 1 AC 553.

[3] Legal Aid, Sentencing and Punishment of Offenders Bill cls 113–17. In what follows I assume that these proposals will be successfully enacted and refer to IPP in the past tense.

mandatory life sentence, while punishment for dangerousness remains an aspect of the proposed extended determinate sentence. I want in particular to explore one possible justification for the presumption of dangerousness. My aim is not to justify any of these sentences, but rather to understand better how they are in practice legitimated. On the one hand, the retention of the presumption of dangerousness in the mandatory life sentence suggests that it continues to enjoy a degree of legitimacy notwithstanding IPP's abolition. On the other, the IPP debacle suggests that there may be certain practicality constraints to this 'precautionary sentencing'.

In exploring precautionary sentencing I will be taking a path through territory that may be more familiar to criminologists than to penal theorists and criminal lawyers. Part of my argument will be that in order to understand the political legitimacy enjoyed by incapacitation in the present, we need to grasp the high degree of scepticism that prevails with respect to longstanding philosophical justifications of punishment.

In the first part of the chapter I argue that IPP can be understood as the application of the precautionary principle to sentencing. I will outline the legal essentials of IPP, considering in more detail the legal test of dangerousness that had to be satisfied before the sentence was imposed and the effective presumption of dangerousness that had to be overcome before the sentence would end. I then give a brief account of the precautionary principle as it has been developed in the sphere of environmental regulation and show that decision-making in IPP was consistent with it. After that I will analyse and elaborate on the arguments for protective sentencing given in the Floud Report, in order to show how applying the precautionary principle to sentencing dangerous prisoners might be justified as punishment for a wrong of dangerousness.

In the second part of the chapter I will argue that it would be a mistake to understand precautionary sentencing as nothing more than a return of traditional consequentialist justifications of punishment. I will suggest that the critical difference between them is the position they ascribe to knowledge, and that this difference indicates that the precautionary principle has arisen at a specific historical moment in which the humanist beliefs that underpin rationalist ethics, like those of utilitarianism, have lost influence. Moreover, I will suggest that the precautionary principle is part of a 'moral order' that has arisen as a direct consequence of the decline of humanism, an order that appears to derive its ethical persuasiveness from a peculiar recycling of older doctrines, combining moral pluralism with a naturalised reworking of the Christian religious imagination.

In the third part I will briefly consider the Coalition Government's reasons for abolishing IPP and the proposed replacement sentences. I will outline the equivocal character of official pronouncements about IPP and argue that the new regime represents not so much a principled rejection of precautionary sentencing as a retreat from some of the practical difficulties that precautionary logic imposes in the criminal justice context.

I IMPRISONMENT FOR PUBLIC PROTECTION

Under the provisions of the Criminal Justice Act 2003 (as amended by the Criminal Justice and Immigration Act 2008), any offender who was convicted of one of a specified range of violent or sexual offences *and* was judged to represent 'a significant risk to members of the public of serious harm occasioned by the commission by him of further specified offences', was liable to a life sentence, 'imprisonment for public protection' or an 'extended sentence' depending on the precise nature of the offence. Extended sentences added periods of release on licence to the normal sentence and were subject to upper limits. We will not consider them further here.[4]

A life sentence or a sentence of imprisonment for public protection could be imposed where the offender who had been adjudged to represent a significant risk of serious harm had also been convicted of an offence that carries a maximum penalty of 10 years or more. Where the maximum was life and 'the court considers that the seriousness of the offence, or the offence and one or more offences associated with it, is such as to justify the imposition of a sentence of imprisonment for life', then a life sentence had to be imposed.[5] Where the maximum is less than life or the court does not consider the offence serious enough to justify a life sentence, an IPP sentence could be imposed.[6] However, an IPP sentence could only be imposed if at the time the offence was committed the offender had previously been convicted of one of the specified range of serious offences or the notional minimum term of the IPP sentence was two years.[7] The IPP sentence itself consisted of a minimum term determined by what is proportional to the seriousness of the offence after which the offender remained in custody until the Parole Board was 'satisfied that it is no longer necessary for the protection of the public that the prisoner should be confined'.[8]

A The Test of Dangerousness

For our purposes, the test for entry to the sentence – that the defendant was judged to represent a 'significant risk' – required that the court was satisfied that the defendant posed a risk to others of death or serious personal injury (whether physical or psychological) that was 'noteworthy' or of 'a considerable amount or importance'.[9] There was, therefore, a radical difference in substance between the two parts of the judge's sentencing decision in an IPP sentence.[10]

[4] They were governed by the Criminal Justice Act 2003 s 227. The rules for life and IPP sentences were different for adults and youth offenders, but I will consider only the rules for adults.

[5] Criminal Justice Act 2003 s 225(2).

[6] ibid s 225(3).

[7] ibid s 225(3A) and (3B).

[8] Crime Sentences Act 1997 s 28(6)(b).

[9] *R v Lang* [2006] 1 WLR 2509.

[10] Despite the similarity of form, see M Wasik, 'The Test for Dangerousness' in ch 11 of this volume.

In order to set the minimum tariff by reference to offence seriousness, the judge had to consider evidence concerning events that the court had been satisfied beyond reasonable doubt had occurred, and other statements of fact about the offender and any victim that the judge regarded as sufficiently credible.[11] In other words, for the purposes of applying the guidelines, the judge would be considering facts that he or she would be justified by the normal standards of criminal justice in regarding as events that actually occurred and experiences and characteristics that certainly existed.

By contrast, to apply the statutory wording concerning dangerousness, the judge had to consider the evidence of a different sort of fact – a risk – and whether that evidence was sufficient to decide that the risk was indeed 'significant' or 'of considerable importance'. A risk is a fact about our state of knowledge concerning something the existence or occurrence of which is not certain but only probable (a 'known unknown' in the Rumsfeldian terminology). Actuarial science in general seeks to order our knowledge of these unknowns. The probability of some frequent and/or clearly patterned events occurring in the future in a given population can be known with a high degree of accuracy. However, even where actuarial predictions are reliable, the problem of taking that data and making accurate clinical predictions of the future actions of a particular individual member of a population are much greater and attended by intractable ethical and methodological disputes among experts.[12] Assessing the risk of future serious offending is notoriously uncertain and subjective.[13] As a consequence, the courts recognise that risk assessment 'is a matter of intuition or . . . a value judgment'.[14] Even if the sentencing judge was not directly undertaking a risk assessment,[15] she was, necessarily, assessing the risk assessments of others in order to make a decision.

When a judge determined that the statutory wording in respect of dangerousness applied to a particular offender, she was making a statement about what might happen between a possible future offender and possible future victims (specifically that the possibility of serious harm was of considerable importance), and not making a statement about what had been done by an actual offender to actual victims, as she was in the matter of offence seriousness.

[11] Where there is a dispute, the defence must prove mitigating circumstances to the civil standard and the Crown aggravating circumstances to the criminal standard, *R v Kerrigan* (1993) 14 Cr App R (S) 179.

[12] See Lucia Zedner's discussion in L Zedner 'Erring on the Side of Safety: Risk Assessment, Expert Knowledge, and the Criminal Court' in ch 10 of this volume.

[13] M Tonry, 'Prediction and Classification: Legal and Ethical Issues' in DM Gottfredson and M Tonry (eds), *Prediction and Classification: Criminal Justice Decision Making* (University of Chicago Press, 1987). In essence, the problem is that the rarer the behaviour in a population, the less accurate actuarial prediction is likely to be in any particular instance, see R Wollert, 'Low Base Rates Limit Expert Certainty when Current Actuarials Are Used to Identify Sexually Violent Predators' (2006) *Psychology, Public Policy and Law* 12, 56.

[14] See *R(Hirst) v Home Secretary and Parole Board* [2002] EWHC 1592 (Admin) at [83] per Moses J.

[15] See Wasik (n 10 above).

B The Presumption of Dangerousness

The decision of the Parole Board in IPP was similar to that of the sentencing judge, except that it took place in the shadow of the sentencing court's original decision to impose the sentence. The consequence was that the emphasis in the decision-making process was reversed with a very significant effect for the offender. Continued imprisonment would be necessary for as long as the board believed that there was a more than minimal risk of further offences dangerous to life or limb.[16] However, unlike the sentencing judge, who had to be satisfied that the risk was *high* enough to necessitate the sentence, the board has to be positively satisfied that the risk was *low* enough that further detention was no longer necessary.[17] The test is not further defined and there is no formal burden of proof on either side, since, as we saw above, this assessment necessarily involved a degree of intuitive judgement. Nevertheless, we have a clear view from the courts as to how the law required the Parole Board to determine the issue. In a case concerning a discretionary life prisoner, Sir Thomas Bingham MR stated the judicial view that the board's judgment requires it to balance:

> the hardship and injustice of continuing to imprison a man who is unlikely to cause serious injury to the public against the need to protect the public against a man who is not unlikely to cause such injury. In other than a clear case this is bound to be a difficult and very anxious judgment. But in the final balance the board is bound to give preponderant weight to the need to protect innocent members of the public against any significant risk of serious injury.[18]

Some years later, sitting in the House of Lords, in a case concerning the application of the test to a mandatory life prisoner seeking release on licence, Lord Bingham re-emphasised the balance of interest where there is uncertainty. He described the determination as an 'administrative process', one in which:

> There is inevitably a balance to be struck between the interest of the individual and the interest of society and I do not think it objectionable, in the case of someone who has once taken life with the intent necessary for murder, to prefer the latter in the case of doubt.[19]

The legal effect of this balancing in conditions of uncertainty is that for the IPP offender to be released, the pre-existing finding of dangerousness by the sentencing court had to be displaced.[20] The House of Lords confirmed this in relation to IPP when it ruled that the 'default position . . . is that the prisoner is

[16] *R v Parole Board ex p Bradley* [1991] 1 WLR 134, 141–42.

[17] *R v Parole Board ex p Lodomez* [1994] COD 525.

[18] *R v Home Sec ex parte Watson* [1996] 1 WLR 906, 916–17.

[19] *R v Lichniak and Pyrah* [2003] 1 AC 903. See also *R (Brooke and Another) v Parole Board* [2008] 1 WLR 1950 [53].

[20] S Livingstone, T Owen and A Macdonald, *Prison Law* (Oxford, Oxford University Press, 2008) 616.

to remain detained unless the Board are satisfied he can be safely released'.[21] Their Lordships denied this was a presumption of dangerousness, but, as Jessica Jacobson and Mike Hough commented, it is not clear what the difference might be.[22]

Although there was no formal burden of proof, the onus was on the prisoner to bring evidence that can displace this presumption of dangerousness. The practical difficulties involved in doing so were very considerable and have been the subject of litigation.[23] As a consequence of these difficulties, the conditions of uncertainty and doubt that will very often prevail at the sentencing stage are likely to remain at the review stage to the detriment of the offender's prospects for release. Nor is it just a practical difficulty. Given a presumption of dangerousness, there must always be some doubt as to whether a person is safe. It is almost impossible to know *for sure* that a person is safe to release. The courts' proposition that the Parole Board should release once the hardship risked to the public has fallen below the hardship actually imposed on the offender will always be subject to some degree of uncertainty.[24] The unanswered question is precisely how much doubt the public should enjoy the benefit of. It is this uncertainty that is the key to understanding the justification for placing the burden of its effects on the offender, and to which we now turn.

IPP deprived an offender of his liberty on the basis that a judge had good grounds to believe that there is a noteworthy possibility that the offender will commit serious criminal harms in the future, and then maintained the detention until the offender could displace the presumption of dangerousness that now applied. There are legal objections to the presumption of dangerousness specifically and moral objections to the entire process.

From the legal point of view, the presumption of dangerousness does not seem to be beyond challenge. The legal grounds for it seem to have been transferred from the case law applying to life prisoners and, as Jill Peay argued, the IPP prisoner seeking release could be thought of as occupying a position much

[21] *James, Lee and Wells v Secretary of State for Justice* [2010] 1 AC 553, Lord Brown at 605. This reasoning is broadly confirmed in at least one relevant European Court of Human Rights (ECHR) decision. In *Comerford v United Kingdom* (App No 293195/95 9 April 1997), the Commission regarded the decision, on the same basis, to release from detention at Her Majesty's pleasure as entailing a finding that the reasons for the original sentence no longer held, and that continued detention would no longer be lawful. For the Commission, the effect is that the offender 'is to be considered to represent a risk unless the contrary is proved'. The Commission ruled that such a presumption did not violate art 5 of the European Convention on Human Rights (ECHR). Moreover, it seems that some scheme to imprison dangerous offenders might even be a necessary aspect of the state's positive obligation to protect the art 2 rights of others (see *Mastromatteo v Italy* (App No 37703/97 24 October 2002) [72]).

[22] J Jacobson and M Hough, *Unjust Deserts: Imprisonment for Public Protection* (Prison Reform Trust, 2010) 44.

[23] *R (Wells) v Parole Board; R (Walker) v Secretary of State for the Home Department* [2008] 1 All ER 138.

[24] See Jacobson and Hough (n 22 above) 44. The practical result is that 'almost five years after the sentence was introduced, no more than around 4 per cent of almost 2,500 post-tariff IPP prisoners . . . have been released', ibid 35.

more like that of a mentally disordered person detained under the Mental Health Act (MHA) 1983 rather than a prisoner seeking release on licence from a life sentence imposed on grounds of offence seriousness.[25] The courts have ruled that where a person is detained under MHA 1983, article 5 of the European Convention on Human Rights (ECHR) requires the detaining authority to prove that continued detention is still necessary with the benefit of doubt going to the detained person.[26] As with the mentally disordered person, the detention of the IPP prisoner after their tariff had expired was justified on the grounds of danger. It is not immediately obvious why the same reasoning that is applied to the mentally disordered should not be applied to the IPP prisoner. One difference with the mentally disordered is, of course, that the IPP prisoner is detained as a dangerous *offender*. What we can say for certain is that, for as long as the presumption of dangerousness applies to a prisoner, a very high standard of public protection against dangerous offenders prevails over the prisoner's interests in liberty.

The moral objection to imprisonment on grounds of dangerousness is well known. On the face of it, these sentences do not appear to be justified on grounds of the offender's desert since their indeterminate element was by definition in excess of what was required by offence seriousness. In its softer version, the objection is that injustice is therefore done to anyone who is imprisoned for a period in excess of the sentence commensurate with the seriousness of the offence committed, but who would not have gone on to commit a subsequent harm. And, given that no risk prediction will be absolutely accurate, there are bound to be some false positives and injustice will inevitably be done to some offenders. The stronger version of the objection is that every offender punished in this way is punished in advance, for a crime they have not committed, and that their moral autonomy is thereby disregarded.[27] A further objection is that if dangerousness is the concern of the sentencer, then applying the sanctions only to offenders seems arbitrary: why not incapacitate anyone who is judged to be a risk regardless of whether or not they have been convicted?

A straightforward utilitarian answer to these problems might be given on the assumption that the risk assessments available to expert witnesses were sufficiently accurate on an actuarial basis. It might then be argued that what an offender deserves is not the issue, and that the incarceration of the dangerous would result in a reduction of subsequent criminal harms that justified the loss of liberty done to all the dangerous people incarcerated (both those who would

[25] See J Peay, *Mental Health and Crime* (London, Routledge, 2010) 133–35.

[26] *R(H) v London and North-East Region Mental Health Review Tribunal* [2002] QB 1.

[27] See A von Hirsch, *Doing Justice: The Choice of Punishments* (New York, Hill & Wang, 1976) 125. Jean Floud and Warren Young deny this possibility, arguing that 'It does not make sense to describe a sentence as punishment for the very actions that it will prevent; for in that case we would be punishing someone not for what he may do but for what, since he is prevented, he is not going to do.' (J Floud and W Young, *Dangerousness and Criminal Justice* (London, Heinemann, 1981) 47).

and those who would not have gone on to (re)offend).[28] However, there are good reasons to doubt that it is simply the political influence of utilitarian thinking that explains the IPP regime of precautionary sentencing in England and Wales. We have already noted the significant doubts that exist about the accuracy of the risk assessments. Moreover, even if from a purely actuarial point of view they were accurate enough, we would still need to account for the effective presumption of dangerousness, a presumption that weighted the scales heavily in favour of public protection in any welfare calculation. Even if these doubts are set aside, IPP appeared after a period in which proportionality had enjoyed significant influence in sentencing,[29] and with IPP, precautionary sentences took the form of an element of incapacitation that was explicitly added on to a carefully calculated proportional element. Moreover, utilitarian arguments notoriously fail to take individuals and their rights very seriously and, on the surface at least, this is at odds with a political and legal culture that has sought to emphasise human rights at the same time as it instituted precautionary sentencing. At the very least, it seems worth looking for some mediating arguments that might re-present consequentialist calculations in some other language more acceptable to a culture of human rights. At any rate, here we will explore a development that is specific to the present period, which might account for the turn to precaution in sentencing and which we might miss if we simply returned to classical utilitarian arguments.

C Imprisonment under the Precautionary Principle

To summarise, offenders were subjected to the IPP regime when there was thought to be a significant risk of them committing serious harms in the future, and they would only be released when the Parole Board was satisfied that the risk to the public was so low that it no longer justified the hardship imposed on the offender. This appears to be a process of risk management. But, as we noted above, it would normally involve a high degree of uncertainty regarding the accuracy of any risk prediction, and in these conditions there was an onus on the offender and a presumption of dangerousness. It is these aspects of the IPP regime that seem to involve the application of the precautionary principle to criminal harms.

The precautionary principle has been widely adopted in environmental law and policy. While explicit advocacy of the principle is for the most part limited to the fields of environmental and public health policy, the influence of precautionary and pre-emptive approaches in different aspects of criminal justice has

[28] See N Walker, *Why Punish?* (Oxford, Oxford University Press, 1991) especially 56–60.

[29] A von Hirsch, A Ashworth and J Roberts, *Principled Sentencing* (Oxford, Hart Publishing, 2010) 102.

been increasingly significant.[30] The analogy between the precautionary principle and the decision rules in IPP is particularly striking. Moreover, *in its own terms*, the application of the principle eliminates the core moral objection to precautionary sentencing. Let's first outline the precautionary principle and its application in IPP before turning to how its application to sentencing might be justified and what common ethical considerations might underlie its adoption in these different fields.

The precautionary principle emerged from German environmental law in the 1970s and has since gained a worldwide influence as a guide to decision-making in environmental regulation. There are many versions of the principle and they are conventionally placed on a spectrum between weak and strong. A weak version is to be found in the UN's 1992 Rio Declaration:

> Where there are threats of serious or irreversible damage, lack of full scientific certainty shall not be used as a reason for postponing cost-effective measures to prevent environmental degradation.[31]

A stronger version is to be found in the 1998 Wingspread Statement on the Precautionary Principle:

> When an activity raises threats of harm to human health or the environment, precautionary measures should be taken even if some cause and effect relationships are not fully established scientifically.[32]

The principle regulates the reasons for action and the basis of a decision, not its outcome.[33] The common element in the different versions is the status of uncertainty concerning the possibility of grave harm: 'Precautionary logic is the logic of uncertainty.'[34] The sort of uncertainties that characterise the decisions to which the principle applies are described by Liz Fisher in the following way:

> decision-makers are not faced with data-gaps but with an ad hoc assemblage of scientific information and hypotheses which comes to few consistent conclusions and is replete with methodological flaws. To talk of probability in such circumstances is neither helpful nor meaningful.[35]

In all versions of the precautionary principle, such uncertainty is never a valid reason for inaction, and in stronger versions it is either a valid or a compelling

[30] For accounts, see R Ericson, *Crime in an Insecure World* (Cambridge, Polity Press, 2007); L Zedner 'Fixing the Future? The Pre-emptive Turn in Criminal Justice' in B McSherry, A Norrie and S Bronitt (eds), *The Redirection of Criminalisation and the Futures of Criminal Law* (Oxford, Hart Publishing, 2009) 44–56; B Hebenton and T Seddon, 'From Dangerousness to Precaution: Managing Sexual and Violent Offenders in an Insecure and Uncertain Age' (2009) *British Journal of Criminology* 343.

[31] Rio Declaration on Environment and Development, United Nations 'Conference on Environment and Development' (1992) principle 15 (available at www.unep.org/Documents.Multilingual/Default.asp?DocumentID=78&ArticleID=1163&l=en).

[32] Available at www.sehn.org/wing.html.

[33] L Fisher, 'Laws of Fear: Beyond the Precautionary Principle' (2006) *Modern Law Review* 69(2) 288, 288 and 290.

[34] Ericson (n 30 above) 22.

[35] Fisher (n 33 above) 290–91.

reason for taking preventive action.[36] James Cameron formulates the principle in a way that can be adopted in three progressively stronger versions as follows:

> The precautionary principle stipulates that where the environmental risks being run by regulatory inaction are in some way (a) uncertain but (b) non-negligible,
>
> [either]
>
> regulatory inaction is unjustified[; or]
>
> regulatory action is justified[; or]
>
> regulatory action is required.[37]

If 'risks of criminal harm' is substituted for 'environmental risks' in Cameron's formulation, the two stages of the IPP regime seem to apply the middle and strongest versions of the principle respectively. Entry into the sentence was governed by the middle-strength principle: where inaction would run a risk of harm of an uncertain[38] and non-negligible degree a judge was *permitted* to (though the judge did not have to) take regulatory action.[39] Exit from the sentence was governed by the high-strength principle: once the sentence was handed down, the presumption of dangerousness applied and the Parole Board *had to* continue that action until the uncertain risk ceased to be non-negligible.[40]

As a decision rule in the face of uncertainty, the precautionary principle validates the elimination of the burden of proof in respect of future harms. Since uncertainty about risk is not a reason not to take action, the possibility of false positives ceases to be a reason not to regulate. As Bill Hebenton and Toby Seddon put it:

[36] Note the difference between prevention and precaution. Prevention may apply where there is a risk but precaution applies only where there is uncertainty concerning a risk. See J Cameron, 'The Precautionary Principle: Core Meaning, Constitutional Framework and Procedures of Implementation' in R Harding and E Fisher, *Perspectives on The Precautionary Principle* (Sydney, The Federation Press, 1999); R von Schomberg, 'The Precautionary Principle and Its Normative Challenges' in E Fisher, J Jones and R von Schomberg (eds), *Implementing the Precautionary Principle: Perspectives and Prospects* (Edward Elgar, 2006) 29.

[37] J Cameron, ibid 36.

[38] Fisher's characterisation of the type of uncertainty that invokes the precautionary principle (text at n 33 above) seems apt for the risk assessment process in respect of criminal dangerousness, at least as it is described by Zedner (n 12 above).

[39] I am assuming in effect that 'noteworthy' and 'of considerable amount or importance' mean the same as 'non-negligible'. The dangerousness test certainly seems to be on all fours with the European Commission's Communication on the Precautionary Principle which stated that it would apply 'where scientific evidence is insufficient, inconclusive or uncertain and preliminary scientific evaluation indicates that there are reasonable grounds for concern that the potentially dangerous effects on the environment, human, animal or plant health may be inconsistent with the high level of protection chosen by the EU' (available at http://ec.europa.eu/dgs/health_consumer/library/pub/pub07_en.pdf).

[40] It might be argued that in some cases appropriate for IPP there would have been no practical uncertainty regarding the risk – that the danger the offender represents was palpable. However, that is to assume precisely what is contested by the stronger of the retributive objections to IPP, that there must always be some uncertainty about the risk insofar as the decision takes the offender seriously as a moral agent.

> Within precautionary logic, margins of error are viewed in a distinctive way. False 'positives' (incorrectly assessing a person as 'dangerous') are part and parcel of being cautious in the face of uncertainty – erring 'on the safe side'. By contrast, false 'negatives' (incorrectly rating a person as 'safe') cannot be tolerated because the consequences of this type of error for public safety and security are seen as potentially catastrophic.[41]

Applying the precautionary principle to sentencing requires the Parole Board, as Lord Bingham put it when he was Master of the Rolls, not to concern itself with the hardship to the offender who is 'unlikely to cause serious injury to the public' for as long as there may be a 'significant risk of serious injury to the public'. Hardship to the offender who will not commit an offence is not a reason not to act because uncertainty about his or her offending is not a reason not to act.

The precautionary principle in environmental law '. . . endorses, or arguably, requires "worst case" environmental planning . . . the worst is assumed about possible environmental outcomes.'[42] Similarly, IPP was concerned with the uncertain risk of death or serious possible injury. With both IPP and precautionary environmental regulation, we have enshrined in legal powers and obligations a requirement to act upon the basis of the uncertain possibility of the worst possible outcomes so as to prevent those outcomes from occurring. There is an obvious difference between the anticipated catastrophes of criminal justice and those of environmental regulation: one refers to a widespread or even global catastrophe, the other to an individual or at least a localised one. But this has not stopped the application of precautionary logic to sentencing: the precautionary principle provides a reasonable way of describing the IPP decision-making process.[43] This does not, of course, provide an answer to the question of how precautionary sentences are to be justified. It rather begs the question as to why using the precautionary principle in sentencing is justified. Why should we view margins of error in respect of potentially dangerous offenders in the way precautionary logic demands? Why should we discount those offenders' moral agency? As Fisher comments, even the weak version of the precautionary principle is:

> quite philosophically complex – by removing the 'facts' as a legitimate basis for decision-making in circumstances of scientific uncertainty, the principle requires public decision-makers to find other legitimate bases for their decisions.[44]

What might those 'legitimate bases' be in the case of IPP?

[41] Hebenton and Seddon (n 30 above) 352.

[42] Cameron (n 36 above) 42.

[43] The IPP scheme conforms remarkably well to other detailed accounts of the precautionary principle: see, for example, Rene von Schomberg's explanation of the principle in R von Schomberg (n 36 above) 37–38; or Stephen M Gardiner's Rawlsian version in S Gardiner, 'A Core Precautionary Principle' (2006) *Journal of Political Philosophy* 14(1), 33 (although in a footnote Gardiner observes that Rawls asserted that the principle was inappropriate for 'small-scale situations', ibid 48).

[44] Fisher (n 33 above) 289.

The key to the answer lies in the shifting of the burden of the *risk of error* that is noted by Hebenton and Seddon. A criminal justice system that is solely concerned with the offender's individual moral responsibility for a criminal harm will require proof of a wrongful act and fault, and will sentence proportionally to the seriousness of the offending behaviour. In such a system, the burden of the *uncertainty of* the risk of future harm caused by the defendant after release is borne by potential future victims. Under IPP's precautionary principle, by contrast, the burden of that uncertainty was borne by the offender. The justice of shifting the burden in this way was the key to Warren Floud and Jean Young's justification of protective sentencing of the dangerous.[45]

D The Wrong of Dangerousness

The 1981 report of the Working Party on Dangerous Offenders, written by Floud and Young, argued in favour of a dangerousness sentencing regime that differed in several ways from IPP.[46] In particular, their report supported only determinate periods of imprisonment for public protection. In effect their argument applies only to the first test in the IPP process (and, as we shall see below, to the proposed extended determinate sentences). Nevertheless, we will pursue it here and consider what further arguments are needed to extend their justification to the indeterminate sentences of IPP.

The key to their justification is the idea that ordinarily, in a free society, the law's subjects have a right to be presumed to be harmless unless it is proved otherwise.[47] They argue that there is no requirement for a free society to extend this presumption to those who have been proved guilty of a serious offence. The presumption may persist in a particular case, but the offender has lost his right to it. For Floud and Young, this explains why protective custody cannot be imposed before an offence is committed and, therefore, why there is no danger of a slippery slope to 'civil preventative detention'.[48] More importantly, they are suggesting that there is a connection between the offence already committed and the preventive detention, a connection that justifies the latter on the grounds of the offender's past wrongdoing:

> what justifies the imposition of preventive measures, if they can be justified, is not simply a prediction of likely outcomes, but that the way they come about is such as to put the potential offender in the wrong. In other words, preventive measures against a risk of willful harm are justifiable only against someone already justly liable to punishment for harmful conduct of the kind to be prevented . . .[49]

[45] J Floud and W Young, *Dangerousness and Criminal Justice* (London, Heinemann, 1981).
[46] ibid 155.
[47] ibid 43–44.
[48] ibid 46.
[49] ibid.

The offender's liability for what he has already done changes the issue concerning preventive detention. It is no longer a question of 'how many innocent persons are to sacrifice their liberty for the extra protection that special sentences for dangerous offenders will provide?' but 'what is the moral choice between the alternative risks: the risk of harm to potential victims or the risk of unnecessarily detaining offenders judged to be dangerous?'[50]

Floud and Young's justification for the protective sentence is that the burden of risk is justly laid on the offender because, by virtue of his offence, the offender has lost the presumption of innocence and thereby lost the right to be presumed harmless.[51] However, this still seems to fall short of an answer to the critical question – what exactly is the wrong that justifies the hard treatment meted out to the offender who has lost the right to be presumed harmless? If it is simply the wrong comprised by the offence for which they have been convicted then their just punishment for that offence has no protective element added on. At any rate, Floud and Young buttress their argument by adding that: '[The offender's] being wrong *by virtue of the risk he represents* is what entitles us to consider imposing on him the risk of unnecessary measures to save the risk of harm to innocent victims.'[52]

For Floud and Young this wrong of representing a risk justified only a protective sentence that was 'proportional to the harm anticipated'.[53] They understood this to mean periods of a determinate length. The seriousness of the wrong could in theory be calculated as a function of the gravity of the harm compounded by probability of its occurrence. But we must remember at this point that the risk calculations involved are in fact clouded in uncertainty. How much confidence can the sentencer have in the level of the anticipated harm, any more than she can have in the likelihood that there will be any harm done at all by the offender? If it is the burden of this *uncertainty* rather than the burden of *risk* that is justly borne by the offender, on account of the offender's wrong consisting of him being the cause of *this* uncertainty, then an indeterminate sentence might seem a peculiarly appropriate, even proportional, response.[54] The wrong of this uncertainty cannot be calculated in the same way, even in theory. The wrong is renewed every day that the defendant remains an uncertain risk. Alternatively, the argument for indeterminacy must be that, once the presumption of harmlessness has been withdrawn, the offender forfeits their right to proportional treatment, at least until he has done enough for the presumption to be restored.[55]

[50] ibid 49.

[51] ibid 46.

[52] ibid (emphasis added). Presumably for Floud and Young this wrong cannot be done by a person who has not committed a serious offence because that person still enjoys a right to be presumed harmless whatever actuarial and clinical predictions may suggest.

[53] ibid 46.

[54] I am grateful to Sandra Marshall for this thought.

[55] I have explored a different aspect of this wrong, as a violation of protected interests in subjective security, in P Ramsay, 'A Political Theory of Imprisonment for Public Protection' in M Tonry (ed), *Retributivism Has a Past: Has It a Future?* (Oxford, Oxford University Press, 2011).

There are many criminal justice and political objections to sentences based on a wrong of dangerousness.[56] Such a wrong implies an obligation not to be dangerous. That is a very demanding obligation, especially for an offender, since it requires that the person subject to it does not do anything that fails to reassure others about their security. However, crucially for present purposes, this wrong, which Floud and Young claim is committed by the serious offender who constitutes an uncertain risk – and which serves as their ultimate justification for a precautionary sentence of some sort – raises normative themes that are consistent with the precautionary principle. For the precautionary principle implies just such a duty to avoid creating a danger to future interests and the concomitant insecurity that that may cause in the present.

II THE ETHICS OF PRECAUTION

According to the Research Findings of Task Force 5 of the European Science Foundation on Environment Science and Society, the influence of the precautionary principle has led to 'a gradual shift . . . to place the burden of proof of environmental sustention on the would-be polluter or alterer of the status quo rather than the victim to cry foul too late'.[57]

If we translate the 'polluter' as the 'dangerous offender', then he is the one who would introduce the risk of harm into the environment and, like the polluter, his dangerousness is the moral basis of placing the onus on him (if not a formal burden of proof) to demonstrate that it would be safe to let him do what he asks (that is, release him). The alternative, which is unacceptable to precautionary thinking, is that the innocent victim of environmental damage/crime may be left 'to cry foul too late'.

There is more than a formal coincidence between the normative concerns of precaution in environmental regulation and criminal justice. One of the attractions of the precautionary principle for its supporters is the attention it pays to the interests and well being of future generations, who would otherwise lack a voice in environmental policy deliberation.[58] Similarly, the precautionary principle in criminal justice promotes the interests of those human individuals who also lack any capacity to protect their own interests because, as yet, they have no certain existence – that is, potential victims of crime. By requiring the offender, like the would-be polluter, to bear the burden of uncertainty, the precautionary principle promotes the interests of the law's 'innocent' but abstract subjects (future generations/potential victims) over those of its 'dangerous' but concrete subjects (would-be polluters/offenders).

[56] See, for example, Zedner (n 12 above); Ramsay ibid.

[57] Cited by Cameron (n 36 above) 29.

[58] See, for example, R Attfield, 'The Precautionary Principle and Moral Values' in T O'Riordan and J Cameron, *Interpreting the Precautionary Principle* (Cameron May, 1994) 159.

Application of the precautionary principle founds the law on the interests of human entities that are known only to the mind, in preference to those that are also perceptible to our senses.[59] To be subjected to the precautionary principle is to have failed in an obligation not to be perceived as a significant if uncertain risk to these abstract entities, a failure that justifies a limitation of rights.

From where does this obligation derive its ethical force? Why should we have an obligation not to be perceived as posing some uncertain risk of harm to others? Why should offenders not have a legal right to go about their business notwithstanding others' perception of the risks their unregulated activity represents? Why should the interests of these abstract persons (who *might* be victimised in future) be coercively enforced to the detriment of the interests of concrete persons who *will* lose their liberty in the present? As the precautionary principle's counterposing of the offender against his or her potential victims suggests, it seems to be the utter powerlessness and vulnerability of the potential victim that provides the answer.[60] The law's abstract potential subjects are vulnerable to the future harms of the dangerous offender, and, insofar as the law's present actual subjects share an interest in avoiding that future harm (because they or some other subject of concern to them may one day occupy the position of that abstract future subject), they too are vulnerable to the *insecurity* that the threat represents.[61] If we recognise a duty to protect the security interests of the vulnerable, then it is this vulnerability that justifies the *burden of uncertainty* being borne by the offender, since only by fulfilling the obligation not to be dangerous (ie, perceived as a risk) will the offender protect the interests of those vulnerable to the potential harm that they might otherwise represent under the high standards of the precautionary principle.

We will return to the assumed vulnerability of the law's normal subjects below, but the justification just given still leaves open the philosophical question of why we ought to protect others from their insecurity as such, from the possibility of harm. Onora O'Neill has suggested that protecting the vulnerable is an ethical principle that can be derived from the universal experience of human vulnerability to harm.[62] Bryan Turner has made a similar outlook the basis of his theory of human rights.[63] Robert Goodin makes a detailed and extensive

[59] In some cases, the uncertain risk will be one of harm to a specific person or persons. In such cases, a wrong of dangerousness and precautionary punishment may involve a balancing of the interests of concrete persons, all of whom are known to the senses. However, there was no requirement that identifiable concrete persons be at risk from an offender before an IPP sentence was imposed.

[60] See also T Arnoldussen, 'Deus Sive Natura: Investigating the Axioms of Precautionary Logic' in M Hildebrandt, A Makinwa and A Oehmichen (eds), *Controlling Security in a Culture of Fear* (Boom, 2010) 81.

[61] For more on the construction of the crime victim as the representative citizen, see P Ramsay, 'Overcriminalization as Vulnerable Citizenship' (2010) *New Criminal Law Review* 13(2) 262.

[62] Though she is careful to restrict it to the sphere of virtue rather than legal obligation, see O O'Neill, *Towards Justice and Virtue: A Constructive Account of Practical Reasoning* (Cambridge, Cambridge University Press, 1996) 192.

[63] B Turner, *Vulnerability and Human Rights* (Penn State Press, 2006).

case for this principle by arguing that it alone can explain the special duties to protect the interests of others that the law has long imposed.[64] Goodin's analysis is focused on the case for the welfare state and foreign aid, but he explicitly extends it to the interests of future generations (and the non-human environment). He claims that this principle, as moral philosophy, is 'fundamentally consequentialist', but is nevertheless 'consistent with most standard forms of nonconsequentialism'.[65]

I do not want to investigate the moral philosophy in any detail here. There are certainly lots of doubts than can be raised. First, it is not clear why the injunction to protect the vulnerable is necessarily a consequentialist principle. We have seen here that it conceivably supports a *wrong* of dangerousness to which precautionary sentencing is a response.[66] Moreover, there must at least be some doubt about the coherence of a consequentialist principle of protecting the vulnerable once it is extended to precautionary legal obligations to protect against causing *uncertain* harms to vulnerable others, as opposed to what we might call 'first-order harms'.[67] Goodin comments that 'As long as there remains something we (individually or collectively) can do to protect the interests of vulnerable future generations, we should do it, *ceteris paribus*.'[68] Critics have, however, doubted that the precautionary principle can ever be applied and all other things remain equal.[69] In the context of precautionary punishment, it is not clear why a justification for the application of the precautionary principle that rests on dangerousness will be limited to dangerous *offenders,* as Floud and Young hoped their determinate sentencing system could be. Anyone who causes insecurity to others could be restricted on the same basis.[70] Another concern is that the application of this principle to provide a duty to reassure others in respect of future criminal victimisation seems particularly problematic when the offender must bear an effective presumption of dangerousness in a process of assessment notorious for its subjectivity.[71] This problem raises the wider doubt as to whether protecting the vulnerable through punishment of the dangerous ought to be thought of in the same way as protecting them through administrative regulation of industrial or scientific activity.

Rather than explore these significant philosophical objections to precautionary sentencing directly, I want to think a bit more here about the social and

[64] R Goodin, *Protecting the Vulnerable: A Reanalysis of our Social Responsibilities* (University of Chicago Press, 1985).

[65] ibid 109–10.

[66] On the protection of the vulnerable through incapacitation of the dangerous as the right thing to do, regardless of its effectiveness in crime prevention, see Ramsay (n 55 above).

[67] H Gross, *A Theory of Criminal Justice* (Oxford, Oxford University Press, 1979) 125.

[68] Goodin (n 64 above) 178.

[69] The possibility that the precautionary principle might prohibit all courses of action as a consequence of the incalculable risk associated with action as well as inaction has been widely noted, see particularly C Sunstein, *Laws of Fear: Beyond the Precautionary Principle* (Cambridge, Cambridge University Press, 2005).

[70] For a discussion see Ramsay (n 55 above).

[71] See Jacobson and Hough (n 22 above) 35–44.

historical sources of precautionary thinking so as to understand better the intellectual and political climate in which the critics of precautionary sentencing must make our arguments. The point I want to pursue is that, regardless of whether or not the protection of this vulnerability is justifiable from a consequentialist point of view, the precautionary principle necessarily entails a very particular way of assessing consequences, and this suggests that the underlying reasons for the influence of the precautionary principle are quite different from those that once supported the utilitarian approach.

A Ignorance as an Ethical Foundation

Insofar as it is a guide to decision-making, utilitarianism depends upon some calculation of the general welfare. The elements of the 'hedonic calculus' include the duration, extent and intensity of the pleasures and pains attendant on a particular decision, and these are to be discounted according to the likelihood of their occurrence and their remoteness in time. However, recall that the precautionary principle sets out from precisely the inability to make that calculation with an adequate degree of certainty. It is this uncertainty about future pains or costs that is the determining factor in precautionary decisions.

The precautionary principle tends to discount the consequences we can be certain of – the present benefits of non-regulation – and to place a high premium on the consequences we cannot be certain of – the future costs of non-regulation. In its stronger versions, the precautionary principle entirely discounts the certain present benefits relative to the uncertain future costs. The principle holds that, for as long as we are unable with confidence to discount those future costs, we are justified in foregoing present benefits.

This determining role of uncertainty represents a very significant ethical shift in the value and place of human knowledge in our decision-making. In the stronger forms of the precautionary principle, decisions are to be determined not by what is known about utility, but by what is *not known* about it. Even if utilitarians can find a way to adapt to this view, to focus on its consequentialist aspect without noticing this shift in emphasis would be to overlook the essential novelty of the precautionary principle.

The precautionary principle's injunction that we should be guided not by our knowledge but by its limitations gives form to a profound and widespread disenchantment with what John Gray describes as 'the Enlightenment project of human self-emancipation through the growth of knowledge'.[72] In the disenchanted view of the Enlightenment project, the growth of scientific knowledge far from liberating human beings is regarded as another source of uncertain risks to the survival of the species. From the unknown consequences of cloning or genetic screening to the feared effects of global warming, the advance of the

[72] J Gray, *Enlightenment's Wake* (London, Routledge, 1995) 232.

human capacity to intervene in natural processes is everywhere thought to threaten disaster. Although the immediate subject matter differs, criminological knowledge has not been immune from similar disenchantment.

As David Garland argues in his influential account, one of the key drivers of criminal justice policy since the 1980s has been the 'pervasive sense' that criminology has failed to give a convincing account of causal mechanisms, leaving the field open to theories that emphasise the need to control criminals and potential criminals.[73] As Garland points out, where 'the criminologies of the welfare state era tended to assume the perfectibility of man', the control theories, that have gained influence on the back of the perceived failure of earlier criminology, reject this Enlightenment optimism and 'begin from a much darker vision of the human condition'.[74] And, as we will shortly see, the precautionary vision with its pervasive emphasis on unregulated human activity as a threat is one aspect of this darker vision. The critical point for understanding IPP is that it is scepticism about the 'Enlightenment project', as opposed to the revival of one of the Enlightenment's variants (utilitarianism), that constitutes the wider intellectual and political context in which to understand the appearance of the precautionary principle in criminal justice.

Disenchantment with the Enlightenment project is disenchantment with a worldview that itself achieved its preeminence, between the eighteenth and twentieth centuries, through disenchantment with older traditional and religious worldviews. It is hard to overestimate the significance of this 'disenchantment with disenchantment'.[75] The end result is that Western societies lack sufficient faith in both their religious traditions *and* in the scientific (or social-scientific) knowledge that displaced those older sources of ethical guidance. In these circumstances, society seems to lack any source of guiding principles, and it is not clear what as a society we ought to do. In criminal justice policy, this intellectual crisis has notoriously been accompanied by a prolonged period of 'volatile and contradictory' policy.[76] The influence of the precautionary principle can be understood as both a symptom of this wider problem and a default solution to it, and this may account for its contemporary influence.

B Precaution as Moral Order

Anthony Giddens has suggested that the solution to the problem of moral order faced by contemporary society is to *embrace* the perceived limitations of

[73] D Garland, *The Culture of Control* (Oxford, Oxford University Press, 2001) 62.

[74] ibid 15.

[75] P Lassman, 'Pluralism and its Discontents: John Gray's Counter Enlightenment' in J Horton and G Newey (eds), *The Political Theory of John Gray* (London, Routledge, 2007) 101. For a fascinating discussion of the issues in a slightly different register, see E Gellner, 'The Rubber Cage: Disenchantment with Disenchantment' in E Gellner, *Culture, Identity and Politics* (Cambridge, Cambridge University Press, 1987).

[76] P O'Malley, 'Volatile and Contradictory Punishment' (1999) 3(2) *Theoretical Criminology* 175.

scientific knowledge and the uncertainty that arises from them. In a book entitled *Beyond Left and Right,* Giddens sought to respond to the final exhaustion, during the late 1980s and early 1990s, of the basic structure of political life that had characterised European societies since the French Revolution; a structure that had disintegrated along with the Enlightenment project. He argued that, by the 1990s, both conservatism and socialism had lost their way, with the former promoting radical change and the latter becoming defensive of the old institutions of the welfare state. In the face of this considerable disorientation in public life, Giddens suggested a new approach, 'we can't return to nature or tradition but, individually and as collective humanity, we can seek to remoralize our lives in the context of a positive acceptance of manufactured uncertainty'.[77]

Giddens's point was that in contemporary circumstances, in which we have lost faith in Enlightenment rationality so that our decisions and our knowledge only seem to 'manufacture uncertainty', we should not indulge either deep green fantasies about a return to a more 'natural' existence,[78] or fundamentalist communitarian fantasies of reinventing abandoned cultural and religious traditions.[79] Rather than nostalgic longing for these illusory sources of certainty, we should reflexively face up to our uncertainty and seek to use it as our guide. Arguably, that is precisely what the precautionary principle does: it provides a moral code by distributing burdens of risk avoidance to those whose actions would 'manufacture' such uncertainty in the absence of the principle's operation.

In subsequent writing on environmental politics, Giddens himself has explicitly rejected the precautionary principle. He sees it as a core proposition of a romantic Green movement, and takes it to mean 'Don't interfere with nature'.[80] Even if that is right,[81] it is important to recognise that, as we have seen, the principle nevertheless provides the basis for moral duties of self-restraint, duties that are grounded in a response to manufactured uncertainty. Incorporating the precautionary principle into law institutionalises a moral order that is based on the disenchantment with the power of human knowledge, or the 'acceptance of manufactured uncertainty'. This might be described as a 'negative' acceptance

[77] A Giddens, *Beyond Left and Right* (Cambridge, Polity Press, 1994) 227.

[78] For Giddens the error of deep ecology is to overlook the reality that humanity has already eliminated nature in the sense of 'objects or processes given independently of human intervention', ibid 206.

[79] As John Gray points out, the more populist versions of the idea of a return to 'tradition' are really atavistic rather than conservative, while the High Tory version is no more than a 'pose'. This is because these 'traditions' are no longer true traditions. Rather what is advocated is a return to practices that have in fact died out in the life of society and have to be reinvented (see n 72 above, ch 5).

[80] A Giddens, *The Politics of Climate Change* (Cambridge, Polity Press, 2009) 6. Giddens also adopts Cass Sunstein's criticisms of the precautionary principle: that it is incoherent because regulatory action carries uncertain risks just as much as failing to regulate and that, in its stronger versions, it is paralysing (ibid 59).

[81] Note that the injunction 'don't interfere with nature' is not necessarily the same proposition as a return to a mythical natural existence that Giddens had earlier rejected. While it assumes that there is something natural that can be and is interfered with, it does not necessarily entail that the postulated 'nature' is something untouched by human activity.

(a defensive response to a threatening problem), rather than the 'positive acceptance' (the embrace of an opportunity as well as a problem) that Giddens advocates.[82] Nevertheless, the precautionary principle enjoys a political influence extending far beyond the green movement because it lays down a system of obligations derived from the 'manufactured uncertainty' that seems to characterise our doubly disenchanted condition of scepticism towards both the 'Enlightenment project' and religious tradition.[83]

These intellectual and historical conditions for the precautionary principle's pervasive influence are worth exploring in more specific detail, in order to get a sense of what is ultimately at stake in the critique of precautionary punishment. The precautionary principle does not impose a system of obligations that is entirely novel. Rather, as the old intellectual order disintegrates, it recycles and recombines those elements of both the liberal and conservative traditions (or, roughly, of the Enlightenment and the anti-Enlightenment) that seem to retain some plausibility despite the broader disenchantment. While it might be more accurate to describe this recombination as a 'collapse of left and right' into each other rather than as a going 'beyond left and right', the reworking of familiar aspects of the old politics in new circumstances is the key to understanding the precautionary principle's grip on the contemporary imagination.

The relationship of the precautionary principle to the broad liberal/left-wing of Enlightenment-era politics is immediately apparent from the account of it already given. The precautionary principle assumes the uncertainty that has been unleashed by modern social and scientific development and, therefore, in line with the modern liberal left's moral pluralism, it entails no return to a particular substantive moral tradition. A moral and legal order incorporating the precautionary principle is very much one that justifies state coercion on the basis of avoiding and preventing harm (which is why it is tempting to look first to the influence of utilitarianism), and its emphasis on ameliorating vulnerability to risk is one with a lineage in the welfare state. What is abandoned from the broadly left-wing tradition is the belief that scientific and material 'progress' will resolve the problems posed by potential harms or 'liberate' humanity from the uncertainty surrounding them.

In place of the 'progressive' outlook of modern liberals and socialists, precautionary logic instead combines moral pluralism with elements of pre-Enlightenment Christian doctrines that have been more associated with conservative and anti-Enlightenment thought. However, the theological basis of these older doctrines is naturalised in the precautionary vision. Tobias

[82] On the climate change question, Giddens prefers cost-benefit analysis to the precautionary principle (n 80 above 58), and, ultimately, he claims to side with the Enlightenment on the value and power of human knowledge (ibid 230), notwithstanding his earlier promotion of the concept of manufactured uncertainty.

[83] In accounting for the political influence of the precautionary principle, Giddens is again content to cite Sunstein's account, which focuses on different ways in which risk is misperceived. Giddens overlooks the way it amounts to an attempt at an ethical response to the problem of manufactured uncertainty, albeit a contentious one that he disapproves of (see ibid 59).

Arnoldussen has argued that the precautionary principle reflects a number of ancient themes in Christian doctrine.[84] In both traditional Christian thinking and the precautionary principle we find the following elements:

- human knowledge is necessarily imperfect and limited, but human pride and disobedience to God/nature, particularly in seeking knowledge of nature, are a potential source of evil/danger that is inherent to humanity;[85]
- the true nature of the world, which ordinary human senses cannot perceive, will be revealed in an apocalyptic event of uncertain proximity;
- a moral doctrine that includes requirements to pay attention to this possibility of catastrophe; to observe certain limits on our present pleasures and our ambitions; to show respect for the interests of the meek and vulnerable, and for the demands of abstract, noumenal beings not known to the senses;
- the proposition that salvation might follow from repentance and embrace of this doctrine.

If these elements of precautionary thinking enjoy deep cultural roots in post-Christian societies, there are also differences with traditional beliefs. It is the specific combination of similarities and differences that explains the principle's influence and real significance. In particular, for Christians, salvation is a matter of divine grace, something that is missing from the precautionary principle. This betokens a difference in the way the two doctrines understand humanity.

We noted above that the precautionary principle is concerned with 'worst case' planning: in environmental law with large-scale catastrophes, in IPP with the localised catastrophe of serious criminal victimisation. To the extent that our law is based on the precautionary principle, it is, like a very traditional Christianity, based on *the ever-present possibility of doom.* Insofar as the law's subjects take moral guidance from its precepts, this is the doctrine that they will internalise. The difference, of course, is that the Christian doomsday heralds the resurrection of the dead; and the salvation of the meek in the hereafter. The catastrophe envisaged by precautionary thinking implies no such eternal salvation; the redemption on offer is no more than the avoidance of disaster.[86] Arnoldussen argues that in the precautionary worldview humanity is returned to something like the 'medium' position between God and the animals that pre-Enlightenment medieval philosophy allotted to us – we are the 'shepherd of ecosystems'.[87] Only now God's love and divine reason, and with them humanity's access to the eternal and universal, have been removed from the picture.[88] By promoting a belief in the proximity of

[84] See T Arnoldussen, 'Precautionary Logic and a Policy of Moderation' (2009) 2(9) *Erasmus Law Review* 259, 276–81, and n 60 above 90–94.

[85] Although in both doctrines some types of knowledge are highly prized: knowledge of the scriptures in Protestantism, for example; knowledge of risk in the precautionary principle.

[86] And, perhaps, the satisfaction of having played one's part in avoiding the catastrophe.

[87] Arnoldussen (n 84 above) 280.

[88] Arnoldussen (n 60 above) 93. It is striking that the precautionary principle lacks not only the Christian virtue of faith but, when applied to sentencing, seems to be short of hope and charity as well.

the approaching end time, but without Christianity's promise of communion with God, the precautionary principle institutionalises the Christian belief in human frailty but without Christianity's humanistic aspect, the privileged place in creation that it reserved for human beings.

The precautionary principle gains political traction from this recycling of elements from both Enlightenment and counter-Enlightenment traditions. Jesus Christ's concern for the meek is replayed as protecting the vulnerable and voiceless from harm; biblical moral doctrines are given up, but what was once seen as a reactionary emphasis on avoiding hubris and observing the limits of human reason is reconstructed as a radical commitment to the future; the ultimate religious figure – the omnipotent, loving God – is edited out, but one of the most powerful works of the Christian imagination, the apocalypse, is given a starring role.

This last aspect of the precautionary principle gives us a clue to one of the key reasons for its rise to global influence, and the decline in faith in the Enlightenment project. Long before the precautionary principle, the apocalyptic imagery of Christianity had already been secularised by the political left. In its socialist and Marxist variants, the Enlightenment commitment to scientific, economic and social progress took a distinctively millennial form in which the present was the precursor to a new era of prosperity and justice that would be ushered in by profound political and social transformation. The exhaustion in practice of the political movement of organised labour has left the millennial imagination without either its socialist political content or the religious content that socialism once secularised. The ideological space evacuated by the optimistic visions of working class politics has been filled with new apocalyptic imaginings denuded of the earlier humanist convictions.

It is in this context of political and intellectual exhaustion that the precautionary principle supplies an ethical framework in which familiar elements of religion are naturalised and combined with elements of Enlightenment doctrine to meet contemporary ideological needs. This is a framework through which a society that has lost faith in the power of both God and human knowledge can nevertheless try to process the problem of 'manufactured uncertainty', a problem that is, at least in part, a consequence of these same spiritual losses.

III AFTER IPP: EXTENDED DETERMINATE SENTENCES AND MANDATORY LIFE

If these are some of the background reasons for the influence of precautionary logic then it might be thought surprising that the Coalition Government that replaced New Labour has moved to abolish IPP. However, it would be premature to regard this moment as the end of the influence of the precautionary principle in criminal justice policy. Neither the Government's policy position nor its legislative proposals amount to an unambiguous and principled rejection of the underlying precautionary logic. They look more like a response to the severe practical problems of implementing precautionary sentencing, especially when budgets are under pressure.

Certainly the proposals will eliminate the severest aspect of IPP. Offenders who meet the IPP criteria will now be subjected to extended determinate sentences. They will be required to serve two-thirds of their nominal sentence, where a normal offender will be eligible for parole half way through.[89] They will be released subject to license and immediate recall for a maximum period of five years for violent offences and eight years for sexual offences.[90] The extra minimum period means that prisoners are still to be punished for the wrong of dangerousness, in a way broadly consistent with Floud and Young's proposals. However, they cannot be imprisoned on a precautionary basis beyond the full period of their sentence. Such offenders will also be controlled and have their liberty limited for a prolonged period by licence conditions that could, if the offender breaches them, result in a return to prison.

For a few very serious offenders, on the other hand, the underlying principle of precautionary sentencing remains in place. In essence, the proposal is that any offender convicted of a second violent or sexual offence where the sentence imposed for both offences on grounds of offence seriousness was 10 years or more must be given a life sentence unless it would be unjust in the particular circumstances to do so.[91] The threshold for imposing the sentence is not explicitly one of dangerousness, but the Minster of Justice, Ken Clarke, made the underlying justification perfectly clear in parliament: 'the new mandatory sentence is mainly intended to reassure those who . . . are worried that the worst offenders might occasionally get out'.[92] The reassurance is supplied by the application of the 'life and limb' test to the life prisoner who is beyond their tariff. But, in these cases, the test will be applied to offenders who have not received a life sentence on grounds of offence seriousness, but on the grounds of the evidence of propensity to commit serious crimes supplied by repeat convictions. Imprisonment under the precautionary principle is therefore retained, albeit for a much smaller group of offenders than that which IPP applied to.

This ambiguity about precautionary sentencing is reflected in the policy development that led to the proposals. Minister of Justice Clarke was tasked with cutting the ministry's budget by 25 per cent. He published a green paper that promoted a renewed emphasis on rehabilitation in sentencing, and proposed narrowing the criteria of IPP, with the overall aim of reducing the number of offenders held in prison.[93] In the Conservative Party, however, Clarke's overall

[89] Legal Aid, Sentencing and Punishment of Offenders Bill cl 116(3).

[90] ibid cl 115(8).

[91] ibid cl 114.

[92] HC Deb, 1 Nov 2011 c788.

[93] Ministry of Justice, *Breaking the Cycle: Effective Punishment, Rehabilitation and Sentencing of Offenders* (2010). The language of security and of controlling threats nevertheless remained prominent in the green paper. The opening paragraph of the Ministerial Introduction, for example, states: 'The safety and security of the law-abiding citizen is a key priority of the Coalition Government. Everyone has a right to feel safe in their home and in their community. When that

emphasis on rehabilitation has been regarded as the suspiciously liberal concern of a politician who seems to belong to another era.[94] Certainly what became the abolition of IPP seemed to require some nimble political footwork.

The repeal provisions were included as last-minute amendments to the Legal Aid, Sentencing and Punishment of Offenders Bill introduced at the report stage of the Bill with just half an hour of debate allocated in the House of Commons. Moreover, the criticisms of IPP made by ministers were, to put it politely, a curious mixture. Prime Minister David Cameron described IPP as 'a scandal' on the grounds that, like any ordinary sentence, they allow for the possibility that a dangerous offender could be released half way through his nominal sentence. He emphasised the 'tough determinate sentences' that IPP was being replaced with.[95] His Minister of Justice, however, took the opposite tack. Clarke argued, more plausibly, that 'We've got 6,000 people languishing in prison, 3,000 of whom have gone beyond the tariff set by the judge, and we haven't the faintest idea when, if ever, they are going to get out.' Significantly, he added, 'It's a gross injustice – a bit of a stain on our system.'[96] In Parliament Clarke emphasised that the heart of the problem is the very demanding nature of the precautionary test that the IPP prisoner had to meet:

> The Parole Board has been given the task of trying to see whether a prisoner could prove that he is no longer a risk to the public. It is almost impossible for the prisoner to prove that, so it is something of a lottery and hardly any are released. We therefore face an impossible problem.[97]

Despite this apparently principled rejection of precautionary sentencing, Clarke nevertheless endorsed applying exactly the same lottery to the narrower group of very serious offenders who would be made subject to mandatory life sentences in order to reassure the public. The 'impossible problem' that Clarke understands precautionary sentencing to represent seems to be as much a practical one of the numbers involved as it is one of the (precautionary) principle of incapacitating dangerous offenders until they can prove that they are safe to release.

Perhaps precautionary sentencing will turn out to be a passing fad of a Labour government that was peculiarly sensitive to the charge of being soft on crime. However, it remains to be seen whether — Ken Clarke notwithstanding, — the

safety is threatened, those responsible should face a swift and effective response.' The passage should not be dismissed on the grounds that it is political boilerplate. It is its very 'taken as read' quality that is important, since its literal meaning encompasses the penal wrong of threatening others' *feelings* of safety.

[94] It is significant to note that on many other aspects of sentencing policy the Legal Aid, Sentencing and Punishment of Offenders Bill was widely interpreted as a political defeat for a minister at the end of his career, see M Ridell, 'Why the U-turn? Because Ken Clarke ran out of road', *Daily Telegraph*, 14 November 2011; D Blackburn, 'Cameron Stamps on Clarke' *Spectator*, 8 June 2011.

[95] HC Deb 26 Oct 2011 c311.

[96] *Today Programme*, BBC Radio 4, 27 October 2011.

[97] HC Deb 1 Nov 2011 c787.

Coalition Government has a markedly greater confidence in Enlightenment humanism than had New Labour. The current Government's policy commitment to rehabilitation and reducing prison numbers seems anything but deeply felt.

IV CONCLUSION

Putting the precautionary principle in its broader historical context, as I have tried to do here, suggests that precautionary institutions may have some capacity to endure. The precautionary principle might be described as an attempt to fill the 'God-shaped hole'. How effectively or attractively it does this, or whether we should try to fill the hole at all, are different questions. On the other hand, the travails of IPP indicate that there are potent practical difficulties with the application of the precautionary principle in criminal justice.

Theorists will divide over how to approach precautionary sentencing. Some will want to keep up a rights-based criticism of measures that preempt future harms through administrative risk management. Others will seek to identify principles that can moderate or restrain the operation of those preemptive measures in the name of justice. All of us will need to understand the nature of the beast. In the precautionary vision, humanity's relation to itself is mediated by existential threat. The ethics of the precautionary principle construct human beings either as potential threats or as 'at risk' from those threats; as the dangerous or the vulnerable. In precautionary industrial, energy or science policies, the existential threat posed by human beings is generalised; in precautionary crime control, the existential threat of the human is individualised. In both spheres, human relations are characterised in terms of threat and vulnerability. With its pervasive emphasis on threat, the precautionary principle is much more pessimistic philosophically than traditional penal consequentialism. Its naturalised vision of humans as either the bearers or the potential victims of catastrophe represents an abandonment not just of the Enlightenment project of mastery through scientific knowledge, but of the entire humanist tradition.

The precautionary construction of humans as either threatening or vulnerable agents amounts to a radical revision of the meaning of our humanity.[98] Unsurprisingly, this transforms the language of rights and duties. In the precautionary vision, rights serve to protect vulnerability and the concomitant obligation is not to be dangerous. If the critics of IPP want to have any political purchase then we will need to rearticulate the citizen's interest in limiting the state's security powers. Part of this will include a critique of the precautionary

[98] Susan Sontag suggested: 'That even an apocalypse can be made to seem part of the ordinary horizon of expectation constitutes an unparalleled violence that is being done to our sense of reality, to our humanity.' S Sontag, *Aids and Its Metaphors* (London, Penguin, 1991) 178–79.

principle in general and its application to criminal justice in particular.[99] But, more broadly, since freedom from state coercion is an interest that was long protected in the language of rights, promoting that interest in a politically effective way in today's circumstances will need to take into account the transformation of the meaning of rights that continues apace under the influence of the broader anti-humanism.

Those who would do business with the precautionary principle, on the other hand, should understand the implications of a principle that justifies legal coercion and control on the grounds of uncertainty about the future that is a consequence of human decisions not yet made. This is a justification that places a vanishingly small value on the risk-taking that is an essential aspect of human freedom.

[99] See also Sunstein (n 69 above); for criminal justice, see Ericson, Zedner, Hebenton and Seddon (n 30 above).

10

*Erring on the Side of Safety: Risk Assessment, Expert Knowledge, and the Criminal Court**

LUCIA ZEDNER

> Any prediction about the future behaviour of human beings (as opposed to the phases of the moon or high water at London Bridge) is necessarily problematical. Reasonable and informed minds may differ, and a judgment is not shown to be wrong or unreasonable because that which is thought likely to happen does not happen. **It would have been irresponsible not to err, if at all, on the side of safety.**[1]

PRUDENCE IS A virtue and it is commonly accepted that where the stakes are high or the threat potentially catastrophic, we should err on the side of safety. So accepted is this conventional wisdom that we scarcely notice that it is an open invitation to blunder. How, otherwise, might we explain Lord Bingham's insistence that it would be 'irresponsible' to do other than to err on the side of safety. After all, it is hardly usual for a Law Lord, still less one rightly recognised as 'the greatest judge of his era', to insist upon his duty to get it wrong.[2]

Why, we might ask, should we be inveighed upon to err at all? One simple answer is that lacking supernatural powers of foresight, time machines, or the 'precog mutants' of Dick's famous short story *Minority Report*,[3] we rely upon technologies and forms of expertise that fall far short of accuracy in assessing

* This chapter is part of the three-year 'Preventive Justice' project I am undertaking with Andrew Ashworth, generously supported by the Arts and Humanities Research Council (AHRC). Project no AH/H015655/1. I am grateful to John O'Grady for first alerting me to the debate within forensic psychiatry about risk assessment, and to Andrew Ashworth, Patrick Tomlin, to participants at the UCL Workshop on 'Seeking Security' (especially Andrew Simester), to members of Aberdeen University Law School and Oxford University Centre for Criminology for commenting on an earlier draft.

[1] *A and Others v Secretary of State for the Home Department* [2004] UKHL 56 at 29, per Lord Bingham (emphasis added).

[2] P Sands, 'Lord Bingham of Cornhill Obituary' in *The Guardian*, available at www.guardian.co.uk/law/2010/sep/11/lord-bingham-of-cornhill-obituary.

[3] PK Dick, *Minority Report* (London, Gollancz, 2002). It is famous not least because it was the inspiration behind Stephen Spielberg's movie of the same name.

risk. As the physicist Niels Bohr is said to have observed, 'Predicting is very difficult, especially about the future.'[4] Lacking total foresight, we are caught between making mistakes that put public safety in peril and making mistakes that impose serious costs or weighty burdens upon those who are deemed to pose a risk. Indeed, we may not even know what mistakes we are making or how the future might be altered by our decisions.

The injunction to err also has a normative basis in the precautionary approach to risk management adopted in many areas of contemporary governance. The precautionary principle, developed originally in the sphere of environmental law but now ubiquitous in modern risk management, shifts the onus of proof on to decision-makers, stating that where there are threats of serious or irreversible damage, lack of full scientific certainty shall not be used as a reason for inaction.[5] Stronger articulations of the principle go further to place the onus on public officials to act even in the face of uncertainty.[6] Its effect is to deny public actors the luxury of inaction against grave risks on the grounds of inadequate or incomplete knowledge. This pressure to act in conditions of uncertainty arguably entails an implicit expectation that modern risk managers ought to be willing to make mistakes in the name of public protection.

The implications of the precautionary approach are far-reaching. Risk has become a common place of modern life: every school trip, building plan, and government policy is subject to risk assessment. The question of how the risks involved can be managed and fairly distributed is hotly debated in disparate spheres, ranging through technology, to drugs, healthcare, and the environment. In the case of crime, the just distribution of risk[7] can most simply be stated as pertaining to the right of the public to live free from risk of wrongful harm or injury versus the right of the individual to live free from the risk of coercive preventive measures. Attempting to steer a course between these interests runs the risk of being deemed 'anti-protectionist' by those who insist upon the right to restrain or detain in the interests of public protection.[8] However, if we recognise that protection against unwarranted interference is owed to the individual, as well as to the public, then the just distribution of risk requires a more careful consideration of the interests in play and the complex issues at stake.

In the case of grave risk to person or property, being willing to err in the interests of public safety is more easily defensible where the costs of those errors fall upon corporations with deep pockets or public bodies adequately endowed to bear the financial or administrative burdens that a precautionary approach imposes. Likewise, less burdensome precautions applied uniformly across the

[4] The attribution is contested but the observation is no less apposite regardless of its authorship.

[5] E Fisher, *Risk Regulation and Administrative Constitutionalism* (Oxford, Hart Publishing, 2007) ch V.

[6] See P Ramsay in ch 9 of this volume.

[7] I borrow the term from J Floud and W Young, *Dangerousness and Criminal Justice* (London, Heinemann, 1981) (better known as the 'Floud Report').

[8] N Walker, 'Harms, Probabilities and Precautions' (1997) 17/4 *Oxford Journal of Legal Studies* 611–20 at 611.

population raise fewer concerns because the resultant restrictions or deprivations are borne equally by all. Precisely because they are widely borne, restrictions that are unfair or unwarranted are more likely to generate effective political resistance. Where the burden of error entails targeted coercive measures or substantial loss of *individual* liberty, however, it is less obvious that we should blithely accept the injunction to err.

This chapter will not address the development and extension of risk-based liability within criminal law or examine the development of civil (or hybrid civil-criminal) preventive orders operating on the margins of the criminal law. Both have been addressed in depth elsewhere.[9] Rather, it focuses on the assessment of individuals as risk subjects within the criminal court. It asks what considerations are in play when individuals are deemed risky, who decides, on what basis, and with what consequences. Where significant restrictions of liberty are in prospect, the chapter takes issue with the claim that it would be irresponsible to do other than err on the side of safety. Instead it argues that the greater the potential incursion upon an individual's liberty, the greater is our collective responsibility not to err at all. Where the question at issue is whether or not the court should incarcerate beyond the proportionate sentence in order to protect the public it is arguable that there is no safe side on which to err since to deprive an individual of their liberty unwarrantedly is itself to commit a grave moral error.

I THE RIGHT TO BE PRESUMED FREE FROM HARMFUL INTENTIONS

The presumption of innocence is rightly considered a fundamental principle of criminal justice.[10] It requires the prosecution to prove all the elements of the offence with which the individual has been charged and to prove that any defence or exception is unfounded before the presumption can be rebutted and an individual found guilty. This core presumption that, in the absence of such proof, one is to be deemed innocent of past offences has been subject to erosions and statutory reversals of the burden of proof, particularly in respect of excuses and exceptions.[11] However, it has also been strengthened by article 6(2) of the European Convention on Human Rights which provides that 'Everyone charged with a criminal offence shall be presumed innocent until proved guilty

[9] A Ashworth and L Zedner, 'Preventive Orders: A Problem of Under-Criminalization?' in RA Duff et al (eds), *The Boundaries of the Criminal Law* (Oxford, Oxford University Press, 2010); A Ashworth and L Zedner, 'Preventive Justice and the Limits of the Criminal Law' in RA Duff and SP Green (eds), *Philosophical Foundations of the Criminal Law* (Oxford, Oxford University Press, 2011).

[10] A Ashworth and M Blake, 'The Presumption of Innocence in English Criminal Law' (1996) *Criminal Law Review* 306–17. V Tadros, 'Rethinking the Presumption of Innocence' (2007) 1 *Criminal Law and Philosophy* 193–213.

[11] A Ashworth, 'Four Threats to the Presumption of Innocence' (2006) 123 *South African Law Journal* 62–96.

according to law.' The nub of this is that each time one appears in the dock, and no matter how many previous convictions, one has the right to be presumed innocent of the present charges until proven otherwise.

How does this fundamental right relate to the assessment of risk within the criminal court? Might it be argued that any assessment of individual risk, insofar as it makes a predictive claim about the probability of future wrongful conduct, does damage to the very principles underpinning the presumption? There is of course a temporal issue to be addressed here: the presumption of innocence relates to crime past, the assessment of risk to crimes future. However, it could be said that every positive risk assessment constitutes a denial of a right to be presumed free of harmful intention and that this denial cannot easily be squared with the maintenance of the right to be presumed innocent of future crimes. On this view, to designate someone as a risk ahead of time is to undermine their right to be presumed innocent into the future. Famously, the Swedish Council of Crime Prevention claimed that sentencing upon the basis of risk assessment amounts to an individual serving 'a sentence for a crime he did not commit' and that the practice 'can be compared to the sentencing of an innocent person'.[12]

An opposing view, enunciated by the Floud Report, is that the right to be presumed free of harmful intentions only applies to those who have yet to offend.[13] As Bottoms and Brownsword observe, for Floud, those who 'have not yet committed any violent act have the right to assume that the State will take no preventive action against them; they are to be presumed free of whatever harmful intentions they may have.'[14] In their view this presumption does not apply to the convicted offender 'since he has already manifested harmful intentions in his present conviction'.[15] Walker states the case even more strongly, arguing that 'someone who has harmed, or tried to harm, another person, can hardly claim a right to the presumption of harmlessness: he has forfeited that right, and given society the right to interfere in his life'.[16] He goes on to claim that the harm someone has caused 'is part of the moral justification for subjecting that person to a precautionary measure'.[17]

Several difficulties arise with this sweeping aside of the right to be presumed free of harmful intentions in the pursuit of public protection. First, given that attrition rates are so high and only a small percentage of offences result in a conviction, it is questionable whether this presumption should apply to all those

[12] National Swedish Council for Crime Prevention, *A New Penal System* (1978) cited in N Walker, 'Ethical and Other Problems' in N Walker (ed), *Dangerous People* (London, Blackstone, 1996) 2.

[13] Floud and Young, *Dangerousness* (n 7 above) 44.

[14] AE Bottoms and R Brownsword, 'The Dangerousness Debate after the Floud Report' (1982) 22 *British Journal of Criminology* 229–54, 236.

[15] ibid 236.

[16] Walker, 'Ethical Problems' (n 12 above) 7. Note that whereas Floud deliberately (and correctly in my view) speaks of the 'right to be presumed free of harmful intentions' in order to limit the discussion to intentional harms, Walker uses the more expansive (and more problematic) 'right to the presumption of harmlessness'.

[17] ibid 7.

yet to be convicted. Second, to say that an offender has 'already manifested harmful intentions in his present conviction' plays fast and loose with the concept of intention, which is not an enduring state of mind but specific to the time and circumstances in which it is formed. A past harmful intention formed in respect of a single circumstance or victim cannot simply be extended into the future. Third, even accepting that there is an important semantic, and perhaps also a moral, gap between the presumption of innocence and the right to be presumed free of harmful intentions, it should surely be acknowledged that forfeiture of the latter has profound implications for the former, particularly since it is unclear whether the forfeiture is to be absolute and irretrievable or not. All this leaves unaddressed the question of whether fundamental rights can be forfeited at all. Fourth, given the potential adverse consequences for the individual, much greater attention needs to be paid to the circumstances, type of crime, and level of seriousness at which the presumption should be foregone.[18] These are not mere matters of academic enquiry but issues of practical import. Where the presumption is foregone the court assumes a right to consider whether the risk the individual poses requires intervention or restraint beyond that which is proportionate to the present offence.

Notwithstanding these, rather obvious, difficulties, the right to be presumed free of harmful intent was withdrawn from the convicted offender in the initial framing of one of the most pernicious of contemporary penal measures: Imprisonment for Public Protection (IPP). Introduced by the Criminal Justice Act 2003 (CJA 2003), the IPP permits indefinite preventive sentences to be imposed on offenders in cases where, according to section 229(1) of the CJA 2003:

> (a) a person has been convicted of a specified offence, and (b) it falls to a court to assess under any of sections 225 to 228 whether there is a significant risk to members of the public of serious harm occasioned by the commission by him of further such offences.[19]

Significantly, under CJA 2003 section 229(3), originally the court not merely withdrew the right to be presumed free of harmful intention but was obliged to presume dangerousness:

> If at the time when that offence was committed the offender was aged 18 or over and had been convicted in any part of the United Kingdom of one or more relevant

[18] Some of these questions are addressed in the Floud Report but for cogent criticism see Bottoms and Brownsword, 'The Dangerousness Debate' (n 14 above) 229–54.

[19] Serious harm is defined in the Act as 'death or serious personal injury, whether physical or psychological'. At the time of writing, the Legal Aid, Sentencing and Punishment of Offenders Bill (2011) is before Parliament, clauses 113–117 of which provide for the abolition of IPP orders and their replacement by Extended Determinate Sentences (EDS) for offenders convicted of serious sexual and violent crimes to be followed by extended periods on licence. If these provisions are enacted, the IPP sentence will no longer be available to the courts. However these changes will not apply retrospectively to those currently serving IPP sentences in prison. On the move to abolish IPP and on the rationale behind the EDS, see Ramsay, this volume pp 193, 214–17.

> offences, the court must assume that there is such a risk as is mentioned in subsection (1)(b).[20]

This reverse burden presumption of risk was to prove deeply controversial, not least because it was over-inclusive[21] and denied the court the ability to exercise discretion in the interests of justice. It did not withstand judicial or parliamentary scrutiny.[22] Within three years of the Act's implementation in 2005, the Criminal Justice and Immigration Act 2008 section 17 removed the obligation to presume risk and restored discretion to the court. As a result IPP sentences are no longer mandatory even when the relevant conditions are fulfilled, but rather are available to judges who are able to exercise their discretion in the light of all the information available to the court. That said, in exercising this discretion the countervailing interest in public protection weighs heavily in the mind of the court[23] and may sway it towards assuming risk. So the key question remains – how is the court to determine who poses a risk sufficient to require preventive measures and who does not?

II APPLYING RISK LABELS

Risk is ubiquitous in criminal law but takes so many forms and connotes such diverse levels of liability that it cannot be said to signify any one thing when spoken of in the criminal court. Sometimes it would appear that the risks in question are simply variables known to be associated with a higher likelihood of future offending. So, for example, particular background characteristics, patterns of behaviour, specific locales, or being a member of a particular demographic or socio-economic group have all been identified as being highly correlated with offending behaviour and used to justify prohibitions said to serve the preventive function of reducing the likelihood of that behaviour. On other occasions the risks in question are forms of conduct deemed inherently presently risky and therefore to be prohibited in their own right such as drinking, drug-taking, or religious extremism. Other risks entail present behaviour which may or may not be risky done with the intent to endanger (such as buying a map of the underground with the intent to bomb it). While other risks still pertain to behaviour that is not presently but only prospectively risky or, more

[20] Though note the section continued 'unless, after taking into account – (a) all such information as is available to it about the nature and circumstances of each of the offences, (b) where appropriate, any information which is before it about any pattern of behaviour of which any of the offences forms part, and c) any information about the offender which is before it, the court considers that it would be unreasonable to conclude that there is such a risk.'

[21] If the offender had ever previously committed any of the 153 offences specified in the schedule to the Act, the court were obliged to presume that the test of significant harm had been reached and that they should be given an IPP sentence. HM Chief Inspector of Prisons & HM Chief Inspector of Probation, *The Indeterminate Sentence for Public Protection: A Thematic Review* (2008) 13.

[22] See HC Justice Committee, *Towards Effective Sentencing* (2008) 18–29.

[23] Walker, 'Harms' (n 8 above) 611–20.

remotely still, only prospectively risky as a result of third party intervention – the shopkeeper who fails to secure his liquor section for example. Perhaps the very word risk is the source of the problem, acting as it does as an umbrella for widely differing perils and degrees of liability. A more discriminating vocabulary would permit greater analytical clarity by distinguishing between present and prospective risks, between agent-dependent and agent-independent risks,[24] and by grading more finely the different levels of culpability, gravity of risk, and degrees of likelihood in play.[25] Only with greater precision can the casual ill-defined reference to risk or, more problematically still, to risky individuals be avoided.

The need to distinguish between different types of risk is made all the more important by the very significant differences in the size or scale of risk in prospect. To talk of risk in broad terms misses the obvious point that risk of personal offence or nuisance is hardly of the same order as risk of personal physical harm which, again, is scarcely the same as risk of nuclear or terrorist attack. In respect of past crimes we have internalised this need to differentiate and have developed sophisticated ordinal scales ranging at the bottom from sub-criminal anti-social, offensive or disorderly behaviour through everyday criminal offences to dangerous violent and sexual offences to terrorism offences and other mass atrocities at the top. The exact placement of particular crimes upon the scale may be contested and their relative ranking subject to reconsideration and revision but that there is such a scale is now accepted.[26] Ordinal ranking of offences is important because the exercise of differentiation is not merely taxonomic; it forms the basis for a proportional system of punishment that ties coercive consequences closely to the gravity of the offence.[27] In respect of risk the need for fine distinctions is no less pressing, both to reflect its scalar nature and the variety of axes upon which it should be assessed. Greater precision is needed not only about the nature and gravity of a risk but also about its likelihood, without which risk assessment may result in a disposal proportionate to the gravity of the prospective risk but wholly disproportionate to the probability of it occurring. Further consideration also needs to be given to the question of whether the probability requirement should vary according to the gravity of the harm in prospect: so in respect of very grave risks a lower probability of occurrence might justify preventive intervention but where the anticipated harm is less grave a higher probability of occurrence should be required.

[24] RA Duff, 'Criminalising Endangerment' in RA Duff, and SP Green (eds), *Defining Crimes: Essays on the Special Part of the Criminal Law* (Oxford, Oxford University Press, 2005) 43–64.

[25] See A Ashworth, *Sentencing and Criminal Justice* (Cambridge, Cambridge University Press, 2010) 152.

[26] See for example, Sentencing Guidelines Council, 'Overarching Principles: Seriousness', available at http://webarchive.nationalarchives.gov.uk/+/http://www.sentencing-guidelines.gov.uk/docs/Seriousness_guideline.pdf.

[27] A von Hirsch and A Ashworth, *Proportionate Sentencing: Exploring the Principles* (Oxford, Oxford University Press, 2005).

At present what exactly is being claimed when risk is assessed in the criminal court is unclear and the basis upon which the assessment is made is far from consistent. Individual risk assessment ranges from advertence to past conduct or, much more narrowly, past convictions; through clinical assessment by experts (typically probation officers, psychologists, or forensic psychiatrists); to predictive actuarial statements that an individual with this particular set of characteristics or belonging to this population group is X per cent likely to go on to commit acts of wrongdoing or criminal harm (I will have more to say about all this below). Whatever its basis, risk assessment entails the immediate application of an enduring (often indelible) label on the individual. Labelling is notoriously problematic in respect of past offending, not least because it adversely affects the way individuals are perceived and treated, and how they come to perceive themselves.[28] Labelling individuals as 'high risk' assigns them to a categorical status that is difficult to escape and, as a consequence, often self-fulfilling. Risk labels are even more problematic than those applied in respect of past offences because being prognostic they tend to fix the future.[29] To apply the label 'high risk' makes the questionable assumption that the individual before the court today is indistinguishable from their future (and perhaps not so risky) self. The further into the future this assumption is extended the more questionable it becomes. It is clearly more problematic to say that someone poses a risk in five years time than to say that he or she poses a risk tomorrow because it leaves open no possibility of change over time. Risk assessments based on past offending behaviour or other fixed criteria are particularly objectionable as they do not allow that the individual might develop in ways that would reasonably qualify them for re-categorisation as less, or not at all, risky.

For all these reasons risk assessment would be troublesome enough if it were simply a label. Yet risk assessment in the criminal court is not simply a descriptive or categorical matter but an instrumental one from which serious consequences – not least stigma and the pains of punishment – follow. It is questionable whether the criminal court is competent or structurally well suited to cope with the dynamic nature of risk because its determinations are typically one-off affairs. In its conventional role (determining liability for past wrongs) this is not a major problem: the criminal court is tasked with ascription of fixed liability. Precisely because the behaviour occurred in the past, saving the emergence of new evidence or procedural impropriety, there is ordinarily no need to revisit that decision at a later date. The judgment is dichotomous (guilty/not guilty) and is made at a particular moment in time. By contrast, because risk is prospective and by nature dynamic, its management necessitates continuing

[28] D Downes and P Rock, *Understanding Deviance*. 4th edn (Oxford, Oxford University Press, 2003) ch 6.

[29] L Zedner, 'Fixing the Future? The Pre-Emptive Turn in Criminal Justice' in S Bronnit, B McSherry, and A Norrie (eds), *Regulating Deviance: The Redirection of Criminalisation and the Futures of Criminal Law* (Oxford, Hart Publishing, 2009).

assessment (at least in respect of those criteria that are fluid rather than static) that will result in determinations very likely to vary over time. This ongoing process sits ill within the structure and workings of the criminal court.[30] For reasons that will be elaborated upon below, a once and for all judgment creates the danger of doing injustice to those whose risk profile may change radically over time.[31]

Notice also that the risk label is applied not only to particular behaviour or conduct but also to people. Whereas in other fields where the object of assessment is a situation, a structure or confluence of circumstances, risk assessment within the criminal court mostly has a single object – the individual in the dock. Particular concerns arise where the question before the court is not 'under what conditions or subject to what triggers is this person at risk of re-offending' but 'does this person pose a risk' or, more problematically still, 'is this person high risk'? Risk assessment of this sort excludes relevant considerations in two important ways. First the individual becomes the sole object of assessment to the exclusion of external circumstances and opportunities. Second, that assessment tends to focus upon one aspect of the defendant's disposition – riskiness – to the exclusion of other considerations (such as character and personal prospects). This narrowing of focus on risk reduces the person, their circumstances, and their capacity for change to a single categorical label or ascription of probability. A trend in recent legislation is the rise of 'risky people' displacing prior attention to risky behaviour and risky scenarios. In many jurisdictions, legislation aimed at controlling risk has successively designated anti-social youths, sexual offenders, dangerous offenders, and suspected terrorists as risk subjects. Yet the basis upon which they are so designated is often problematic. For example, in respect of IPP, the Criminal Justice Act 2003 section 229(1) states that an offender is to be deemed dangerous if *'the court is of the opinion that there is a significant risk to members of the public of serious harm occasioned by the commission by him of further specified offences'.* And yet the structured OASys risk assessment tool,[32] upon the basis of which the court often makes its determination, assesses likelihood of reconviction in terms of 'low', 'medium' or 'high' risk and assesses 'risk of serious harm' as 'low', 'medium', 'high' or 'very high'. Despite claims that there is 'a measure of compatibility' between these terms,[33] it is quite unclear how the categorisations generated by

[30] M Shapiro, *Courts: a Comparative and Political Analysis* (Chicago, University of Chicago Press, 1981) ch 1.

[31] M Brown, 'Calculations of Risk in Contemporary Penal Practice' in J Pratt and M Brown (eds), *Dangerous Offenders* (London, Routledge, 2000); P Maurutto and K Hannah-Moffat, 'Assembling Risk and the Restructuring of Penal Control' (2006) 46 *British Journal of Criminology* 438–54; R McLeod, A Sweeting and R Evans, *Improving the Structure and Content of Psychiatric Reports for Sentencing: Research to Develop Good Practice Guidance* (London, Ministry of Justice, 2010) 17.

[32] See HMSO Prison Service PSO2205 *Offender Assessment and Sentence Management-OASys* at www.justice.gov.uk.

[33] HM Chief Inspector of Prisons, *The Indeterminate Sentence for Public Protection* (2008) 14. See www.ohrn.nhs.uk/resource/policy/IPP.pdf.

the assessment tools relate to the category laid down in the legislation.[34] Unsurprisingly, the courts have struggled to come up with a satisfactory definition of 'significant risk' under the Act. In the leading case of *Lang*,[35] the Court of Appeal held that 'significant risk' means 'noteworthy, of considerable amount or importance' – but it can hardly be said that this definition makes the task of the court easier. Perhaps this rather lame resort to the dictionary betokens a declaration of defeat in the face of the difficulties posed by the statutory provisions.[36] In *Pedley, Martin and Hamadi*,[37] the Court confirmed the indication given in *Lang* that a 'significant risk' presented a higher threshold than a mere possibility of occurrence but, again, did not think that any further definition of the term would be helpful. In particular, they rejected the invitation of counsel for the appellants to re-define it in terms of numerical probability or any other percentage of likelihood. So the glaring disjuncture between the use of numerical risk assessment tools and the legal definition of risk remains.[38]

In *Johnson*,[39] the Court of Appeal, following the judgment in *Lang*, addressed the relationship between assessment of future risk and the present offence. The Court held that IPP was concerned with **future** risk and the **future** protection of the public, and not with punishing the present offending. It also held that it did not automatically follow from the absence of actual harm caused by an offender to date, that the risk that he would cause serious harm in the future was negligible.[40] There may, of course, be legitimate reason to conclude that an individual who has not yet caused serious harm may, nonetheless, pose a significant risk of serious harm for the future. Yet the figures on the use of IPP suggest a worrying readiness to reach this conclusion. According to evidence given by the Parole Board to the House of Commons Justice Committee, prior to 2008, half of IPP

[34] Prison Reform Trust (PRT), *Unjust Deserts: Imprisonment for Public Protection* (London, PRT, 2010) 26.

[35] *R v Lang [2005] EWCA Crim 2864.*

[36] Significantly, the judgment in Lang concludes: 'It would be inappropriate to conclude these proceedings without expressing our sympathy with all those sentencers whose decisions have been the subject of appeal to this Court. The fact that, in many cases, the sentencers were unsuccessful in finding their way through the provisions of this Act, which we have already described as labyrinthine, is a criticism not of them but of those who produced these astonishingly complex provisions. Whether now or in the fullness of time the public will benefit from sentencing provisions of such complexity is not for us to say. But it does seem to us that there is much to be said for a sentencing system which is intelligible to the general public as well as decipherable, with difficulty by the judiciary.' *R v Lang [2005] EWCA Crim 2864.*

[37] *Pedley, Martin and Hamadi [2009] EWCA Crim 840.* The Court also found that a sentence of IPP imposed when the judge is satisfied that the defendant poses a significant risk of serious harm to the public is wholly compatible with both arts 3 and 5(1)(a) of the European Convention. See further www.cps.gov.uk/legal/s_to_u/sentencing_and_dangerous_offenders/#a01.

[38] More worryingly still it appears that not all those sentenced to IPP orders are subject to formal risk assessment. A study by HM Inspector of Prisons found that of 48 offenders subject to IPP, three had no pre-sentence report at all and a further five had no OASys assessment completed before sentencing. Of those upon whom reports had been completed, HMCI concluded that the risk had been falsely inflated in 16 cases and that of the 48 the risks posed could have been managed by a different sentence in 19 cases. HM Chief Inspector of Prisons (n 33 above)19.

[39] *R v Johnson [2006] EWCA Crim 2486.*

[40] ibid.

prisoners received a tariff sentence of 20 months or less and 20 per cent received a tariff sentence of less than 18 months.[41] According to the Prison Reform Trust, in the first years of the IPP some individuals were given tariff sentences 'of no more than a few months or even weeks'.[42] Of course the justification for imposing extended sentences on these relatively low tariff offenders was precisely the future risk they were deemed to pose. However, alarm bells ought to ring where 'a significant risk to members of the public of serious harm' is so routinely found in respect of those whose present offences merited such short sentences. No doubt in recognition of the fact that offenders with very low tariff sentences were so regularly sentenced to indefinite detention, the Criminal Justice and Immigration Act 2008 required that an IPP order could be imposed only if the tariff sentence were two years or more.[43] Although the two year minimum tariff is to be welcomed, it remains unclear why two years, rather than any other period, should be deemed an appropriate lower threshold.[44] Furthermore this amendment was not applied retrospectively so those with tariff terms under two years already serving IPP sentences remain in prison. The implications are not trivial. Although 'it was only intended and expected to be used in a limited number of cases', at the end of March 2011 the number of IPP sentenced prisoners in custody was 6,550 .[45] Around 3,500 of these have already completed their minimum custodial terms.[46] Five years after their introduction only 4 per cent of these post-tariff IPP prisoners have been released.[47] These striking figures attest to the relative ease of entering the high risk category resulting in indefinite incarceration and the extreme difficulty of escaping that categorisation and thereby securing one's release once it has been made. Recognising that risk assessments are not merely classificatory but instrumental invites closer attention to the ways in which they are used by the courts and to what ends. We have seen how the IPP sentence deploys risk assessment to justify incarceration beyond the tariff term of imprisonment. Risk assessment also plays an important role in pre-sentence

[41] HC Justice Committee, *Towards Effective Sentencing* (2008) 21. See www.publications.parliament.uk/pa/cm200708/cmselect/cmjust/184/184.pdf

[42] Prison Reform Trust, *Unjust Deserts* (n 34 above) 24.

[43] The Criminal Justice & Immigration Act 2008 provided that IPP may be imposed only where either of two conditions is met: either the immediate offence would attract a notional minimum term of at least two years; or the offender has on a previous occasion been convicted of one of the offences in the extensive list set out in the new sch 15A to the 2003 Act.

[44] The Prison Reform Trust (PRT) condemns it as an 'arbitrary threshold' (though of course any threshold would likewise be arbitrary). More importantly, the PRT suggests it is too low on the grounds that the offence committed has not been deemed serious enough in itself to warrant an indeterminate sentence. Prison Reform Trust, *Unjust Deserts* (n 34 above) 23. Note also that where an offender has a previous conviction for one of 22 specified very serious violent or sexual offences, an IPP order may be imposed without this minimum tariff. The House of Commons Justice Committee comment: 'We are unclear as to the rationale for this particular distinction'. HC Justice Committee, *Towards Effective Sentencing* (n 41 above) 26.

[45] Ministry of Justice (MOJ), *Provisional figures relating to offenders serving indeterminate sentence of imprisonment for public protection (IPPs)* 2. www.justice.gov.uk/downloads/publications/statistics-and-data/mojstats/provisional-ipp-figures.pdf.

[46] ibid 3.

[47] Prison Reform Trust, *Unjust Deserts* (n 34 above) 35.

reports used in the allocation of non-custodial penal measures under the Community Sentence. Risk assessment provides the basis for and justification of a growing array of civil and hybrid civil-criminal preventive orders such as Anti-Social Behaviour Orders (ASBOs), Control Orders,[48] Serious Crime Prevention Orders, and Sexual Offences Prevention Orders. Technically non-punitive, but highly coercive nonetheless, is the use of risk assessment as a basis for incapacitative civil detention, for example the civil commitment of sexual offenders in the US.[49]

As this brief overview makes clear, risk assessment is central to court decisions concerning coercive measures that intrude on individual liberty beyond the tariff term or proportional punishment. Recognising risk assessment as instrumental in licensing state coercion beyond that justified on punitive grounds makes it all the more important that its foundations are methodologically sound and morally defensible. More will be said on the methodological questions below; for the moment let us consider what moral claims are being made when risk is assessed for preventive purposes.

III JUSTIFYING INTERVENTION ON GROUNDS OF RISK

Coercive intervention or the imposition of penal sanctions by the state for past behaviour is recognised as a prima facie wrong in need of special justification.[50] Where the ground for coercive intervention is future risk, the question of justification is no less pressing. If, and to the extent that, simply posing a risk can be seen as harmful to the interests of others, then intervention might be justified on retributivist grounds. This is most plausibly defended as a form of 'present retributivism', whereby the individual is censured and sanctioned for the harm inherent in the risk the individual presently poses.[51] Where an individual poses a significant risk of serious harm to others he or she reduces their welfare whether the risk eventuates or not: either because the individual damages their subjective security[52] or because he or she takes unacceptable risks with their safety. Drink driving is a case in point. It can be argued that a retributive response is justifiable on this basis alone but the corresponding penalty must be proportional to the actual reduction of welfare suffered and the wrong done. Less plausible is the attempt to justify coercive intervention as a form of prospective retributivism,

[48] Now relabelled 'terrorist, prevention and investigation measures' or TPIMs. See 'Control Orders have been Rebranded. Big Problems Remain' *The Guardian* 28 January 2011, available at www.guardian.co.uk/commentisfree/libertycentral/2011/jan/28/control-orders-protection-of-freedoms- bill.

[49] E Janus, 'The Preventive State, Terrorists and Sexual Predators: Countering the Threat of a New Outsider Jurisprudence' (2004) 40 *Criminal Law Bulletin* 576.

[50] RA Duff and D Garland (eds), *A Reader on Punishment* (Oxford, Oxford University Press, 1994) 2.

[51] C Finkelstein, 'Is Risk a Harm?' (2003) 151 *University of Pennsylvania Law Review* 963–1001.

[52] L Zedner, *Security* (London, Routledge, 2009) 16–19.

whereby the individual is pre-punished for what he or she will in future do.[53] Although this approach has the merit of imposing a form of prospective proportionality as a restraint on any intervention by limiting it to the gravity of the risk and the likelihood of it occurring, the glaring problem is that the individual is deemed punishable for what he or she has not yet done and may never do.[54]

Coercive intervention against risky individuals is more plausibly justified on instrumental or consequentialist than retributive grounds. Intervention to eliminate or reduce future risks can be defended as a form of crime prevention or prospective crime reduction. Yet even here the justification is questionable and relies upon three separate claims. First, that an individual presents an unacceptable risk and that the court is competent to determine this level of riskiness. Second, that there is a causal relationship between the assessment of an individual's riskiness and the proposed intervention such that the intervention can plausibly be said to be reductive of the risk. Third, that the individual's riskiness requires this level of coercive intrusion and that no other or lesser means is equal to the task. In short, only through this degree of coercive intervention can this riskiness be addressed, minimised, or eliminated. Absent this prospective efficacy, in minimising future risks the intervention would not be justified. So the efficacy claim depends upon a subsidiary claim that the risk in question is malleable and, by intervention, amenable to management and reduction. The difficulty here is that, as observed above, the criminal court can only make a once in time determination as to risk. Yet, if the very grounds for intervention are that the risk is fluid and malleable over time, its assessment must be conducted over time also. Of course the criminal court typically deals with this problem by leaving the risk reductive part of an intervention open-ended, for example, by way of indeterminate sentence. In cases of indeterminate imprisonment it entrusts the power of release to the Parole Board. This is not the place to explore the workings of the Parole Board; suffice to say here that although it is ordinarily thought of and thereby justified as a body charged with determining release, its decisions also have the effect of determining and thereby prolonging the length of sentence. By deploying risk as the justification for indeterminate sentencing, the criminal court delegates its coercive power to a body that is both inadequately resourced to bear the burden of making determinations as to release and highly risk averse.[55]

Of the three claims outlined above (i) that the criminal court is competent to determine risk, ii) that the proposed intervention is reductive of risk and (iii) that no lesser means is equal to the task, I propose now to consider only (i).

[53] C New, 'Time and Punishment' (1992) 52 *Analysis* 35–40; L Zedner, 'Preventive Justice or Pre-Punishment? The Case of Control Orders' 59 (2007) *Current Legal Problems* 174–203.

[54] S Smilansky, 'The Time to Punish' (1994) 54/1 *Analysis* 50–53.

[55] Not least because it is required to be so: 'the Parole Board is only able to release a prisoner where it is satisfied that the risk of doing so is considered to be no more than minimal'. To address this, the Government is considering introducing a new test for the Parole Board that would deny release only to 'those who clearly pose a very serious risk of future harm'. Ministry of Justice, *Breaking the Cycle* (n 45 above) 56.

The other two are no less important, but, logically, they come into play only if (i) can first be established.

IV RE-ASSESSING RISK ASSESSMENT

In the early 1990s, Feeley and Simon published seminal articles that heralded the advent of 'the new penology' and 'actuarial justice'.[56] In these works they raised concerns about the validity of risk assessment and the implications of its deployment in the criminal court. Those warning bells rang loudly in academic circles and spawned a rich literature dedicated to exploring the perils of risk assessment as a tool of crime control.[57] They did little, however, to halt the development of actuarial risk assessment instruments (ARAIs) that rapidly became entrenched in the daily workings of the criminal court. Intriguingly, a more recent work by Simon appears to adopt a more sanguine view of the capacity of ARAIs to predict risk accurately.[58] As enormous sums and intellectual resources are invested in the development of ever more sophisticated tools, Simon sees room for optimism in the fact that as risk assessment becomes more 'scientific', it is subject to the restraints self-imposed by scientific method. He cites the $8 million MacArthur study[59] as an example of a sophisticated research study whose methods more nearly meet the standards pertaining in medical research and whose tools provide a more reliable basis for predicting violence than was hitherto available. He also welcomes the replacement of problematic dichotomous designations (dangerous/not dangerous) by assessments that claim only to determine whether an individual falls above a designated threshold for risk and by probabilistic forecasts that there is an X per cent chance of future violence.[60]

What are we to make of these plaudits from one of the fiercest critics of actuarial justice? Granted, the use of probabilistic forecasts gets round the problem of false positives because it is not dependent upon making a claim that a given offender will or will not offend. It is merely a statement of likelihood about that population sample's propensity for violence or other offence. The obvious problem, however, is that probabilistic assessments continue to form the basis for

[56] M Feeley and J Simon, 'The New Penology: Notes on the Emerging Strategy of Corrections and Its Implications' (1992) 30/4 *Criminology* 449–74; M Feeley and J Simon, 'Actuarial Justice: The Emerging New Criminal Law' in D Nelken (ed), *The Futures of Criminology* (London, Sage, 1994) 173–201.

[57] For example, B Harcourt, *Against Prediction: Profiling, Policing, and Punishing in an Actuarial Age* (Chicago, University of Chicago Press, 2007); P O'Malley (ed), *Crime and the Risk Society* (Aldershot, Ashgate, 1998); P O'Malley, *Risk, Uncertainty and Government* (London, The Glasshouse Press, 2004).

[58] J Simon, 'Reversal of Fortune: The Resurgence of Individual Risk Assessment in Criminal Justice' (2005) 1 *Annual Review of Law and Social Science* 397–421 especially 411ff.

[59] J Monahan et al, *Rethinking Risk Assessment: The MacArthur Study of Mental Disorder and Violence* (New York, Oxford University Press, 2001).

[60] Simon, 'Reversal of Fortune' (n 58 above) 413.

dichotomous decisions, such as whether to impose a fixed term or indeterminate (and potentially severely disproportionate) sentence or not. Being able to state with any confidence that there is a 40 per cent risk of future violence in a given population group is clearly better than no knowledge but it remains insufficient to underwrite the decision to deprive an individual of liberty indefinitely. Another danger is that these assessments are impossible to refute since non-offending does not discredit or disprove the assessment, since the claim is not that a given offender *will* offend but merely that there is a 40 per cent risk of those with the offender's characteristics doing so.

No less problematic is Feeley and Simon's claim that the rise of the 'new penology'[61] entailed a shift from individual to aggregate determinations of risk and to the management of risky populations. Although the rise of mass surveillance and other aggregate risk measures go some way to bearing out this claim, in the dock of the criminal court a lone individual remains the focus of risk assessment. Here an acute tension arises between the use of ARAIs as means of assessing categorical probabilities and the need for an individualised risk assessment in respect of a single person against whom coercive measures are contemplated. As Peay observes, 'Academics and policy-makers have been fiercely divided' on the question of how one squares 'the difference between risk factors associated with groups of people who have common characteristics . . . and the determination of whether any one individual within that group will be amongst those where risk is realized'.[62]

Let us consider for a moment what ARAIs are designed to do. ARAIs are tools with which to assess the probability that those belonging to a particular class or population will re-offend or pose a threat of future violence. The assessment is an aggregate one that maintains that of population X, Y per cent will re-offend. Even in respect of their capacity to make this aggregate claim difficult methodological issues arise concerning the size of sample, the selection of the population, and the margin of error.[63] There are also serious questions about the impartiality of ARAIs, particularly when applied to members of minority populations for whom these standardised tools may fail to provide a reliable assessment.[64] More problematic still is the application of aggregate prediction tools to the individual. As Hart and colleagues rightly observe, 'moving the focus of analysis from groups to individuals changes the way in which risk is conceptualised'.[65] Group risk assessments are predictive statements about the proportion of people within a given population who will offend: here the

[61] Feeley and Simon, 'Actuarial Justice' (n 56 above) 178.

[62] J Peay, 'Mentally Disordered Offenders' in M Maguire, R Morgan, and R Reiner (eds), *The Oxford Handbook of Criminology* (Oxford, Oxford University Press, 2007) 496–527, 520.

[63] SD Hart, C Michie, and DJ Cooke, 'Precision of Actuarial Risk Assessment Instruments: Evaluating The "Margins of Error" Of Group v Individual Predictions of Violence' (2007) 190 *Journal of Psychiatry* 60–65.

[64] EEH Griffith, 'Ethics in Forensic Psychiatry: A Cultural Response to Stone and Appelbaum' (1997) 26 *Journal of the American Academy of Psychiatry and the Law* 171–84.

[65] Hart, Michie, and Cooke, 'Precision of Actuarial Risk Assessment' (n 63 above) 60–65, 61.

margin of error is uncertainty regarding that proportion. When applied to the individual, the question shifts to become one of how likely that *particular individual* is to reoffend. Hart and colleagues argued that 'the margin of error or uncertainty for an individual prediction is not the same as – and indeed, logically, must be considerably greater than – that for groups'.[66] Yet it is questionable whether one can distinguish between aggregate and individual risk assessment in this way because, as their critics were quick to point out, 'if all one knows about an individual is his membership of a risk group what can "individual risk" mean?'[67] In response Hart and colleagues were obliged to concede that individual risk is 'unknown or incalculable' precisely because the ARAIs are constructed in such a way as to make it impossible to make statements about individual risk. The key issue then is should ARAIs be regarded as providing data that makes it possible to 'help us make better decisions that we otherwise could'[68] or does the aggregate basis upon which ARAIs calculate risk render it indefensible to apply them to individuals? Judging by the highly technical debates and differences of opinion in the forensic psychiatry literature, the jury seems to be out on this question. Although use of ARAIs raises such important and, as yet unresolved, methodological questions about scientific validity that give rise to serious moral dilemmas about their use, these have received curiously little attention in legal or criminological circles.

V WHO IS TO DECIDE? PSYCHIATRIC VERSUS LEGAL DETERMINATIONS

A further difficulty is that, although much of the criminological literature presumes the dominance of ARAIs as technical tools of risk knowledge,[69] professional experts retain a key role in interpreting actuarial data for the criminal court.[70] In making risk assessments of individuals facing sentence by the court, these experts do not simply read off the data the ARAIs spew out but interpret and apply it, in no small part using their professional judgement.[71] Generally, ARAIs are interpreted by probation officers. Whether or not they have the statistical expertise to interpret this complex data is subject to little scrutiny. Given the close correlation between mental illness and dangerousness, psychologists and forensic psychiatrists also play a key role as expert witnesses called upon by the court to offer authoritative determinations as to the threat posed by

[66] ibid 61.

[67] D Mossman and T Sellke, 'Avoiding Errors About "Margins of Error"' (2007) 191 *British Journal of Psychiatry* 561–62, 561. See also GT Harris, ME Rice, and VL Quinsey, 'Shall Evidence-Based Risk Assessment Be Abandoned?' 192 (2008) *The British Journal of Psychiatry* 154.

[68] Mossman and Sellke, 'Avoiding Errors About "Margins of Error"' (2007) 561–62, 561.

[69] Harcourt, *Against Prediction* (n 57 above) 32.

[70] B Hebenton and T Seddon, 'From Dangerousness to Precaution: Managing Sexual and Violent Offenders in an Insecure and Uncertain Age' (2009) 49 *British Journal of Criminology* 343–62, 351.

[71] So much so that Ansbro observes 'it is somewhat artificial to see actuarial and clinical information as mutually exclusive'. M Ansbro 'The Nuts and Bolt of Risk Assessment: When the Clinical and Actuarial Conflict' (2010) 49 *The Howard Journal of Criminal Justice* 252–68, 254.

putatively dangerous offenders.[72] Recent academic debates in criminal law and criminology have focused almost entirely on the challenges of actuarial justice[73] and have paid little heed to the continuing importance of clinical experts in court.[74] Parallel debates in psychiatry about the dilemmas posed by the making of clinical determinations of risk in the criminal court[75] also remain largely unheeded by criminal lawyers. This is a worrying oversight because these debates reveal psychiatrists to be alert to important moral and jurisprudential issues that have largely escaped lawyerly notice.

A primary concern for psychiatry is that risk assessments are presented to the court with as much flourish as scientific evidence, despite the fact that their validity is fiercely debated within the profession. Psychiatrists are called as expert witnesses and their medical qualifications, experience, and skills are routinely recounted by barristers in glowing terms ahead of their cross-examination as if to pre-empt any challenge to their judgement. Like other witnesses they are called upon to tell the truth but what constitutes truth here is of a different order than, for example, the recollections of a witness about a past event. Instead the truth they are called upon to tell is a complex and often highly contested reading of actuarial and clinical data that makes claims about future conduct that is as yet unknowable. In a setting that attributes criminal liability for past offences only when the court is satisfied beyond reasonable doubt, the qualms and questions raised within the profession concerning the use of ARAIs to predict future risk are worrisome. Little surprise then that psychiatrists continue to ask 'Does psychiatry have anything true to say that the courts should listen to?'[76] Or that, despite the growing sophistication of actuarial tools, there are continuing heated and often acrimonious debates within the profession about what reliance can be placed upon them.[77]

[72] McLeod et al, *Improving Psychiatric Reports for Sentencing* (n 31 above) 23.

[73] M Feeley, 'Actuarial Justice and the Modern State' in G Bruinsma, H Elffers, and J De Keijser (eds), *Punishment, Places, and Perpetrators: Developments in Criminology and Criminal Justice Research* (Devon, Cullompton, Willan Publishing, 2004) 62–77; B Harcourt, 'The Shaping of Chance: Actuarial Models and Criminal Profiling at the Turn of the Twenty-First Century' (2003) 70/105 *The University of Chicago Law Review* 105–28; Harcourt, *Against Prediction* (n 57 above); R Wandall, 'Actuarial Risk Assessment: The Loss of Recognition of the Individual Offender' (2006) 5 *Law, Probability and Risk* 175–200.

[74] This is so despite the fact that the Law Commission has publically voiced its concerns about the validity of expert evidence and about the ability of judges, advocates and jurors to appreciate its limitations. The Law Commission, 'The Admissibility of Expert Evidence in Criminal Proceedings in England and Wales' (London, The Law Commission, 2009). This Consultation Paper proposes a new statutory admissibility test for the reliability of expert evidence to be applied by the judiciary.

[75] For an overview see N Eastman, 'The Psychiatrist, Courts and Sentencing: The Impact of Extended Sentencing on the Ethical Framework of Forensic Psychiatry' (2005) 29 *The Psychiatrist* 73–77.

[76] A Stone, 'The Ethical Boundaries of Forensic Psychiatry: A View from the Ivory Tower' (2008) 36/2 *Journal of the American Academy of Psychiatry and the Law* 167–74. (Reprint of a seminal article first published in 1984).

[77] Hart et al, 'Precision of Actuarial Risk Assessment Instruments' (n 63 above) 60–65; Harris et al, 'Evidence-Based Risk Assessment' (n 67 above) 154. A Buchanan, 'Risk of Violence by Psychiatric Patients: Beyond The "Actuarial Versus Clinical" Assessment Debate' (2008) 59/2 *Psychiatric Services* 184–90.

Lurking behind debate about risk assessment is an often anguished self-examination of whether or at what level or in what manner it is skewed by professional value judgements about what ought to result.[78] For risk assessments in the criminal court are not merely bland statements of probability but made in full knowledge of their consequences for the individual liberty. Clinicians appear well aware that predictive risk assessments sit uneasily with the liberal legal presumption of individual moral responsibility. Several concerns arise. To the extent that ARAIs deal in the aggregate probabilities of risky behaviour by cohorts of offenders, they do not treat each individual as morally autonomous.[79] In making claims to predict the future, risk assessment engages in a determinism that is erosive of the presumption of free will underpinning moral responsibility. Some claim that expert testimony is not predictive but merely descriptive and deny that free will is a necessary condition of legal responsibility.[80] Despite these claims, the danger remains that risk assessment entails a degree of determinism injurious to individual moral autonomy and the right to be author of one's fate in a manner consistent with a liberal legal order.[81]

The psychiatric profession identifies a further set of ethical dilemmas concerning the conflict of duties they owe to their patients and to the court. The role of the psychiatrist as physician is ordinarily to act in the best interests of his or her patient by pursuing the optimal therapeutic outcome. However, where forensic psychiatrists are called upon as expert witnesses, they fulfil a dual role[82] – as physician to their patient and as advisor to a court engaged in upholding the public interest in protection. An irresolvable tension thus arises between their medical/clinical and their court expert roles that generate dilemmas with serious implications for their testimony. On the one hand psychiatrists recognise the danger that they may be tempted to conceal or twist data in a bid to serve the best interests of their patient, for example to ensure a welfare or treatment based disposal rather than a punitive one. On the other they worry that their duty to the court and the interests of justice may incline them to offer assessments that constitute an abrogation of their duty to promote the best interests of their patient. Putting truth or justice before patient welfare raises a conflict of interests between their obligations to law and to doctoring. For some, like Stone, testifying in court entails taking 'a grave moral risk'.[83] For others, like Appelbaum, presenting evidence to court is a primary task of the forensic

[78] N Eastman, 'Public Health Psychiatry or Crime Prevention' (1999) 318 *British Medical Journal* 549 –51; Eastman, 'The Psychiatrist, Courts and Sentencing' (n 75 above) 73–77; J O'Grady, 'Psychiatry and Ethics in UK Criminal Sentencing' in A Buchanan and MA Norco (eds) *The Psychiatric Report* (New York, Cambridge University Press, 2011).

[79] Wandall, 'Actuarial Risk Assessment' (n 73 above) 175–200.

[80] S Morse, 'The Non-Problem of Free Will in Forensic Psychiatry and Psychology' (2007) 25 *Behavioral Sciences & the Law* 203–20.

[81] A Brudner, *Punishment and Freedom: A Liberal Theory of Penal Justice* (Oxford, Oxford University Press, 2009) 140ff.

[82] O'Grady, 'Psychiatry and Ethics' (n 78 above).

[83] GH Miller, 'Alan Stone and the Ethics of Forensic Psychiatry: An Overview' (2008) 36/2 *Journal of the American Academy of Psychiatry and the Law* 191–94, 191.

psychiatrist and one that is governed by a different ethic based not on beneficence but on truth telling.[84] At the risk of over-generalisation, it seems that American psychiatrists are more at ease in their 'forensic' role, seeing themselves first and foremost as servants of the court to whom obligations are owed over and above individual patient welfare.[85] By contrast, British psychiatrists appear more conflicted about the tension between their professional training and self-identification as doctors devoted to patient welfare and the opposing demands on them as expert witnesses, particularly where long-term or indefinite incarceration is in view. Gunn puts it simply: 'I find it very difficult to understand how a doctor can stop being a doctor.'[86] For those who see themselves first and foremost as doctors, the shift to truth-teller, acting in the interests of justice or public protection, sits very uneasily with their clinical role and therapeutic obligations.

Little of these concerns seem to have filtered into contemporary legal or criminological debates about risk assessment. Yet the dilemmas voiced by forensic psychiatrists cannot safely be dismissed as internal professional debates of no interest or relevance to law. These conflicted loyalties stand behind and inevitably inform clinical interpretation of the ARAI results, the reports written by expert witnesses, and the answers they give under cross-examination. A clinician who is persuaded that his or her patient's best interests would not be served by long-term incarceration may feel a strong pressure to down play indicators of future dangerousness. Equally clinicians whose primary loyalty is to the court may find themselves acting as double agents, gleaning information from patients only to use it against them in court. This uncomfortable situation is only partially assuaged by making clear to patients the nature of the expert witnesses' obligations to the court.[87] Some psychiatrists even refuse to examine defendants in person in order to avoid creating a doctor-patient relationship. They seek thereby to minimise possible conflicts of interest by generating no false expectations and engaging in no deception to *their* patient.[88] However, in resolving one problem this ruse only creates another: namely how much reliance can be placed upon a risk assessment made remotely.

No less fraught is the conflict that arises between individual patient welfare and the larger public health interest in protection from violent attack or other harm. Even those psychiatrists who have no difficulty in privileging their medical over their forensic obligations find themselves torn by the divergent interests

[84] PS Appelbaum, 'Psychiatric Ethics in the Courtroom' (1984) 12/3 *Bulletin of the American Academy of Psychiatry and Law* 225–31.

[85] Eastman, 'Psychiatrist, Courts and Sentencing' (n 75 above) 73–77, 75.

[86] J Gunn, 'Future Directions for Treatment in Forensic Psychiatry' (2000) 176 *British Journal of Psychiatry* 332–38, 337.

[87] See the differences of opinion between: Stone, 'Ethical Boundaries of Forensic Psychiatry' (n 76 above) 167–74; PS Appelbaum, 'Ethics and Forensic Psychiatry: Translating Principles into Practice' (2008) 36 *Journal of the American Academy of Psychiatry and the Law* 195–200.

[88] A Stone, 'Ethical Boundaries of Forensic Psychiatry' (n 76 above) 167–74, 172.

of individual versus public welfare.[89] The ethical duty of care to the individual is here challenged by the countervailing duty of care to the health and well-being of the public at large.

The crunch of disciplines that sounds so loudly when a psychiatrist walks into a criminal court reverberates not only within the psychiatric profession. An equally important, but again largely unasked, question is how well suited lawyers and law courts are to assessing and judging the validity of scientific evidence? Unless they happen to have a scientific background or training in statistics, lawyers typically lack the ability test claims as to scientific validity or statistical significance or to challenge a psychiatric diagnosis of pathology. Instead the criminal court seems to take the claims of science on trust, even as psychiatrists question the scientific status of their discipline and their diagnoses, as they dispute the reliability of ARAIs and the use that can be made of them, and as they publicly debate their role in court and even question their own competence.

Precisely because psychiatrists are called as expert witnesses and their testimony is privileged as the telling of a scientific truth that is independent and impartial, they may be seen a quasi inquisitorial intrusion on the adversarial process. Although there is little reason to doubt that those called upon to testify as experts do seek to tell the truth such as they honestly believe it to be, the effect of being designated as experts risks placing their testimony beyond challenge. So much is made in court of an expert witness's professional or medical credentials and the validity of the ARAIs upon which they draw it is little wonder that the impartial authority of their risk assessment comes to be accepted uncritically. Unless they are equally well versed in the intricacies of statistic inference and psychiatric diagnosis, lawyers may lack the expertise to challenge expert evidence or cast sufficient doubt in the minds of jurors to question its apparent unassailability. The calling of expert witnesses for both sides may render their respective allegiances transparent and diminish the conflicts of interest in play. However, use of partisan expert witnesses introduces the further difficulty that, in fulfilment of their partisan role, witnesses make one-sided assessments whose partiality remains obscured by pretensions to scientific reliability and truth-telling.

Greater awareness among criminal lawyers would alert the court to the contested status of ARAIs and difficulties of interpreting their data that are already so hotly debated within the psychiatric profession.[90] Inviting experts for each side to comment upon the validity of the other's testimony would also help to expose the limits and uncertainties inherent in their respective assessments. And yet a lack of authoritative determination by the experts brings new dangers: creating a power vacuum that others may be quick to fill. Take, for example, the

[89] N Eastman, 'Public Health Psychiatry or Crime Prevention' (1999) 318 *British Medical Journal* 549–51.

[90] For example, research that suggests practitioners find it easier to override a low ARAI score than to override a high one. Ansbro, 'The Nuts and Bolts of Risk Assessment' (n 71 above) 266.

emergence of 'Dangerous Severe Personality Disorder' (DSPD), a label that is contested in medical circles but that has been adopted as a basis for underwriting preventive detention policies.[91] As Gunn observes, '[p]sychiatry is confused and illogical in its approach to the concepts embodied under the broad umbrella of personality disorder' and he speculates whether the profession's 'philosophical muddle about terminology and the concepts behind the terminology handed politicians new devices for social control?'[92] Despite a woeful lack of clarity about what DSPD might mean, how exactly it is to be identified, how it might be treated, or if it is treatable, this construction, bolstered by public concern about dangerous offenders, has been central to legislative developments like the introduction of Imprisonment for Public Protection. As we have seen, IPP has permitted the imposition of thousands of indeterminate sentences and had a very significant impact on the overall size of the prison population. Yet as Peay observes of DSPD, 'there is no agreed definition, no clear diagnosis, no agreed treatment, no means of assessing when the predicted risk may have been reduced'.[93]

If psychiatrists are concerned about the ways in which their assessments of risk feed into determinations by the court, practising lawyers are becoming uneasy about what use they ought to make of the products of actuarial risk assessment and expert analysis. In their damning report on IPP, the Prison Reform Trust cite legal respondents who describe actuarial determinations of risk as 'formulaic', mechanistic', 'sausage-machine-ish', they decry the practice of 'trying to make statistical something that is actually a guess', and deplore the fact that they are not helped 'in their difficult task by tick-box assessments'.[94] They have little more faith in the 'quasi-scientific' claims made upon the basis of 'necessarily subjective judgment' by clinicians.[95] And yet, running seamlessly alongside this scepticism and anxiety, is an enormous and terrifying confidence evinced by judges about their own ability to assess risk.[96] By way of illustration, take just a few of the responses made by judges interviewed by the Prison Reform Trust:[97]

[91] T Seddon, 'Dangerous Liaisons: Personality Disorder and the Politics of Risk' (2008) 10 *Theoretical Criminology* 301–17.

[92] J Gunn, 'Future Directions for Treatment in Forensic Psychiatry' (2000) 176 *British Journal of Psychiatry* 332–38, 336.

[93] Peay, 'Mentally Disordered Offenders' (2007) 496–527, 519.

[94] Prison Reform Trust, *Unjust Deserts* (n 34 above) 25–27.

[95] ibid.

[96] The extent of judicial licence to determine risk is made clear in the national guide for IPP, issued by the National Offender Management Service (NOMS) in June 2005, which stated: 'it will ultimately be a matter for the court how they form their opinion of risk, but Section 156(3)(a) of the act requires the court to obtain a PSR before forming any opinion on risk which would inform sentencing under the provision, unless the court believes no question of significant risk arises, or the offender is so obviously dangerous as for it to be indisputable.' Given the degree of judicial self-confidence evidenced by the following quotes, the words 'so obviously dangerous' can only be read as a hostage to fortune. www.justice.gov.uk/inspectorates/hmi-probation/.../IPP_report_final_2-rps.pdf.

[97] Prison Reform Trust, *Unjust Deserts* (n 34 above) 29.

> 'You kind of know instinctively if someone is dangerous or not . . . Follow your instincts – they're probably right.
>
> Usually it's overwhelming [that an offender is dangerous. I only pass [an IPP] if I'm absolutely 100 per cent sure, and usually they stare out at you.
>
> I don't think I've found any difficulties [in assessing risk]. . . . You have to have that comforting belief in your abilities if you're going to be a judge, don't you!
>
> [Risk assessment] is an instinctive thing. . . . It's a value judgment, isn't it, and the decision is as good as the person making the value judgment.
>
> There are some people, particularly after a trial and you've watched them in the witness box, and you've seen the person and felt the presence – and you know.'[98]

Quite possibly the British case is singular but these quotes surely call into question Jonathan Simon's optimistic view that '[t]oday, risk assessment has established a new scientific paradigm that is in a position to reshape much of practice.'[99] However scientific the tools and the data they produce (and this remains debatable), recognising the role of human agency suggests a rather less sanguine conclusion.

VI CONCLUSION

This chapter has explored the idea that as individuals we have a right to be presumed free from harmful intentions. It has asked when, under what conditions, and why that presumption might be rebutted. To allow that the presumption is rebuttable in cases of significant risk only raises questions about what constitutes a significant risk, if it can safely be determined, and if so how, by whom, at what level of probability, and in respect of harms of what gravity? It has suggested that more finely graded conceptions of risk might ensure that measures taken are proportionate to the likelihood as well as to the gravity of the prospective risk. It has also pointed out some difficulties entailed in determining who or what the subjects of risk assessment are. It has explored some hazards entailed in using actuarial data, focusing on questions of interpretation and the difficulties they throw up, particularly for clinicians. This in turn has raised difficult questions about the role of expert witnesses and the status of clinical judgment in the criminal court. At the heart of these lie heated debates in forensic psychiatry about what it is possible to learn about risk from ARAIs and, in particular, whether an assessment of individual risk can safely be derived from aggregate data. Although there is much more to be said about questions of

[98] Responses such as these raise serious questions about the advisability of the Law Commission's proposal to enhance the judiciary's role as 'gate-keepers' for the admissibility of expert evidence using a new statutory test. The Law Commission, *The Admissibility of Expert Evidence in Criminal Proceedings in England and Wales* (London, The Law Commission, 2009) 43–46. For a critical evaluation see A Samuels, 'The Admissibility of Expert Evidence in Criminal Proceedings' (2009) *Criminal Law and Justice Weekly* at www.criminallawandjustice.co.uk/index.php?/Analysis/the-admissibility-of-expert-evidence-in-criminal-proceedings.html.

[99] Simon, 'Reversal of Fortune' (n 58 above) 417.

validity, confidence intervals, and margins of error, quite enough has been said here to make worryingly clear that risk tools, risk data, and their interpretation are so contested as to render judgments based upon them a source of concern. A recent government consultation paper admits as much, observing:

> The limitations in our ability to predict future serious offending also calls into question the whole basis on which many offenders are sentenced to IPPs and, among those who are already serving these sentences, which of them are suitable for release.[100]

This recognition of our limited ability to predict risk is an important factor behind the proposed abolition of the IPP sentence. Another key driver is the mounting political embarrassment posed by the large numbers of IPP prisoners unable to persuade the Parole Board that they can safely be released. As Minister of Justice Ken Clarke was obliged to acknowledge in Parliament, the IPP is 'a punishment that leaves a rather randomly selected group to languish indefinitely in prison' and he conceded that: 'we have to reflect . . . on whether we have been giving the Parole Board an almost impossible task. It is no good pretending that it can come to a scientifically certain conclusion in each case'.[101] It is doubly ironic therefore that abolition will not apply retrospectively to those 6,550 prisoners already serving IPP sentences. The injunction to 'err on the side of safety' in this case has proved to be an invitation to error of major proportions and, even if as looks likely the IPP is abolished, a continuing source of injustice. When impelled in future to err on the side of safety, should we not pause to ask quite how big an error we are willing to make and to what end?

[100] Ministry of Justice, *Breaking the Cycle* (n 45 above) 55.
[101] HC Deb 1 Nov 2011 787, 791.

11

The Test for Dangerousness

MARTIN WASIK

I BACKGROUND

SECTIONS 224 TO 236 and schedules 15 and 15A of the Criminal Justice Act (CJA) 2003 provide measures for sentencing 'dangerous offenders'. The original scheme came into effect on 4 April 2005 and applies to offences committed on or after that date. This was the latest attempt to create sentencing provisions in England and Wales targeted at this particular group of offenders, and forms part of a long history of failure.[1] Protective sentencing of this kind has been bedevilled by over-inclusiveness (catching minor persistent offenders as well as the more serious) and the high false positive rate involved in prediction of future serious lawbreaking.[2] The 2003 Act replaced previous provisions for the imposition of 'longer-than-commensurate' sentences, created by the CJA 1991, and the 'automatic' life sentence for the second serious offence, introduced in 1997. The new scheme was different from what went before, but far worse, in that it was broader (many more offences would now bring offenders within the scope of such sentences) and less flexible (restricting judicial discretion to dis-apply the provisions where necessary). In what follows, in order to keep this chapter within reasonable bounds, I shall consider those parts of the scheme which apply to offenders aged 18 and over and leave on one side the different arrangements applicable to young offenders. I shall focus on the sentences of life imprisonment and imprisonment for public protection (IPP), with lesser attention being given to the somewhat different provisions of the 'extended sentence'. The test for dangerousness, which is the topic of my chapter, is relevant and applicable to all three sentences.

[1] See L Radzinowicz and R Hood, 'Incapacitating the Habitual Criminal: The English Experience' (1980) *Michigan Law Review* 1305.

[2] There is a substantial literature on both the effectiveness, and ethics, of different forms of incapacitative sentencing policies. See for example the essays gathered in Andrew von Hirsch, Andrew Ashworth and Julian Roberts, *Principled Sentencing; Readings on Theory and Policy*, 3rd edn (Oxford, Hart Publishing, 2009) ch 3.

II THE ORIGINAL DANGEROUS OFFENDER SCHEME

The original scheme applied to an offender convicted of a 'specified sexual offence' or a 'specified violent offence', where the court is of the opinion that 'there is a significant risk to members of the public of serious harm occasioned by the commission by him of further specified offences'. All 'specified offences' are listed in schedule 15 to the CJA 2003, and there is a very large number of them – 153 in total.[3] The original scheme, in general terms, provided that (i) if the offence of conviction was a specified offence with a maximum penalty of between 2 and 10 years and the offender was found to be dangerous, the offender *must* receive an 'extended sentence' (a form of determinate sentence with a release date determined by the Parole Board and an extended licence period[4]). If the offence of conviction carried a maximum sentence of 10 years or more (known as a 'serious specified offence' – there are 96 such offences listed in the statute) and the offender was found to be dangerous, the offender *must* receive either a life sentence[5] or a sentence of IPP. There was also a presumption of dangerousness in the case of offenders aged 18 or over. If the offender convicted of the specified offence had previously been convicted of one or more specified offences, the court *must assume* that the offender is dangerous (ie poses a 'significant risk . . .') unless the court considered that it would be *unreasonable* to conclude that there was such a risk. For a life sentence or IPP, the sentencing judge must fix a 'minimum term',[6] which must be served *in full* before the offender can first be considered for release on licence. The minimum term is calculated by taking the 'notional determinate sentence' appropriate for the offence, and dividing it by two.[7] Life sentences and IPP are indeterminate sentences and will last for the rest of the offender's life unless the Parole Board is satisfied that detention is no longer necessary for the protection of the public and releases the offender, from which point the offender will be on licence and subject to recall to prison.

The scheme caused very great difficulty. There were three reasons for this. First, it was drafted in an over-inclusive and inflexible way, leaving insufficient room for judges to exercise proper judgment. The shortcomings were made apparent to judges through the compulsory training on the CJA 2003 which all practitioners received. Lectures from Dr Thomas at these Judicial Studies Board

[3] As originally drafted, 65 specified violent offences and 88 specified sexual offences. Further offences were added by the Coroners and Justice Act 2009 s138.

[4] Of up to 5 years if it was a specified violent offence and up to 8 years if it was a specified sexual offence. The 'new-style' extended sentence in the CJA 2003 must be distinguished from the 'old-style' extended sentence under the Powers of Criminal Courts (Sentencing) Act 2000 s 85.

[5] Provided the offence carries life as its maximum.

[6] Under the Powers of Criminal Courts (Sentencing) Act 2000 s 82A.

[7] Divided by two because (in general terms) an offender serves half of a determinate sentence before being released while an offender serves the whole of a minimum term. The calculation is also affected by other matters, such as days served by the offender on remand, or on qualifying curfew. Such days are normally deducted (PCC(S)A 2000 ss 240 and 240A).

seminars made it obvious to all that the provisions, if applied literally, would result in thousands of offenders being given indeterminate sentences in circumstances where their offence of conviction would make that hard to justify on any common sense basis. The statute relied upon the maximum penalty of the offence of conviction as the measure of offence seriousness, but of course it should have been realised that maximum penalties are set very high in England and Wales, so as to allow for the worst example of the offence that is likely to occur, and the 'standard case' offence will tend to attract a sentence much lower than the maximum. The Court of Appeal, to its credit, moved quickly to assist judges with the new scheme and, in *Lang*,[8] Rose LJ interpreted the provisions in such a way as to give judges the greatest possible leeway consistent with their duty to apply the words of the statute. There was, however, no getting away from the mandatory terms in which the legislation was cast, nor from the limited discretion to avoid the operation of the presumption of dangerousness. The second reason that the scheme caused difficulty was its complexity. Perhaps practitioners and judges, after appropriate training, ought to have been able to get this right, but there was the need for the Court of Appeal to correct a significant number of mistakes made by sentencing judges. *Lang* itself dealt with 13 separate cases.[9]

Flowcharts were published by the Sentencing Guidelines Council to keep sentencers on track. Offenders being sentenced for several offences at the same time, one or more of which were specified offences and others of which were not, prompted particular difficulty and occasioned a number of appeals.[10] The third reason was the 'deplorable failure' by the government to provide the systems and resources necessary to ensure that prisoners sentenced under the new regime were assessed properly and had the opportunity to demonstrate to the Parole Board, by the time of expiry of the minimum term, that it was no longer necessary for the protection of the public that they should remain in detention. The House of Lords found in *Wells v Parole Board*[11] that the Secretary of State was in breach of his public law duty to provide adequate rehabilitative programmes in prison for offenders sentenced to IPP, although the House stopped short of deciding that detention after expiry of the minimum term was unlawful. Lord Carswell pointed out that the dangerous offender provisions were yet another example of over-prescriptive sentencing legislation, especially when 'Pelion was piled upon Ossa' and the government decided that the whole scheme had to be resource-neutral. The facilities necessary for IPP prisoners to demonstrate their fitness for release were simply not made available.[12]

[8] *Lang* [2006] 1 WLR 2509. See also *Johnson* [2007] 1Cr App R (S) 112.

[9] In *Reynolds* [2007] 2 Cr App R (S) 553, the Court of Appeal dealt with a further eight cases.

[10] For a mind-boggling analysis of the intricacies of these provisions see C [2007] 2 Cr App R (S) 627.

[11] *Wells v Parole Board* [2009] 2 WLR 1149.

[12] ibid [23]. See further Nicola Padfield, 'The Future of Parole' *Archbold News*, 4 November 2009 p 6 and the chapter by Lucia Zedner in ch 10 of this volume.

Despite the best efforts of the Court of Appeal in *Lang*, it was inevitable that many more defendants would receive indeterminate sentences than before, and that soon proved to be the case. To give one example, a conviction for a street robbery by an offender with a previous conviction for assault occasioning actual bodily harm would trigger the presumption of dangerousness. Let us assume that the robber used a knife to threaten the victim, but there was no injury. Applying the relevant Sentencing Guidelines Council Guidelines,[13] the sentence range for the robbery is between two and seven years. The starting point is four years, but with one-third reduction from those figures for a guilty plea at the first reasonable opportunity. The judge might properly take a notional determinate sentence of three years, giving a minimum term of 18 months, less time served on remand. The 18 months would have to be served in full, and after that time release is a matter for the parole authorities. When the impact of increased numbers was felt on the prison population, protests were heard from the Parole Board. The Board was overwhelmed by weight of numbers and, in particular, was often unable to make any proper risk assessment on offenders given their short minimum terms simply because there was not enough time to do so. Half of offenders given IPP were receiving a minimum term of 20 months or less and 20 per cent had been given an 18 month minimum term. It was pretty rich to blame the judges, rather than the legislators, for this, but that is what happened.[14]

III THE REVISED DANGEROUS OFFENDER SCHEME

The original scheme was significantly amended by the Criminal Justice and Immigration Act 2008, sections 13 to 18 and schedule 5, which came into force on 14 July 2008.[15] First, the presumption of dangerousness was abolished, and I say no more about that in this chapter.[16] Second, if the serious specified offence does not carry life as its maximum penalty, or if it does but the court considers that its seriousness does not justify a life sentence, the court *may* (rather than *must*) impose a sentence of IPP, *but only* where the condition in section 225(3A) *or* the condition in section 225(3B) is made out. The former condition is where, at the time of the offence, the offender had been convicted of an offence which is listed in schedule 15A. This is a new schedule, with a small number of very serious offences, such as murder, manslaughter, armed robbery and the like.[17] The latter condition is that, if the court were to impose IPP, the nominal deter-

[13] Sentencing Guidelines Council (SGC), 'Definitive Guideline on *Robbery*' (SGC, July 2006) and '*Reduction of Sentence for a Guilty Plea*' (revised guideline July 2007).

[14] Richard Ford, 'Judges Use Never-Ending Sentences too Often, Complains Parole Chief' *The Times*, 10 January 2007.

[15] R Epstein and B Mitchell, 'Indeterminate Imprisonment for Public Protection and the Impact of the 2008 Reforms' (2009) 173 *JPN* 311.

[16] 'No court will mourn its departure', according to Lord Judge CJ in *AG's Reference (No 55 of 2008)(C)* [2009] 2 Cr App R (S) 22.

[17] See further *Gore* [2010] EWCA Crim 369, [2010] 2 Cr App R (S) 93.

minate sentence would be *at least four years*, so that the minimum term would be for *at least two years*. This means that the dangerous offender provisions are now only available when the instant offence crosses a specified threshold of seriousness, rather than being triggered simply by the maximum penalty carried by that offence. A similar change has been made in respect of the extended sentence, so that an extended sentence can only be passed where the proportionate determinate sentence for the instant offence would have been at least four years, and the extended sentence also ceased to be limited to specified offences with a maximum penalty of less than 10 years. Another change to the extended sentence is that from 2008, release from the custodial part of the sentence becomes automatic at the half way point, rather than being a matter for the Parole Board.[18] The period on licence continues, as before, right up until the end of the extension period.[19]

These changes are clearly designed to reduce the number of offenders eligible for indeterminate sentences, and the changes have been widely welcomed, not least by judges who have to apply them. It is obviously intended that the numbers of offenders so sentenced will fall significantly as a result of these statutory amendments, although the most recent indications are that this effect has not been as clear as anticipated. The changes made by the 2008 Act are not retrospective, so IPP prisoners with a minimum term of less than two years who had been convicted before the passing of the 2008 Act are still held under the original terms of the CJA. The 2008 Act changes will therefore reduce the flow of new IPP prisoners but will do little to reduce the backlog of prisoners sentenced before those changes.[20] As is explained towards the end of this chapter, more radical changes are now in train. The Coalition Government in 2010 consulted on further restricting IPP, so it would be available only where the instant offence would otherwise have attracted a determinate sentence of 10 years or more. At the time of writing the Legal Aid, Sentencing and Punishment of Offences Bill 2011 is being debated by Parliament. If the relevant provisions in the Bill are enacted as they currently stand, IPP will be repealed completely and replaced with a new form of indeterminate sentence available only where the defendant qualifies as dangerous, the seriousness of the instant offence would justify a determinate sentence of at least 10 years *and* the defendant has previously served a sentence of that duration. The new sentence (termed a life sentence for the second listed offence) will still require a finding by the judge that the defendant is dangerous and the new law will retain the same wording for that test. It is, then, to the test for dangerousness that we now turn.

[18] It was said in *Lang* that uncertainty over the release date in an extended sentence meant that consecutive extended sentences should be avoided, but since the law has been amended the restriction on imposing consecutive sentences has been relaxed: *Pinnell* [2010] EWCA Crim 2848.

[19] *Burt* [2006] 2 Cr App R (S) 35.

[20] See Jessica Jacobson and Mike Hough, *Unjust Deserts: The Indeterminate Sentence for Public Protection* (Prison Reform Trust and Institute for Criminal Policy Research at King's College London, 2010).

IV THE TEST FOR DANGEROUSNESS

Defining the dangerous offender in a just and appropriate manner has been an enduring problem.[21] Section 229 of the 2003 Act is central for our purposes, because it deals with the necessary standard for the assessment of dangerousness: to establish whether the offender poses 'a significant risk to members of the public of serious harm occasioned by the commission by him of further specified offences'. The Court of Appeal in *Lang* provided guidance on the meaning of this phrase, as well as on the operation of the scheme more generally. Much of what was said in *Lang* remains valid, but of course the judgment has to be read in light of the 2008 Act amendments. Guidance on the operation of the amended scheme can be found in *AG's Reference (No 55 of 2008)*.[22] It is clear that any test for the determination of risk involves a number of different dimensions. These include – (i) the nature of the anticipated harm, (ii) the likelihood of its occurring, and (iii) the magnitude of the harm should that risk materialise. All these issues have to be informed by the seriousness of the instant offence, whether (as in the original scheme) by reference to the maximum penalty available or (as in the revised scheme) by reference to the instant offence being serious enough to attract a sentence of at least four years. They also have to be seen in light of the defendant's criminal history, since past misconduct is generally taken to be the best predictor of future misconduct. Let us now turn to consider the dangerousness test in the 2003 Act, as interpreted and applied by the courts.

A Significant Risk

According to *Lang*, the requirement that a risk be 'significant' means that it is 'more than a possibility' – it must be 'noteworthy; of considerable amount or importance'. It may be thought that this gloss on the meaning of 'significant' is not particularly helpful. The two parts of the statement do not sit happily together. 'Noteworthy' seems to suggest a lower threshold of concern than 'considerable amount or importance'. The former term is closer to 'significant', while the latter is nearer to 'substantial'. Parliament might have used the word 'substantial' but chose not to do so, preferring 'significant'.[23] 'Significant' may be re-written as 'not insignificant'. Compare this language with the terms employed to describe UK terrorism threat levels,[24] which range from 'low',

[21] See Mark H Moore, Susan R Estrich, Daniel McGillis and William Spelman, *Dangerous Offenders: The Elusive Target of Justice* (Harvard, Harvard University Press, 1984) ch 2.

[22] *AG's Reference (No 55 of 2008)* [2008] EWCA Crim 2790.

[23] Andrew Ashworth, *Sentencing and Criminal Justice*, 5th edn (Cambridge, Cambridge University Press, 2010) 234.

[24] See www.homeoffice.gov.uk/counter-terrorism/current-threat-level.

through to 'moderate', 'substantial' and then 'severe', to 'critical'. 'Substantial' is in the middle of this range,[25] and although the term 'significant' is not used, it would seem naturally to fit somewhere in the same part of the scale as 'moderate'.[26] In *Pedley*,[27] the Court of Appeal considered arguments advanced by the defence that 'significant risk' should be construed to mean 'more likely than not to follow' or, alternatively, 'in the order of 35–50 per cent probability' because, it was claimed, any lesser threshold would infringe article 3 (disproportionate punishment) or article 5(1) (arbitrary punishment) of the European Convention on Human Rights (ECHR). The Court firmly rejected these contentions, and deprecated any attempt to re-define 'significant risk' in terms of a percentage likelihood, whether 'more probable than not' or any other formula. The Court also rejected the suggestion that the earlier case of *Johnson*[28] had said that 'significant' risk was met whenever the risk was more than negligible. *Pedley* reaffirms that '*some* risk is not enough: it must be a *significant* risk' (emphasis added). The unwillingness of the Court of Appeal to be tempted down the route of defining 'significant risk' has echoes of a similar reluctance to place mathematical value on the meaning of proof beyond reasonable doubt.[29]

B Significant Risk of Serious Harm

There must be a 'significant risk' of 'serious harm', and 'serious harm' is defined in the Act as 'death or serious personal injury, whether physical or psychological'. This is a very similar test to that which applied in the context of 'longer-than-commensurate' sentences under the earlier legislation. The fact that the offender is foreseen as committing a 'specified offence' does not mean that the test is satisfied unless such an offence is foreseen as resulting in 'serious harm', so defined. According to Rose LJ in *Lang*, if the offence which is foreseen is not a serious specified offence then it will be rare that there is a 'significant risk of serious harm'. In *Terrell*,[30] the Court said that 'serious personal injury' had to be read in the context of the word 'death', with which it had been coupled. The effect of these judicial comments is to narrow somewhat the scope of the provisions. The Court in *Pedley*[31] suggested that there was flexibility within the notion of 'significant risk of serious harm' in that a lower probability of particularly serious harm may be 'significant', but a somewhat greater probability

[25] Further explanation is that 'severe' means a terrorist attack is 'highly likely', and 'substantial' means a terrorist attack is 'a strong possibility'.

[26] The equivalent scale in the United States is designed to reflect the appropriate level of protective measures that citizens should take, and ranges from 'low', through to 'guarded', 'elevated' and 'high' to 'severe': www.dhs.gov/files/programes/Copy_of_press_release_0046.shm.

[27] *Pedley* [2010] 1 Cr App R (S) 24.

[28] *Johnson* [2009] 1 WLR 608.

[29] According to *Ching* (1976) 63 Cr App R 7, 11, 'if judges stopped trying to define that which is almost impossible to define there would be fewer appeals'.

[30] *Terrell* [2008] Cr App R (S) 49.

[31] *Pedley* [2010] 1 Cr App R (S) 24.

of less serious harm may not be. There is clearly some interplay between the magnitude of the anticipated harm and the likelihood of its occurring. However, this should not be taken too far. A finding of dangerousness cannot be justified within the terms of the statute either on the basis of a low risk of grave harm or a very substantial risk of less serious harm.

C To Members of the Public

According to *Lang*, the reference to risk to members of the public is a general term, and should not be construed to exclude any particular group of citizens, such as prison officers or mental hospital staff. It is perhaps the classic image of the dangerous offender that he or she represents a diffuse and general risk of perpetrating violence upon strangers. However, risk can be made out where it exists not in relation to the public at large, but in respect of a particular individual (such as the offender's ex-partner) or a small group of individuals (such as anyone forming a relationship with the offender's ex-partner).[32] If the risk posed by the offender is more narrowly focused in this way, it may be that if the person or persons at risk have now been moved to a place of safety then the offender should no longer be regarded as dangerous. The generality or specificity of the risk posed by the defendant is an issue little explored in the cases on IPP, presumably because in most cases the risk posed is quite diffuse and in any event the custodial sentence will protect specific potential victims as well as the generality. In the related context of sexual offence prevention orders (SOPOs), which are considered further below, the Court of Appeal has said that the nature and extent of the risk posed by the defendant must be properly taken into account. The case law on SOPOs shows, for example, that if the defendant represents a risk to children of a particular age or gender, any preventive conditions should be limited so as only to restrict the defendant's access to children of that group.[33] SOPOs can be combined with custodial sentences, but are mainly appropriate where the defendant is in the community and limitations need to be placed upon his or her activities in order to protect persons at risk, or a specific category of persons at risk.

D By the Commission by Him of Further Specified Offences

The test refers to 'further specified offences', rather than to 'a further specified offence', which could be taken to mean that the court must foresee the commis-

[32] See, for example *Hashi* (1995) 16 Cr App R (S) 121 and *S* (1994) 15 Cr App R (S) 765, both pre-Act authorities but decided in relation to similar wording. Logically, risk to 'members of the public' is a wider term than risk to 'others', and presumably should be taken to include risk to the offender his or herself. Rose LJ apparently took that view in *Lang*.

[33] *Barley* [2009] 2 Cr App R (S) 5; *Buchanan* [2010] EWCA Crim 1316.

sion of more than one future such offence. The words have not been interpreted in this way, however, and are probably designed to capture the idea of a general future risk. The test also requires the anticipation of such future offending *by* the offender. This will hardly ever be controversial, since clearly it is the risk posed by the defendant his or herself that matters, but in *Owen*, discussed next, the Court of Appeal had to consider the dangerousness of a defendant who had failed to intervene when others abused and killed a young child. It can be seen that the 'significant risk' must relate to the commission of further 'specified' offences, rather than further 'serious specified' offences, but see the limiting comment from *Lang* at B above. If the foreseen specified offence is serious, there will be some cases (but by no means all) where there is a significant risk of serious harm. As pointed out in *Lang*, robbery is a serious specified offence, but one which can be committed in a wide variety of ways, some of which do not give rise to a significant risk of serious harm. Both the Sentencing Guidelines Council and the Court of Appeal have noted that courts should be particularly careful before concluding that a young offender is 'dangerous', given that young people change and develop through maturity and this may be highly relevant in assessing what their future conduct may be.[34]

V THE INFORMATION BASE

It will be clear from has been said so far that when assessing dangerousness for the purpose of these statutory provisions, a variety of information needs to be considered, including

(a) the nature and circumstances of the offence,
(b) the nature and circumstances of other offences committed by the offender,
(c) any pattern of behaviour of which the offence forms part, and
(d) any information about the offender which is before the court.

These considerations are all expressly set out in section 229(2). The first is expressed in mandatory terms. The court *may* take any of the others into account, but nothing seems to turn on this difference in wording. The court will, in each case, be relying on a number of sources of information – the facts of the offence (especially where these have emerged in the course of a contested trial), the other offences including previous convictions, and the contents of (and especially the risk assessment within) a pre-sentence report. Sometimes, where there is a suggested mental abnormality on the part of the offender, there will need to be a psychiatric report before a risk assessment is made.[35]

[34] *JW* [2009] 2 Cr App R (S) 94.

[35] It seems that a high percentage of IPP prisoners suffer from mental health problems: Sainsbury Centre for Mental Health, 'In the Dark: the Mental Health Implications of Imprisonment for Public Protection' (Centre for Mental Health, 2008). One in five had received psychiatric treatment in the past, and more than half of IPP prisoners had problems of 'emotional wellbeing'.

Strictly, it is not a requirement for eligibility for IPP that the offender has previous convictions and, in principle, a first offender might qualify.[36] This aspect of the English scheme is very unusual – virtually all dangerous offender laws rely explicitly on the defendant's record of committing prior serious offences and/or serving significant prior custodial terms, within a specified recent period.[37] In practice it is highly unusual for a finding of dangerousness to be made in respect of a first offender. The English scheme says that, where there are previous offences, in the assessment of dangerousness it is *not* just previous *specified* offences which are relevant. All offences on the record may be relevant, including those committed before the 2003 Act provisions came into force,[38] especially where they reveal an escalating pattern of seriousness. Nor is it necessary that serious harm (or, indeed, any harm) has been caused by the past offence(s), since that may simply have been a matter of good fortune. Clearly, however, where harm has already occurred it will be somewhat easier to find that there is a significant risk of serious harm occurring in the future. Usually it is the circumstances of the earlier offences, rather than simply the fact of their existence, which will inform the decision on risk. So, wherever possible, counsel must be in a position to describe the facts of the earlier convictions.[39] If relevant information is not to hand, a judge should not normally pass an IPP without it – an adjournment may well be necessary for the information to be obtained.[40]

The use of the word 'information' in section 229 has been considered by the Court of Appeal on a number of occasions, and it has become clear that in assessing dangerousness the sentencing court should not confine itself to evidence which has been established to the criminal standard.[41] This is controversial. Normally finding of facts by the judge at the sentencing stage which are adverse to the defendant must be established to the criminal standard of proof.[42] In *Hillman*,[43] however, the Court said that it was appropriate for a judge to rely upon a synopsis of material prepared by the prosecution containing details of alleged misconduct by the defendant which had earlier resulted in the making of an anti-social behaviour order against him. The Court said that although this material had never been tested in cross-examination, it was sufficiently 'hard' information and could be relied on. In *Considine*[44] the Court confirmed that

[36] According to Lord Judge CJ in *Johnson* [2007] 1 Cr App R (S) 112, 'A man of good character may properly qualify for this sentence.' An example is *Troninas* [2012] 1 Cr App R (S) 20.

[37] See Moore et al (n 22 above) 56: 'Justice compels a special interest in dangerous offenders because those who have committed crimes repeatedly have clearly revealed their guilt through a pattern of criminal activity that merits special attention.'

[38] *Stannard* [2009] 2 Cr App R (S) 21.

[39] *Johnson* [2007] 1 Cr App R (S) 112.

[40] *Bryan* [2007] 1 Cr App R (S) 53, though see further *Johnson* [2007] 1 Cr App R (S) 112, where Lord Judge CJ said that if the Crown is not in a position to challenge the defence version of the facts, the court may proceed on the information it has.

[41] *Considine* [2007] EWCA Crim 1166.

[42] *Kerrigan* (1993) 14 Cr App R (S) 179.

[43] *Hillman* [2006] 2 Cr App R (S) 565.

[44] *Considine* [2008] 1 Cr App R (DS) 41.

there was no reason to distinguish for these purposes between formal evidence and material 'which comes before the court through some different route' such as a psychiatric report or a pre-sentence report. The use by the National Probation Service of statistical tools for the assessment of dangerousness has been held to be both necessary and appropriate by the Court of Appeal.[45] Indeed the Court has made it clear that the risk analysis in the pre-sentence report will often be crucial when sentencing a dangerous offender, but the decision whether or not to impose such a sentence remains one for the court. The sentencer may disagree with the probation assessment, but would be expected to warn counsel that this was in the offing, to give both counsel the opportunity to address the court on the issue and then, of course, to give clear reasons for taking a different line.[46] It may sometimes be appropriate to call the report writer to be cross-examined on the issue of risk,[47] but the case law generally discourages this.

The risk assessment for adult offenders is generated by way of a programme called OASys, the Offender Assessment System, developed by the probation service and in operation nationally.[48] For young offenders there is a different assessment framework, known as Asset.[49] OASys requires the probation officer producing the report to input data into 12 separate fields (such as offending information, lifestyle and associates, drug misuse, alcohol misuse, emotional well-being, thinking and behaviour), each of which carries a numerical weighting depending on general research evidence as to its predictive value in terms of reconviction. Completion of the sections generates a numerical risk score. There is also an optional self-assessment form which provides the offender's own perspective on his or her offending behaviour. Completion of the form may alert the officer to the need for additional and more specific assessment, such as violent offender assessment, mental health assessment, or dangerous and severe personality assessment. OASys is designed to address specific risks, including harm to the public, harm to known adults, and harm to children. Levels of risk of serious harm are generated, which range from low, through medium and high, to very high. If the offender falls within the upper two categories the pre-sentence report will conclude with a risk management plan for consideration by the sentencer. While the decision in *Considine* permits the judge to consider a broader range of information about the offender than would be admissible in evidence, it will be seen that the information relied upon in the pre-sentence report goes well beyond that. Evidence of the offender's lifestyle and associates, history of drug misuse and employment, and so on will have been obtained from the defendant his or herself or from others, but cannot be described as 'hard' information. Through the sentencing court's

[45] *Boswell* [2007] EWCA Crim 1587; *Griffin* [2008] 2 Cr App R (S) 61.

[46] *Pluck* [2007] 1 Cr App R (S) 43.

[47] *S* [2006] 2 Cr App R (S) 224.

[48] See the National Probation Service, *Probation Bench Handbook*, 2nd edn (London, National Offender Management Service, 2007).

[49] Details can be found on the Youth Justice Board website at www.yjb.gov.uk.

reliance on the pre-sentence report, however, it can become crucial in the decision over dangerousness.

The OASys scheme has been criticised by Lancaster and Lumb[50] as relying too heavily on static risk factors and underestimating individual agency and motivation in the context of changing circumstances over time. The authors say that static risk factors

> can produce worrying risk assessments which remain fixed . . . whereas for clinicians it is the need to engage in a process to actively reduce the probability of violence which should be paramount, hence requiring a greater focus on dynamic variables.[51]

Clearly, any assessment of risk must be subject to change and reassessment over time as the offender, and surrounding circumstances, change. However, as explained below, the respective risk assessment roles of the judge and the clinician are very different, and judges are making an assessment of risk at a fixed point in time. Then the judge's task is to fix the minimum term to be served, purely in accordance with the seriousness of the offending. What may or may not happen after the expiry of the minimum term is simply not a matter for the judge. The judge may make observations in his or her sentencing remarks relevant to the nature and degree of the risk posed by the offender, and these will be retained in the file which will later be considered by the Parole Board, but the judge's observations are simply that, and are in no way binding upon the Board when making its decision over release.

VI THREE EXAMPLES

It is helpful next to consider three specific examples of the application of the dangerousness test. The Court of Appeal has said that it will be slow to depart from the judge's assessment of dangerousness, especially where there has been a contested trial and the judge has had the opportunity to observe the defendant and perhaps to hear him or her give evidence,[52] but there are cases where on appeal the Court has reviewed all the information which was available to the judge and found itself unable to support the original finding.

The first case is *Owen*.[53] The defendant was one of three people convicted by a jury in respect of the death of baby Peter, a case which attracted a huge amount of publicity and media interest at the time. Peter's mother and her boyfriend had been living together with the mother's four children for over a year

[50] E Lancaster and J Lumb, 'The Assessment of Risk in the National Probation Service of England and Wales' in B Hudson (ed), *Justice in the Risk Society* (London, Sage, 2006) 285.

[51] M Nash and A Williams, *The Anatomy of Serious Further Offending* (Oxford, Oxford University Press, 2008) 78.

[52] According to Lord Judge CJ in *Johnson* [2007] 1 Cr App R (S) 112, 'this court will not normally interfere with the conclusions reached by a sentencer who has accurately identified the relevant principles, and applied his mind to the relevant facts.'

[53] *Owen* [2009] EWCA Crim 2259.

before Peter died. The defendant, who was the brother of the boyfriend, moved into the household about five weeks before Peter's death. Peter's mother, her boyfriend, and the defendant were all convicted of the offence of causing or allowing the death of a child, contrary to section 5 of the Domestic Violence, Crime and Victims Act 2004. The mother received a sentence of IPP with a minimum term of five years and her boyfriend received a determinate sentence of imprisonment of 12 years. The sentence passed on the defendant, aged 37, was one of IPP with a minimum term of three years. The defendant appealed. The Court of Appeal said that the sole issue in the appeal was whether there was a sound basis for the judge's finding that the defendant represented a significant risk to the public of serious harm in the future from the commission of further specified offences. Hughes LJ considered in detail the material which had been before the judge, including the defendant's previous convictions (there were four, for theft and burglary committed when he was aged 16 and 18, carrying an offensive weapon when he was 20 and, when he was 33, two more burglaries and an offence of arson, for none of which he had served a custodial sentence) and the pre-sentence report, the tentative adverse conclusion and some of the factual contents of which were seriously in dispute. The Court of Appeal noted that the offence was 'deeply unpleasant because a completely innocent child whom he could have protected was not protected by him against harm by others', but that although there was *some* possible potential to commit an offence in future which *might* cause harm and, it *may be,* serious harm, to someone, *some* risk is not the test. 'The test is the existence of a serious risk, enough to warrant a sentence which may never end. This man has no history of either violence or exploitative or dangerous sexual offending'. The indeterminate sentence was quashed and a determinate sentence of six years was substituted

The second example is *AG's Reference (No 14 of 2009)(Morgan).*[54] The defendant, aged 38, was convicted of wounding with intent and robbery. He, acting together with a second defendant, had attacked the client of a prostitute, hitting him on the head repeatedly with a piece of wood, causing a depressed fracture of the skull and consequent brain injury with serious long-term effects. When the victim had been rendered unconscious the defendants stole from him cash and a bank card. In the past the defendant had been sentenced to various terms of imprisonment for carrying a firearm with intent, robbery, burglary, and possession of a bladed instrument. The author of the pre-sentence report indicated that the defendant's risk of re-offending was high and the risk to the public of serious harm was high. The judge concluded, however, that the criteria for an indeterminate sentence were not met, and sentenced the defendant to a total of nine years' imprisonment. The Attorney General asked the Court to review the sentence on the basis that it was unduly lenient and that an indeterminate sentence should have been passed. Hallett LJ in the Court of Appeal said that there was force in the argument that the Court should be slow to interfere with

[54] *AG's Reference (No 14 of 2009)(Morgan)* [2010] 1 Cr App R (S) 17.

the decision of a trial judge in these circumstances, but it was unclear why the judge had departed from the probation officer's assessment and that 'in our judgment, everything points to the fact that this offender is dangerous: his repeated violent offending, his involvement in yet another robbery in which weapons were used, and his active participation in an appallingly savage beating'. Her Ladyship said that a sentence of IPP was amply justified, and that since the nominal determinate sentence was at least 12 years, the minimum term in the IPP should be six years.

A third case is *Barton*[55] which, it is submitted, is very close to the line. The defendant entered a shop and produced a knife with which he threatened to stab the shopkeeper, a Mr Carey. He demanded money until, in the face of repeated threats, the shopkeeper opened the till and handed over £670. The defendant then forced Mr Carey to accompany him out of the shop and to lock the door behind him. The defendant led him along a pathway and told him that he had already killed his wife. He said this several times and gestured with the knife. Mr Carey shouted to another passer-by for help, and when that man came over the defendant ran away. It was clear from the victim's personal statement that these events had deeply affected the victim's life, and he needed to undergo counselling and was fearful of being on his own. This was the defendant's third conviction for robbery. In the first robbery he had taken hold of a young woman and threatened her with an imitation firearm. In the second robbery he (together with two others) restrained the victim and removed his property, repeated the offence on a second victim, and assaulted a third. The writer of the pre-sentence report assessed the defendant as presenting a high risk of harm to the public. The judge noted various relevant aggravating features of the case but took into account that no physical harm had been inflicted on the latest victim. He said, rather tellingly, that 'It is plain that you will re-offend in much the same way in future, and I fear for anyone who is the victim of your fourth robbery . . .'. The judge found that neither a determinate sentence, nor an extended sentence, would achieve the appropriate protection for the public from the risk posed by the defendant, and passed a sentence of IPP with a minimum term of two years and eight months. The Court of Appeal considered all the material available to the judge and the judge's detailed sentencing remarks. The Court concluded that while the defendant had committed a number of serious offences, such offences do not always cause serious harm within the meaning of the statute, and he had not in fact caused serious harm. The judge's statement that he feared for the next robbery victim did not, in its language, meet the statutory threshold. The material before the judge did not meet the level which was required for IPP or an extended sentence. The indeterminate sentence was quashed and the Court substituted a determinate sentence of five years and four months.

[55] *Barton* [2010] EWCA Crim 2139.

VII JUDGES AND THE ASSESSMENT OF RISK

The assessment of risk obviously involves anticipation of a future event. This is, in general terms, the process the judges are involved in. The Court of Appeal has stressed that, when applying the dangerous offender scheme, judges are concerned with future risk and public protection rather than punishment for past offences.[56] In one sense this is clearly true – an indeterminate sentence should not be imposed simply as the means to mark the seriousness of an offence. However judges, unlike clinicians, are not required to make a full risk assessment, nor are they required to estimate for how long the offender will continue to represent the requisite degree of danger, nor to suggest the nature or extent of necessary interventions. Still less are judges required to engage in some 'crystal-ball gazing' exercise. The judge is concerned with whether, at the point of sentence, the offender crosses a certain threshold, as defined in the 2003 Act, and so in that sense, they are engaged in answering a yes/no question – whether the offender qualifies as 'dangerous' or not. The House of Lords in *Smith*[57] upheld the decision of the trial judge to impose IPP on a man already serving a life sentence. Smith had been released on licence, but had then committed a further serious crime. Although the original life sentence was still in place and Smith had been returned to prison under that sentence, it was held that it had been right for the judge to make a fresh determination of Smith's dangerousness at the time of passing the new sentence. Much of the evidence relevant to the dangerousness test is the kind of evidence that judges are familiar with, and feel reasonably comfortable to assess (the full facts and circumstances of the current offence, the facts and circumstances of previous offences). The rest of the evidence, in the form of reports, they are also well used to considering when making other sentencing judgments. Quite apart from the dangerous offender provisions, protection of the public is a standard statutory purpose of sentencing[58] and, according to one leading decision of the Court of Appeal, it underpins all the other purposes of sentencing.[59]

If risk factors in relation to the offender change over time, as they generally will, that is a matter for the executive authorities and not for the judge. The only possible exception to this is where on appeal against sentence there is more up-to-date information available to the Court of Appeal. There is a long-standing tension in cases where the Court of Appeal allows an appeal against sentence in a case where no criticism can be made of the original sentence, but where events have moved on in the meantime. In such cases the Court of Appeal

[56] According to Lord Judge CJ in *Johnson* [2007] 1 Cr App R (S) 112, 'Although punitive in its effect, with far-reaching consequences for the offender on whom it is imposed, strictly speaking it does not represent punishment for past offending.'

[57] [2011] UKSC 37.

[58] Criminal Justice Act 2003 s 142(1).

[59] *Howells* [1999] 1 Cr App R (S) 98 (Lord Bingham CJ). See also *Wilkinson* [2010] 1 Cr App R (S) 100.

acts less as an appeal tribunal determining whether the sentence was manifestly excessive or wrong in principle, but more like the Parole Board. In the specific context of the test for dangerousness, however, the Court of Appeal in the important case of *Beesley*[60] has made it clear that, if the sentencing judge has applied the dangerousness test properly, then the fact that the risk posed by the defendant may have diminished to some extent while he has been in prison (whether by attending courses, undergoing treatment, or for some other reason), it would not be right for the Court to interfere with the assessment of dangerousness made at the point of sentence. The Court rejected three separate appeals in *Beesley* on that basis.

VIII THRESHOLDS OF RISK / SERIOUSNESS

All available sentencing options must have been considered and dismissed by the judge before the dangerous offender provisions come into play at all. The judge decides whether the test for dangerousness is made out. If it is not, a community sentence with appropriate requirements, or a commensurate determinate sentence with appropriate licence conditions, is imposed.[61] If the test *is* made out, there are still choices to be made, between the extended sentence, IPP and (where available) the discretionary life sentence. These sentences can properly be seen as a hierarchy of disposals. Since the 2008 Act amendments to the dangerous offender scheme, there is the further threshold requirement that before an indeterminate sentence can be passed the offence itself must be sufficiently serious to justify a notional determinate sentence of four years. These various thresholds comprise an uneasy mix between risk-based and seriousness-based considerations.

The first threshold determines whether the dangerousness test has been passed at all.[62] A particularly useful decision is that of *Terrell*.[63] The defendant had pleaded guilty before magistrates to making indecent images of a child, and had been committed to Crown Court for sentence. The Court of Appeal quashed a sentence of IPP, despite the fact that the statutory presumption of dangerousness had operated in that case. Although there was a clear risk that the offender might re-offend in a similar way in future, there had been no evidence before the judge that his offending would escalate to photographing

[60] *Beesley, Coyle & Rehman* [2012] 1 Cr App R (S) 15. See also *Grant* [2010] EWCA Crim 3103.

[61] In *AG's Ref (No 55 of 2008)(C)* [2009] 2 Cr App R (S) 142, Lord Judge CJ said that in deciding whether an IPP should be passed, the suitability of all other available means of providing public protection must be considered, and if an overall sentencing package short of IPP could be found, IPP should not be used.

[62] As Lord Judge CJ put it in *AG's Reference (No 55 of 2008)(C)* [2009] 2 Cr App R (S) 22, 'Such an offender, whatever the nuisance he represents, would not present a significant risk of serious harm to the public. The individual who does not pose such risk should be dealt with by an appropriate determinate sentence or community order to which additional protective conditions may be attached.'

[63] *Terrell* [2008] 2 Cr App R (S) 49.

children, or to child abuse. It could not therefore be said that the offender represented a 'significant risk . . . of serious harm' where 'serious harm' meant death or personal injury, the latter phrase being deliberately coloured by the word 'death'.[64] The Court of Appeal went on to advocate the use of a determinate custodial sentence in this case coupled with a SOPO. The Court said that the threshold of dangerousness for a sentence of IPP was higher than that required for a SOPO, and that the restrictions available under a SOPO should always be in the judge's mind when considering whether IPP had to be invoked in a particular case. The particular decision in *Terrell* has been followed in several later cases, including *Waller*,[65] although the Court stressed in that case that *Terrell* did not mean that an IPP could never be appropriate for a defendant who downloaded child pornography. The test for applicability of a SOPO is whether such an order is 'necessary' 'for the purpose of protecting the public or any particular members of the public from serious sexual harm from the defendant'.[66] This in turn means protecting the public from 'serious physical or psychological harm, caused by the defendant committing one or more offences listed in schedule 3'.[67] The order may prohibit the offender from doing anything described in the order, provided that such proscriptions are 'necessary' for the stated statutory purpose. The order must last for at least five years, or until further order.[68] Clearly the SOPO is narrower than IPP in that it is confined to sexual offences rather than including violent offences as well, but in terms of the dangerousness test the differences between the two are quite narrow. The element of risk for the purpose of the dangerous offender provisions must be 'significant', but that word does not appear in relation to a SOPO, and the envisioned harm under the dangerous offender provisions must relate to 'death or serious personal injury' whereas under a SOPO it is 'serious physical or psychological harm'. Again, the imposition of a SOPO involves the judge in making an assessment of risk primarily on the basis of current and past offending, applying the stated criteria as the threshold test. There has been a steady stream of appeals to the Court of Appeal on the question of whether the offender represents a risk of sufficient magnitude to justify the imposition of a SOPO at all,[69] or whether the nature and degree of the risk that the offender poses is sufficient to justify the insertion of particular prohibitions in the SOPO, such as banning the offender from accessing the internet, either entirely or permitting access only for specific purposes.[70] The question whether a SOPO can, or should, be imposed as an adjunct

[64] Contrast the reasoning in *Collard* [2005] 1 Cr App R (S) 34, where it had been held that downloading of indecent images of children might cause serious psychological injury to a child, arising not only from what the child had been forced to do, but also from the knowledge that the images were available on the internet and that others could see what had been done.

[65] *Waller* [2010] 2 Cr App R (S) 101; see also *Sackman* [2010] 2 Cr App R (S) 56.

[66] Sexual Offences Act 2003 s104(1).

[67] *ibid* s 106(3).

[68] *ibid* s 107(1).

[69] *Halloren* [2004] 2 Cr App R (S) 57.

[70] See Ian Walden and Martin Wasik, 'The Internet: Access Denied / controlled' [2011] *Criminal Law Review* 377–87.

to an IPP has been considered in several cases,[71] but the recent leading decision in *Smith*[72] states that the 'usual rule is that an indeterminate sentence needs no SOPO'. This is no doubt because the terms of a SOPO are set at the point of sentence, and these may well be obsolete or unnecessary by the time the defendant is released from prison.

The next issue, if the dangerousness test is passed, is whether the offence in itself (considerations of dangerousness apart) would have justified a commensurate sentence of at least four years. There have been a number of appeals to the Court of Appeal on this issue, but it is clear that this is purely a matter of gauging offence seriousness, and is nothing to do with risk prediction. According to Lord Judge CJ, '. . . courts will no doubt ensure that longer than appropriate sentences are not imposed in order to avoid the restriction.'[73] To give just two examples, in *Birkett*[74] the Court varied a sentence of IPP for arson being reckless whether life was endangered to a determinate sentence of three years, saying that on ordinary principles the offence could not justify four years, and in *Ashworth*[75] the Court quashed an IPP and substituted a sentence of two years for false imprisonment. The four-year threshold is welcome in the sense of restricting the use of IPP generally, but of course is of questionable logic in the context of predicting future offending. A defendant might have a string of previous convictions for offences such as malicious wounding, assault occasioning actual bodily harm and possession of an offensive weapon. The defendant may now fall to be sentenced after pleading guilty to a section 18 wounding and the court may take the view that the test for dangerousness is passed and an IPP is appropriate and necessary. However, an IPP cannot be passed because the instant offence viewed in isolation would not have attracted a determinate sentence of four years on a timely guilty plea, or six years on conviction after a trial. Matters become more complex when the defendant is being sentenced for several associated offences, one or more of which are specified offences and one or more of which are not. The Court of Appeal has held that in this situation it is proper to aggregate the seriousness of all the offences in setting the minimum term and, in particular, in deciding whether the offending, looked at in this way, reaches the threshold of a notional determinate sentence of four years.[76]

The next distinction to be drawn is that between the extended sentence and IPP, and this has always been somewhat obscure. The extended sentence is the less severe sentence, and where the sentencer has a choice the extended sentence

[71] According to *Bolton* [2010] EWCA Crim 1177 and *L* [2010] EWCA Crim 2046, the sentences must be regarded as mutually exclusive; according to *N* [2010] EWCA Crim 1624 they can, and often should, be combined together.

[72] *Smith (Steven)* [2011] EWCA Crim 1772.

[73] *AG's Reference (No 55 of 2008)(C)* [2009] 2 Cr App R (S) 22.

[74] *Birkett* [2010] 2 Cr App R (S) 5.

[75] *Ashworth* [2010] 1 Cr App R (S) 15.

[76] For the sentence of IPP see *Delucca* [2010] EWCA Crim 710. The same approach is applicable to the extended sentence: *Pinnell* [2010] EWCA Crim 2848.

should be selected where it would achieve sufficient protection of the public.[77] The dangerousness test applies to the extended sentence in exactly the same way as it does to IPP. Since the 2008 Act both sentences are available whatever the maximum penalty which attaches to the specified offence. The two sentences, however, operate differently. An extended sentence comprises a custodial term of at least four years which is proportionate to the seriousness of the offence, and an extended licence period. Licence can last for up to five years in the case of a specified violent offence and up to eight years in the case of a specified sexual offence. Presumably the judge must decide whether, in the case of a dangerous offender, an extended licence period would be enough to protect the public, or whether IPP is required. This is a rather fine-grained judgment about the magnitude of future risk, and it may be doubted whether such a judgment can be made with any degree of confidence. Under the original 2003 Act scheme, release from the custodial part of the sentence was a matter for the parole board, but since the 2008 Act changes an offender under an extended sentence is released automatically at the half way point of the custodial term. The extended sentence now offers less protection for the public than was the case before the Act when the parole board had discretion to keep the offender in custody.[78] Ashworth[79] refers to this change as a 'strange dilution of the public protection function' of the sentence. However, 'if an extended sentence with, if required, the support of other orders, can achieve appropriate public protection against the risk posed by the individual offender, the extended sentence rather than IPP should be ordered.'[80]

The final issue to be determined by the judge, once the dangerousness threshold has been passed and an extended sentence is ruled out, is the choice between IPP and (if the offence carries life as its maximum) a discretionary life sentence. In either case the judge must set a minimum term which must be served in full before early release of the defendant can be considered. While both the life sentence and IPP are protective sentences it is clear that the minimum term should reflect the degree of punishment and retribution appropriate to the offence, and not the dangerousness of the offender.[81] The life sentence in its discretionary form (as opposed to the special case of murder) has been used for many years and, prior to the 2003 Act changes, there was a long-established Court of Appeal sentencing jurisprudence as to when a life sentence should properly be used. The criteria essentially were that the offence committed was in itself serious enough to require a very long sentence, that the defendant was a person who would probably re-offend and present a grave danger to the public, and was

[77] *AG's Reference (No 55 of 2008)(R v C)* [2009] 2 Cr App R (S) 22.

[78] A point noted in *Bretton* [2010] EWCA Crim 207.

[79] Andrew Ashworth, *Sentencing and Criminal Justice*, 5th edn (Cambridge, Cambridge University Press, 2010) 233.

[80] *AG's Reference (No 55 of 2008)(C)* [2009] 2 Cr App R (S) 22 (Lord Judge CJ).

[81] This is clear from the wording of the statutory provision s 82A of the Powers of Criminal Courts (Sentencing) Act 2000. See also *Hogg* [2008] 1 Cr App R (S) 22 and *Wilson* [2010] 1 Cr App R (S) 11.

someone who would remain dangerous for a long and / or uncertain period of time.[82] Initially, in *Lang*, the Court of Appeal took the view that this position had not been changed by Parliament.[83] Latterly, however, it has come to be accepted that the sentences of life imprisonment and IPP overlap to a very large degree, such that they are almost identical in their practical effects.[84] It is clear that IPP is not a heavier sentence than a life sentence.[85] The IPP sentence covers most but not all of the ground, and the discretionary life sentence is now confined to a small number of residual cases. The criteria for determining which residual cases should still attract a life sentence took some time to emerge. It might be thought, logically, those offenders regarded in some way as being 'exceptionally dangerous', over and above the risk threshold essential to justify IPP, ought to qualify for life sentence. The test adopted by the Court of Appeal, however, is once again more to do with seriousness than risk. In the leading case of *Kehoe*,[86] the Court of Appeal said that the life sentence should now be reserved for those cases where the culpability of the offender is exceptionally high, or the offence itself particularly grave. Strikingly, in *Wilkinson*[87] the Court of Appeal added that a life sentence should be considered where the seriousness of the crime is such that a life sentence would have denunciatory value, to reflect public abhorrence of the particular crime. A distinction between the life sentence and IPP is that the sentencing court may decide in the case of the former but not the latter to make an order[88] that the early release provisions should not apply at all, ie that the offender should remain in prison for the rest of his or her life. Such an order should, according to the Court of Appeal, be made only in a case of the 'utmost gravity'.[89]

IX CONCLUSION

It seems likely that there will continue to be provisions in English law for the sentencing of dangerous offenders. The 2003 Act provisions were poorly drafted and over-inclusive, and have perpetrated great injustice. Their effect has been summed up by Dr David Thomas as 'catastrophic', and the 'worst disaster (so

[82] *Hodgson* (1968) 52 Cr App R 113; *de Havilland* (1983) 5 Cr App R (S) 109; *AG's Reference (No 32 of 1996)* [1997] 1 Cr App R (S) 263.

[83] *Lang* was followed and applied on this point in a number of cases, including *Cross* [2009] 1 Cr App R (S) 34.

[84] The only difference between the sentences seems to be that in the case of IPP the parole board may, under the Crime (Sentences) Act 1997 s 31A direct the secretary of state to order that a prisoner's licence may cease to have effect after a period of at least 10 years has elapsed following the prisoner's release from custody. No such provision is available in the context of a life sentence.

[85] *Gorman* [2009] 2 Cr App R (S) 36.

[86] *Kehoe* [2009] 1 Cr App R (S) 9.

[87] *AG's Reference (No 43 of 2009)(R v Bennett); R v Wilkinson* [2010] 1 Cr App R (S) 100.

[88] Powers of Criminal Courts (Sentencing) Act 2000 s 82A(4).

[89] *Wilson* [2010] 1 Cr App R (S) 11.

far) in penal history'.[90] The Coalition Government's Green Paper on Sentencing, published in 2010, is mealy-mouthed by comparison, stating merely that IPP 'was only intended and expected to be used in a limited number of cases' and 'has been used on a much wider basis than expected'.[91] This is clearly a gross under-statement of what has occurred. The Coalition also recognised 'the limitations in our ability to predict serious future offending'.[92] This might have led on to a proposal to abandon the whole exercise of predictive indeterminate sentencing. The proposal, however, was to retain it, but only for 'the most dangerous offenders'[93] triggered only where the instant offence would otherwise have attracted a determinate sentence of 10 years or more. At the time of writing the Legal Aid, Sentencing, and Punishment of Offenders Bill is before Parliament. Chapter 5 deals with dangerous offenders, and proposes a very significant further restriction on the availability of the indeterminate sentence. The Bill proposes to replace IPP entirely, with a new sentence of 'life sentence for the second listed offence'. The name of the new sentence is unfortunately redolent of another failed sentence for dangerous offenders – section 109 of the Powers of Criminal Courts (Sentencing) Act 2000 – which created considerable difficulty to start with before being emasculated by the Court of Appeal[94] and then repealed to make way for the more far-reaching (and more disastrous) dangerous offender provisions of the 2003 Act. The Bill as currently drafted, however, would permit the passing of such a life sentence only where a defendant aged 18 or over is convicted of an offence which would otherwise merit a determinate sentence of 10 years or more *and* the defendant has previously served a sentence of such a length. Determinate sentences of 10 years or more are rare in English sentencing practice, and it seems that there will be *very few* defendants who will in fact be eligible for the new disposal. Even for those who do qualify, judges are given a power to avoid the operation of the provision if to impose such a sentence would in the circumstances be 'unjust'. The extended sentence is set to be retained, in very similar form, limited to cases either where the offence of conviction is listed in schedule 15B or where the proportionate determinate sentence would be four years or more. The 'dangerousness test', and the assessment of dangerousness in section 229, which have been the subject of this chapter, are retained in their entirety for both of these sentences, so that many of the issues discussed in this chapter will continue to apply, albeit in significantly fewer cases. It should be clear from the tangled history of IPP that, if we are to have such provisions at all, they must be very sharply focused, directed towards identifying a small group of exceptionally dangerous offenders. The current offence must in itself be very serious (measured by way of the commensurate determine

[90] *Sentencing News*, 27 February 2008 pp 6, 9.

[91] Ministry of Justice, *Breaking the Cycle: Effective Punishment, Rehabilitation, and Sentencing of Offenders* (December 2010), para 184.

[92] ibid para 186.

[93] ibid para 183.

[94] In *Offen* [2001] 1 WLR 253.

sentence which it would attract rather than the maximum penalty which it carries), and seen in light of the nature and extent of prior criminal conduct. In respect of those few offenders who are dealt with by way of indeterminate sentences, those sentences must be properly catered for in the penal regime and must be fully funded, offering for all except a very few obdurate recidivists the opportunity to demonstrate, once their period of punishment has been served, that they are no longer a risk to the public.

12

Culpability in Self-defence and Crime Prevention

JONATHAN ROGERS*

IN THIS CHAPTER we are concerned with the assessment of 'reasonable force' in self-defence and related law-enforcement defences.[1] Its focus is on the use of force by state officials to meet putative threats. It would not be new to say that the current law as it applies in criminal proceedings is unsatisfactory, but I hope to offer some fresh observations as to *why* it works so badly and to suggest why we should be rethinking the culpability of those who use strictly unnecessary force. We shall concentrate on the liability of the individual state agent who uses force, but at the same time, we will note the difficulties in holding police officers to account for excessive uses of force. This is one area where the substantive law should have regard to difficulties in practice, not only in the case of armed operations, but also in everyday matters such as the restraints on persons who resist arrest, which may also readily prove fatal. Our priority will not be to suggest rules of engagement or anything of the sort, but rather to discuss when persons can be blamed for using excessive force, and the conclusions here will be applicable to private citizens too.

One main theme is that the substantive law works mechanically. It imposes tests of necessity and proportionality, but courts are reluctant to withdraw a defence from the defendant (D[2]) who did at least act under the apprehension of danger, which would thus condemn D to be labelled as a murderer (or otherwise depending on the consequences of D's force). So these tests are loosely applied in practice, and D is also judged on the facts as D believed them to be even if D

* I wish to thank all the participants who commented on an early version of this chapter at the Conference on Seeking Security, hosted by University College London's Centre for Criminal Law in September 2010, and in particular Bob Sullivan who commented on a later version. As ever, the final contents are my own responsibility.

[1] Subject to the context, I will use the generic term 'self-defence' to embrace the related defences of crime prevention, effecting an arrest, preventing the escape of a prisoner from lawful custody, etc. It should be noted that many confrontations which start out as an attempt to (say) prevent an offence can transform into self-defence cases where the suspect threatens the life of the officer.

[2] We shall use 'D' to refer to the defendant, the person who used force and seeks a defence, and 'V' is the subject of the force, who may or may not have been an innocent person.

made an absurd mistake. However, nothing is said of D's possible use of force as an assertion of power, nor to what may be termed an 'attitude of unaccountability'. Yet these factors may in some cases be of greater moral significance to assessing D's culpability than the short time available for D to decide what to do. We shall argue that where D's culpability is in issue, as it should be when D has harmed an innocent person or used excessive force to avert a suspected or 'real' danger, then a finding that (besides preventing the offence) D was substantially motivated to assert power through use of force, or was indifferent to the proper measure of force, should be fatal. It may be that these elements of culpability will frequently be difficult to prove. However, the law is improved by requiring investigators to ask the morally pertinent questions, and by ensuring that outcomes are readily explicable to the public, even if the rate of successful prosecutions does not markedly increase.

The emphasis on culpability means that we will not be discussing how the defences should operate in civil proceedings. The theoretical underpinning of these defences in tort and crime should differ,[3] and the motives which we shall suggest are condemnable in the criminal courts might have no natural place in the law of tort. Similarly, we will not discuss directly the test of 'absolute necessity' which a state agent must satisfy in order to comply with article 2 (2) of the European Convention on Human Rights (ECHR)[4] when the agent has killed a suspect in self-defence or crime prevention, because again there is no necessary correlation between this test and the standard of reasonableness set by the criminal law which in principle is for Member States to determine.[5] It is however worth making immediately two points which should serve as essential background to our discussions of the criminal law. First, as well as having a greater chance of defeating self-defence in civil proceedings on account of the more stringent approach to mistakes, a civil remedy may lie in negligence. Typically this arises where D (or more likely, D's superiors) has carelessly prepared for an encounter with a dangerous person so as to increase the necessity to use fatal force in the event of an armed confrontation.[6] Usually, victims of mistaken uses

[3] As illustrated by the decision that in civil proceedings, any mistaken belief by D that V poses an imminent threat will have to be based on reasonable grounds: *Ashley v Chief Constable of Sussex Police* [2008] UKHL 25.

[4] Article 3 is silent on any justifications for inhuman or degrading treatment, but the Court seems to read in by necessary implication the same allowances for self-defence, etc that append to art 2. See *Rivas v France* (Application No 59584/00), 1 April 2004, commented on by Ashworth, 'Case and Comment on Rivas v France' (2005) *Crim LR* 305ff.

[5] See J Rogers, 'Applying the Doctrine of Positive Obligations in the European Convention on Human Rights to Domestic Substantive Criminal Law in Domestic Proceedings' (2003) *Crim LR* 690.

[6] In *McCann v United Kingdom* [1996] 21 EHRR 97, the European Court of Human Rights (ECtHR) was clear that duties are owed even to active terrorist suspects to be careful in planning the timing and context of their arrests so as to minimise the likelihood that lethal force will be thought to be needed. For suggestions that criminal liability on the part of senior officers may be warranted in some cases of egregious failure, see *Isaveya v Russia* (2005) 41 EHRR 791, *Juozaitiene v Lithuania* (2008) 47 EHRR 1194. However, the police cannot be liable for corporate manslaughter in relation to 'operations for dealing with terrorism, civil unrest or serious disorder' or operations which

of force receive settlements by one remedy or another, not least because the police may not wish to be forced to disclose the contents of intelligence briefings which may have been passed onto the officers on the ground. So, whilst no policeman on the mainland has been found liable in a criminal court for the use of firearm in the purported execution of his or her duty,[7] the record of out of court settlements shows a different picture entirely.[8] Second, whilst article 2(2) ECHR does not automatically affect our criminal law, the European Court of Human Rights (ECtHR) could conceivably find that our overall record[9] of punishing excessive uses of force to be so bad that we incur a positive obligation to amend the substantive law[10] to deter future excesses. Should this ever happen,[11] then the decision as to how to amend it would still remain with the United Kingdom, and in that eventuality, the arguments in this chapter about the rethinking of our criminal law would be relevant to meeting human rights obligations after all.

The rest of the chapter will be subdivided as follows. In part I I will introduce the law of self-defence as it currently applies in criminal trials, and suggest that it suffers from its emphasis on D's cognitive process, and from its tendency to isolate D's use of force. In part II, I will discuss the importance of condemning the motive to use force in order to assert power, and also what may be called an attitude of unaccountability. I shall then consider how these elements of

'involve the carrying on of policing or law-enforcement activities': Corporate Manslaughter and Corporate Homicide Act 2007 s 5(2) a, b.

[7] See the list of cases at www.independent.co.uk/news/uk/crime/shot-dead-by-police-30-officers-convicted-0-511859.html.

[8] Most victims of mistaken shootings receive compensation. The pattern is replicated in cases of alleged police brutality. Perhaps the most disturbing case of recent times is the acquittal of four police officers who were acquitted of assault occasioning actual bodily harm when arresting the terrorist suspect Babar Ahmad. Unknown to the jury, the Metropolitan Police had already paid compensation over the incident to Ahmad, and accompanied it with an acknowledgment that he had been subjected to 'a serious, gratuitous and prolonged' assault: www.guardian.co.uk/uk/2011/jun/03/police-not-guilty-babar-ahmad. For an informed discussion of comparable cases, many of which also have racist elements, see A Sanders and R Young, *Criminal Justice*, 3rd edn (Oxford, Oxford University Press, 2007) ch 12.3.

[9] Thus, our law of chastisement was condemned in *A v United Kingdom* (1999) 27 EHRR 611 when it emerged that, despite several cases of serious bodily harm against children being prosecuted over 30 years, on only eight occasions had a jury apparently rejected a defence of chastisement.

[10] I say only that this is conceivable. In many cases involving state agents, impediments to prosecution turn out to be faulty investigations, and here an adjectival remedy under art 2 may be easier to establish: see eg *Jordan v United Kingdom, Kelly et al v United Kingdom* (2001) 11 BHRC 1.

[11] The point has not yet been decided. In the leading case *McCann* the indication that the criminal law was not substantially at variance with art 2 was foremost a way of defending the effectiveness *of the inquest* in that particular case (where in any event, the argument raged over a shoot-to-kill policy on IRA suspects regardless of perception of threat). Indeed the Court explicitly said that it was not considering the compatibility of the criminal law on self-defence in Gibraltar, [155] and [173]. In *R (Bennett) v HM Coroner for Inner London* [2006] EWHC Admin 196, Collins J thought that our criminal law was compatible with art 2, but by deference to the lack of any condemnation in Strasbourg ([25]) and again the matter arose in relation to how an inquest should proceed. Only in *Caraher v United Kingdom* (App No 24520/94) might the compatibility of our criminal law have been directly in issue; but the ECtHR seemed to misunderstand this and simply referred quickly to *McCann*.

culpability might affect our treatment of mistakes of fact, and of excessive force. In part III, I discuss the prevention of non-imminent offences, and in part IV I argue that the same elements of culpability should apply to private citizens as well as to state agents.

I THE RULES AND DEFICIENCIES IN THE CRIMINAL LAW

The law as it applies to criminal proceedings has recently been codified in section 76 of the Criminal Justice and Immigration Act 2008 (hereafter, 'CJIA'"). This section provides:

76 Reasonable force for purposes of self-defence etc.

(1) This section applies where in proceedings for an offence –

(a) an issue arises as to whether a person charged with the offence ("D") is entitled to rely on a defence within subsection (2), and
(b) the question arises whether the degree of force used by D against a person ("V") was reasonable in the circumstances.

(2) The defences are –

(a) the common law defence of self-defence; and
(b) the defences provided by section 3(1) of the Criminal Law Act 1967 (c. 58) or section 3(1) of the Criminal Law Act (Northern Ireland) 1967 (c. 18 (N.I.)) (use of force in prevention of crime or making arrest).

(3) The question whether the degree of force used by D was reasonable in the circumstances is to be decided by reference to the circumstances as D believed them to be, and subsections (4) to (8) also apply in connection with deciding that question.

(4) If D claims to have held a particular belief as regards the existence of any circumstances –

(a) the reasonableness or otherwise of that belief is relevant to the question whether D genuinely held it; but
(b) if it is determined that D did genuinely hold it, D is entitled to rely on it for the purposes of subsection (3), whether or not –

(i) it was mistaken, or
(ii) (if it was mistaken) the mistake was a reasonable one to have made.

(5) But subsection (4)(b) does not enable D to rely on any mistaken belief attributable to intoxication that was voluntarily induced.

(6) The degree of force used by D is not to be regarded as having been reasonable in the circumstances as D believed them to be if it was disproportionate in those circumstances.

(7) In deciding the question mentioned in subsection (3) the following considerations are to be taken into account (so far as relevant in the circumstances of the case) –

(a) that a person acting for a legitimate purpose may not be able to weigh to a nicety the exact measure of any necessary action; and
(b) that evidence of a person's having only done what the person honestly and instinctively thought was necessary for a legitimate purpose constitutes strong evidence that only reasonable action was taken by that person for that purpose.

(8) Subsection (7) is not to be read as preventing other matters from being taken into account where they are relevant to deciding the question mentioned in subsection (3).
(9) This section is intended to clarify the operation of the existing defences mentioned in subsection (2).
(10) In this section –

(a) "legitimate purpose" means –

(i) the purpose of self-defence under the common law, or
(ii) the prevention of crime or effecting or assisting in the lawful arrest of persons mentioned in the provisions referred to in subsection (2)(b);

(b) references to self-defence include acting in defence of another person; and
(c) references to the degree of force used are to the type and amount of force used.

The effect of this provision is no more than to consolidate common law principles.[12] We can see that the first task in any case is (still) to identify the facts as believed by the defendant, regardless whether it was reasonable for D to believe what D did.[13] Then the tribunal of fact considers whether D used 'reasonable force' on D's putative facts, and this is commonly understood to mean that D's force must have been necessary (no lesser measure would have warded off the putative threat) and proportionate (the harm done to the victim must be comparable with that which D might have inflicted, if let alone). However, there are two ways in which this test is compromised, both of which prefer the defendant's interests to those of the victim's. First, section 76 (7) (a) is intended as a reminder *to the court* that the necessity of force should not be judged in hindsight. So, D may have injured V already but may be unsure of the extent to which V has been incapacitated and may fear another wave of attack if D lets 'his or her guard down. If D pursues the attack a bit further, but medical evidence later shows that V was already incapacitated, then that evidence should not necessarily be fatal. By contrast, section 76 (7) (b) is concerned with whether the self-defender might *deserve* a liberal application of the necessity test *even without the benefit of hindsight*. This 'fudge factor' is to be granted to the defendant who acts 'honestly and instinctively'.

In many cases both parts of section 76(7) will apply: it might not have been obvious (to anyone) at the time that option (a) was available, and in the heat of

[12] *R v Keane, R v McGrath* [2010] EWCA Crim 2514 [6]. See later IV.
[13] Criminal Justice and Immigration Act 2008 (CJIA) s 76 (4).

the moment, the honest defender may be forgiven for having overlooked option (b) and so D's preferred option (c) – the most harmful of all – may yet be denoted 'reasonable'. It is assumed that the test of necessity continues to refer only to the 'immediate' circumstances in which D uses force.[14] The only discernible 'prior fault' rule at common law, and which seems to have survived the CJIA, is that a person who deliberately provoked another to aggression *in order to have an opportunity* for self-defence should lose that defence.[15]

The effect of these principles is that when D does believe that V has a gun or explosive and that V intends to use it imminently, then this belief is de facto likely to be determinative of the lawfulness of anything D might do to prevent the apprehended attack. It is against this background that we have witnessed high-profile shootings by police officers of persons who, when shot, have been found to be 'armed' with, variously, a torch,[16] a cigarette lighter,[17] a broken coffee table leg,[18] or who have been carrying nothing, either when dressed[19] or even when naked.[20] That the mistake may[21] have been made is commonly thought to be virtually impossible to disprove, and in almost all of these cases the use of force was assumed by the Independent Police Complaints Commision (IPCC) or the Crown Prosecution Service (CPS) to be lawful. Nor does it matter if the police caused the suspect to act in a way which made the police (mistakenly) fear for their lives, for unless they did so with the intention of creating an opportunity for self-defence (again, almost impossible to disprove) then their 'prior fault' will not forfeit a defence. Thus, when an inquest jury found a verdict of unlawful killing in relation to the unarmed Harry Stanley, who was walking home carrying a table leg in a plastic bag but turned around when police officers challenged him, the verdict was quashed on judicial review. Leveson J (as he then was) held that the jury should not have been left to consider a verdict of unlawful killing, given what seemed to be irrebuttable evidence of self-defence. He reasoned thus:

> First, the police were properly responding to information that a man was carrying a sawn-off shot gun; they were required by their duty to put themselves in what was,

[14] *Farrell v Secretary of State for Defence* [1980] WLR 172, 178–79.

[15] *Mason's Case* (1756) Foster 132. By statute, this forfeits the *partial* defence to murder based on fear: Coroners and Justice Act 2009 s 55 (6) a. It is curious that the same Ministry of Justice had enacted no equivalent provision in the CJIA 2008, thus leaving us merely with very old common law instead. See now *R v Rashford* [2005] EWCA Crim 3377, and the *post* CJIA case *R v McGrath* [2010] EWCA Crim 2514.

[16] *Brady v United Kingdom* (App No 55151/00) 3 April 2001.

[17] The shooting of Derek Bennett (n 11 above).

[18] The shooting of Harry Stanley: see below.

[19] The shooting of Jean Charles de Menezes, discussed below. This was also the case of the IRA terrorists shot in Gibraltar, although one SAS soldier testified that he thought that one suspect had looked at him with a 'sudden look of recognition', and that had prompted a belief that he might reach into his pocket to detonate an explosive device: *McCann v United Kingdom* (n 6 above) [61].

[20] The shooting of James Ashley (n 3 above).

[21] In criminal proceedings, the prosecution must disprove self-defence, assuming there to be some coherent evidence such as to raise it in the first place. In civil law, the burden lies on the defendant, which is another reason why so many cases are settled.

> potentially, harm's way; they had not embarked on a frolic looking for trouble. Second, if the family's challenge to Chief Inspector Sharman is right, within 19 seconds of reporting his presence at the scene, Mr Stanley had been shot: on any showing, very little time elapsed for considered and measured decisions. Third, although Mr Stanley appears to have been walking away from the officers, he had certainly turned sufficiently to receive the shot to the side of his head . . . whichever way Mr Stanley turned, he had turned round.
>
> . . .
>
> [The respondent] postulated the possibility that the officers had fired prematurely in panic or fear, perhaps because they had permitted themselves to be exposed and had not waited for backup. But if they were in panic or fear, it is necessary to ask in panic or fear of what? The most likely answer is that they were in panic or fear of being shot. In reply, Mr Lawson observed that if they were in fear, that was very close to establishing lawful killing, particularly bearing in mind that the test is subjective and it does not matter that their fear is irrational, unreasonable or arises because they have wrongly exposed themselves. Whether 'very close' or not, it does not establish that verdict because panic may lead to a reaction without there being a fear of imminent threat but it is certainly an important background fact.
>
> . . .
>
> [But] I am concerned that by challenging Mr Stanley from behind, without having taken cover, the officers ran the risk that he would turn round to see what was going on and react in a way that could create a real risk of a misunderstanding as to his intentions. That risk is particularly acute if, as was the event, Mr Stanley was unarmed and might even have been unaware that the challenge was addressed to him. Whether or not a misunderstanding on the part of the officers may be justifiable, they did in fact misunderstand Mr Stanley's reaction and, as a result, he lost his life.[22]

Some writers argue that the principles of self-defence are supplemented in homicide cases by the offence of gross negligence manslaughter.[23] The argument is that if D succeeds in self-defence on a murder charge because a mistake was made about V's intentions (and used reasonable force on that basis) then D might still be liable for gross negligence manslaughter if the mistake was unreasonable and in breach of a duty of care to D's victim. However, this seems doubtful. If 'gross' negligence denotes a standard of negligence so high that it warrants criminal conviction,[24] then it would be odd, even contradictory, to convict the defendant under this rubric – if D's mistake were so bad as to be deserving of criminal condemnation, then why would D's plea of (mistaken) self-defence have succeeded? One notes that no charges have been brought for gross negligence manslaughter on this basis, and it is submitted that the apparent scepticism of the CPS in this area is justified.

[22] *Sharman v HM Coroner for Inner North London & Anor* [2005] EWHC 857 (Admin) [39]–[40], [55], summarily confirmed on appeal [2005] EWCA Civ 967.

[23] Most prominently, the late Professor Sir JC Smith, 'The Use of Force in Public or Private Defence and Article 2' (2002) *Crim LR* 958.

[24] Which it does: *R v Adomako* [1995] 1 AC 171.

A Two Problems

We suggest that the law suffers from two problems. First, it focuses on whether D believes that there is a need to use force, and whether the defendant believes he or she is acting reasonably; but the analysis stops as soon as it reaches a (possibly) affirmative answer. We call this 'the cognitive problem'. Second, it tends to treat each occasion of self-defence as a separate incident and an individual event, even if D acted as part of a team and was experienced in the use of force. We call this 'the isolation problem'. Together, they combine to contribute to a crisis of accountability.

i The Cognitive Problem

As we have seen, much depends on D's beliefs: if D believes that a personal attack is about to occur, then the case continues on that flawed basis. An erroneous belief that D used reasonable force in those circumstances does not quite exculpate D in law, but juries must take D's 'honest and instinctive' thoughts as 'strong evidence' that D acted reasonably. Indeed, it is probably not just mistaken *beliefs* that are permitted. Although only the word 'belief' is used in law reports, and accordingly also in the prepared statements of defendants, it must surely be the case that a strong *suspicion* that V is about to kill another or to detonate an explosive device will also suffice.[25] Most self-defence actions occur where there is so little time for reflection that it is unrealistic to speak of firm beliefs, and many defendants will know that they do not know the full facts but need to take an instant decision whether to trust their instincts.[26] It is perhaps with this in mind that at common law, the ability to rely entirely on mistakes of V's intentions[27] was mitigated by a rule that a mistake caused by intoxication could not be relied on.[28]

However, the moral significance of both kinds of mistakes (of V's intentions, and of the force that may properly be used to meet the possible threat), taken by themselves, is exaggerated. It is submitted that a mistaken belief that V poses a threat is only morally compelling when D is not otherwise interested in using

[25] The common law did recognise a distinction between mistaken beliefs on consent and mistaken suspicions in the law of rape: *R v Satnam and Kewell* (1984) 78 Cr App R 149, and doubtless the word 'belief' in s 1(1) c of the Sexual Offences Act 2003 will be interpreted strictly. However, mistakes about consent and mistakes about another's aggressive intentions are quite different. The classic article on the difference is J Horder, 'Cognition, Emotion and Criminal Culpability' (1990) 106 *LQR* 469.

[26] See K Simons, 'Self-Defence: Reasonable Beliefs or Reasonable Self-Control?' (2008) 11 (1) *New Criminal Law Review* 51, who seems to assume an unduly strict interpretation of the word 'belief'.

[27] *R v Williams (Gladstone)* (1984) 78 Cr App R 276, confirmed by the Privy Council in *Beckford v R* [1988] 1 AC 130.

[28] *R v Hatton* [2006] 1 Cr App R 16, now consolidated in s 76(5) of the CJIA.

violence against V for other purposes. If D might have other motivations, then we should need to be sure that the defendant did not believe 'what he wanted to believe' when D made the mistake. Yet, the possibility that some state agents who are trained in the use of force may become more prone (consciously or subconsciously) to wrongly apprehend trouble *as though to justify being violent* – ie, doing what they have been trained primarily to do[29] – seems to be lost. In contrast, the law, focusing only on the cognitive process and not the deeper motivations and attitudes of D, refuses to entertain any mistake caused by intoxication, even though the defendant (even when drunk) may still have been vehemently opposed to violence. So if a woman who walks home late at night, after having drunk some alcohol, consequently mistakenly believes that a man who is following her must be intending to rape her, she might be punished for trusting her intuitions when she uses defensive force.[30] It seems clear that the opposite results should be reached in both cases, but to do this, the law needs to free itself from its cognitive shackles. When ascertaining *mens rea*, it is all very well to focus on what D intended or foresaw (save when drunk) and to ask nothing more, but culpability often works differently in exculpatory defences.[31]

If this is right, then it is not enough to reform the law to require *reasonable* mistakes in the intentions of V.[32] For a start, where D acts in an emergency, it seems almost inevitable that any such test of 'reasonableness' will apply in D's favour. Thus, the House of Lords seemed to be quite unsure whether the Ashley family would succeed in showing that PC Sherwood did not have a reasonable belief in the need for self-defence in any subsequent civil proceedings,[33] even though V, who was confronted at 4.20 am at home, was naked when shot and is not thought to have uttered any threat. A similar pattern arises in the series of cases brought to Strasbourg where state liability under article 2 of the ECHR in relation to killings by state agents would accrue unless there were 'reasonable grounds' for any mistake.[34] However more importantly, the unreasonableness of a mistake is not an accurate measure of culpability.

[29] To use the contemporaneous words of a former constable 'a member of the Territorial Support Group . . . spends his days waiting for action, and far too many officers join seeking excitement and physical confrontation': www.newstatesman.com/law-andreform/2009/04/dream-job-officers-leave.

[30] See J Rogers, 'Let the Drunkard Lie!' (2005) 155 *NLJ* 1892.

[31] For related arguments, see J Horder, 'On the Irrelevance of Motive in Criminal Law' in J Horder (ed), *Oxford Essays in Jurisprudence*, 4th series (Oxford, Oxford University Press, 2000).

[32] *cf* A Ashworth in *Principles of Criminal Law*, 6th edn (Oxford, Oxford University Press, 2009) 125; A Ashworth, B Emmerson, A Macdonald, *Human Rights and Criminal Justice*, 2nd edn (London, Sweet & Maxwell, 2007) 750–57; F Leverick, *Killing in Self-Defence* (Oxford, Oxford University Press, 2006) ch 10.

[33] (n 3 above) [27] (per Lord Scott).

[34] Leverick (n 32 above) 186–90 discusses a range of cases from signatory countries involving the shooting of unarmed persons. In all but one particularly extreme case (*Gul v Turkey* (2002) 34 EHRR 28), the ECtHR found the mistake to be 'reasonable', sometimes emphasising that it 'could not substitute its own assessment for that of the officers who were required to react in the heat of the moment': *Andronicou and Constantinou v Cyprus* (1998) 25 EHRR 491 [192].

Similarly, the weight of D's belief that he or she acted reasonably because he acted 'instinctively', which seems to go without saying in most cases,[35] should only take D so far. Those who are disposed to violence for other reasons, such as the man who beats his wife at home, are presumably more likely to believe that they act reasonably when using force to detain an arrested person at night. Those who use force in the line of duty may also become accustomed to doing so, and where bad habits are not cured at an early stage, they may well hold honest beliefs that what they do is lawful.[36] The possibility that some excesses of force may become routine and tolerated as a matter of convenience has been illustrated by the revelation of the use of excessive restraints in children's prisons. When one inmate committed suicide after being subjected to a technique of distraction (involving an assault) by a member of staff, which was subsequently conceded to meet the threshold of article 3 of the ECHR, the Divisional Court ordered the inquest to resume because, inter alia:

> It was clear from the evidence that the way Adam was treated was not unique in Hassockfield. . . . In the lengthy log of injuries to trainees for the 12 months before Adam's death, the court has identified 26 occasions where injuries caused by the nose distraction technique were recorded; on 7 of these occasions the record was of painful nose only, on the remaining 19 occasions nose bleeds due to distraction technique were recorded. . . . This was not a one-off error of understanding but a persistent practice, duly recorded, in dealing with children in detention in breach of the law, the rules, the STC contract and the training manual as well as the in-house rules. . . .
>
> Mr Bowers' evidence at the inquest as to the consequences if children were being routinely assaulted now needs revisiting . . .[37]

A subsequent inquest jury found that Adam was unlawfully killed,[38] since there was not any arguable defence open on the facts (the technique was employed to maintain discipline and not to prevent any imminent offence). However, we might note that the jury also thought that those who used distraction techniques had thought that they were acting lawfully. So if the same technique had been used to prevent a minor offence, thus raising the issue of whether reasonable force had been used, it is possible that their claim of sincerity might have amounted to an honest and instinctive belief that they were using reasonable force, with a likely acquittal if the case were prosecuted.

[35] See *Attorney-General for Northern Ireland's Reference (No 1 Of 1975)* [1977] AC 105, 138, where allowance was given to soldiers acting in situations where there was no present danger. Ashworth expresses doubts that this test, perhaps designed with private citizens in mind, should apply equally to state agents: *Principles of Criminal Law*, 6th edn (Oxford, Oxford University Press, 2009) 126.

[36] It is common for police officers on trial to say that 'they would do the same thing again', and whilst such statements may be part of an assertive defence strategy, they may also have an uncomfortable ring of truth. See the account of one case where a jury found that a man was unlawfully killed by excessive restraint measures: www.tribunemagazine.co.uk/2010/03/how-the-police-killed-mikey-powell/.

[37] *R (on the application of Pounder) v HM Coroner for North and South Districts of Durham and Darlington* [2009] EWHC 76 (Admin) [67]–[68].

[38] See www.independent.co.uk/news/uk/crime/unlawful-use-of-force-contributed-to-boys-custody-death-2196148.html.

ii The Isolation Problem

State agents are trained in the use of force but advised that any action they take is at their own responsibility. This is constitutionally correct.[39] It is also clear that when an officer acts in self-defence, the officer must believe the relevant facts, eg that V is armed and dangerous, and the officer cannot rely simply on an earlier briefing that this is a possibility.[40] However, as already seen, the subjective tests employed in assessing the use of reasonable force tend to undermine this responsibility. Whilst the officer can point to his or her instructions or training as evidence that he or she acted honestly and instinctively, it does not seem that the officer's standard instructions can be used *against* him or her when the officer deviates from them.[41] The point has no legal relevance since it is only the jury who decides whether the force the officer used was reasonable or not.[42] Not only is the jury invited to decide the reasonableness of the force used with little or no expert assistance or reference point, but the incident is presented to them as though it were isolated in the career of the officer his or herself. Thus, the jury were not told of an astonishing 70 independent complaints made against the six officers accused of a gratuitous attack on Babar Ahmad, which were mainly in relation to violence against other black or Asian suspects.[43] Since none of these complaints were substantiated, one can see why they might not have been admissible as bad character evidence. However, it should be a challenge for law reformers to find a way which legitimately gives such disturbing background evidence some substantive legal relevance. We will return to this in part II.

The twin problems of cognition and isolation contribute towards a lack of public accountability. To be sure, there are other reasons for this crisis in accountability, including a lack of rigour in investigations[44] and (what appear to be) deep flaws in the police investigations system,[45] which no doubt help to

[39] 'With us, every official, from the Prime Minister down to a constable or a collector of taxes, is under the same responsibility for every act done without legal justification as any other citizen': A Dicey, *An Introduction to the Study of the Law of the Constitution*, 6th edn (London, Macmillan, 1902) 189–90.

[40] Nor does the briefing necessarily give the officer 'reasonable grounds' for believing its contents. The arresting officer must have some idea of the basis for the suspicion of his or her superiors: *O'Hara v Chief Constable of the RUC* [1997] AC 286.

[41] Unlike the Codes of Practice issued under the Police and Criminal Evidence Act 1984 (PACE), there is no legal provision stating the evidential significance of departure from them.

[42] The independence of the court was well established in Irish cases concerning alleged excesses by the security forces: eg *Lynch v Fitzgerald* [1938] IR 382, 399 (Hanna J): *R v Hegarty* [1986] NIJB 25, 46 (Hutton J).

[43] See www.guardian.co.uk/commentisfree/2011/jun/05/babar-ahmad-metropolitan-police-ipcc.

[44] For example, officers who have shot an innocent suspect are not routinely arrested and, until recently, other officers at the scene were afforded an opportunity to exchange notes before anyone was questioned. See the unsuccessful challenge to this former practice in *R (Saunders) v IPCC* [2008] EWHC 2372 (Admin). See further the criticisms of the IPCC relating to the aftermath of the shooting of Jean Charles de Menezes: www.ipcc.gov.uk/en/Pages/the_stockwell_investigation.aspx.

[45] See Amnesty International, 'Deaths in Police Custody: Lack of Police Accountability' (Amnesty International, 2000), accessible at www.amnesty.org/en/library/info/EUR45/042/2000/en; G Smith, 'Rethinking Police Complaints' (2004) 44 *BJ Crim* 15. See too an account of a recent crisis at the IPCC arising out of series of decisions where the versions of the police were said to be accepted

explain why an accused officer might have a long trail of unsubstantiated complaints behind him or her. Undoubtedly, some shift at a political level towards maintaining a credible system of investigation (including extra resources) will be needed, perhaps especially in relation to some sections of our forces.[46] However, we should not let the substantive law off the hook. It plays a substantial part in causing the accountability crisis by simply asking *what* the officer believed, and not *why* the officer perceived V to pose a threat, nor *why* the officer thought arguably excessive force was in fact reasonable.

II SELF-DEFENCE, VIOLENCE AND LEGAL PRINCIPLES

Self-defence and related defences apply more or less exclusively to offences of violence. So where they fail, D is convicted and condemned for a violent offence in the same way as one who acted purely malevolently. This alone should suggest to us that, provided that D was in some way motivated to act in self-defence, etc then D's defence should only fail where D acted with a culpable attitude towards the use of violence. The current law does not do this, other than its reliance on the defendant's 'honest and instinctive' reactions, criticised already in part I. In this part, we will ponder further what sort of culpability we should be looking for when self-defence in relied on in criminal proceedings, such that we can fairly label and punish the self-defender for a violent offence if culpable.

It should be noted that in some self-defence cases, culpability will not be in issue. Where the jury accepts that D used reasonable force against a true aggressor, such that they are not making any allowance for any mistake or over-reaction, then they should accept that the defence is made out; the law seems to require that D must have believed in justifying circumstances at the time[47] but nothing more. There is strong philosophical support for the idea that D must also in some way be *motivated* to act for the justifying purpose[48] but it is unclear whether this represents the law. Certainly if there is some evidence that D acted in order to meet the threat, we would not expect D's defence to fail if D had competing motives too. Equally, where D grossly over-reacted, such as by knowingly shooting a shoplifter in the back, then the defence can be rejected without

without challenge: 'Crisis at Police Watchdog as Lawyers Resign' www.guardian.co.uk/politics/2008/feb/25/police.law1.

[46] The Territorial Support Group, which is used to dispel riots and in armed raids around the capital, received a staggering 2,280 complains for 'oppressive behaviour' between 2005 and 2009. See www.guardian.co.uk/politics/2009/nov/06/police-scotland-yard-riot-squad. This was the section from which came the officers who were charged over the injuries to Babar Ahmad, and also the officer who allegedly pushed Ian Tomlinson to his death. cp n 8 and n 29 above.

[47] *R v Dadson* (1850) 4 Cox CC 358.

[48] See J Gardner, 'Justifications and Reasons' in A Simester and A Smith (eds), *Harm and Culpability* (Oxford, Oxford University Press, 1996) and V Tadros, *Criminal Responsibility* (Oxford, Oxford University Press, 2005) ch 10.

further ado, as though culpability is already established.[49] However, we are concerned instead with cases 'in the middle', where V has been wrongly harmed, but where D makes a mistake, or has acted not strictly reasonably. Here it is proper that D's attitude towards using force should be assessed as being substantively relevant, and competing motives should become relevant too. However in saying this, I do not propose remodelling defences according to their classification as justifications and excuses, with different rules attaching to each doctrine. The traditional unitary approach in my view is theoretically proper[50] and in any case pragmatically essential for anyone thinking potentially in terms of concrete law reform.[51] So the proposal here is that where the prosecution accepts that D might have been motivated in some way to use force in self-defence, and used excessive force (whether or not due to mistake) *but* did not grossly overreact, then they should need to lead additional evidence showing a culpable motive or attitude on the part of D.

A One Culpable Motivation and One Culpable Attitude

It is suggested that culpability should be regarded as present *either* where D was motivated to assert power, *or* where D acted with the attitude that he or she was de facto unaccountable, both to the victim and to the wider community, for his or her actions. We will start to think in these broad terms though it may be that the law will need to find simpler language in which to express these concepts.

We start with the culpable motivation. It is enough to criminalise offences against the person to point towards the physical harm done and the disrespect to the victim's autonomy. They involve also typically intimidation, humiliation and injury. However, further wrongs are done. Those who use violence often do so because they are motivated to assert power over their victims. This may take the form of a feeling of respect, or control over the lifestyle and choices of other people which cannot be gained in any other way, a phenomenon well recognised in the literature on domestic violence,[52] or to establish 'territory' to the exclusion of others as in some gang-related violence. Alternatively, it may be used to convey hatred or misunderstanding of those who are felt to be different, as in cases of racist assaults or other forms of bullying. In cases of self-defence, a likely motivation to assert power will be that D wishes not just to prevent V's anticipated offence but to add his or her own form of extra-judicial punishment

[49] Should any defendant think that this is reasonable, it is better to look more deeply at the defendant's criminal agency altogether.

[50] For a brief discussion of how ardent justification and excuse adherents can 'tie themselves in knots', see my review of Leverick's book, 'Review of Killing in Self-Defence' (2008) 124 *LQR* 172–75.

[51] The original article in this field is K Greenawalt, 'The Perplexing Borders of Justification and Excuse' (1984) 84 *Columbia LR* 1897.

[52] See J Babcock, J Waltz, N Jacobson, J Gottman, 'Power and Violence: The Relation between Communication Patterns, Power Discrepancies, and Domestic Violence' (1993) 61 (1) *Journal of Consulting and Clinical Psychology* 40–50.

for it (or for other offences which D might assume that V has committed in the past, should V be thought to have a criminal lifestyle). Similarly, we might note the allied distinction between *overpowering V with force* and *exerting power over V by the use of force*: the latter occurs when D uses force so as to intimidate V or others on an ongoing basis, and not just in order to deter V from imminent or future offences. In all these cases D uses the occasion for self-defence as an opportunity to assert power, and in appropriate cases this attitude is sufficiently culpable to merit forfeiting the defence and being labelled as a violent offender.

We may also identify a culpable attitude on the part of the defendant who uses force in the belief that the defendant is already de facto above the law in respect of any excesses of force that might be perpetrated on the victim. We might call this the attitude of unaccountability', whereby D acts with the perspective that he or she should not, or at least will not, be required to explain to either the victim or the wider community why use of force should be regarded as reasonable. This attitude may exist may be because D knows or believes that his or her actions will not be investigated with proper rigour; or it may be because others in similar positions have been absolved of liability. It may well be found in cases where the victim, like Babar Ahmad, is a terrorist suspect whose testimony might not be expected to carry much weight.

More importantly, and in contrast to the cognitive approach, D may be blamed for thinking him or herself to be unaccountable even if D had been trained to act in the manner in which he or she did. It depends on D's attitude. In some cases, especially those involving more experienced officers, there may yet be misgivings about the training; the supposed safety of a technique of restraint, for example, may not fully accord with the defendant's own experience. The defendant is culpable if he or she nonetheless continues to apply it out of convenience, believes that he or she is somehow accountable only to superiors and not also to the wider community (a representative sample of which would already have found the defendant's use of force to be excessive when considering his or her attitude). The point is that the defendant must be prepared to account for his or her actions when they are performed; and that accountability involves an explanation that goes beyond unquestioning acceptance of what the defendant has been told to do. On the other hand, there may be some cases where D is so inexperienced in his or her job, and so reliant on the training, that we cannot infer that D felt unaccountable. However, the longer D stays in his or her job, the more we might expect D to assert independence and take a critical approach to what he or she is being asked to do.

These two elements of culpability are distinct, though they may coincide in many cases. The culpable motivation focuses on reasons D has to assert power over V in particular; the culpable attitude is one of defiance to the wider community. For the culpable attitude, it is not necessary that D should regard V's interests as inferior or that D should be indifferent to V's unnecessary suffering, though such an attitude will certainly tend to signify unwillingness to attempt publicly to account for his or her actions. These culpable approaches should even be considered as relevant to any exculpatory defence raised to an offence of violence. Perhaps this is the greatest concern over the defence of parental chastisement; virtually all cases probably involve the use of violence to assert control or to gain respect from a recalcitrant child, or at least the use of violence on the basis that D should never have to account for it. The present author once argued that chastisement as a defence could only be legitimate if D could suggest that he or she felt compelled as a parent to correct some misdemeanour and that the use of physical punishment was part of a coherent strategy towards that end.[53] That still seems plausible, since the elements of power through violence and indifference to the effects of violence might then be absent.

The translation of these culpable attitudes into workable and comprehensible rules is likely to be a task which will require further refinement. It is suggested here that the motivation to assert power, might be narrowed down in the context of self-defence, etc to refer to a substantial motivation to use force to *punish* V, even if the motive to prevent V's anticipated attack was also present. Here, the term punishment may be interpreted broadly, as a reference not just to punishment for what V is currently suspected of doing, but of anything else (including lawful actions) of which D might disapprove. Similarly, instead of speaking of the unfamiliar-sounding 'attitude of unaccountability', we may define the culpable attitude in question as being one of 'indifference to the necessity of D's actions' (as the jury will have decided the issue in some way against the defendant). It is submitted that where either motivation or attitude can be proven to be linked to any mistake of V's intentions or to any excessive use of force (as the jury may perceive it) then the defence should fail. Further, these indicators of culpability may replace other principles in the areas of mistakes and excesses of force (that are not gross excesses).

Thus, in cases of mistakes, where D may have genuinely suspected V to pose a threat the jury should look closer at the reasons why the mistake was made and they may find those reasons to be informed by a deeper desire to *wish* that V were posing a threat so that an opportunity to use force to punish V might arise.[54] However, it is the underlying motivation for the mistake that the jury should be looking for. Mistakes that are blameworthy in other respects but not prompted by any motivation to punish or any attitude of unaccountability should still be allowed. That will probably be the case with the drunken woman who believes that a man who is following her intends to rape her. Cases with a racist element should be harder. In a case where an officer believes that ethnic minority men are more likely to be part of an underground gang and to have weapons, and mistakenly believes that this applies to V, the question to ask is whether the mistake was caused by a desire to have the opportunity to use force against black people; the (racist-driven) desire to use force on the basis of the assessment of the threat is

[53] J Rogers, 'A Criminal Lawyer's Response to Chastisement in the European Court of Human Rights' (2002) *Crim LR* 98.

[54] See n 29 above.

critical, not the mere fact that racial stereotyping caused the mistake in itself.[55] It is not so unusual for juries to consider competing motivations of defendants,[56] nor is it unusual for them to decide whether certain motivating factors had a 'substantial' effect upon their actions.[57] If it finds that D was substantially motivated by an opportunity to use force to punish or degrade a black man, they are likely to find that this caused a mistaken appraisal of the facts.

Similarly, when it comes to measuring reasonable force, we should continue to judge the necessity to act without the benefit of hindsight, meaning for example that unknown vulnerabilities of victims should not be taken into account. However, it is submitted that no extra leeway should be shown to defendants who used excessive force, even if they did 'instinctively' over-react in the heat of the moment. Instead, where a jury finds that D did not act strictly in accordance with necessity (but neither that D acted grossly disproportionately), then it should deny the defence if, *but only if*, it finds that D was motivated to punish V, or that D showed indifference to whether reasonable force was used. It should only be as a matter of trial tactics that D may argue that, as the Privy Council in *Palmer* put it, D acted 'in a moment of unexpected anguish',[58] since a jury which accepted this characterisation of the case would often have little or no room to find that D wished to punish V or was indifferent to the proper amount of force, and D would enjoy the benefit of the doubt on the matter.

B Evidence of the Culpable Motive and Attitude

One may wonder how much difference the recognition of these culpable elements might make. The answer to this starts with consideration of the range of evidence that might be relevant to establishing them, not all of which would be relevant to any distinct legal issue under the present law.

[55] See further S Garvey, 'Self-Defence and the Mistaken Racist' (2008) 11 (1) *New Criminal Law Review* 119, who argues that even if one can be blamed for racist beliefs, including a failure to rectify them over time, the core belief in self-defence cases is a perception of urgent peril and then 'He has no [direct] control over whether he forms that belief at that moment or not', at 160. However, Garvey's main argument is that racism is a character flaw for which D cannot be punished; a better way of putting this is to say that self-defence should be withdrawn on the basis of culpable attitudes towards the use of violence rather than on the basis of non-specific character defects.

[56] Thus, D may have a partial defence to murder if he kills through 'fear of serious of violence' but not where, in the event, 'D acted in a considered desire for revenge': Coroners and Justice Act 2009 s 1(4).

[57] The issue may arise in cases of diminished responsibility when deciding whether D's abnormality of mental functioning 'causes, or is a significant contributory factor in causing, D to carry out that conduct': Homicide Act 1957 s 2 (1B). In duress cases, the jury should have to think that D was significantly motivated by the threat, and not mainly by other motivations, such as a share of the profits from the planned crime: *R v Valderrama-Vega* (1985) *Crim LR* 220. It also arises where D denies *mens rea* but there are competing explanations of diseases of the mind, automatism and intoxication underlying D's actions.

[58] *Palmer* [1971] AC 814, 832.

It would probably be easier to find evidence of a substantial (independent) motive to use violence by way of punishment. This may take the form of past dealings between D and V or because D has repeatedly expressed a hatred on social occasions of black people (or law breakers, etc). Refusal to listen to V's attempts to show that V was unarmed may sometimes give way to an inference that D preferred to believe 'what he wanted to believe' about V's intentions. Moreover, evidence of the extensive nature of D's injuries may raise an inference of an intent to inflict pain rather than mere restraint; and where D held a mistaken belief in danger, the fact that D may have done so on unreasonable grounds may enable a jury to infer that D's decision to use force was prompted substantially by other violent motives, even if self-defence is accepted to have been at least part of the explanation. Evidence of past acts of violence, whether or not in the context of self-defence, should also be admissible but only to the extent that one may infer from them that D presently intended to use force by way of punishment, and it may be best that in such cases, previous complainants should testify in person (this is likely to be essential in any case, unless the previous complaint was substantiated). However, it would be improper to draw inferences about D's substantial motivation to use force by way of punishment by reference to those of D's associates, that is to say that soldiers or police officers who come from sections of their forces who have acquired (rightly or wrongly) a reputation for violence[59] should not be tried on the basis of guilt by association.[60]

Establishing indifference to the propriety of force may also be shown primarily by evidence arising from the event itself. Unexplained failures to warn a suspect before engaging him or her, and the failure to adjust to the vulnerabilities of the victim when they become evident, are two common ways in which an adverse inference can be drawn. Departure from training is more clearly relevant here than under the current law. However, indifference might also be evidenced from previous complaints of similar excesses against the officer, even if the officer had not been prosecuted or disciplined over the incidents. This might only be permitted if the jury (which will after all have found the use of force to have been somewhat excessive) considers that D might have been expected to have adapted conduct in the light of experience, and infers from D's failure to adapt that D is not sufficiently concerned whether his or her force can be said to be justified since D feels that in any event no consequences will arise. One

[59] Lord Saville thought that General Ford could be criticised for deploying 1 PARA on Bloody Sunday 'on the ground that 1 PARA was a force with a reputation for using excessive physical violence': Saville, 'Report of the Bloody Sunday Inquiry' at para 4.8 (www.bloody-sunda-inquiry.org/) (London, HMSO, 2010). Even so, his Lordship found that only some members of that regiment could be shown to have acted criminally that day (paras 3.101–3.106).

[60] However, potentially the evidence could be relevant to rebut any misleading defence claim that everyone in D's regiment is trained to avoid, and not to glorify, violence against civilians. See *R v Sawoniuk* [2000] 2 Cr App R 220. The argument now would be that the misconduct of others would be important explanatory evidence in understanding the background: Criminal Justice Act 2003 s 100(1) a.

further benefit from this approach is that it allows some relief from the purported failures of the IPCC to hold accountable officers for violent acts because it allows previous complaints to become relevant even when they have not been substantiated. This is not a question of establishing bad character by innuendo; rather, the very fact that D has had so many complaints against him or her rejected pre-emptorily may lead to the inference that D started to feel invulnerable to any kind of investigation, and that in turn may have allowed D to become increasingly casual about the necessity of his or her actions. As will already be clear, this may have made a difference to the case of the officers who were charged over the injuries to Babar Ahmad. The fact that D joined a unit with a reputation for violence may itself be relevant to D's general indifference to the use of reasonable force. This may mean that the reputation of D's fellow officers is relevant to establishing D's own culpable attitude of indifference but it should not be relevant to establishing D's own motives to use force in order to punish. This is worth noting if only to suggest that the two elements of culpability are probably best kept separate.

An attitude of indifference may also be supported by findings that the officer lied to investigators, if this shows an assumption that the officer's account will be believed without further ado.[61] However, we should be careful here to be sure that lies were suggestive of a feeling that the investigation is of no consequence because the result is pre-determined, *and* that this reflected an attitude which D would have had at the time of his or her use of force. This will not always be the case. For example, the firearms officers who were in the underground carriage where Jean Charles de Menezes (the wrongly suspected would-be suicide bomber) were found to have lied by the inquest jury when they compared notes and uniformly testified that a warning was shouted before the shooting.[62] However, this should not have influenced the inquest jury. For a start, it is not clear that this failure in any event undermined the reasonableness of their actions,[63] and culpable motives should only come into play if they acted excessively on the facts as they thought them to be. However, even if they did act excessively by not shouting a warning, the lie does not go far to showing that they had been indifferent to the necessity of what they were doing. More probably they thought that the apparent hunting down and assassination of an innocent man would look so shocking to the lay public that they felt under pressure

[61] This is perhaps particularly so where the officer falsely blames the victim. See S Box and K Russell, 'The Politics of Discreditability: Disarming Complaints against the Police' (1975) 23 *Soc Rev* 315, arguing that 'condemning the condemners' and 'denying the victim' are typical ways in which the police neutralise complaints, even and especially to themselves.

[62] The IPCC had also disbelieved this assertion, and found that the fact that every officer on the train had asserted it pointed to collusion (as noted in the *Saunders* case, n 44 above).

[63] It would have been thought that almost any kind of bodily movement may set off at least one of the explosives. The continuing danger posed by injured suspects was reasonably well-established even before the 'Kratos' policy of shooting suicide bombers in the head: see P Waddington, '"Overkill" or "Minimum Force"?' (1990) *Crim LR* 695. The IPCC itself did not think that this failure was inconsistent with the use of reasonable force in these circumstances.

to suggest that they had done everything possible to avert the tragedy. The lie was a misjudgement in tactical terms, but sheds little light on the attitude of the individual officer at the time when he shot Mr de Menezes.

It may be that while evidence of the culpable elements may be found, they may not yet be persuasive. However, if the evidence has objective merit, it may at least suffice for more prosecutions to start, and to be put to a jury. One of the more troublesome cases has been that of PC Sherwood who shot and killed James Ashley. PC Sherwood was involved with a number of officers in a drugs raid at Ashley's flat and had been told of the possibility that one of Ashley's associates might be there and if so, would likely be armed. The officers broke down the door at 4am and, with the flat in darkness, Sherwood proceeded to the bedroom with his gun, ready to shoot. It remains unclear what happened in the ensuing seconds to have caused him to believe that someone in Ashley's bedroom was preparing to shoot him as he entered; Ashley had just got out of bed and was naked when shot. Sherwood's trial for murder was stopped because the prosecution was unable to offer evidence to rebut the possibility that he did mistakenly believe that Ashley was armed and about to shoot. However, it was suggested in the subsequent civil litigation that he might have had a history of violence and alcohol abuse,[64] and he had until recently had his licence to carry a firearm revoked.[65] Under the proposals here, the evidence of past misbehaviour, if sufficiently cogent and combined with the apparently 'trigger-happy' nature in which Sherwood rushed to Ashley's bedroom, may legitimately have paved the way for an inference that his desire for a battle prompted his mistake. Had there then been a case to answer, then Sherwood would have had to decide whether to testify, exposing himself to cross-examination about his motivations if he decided to do so. He may yet have acquitted himself; by all accounts he was horrified by what he had done, and his 'Bermuda method' of approaching the operation was done in pursuance of instructions,[66] which might at least negate an inference that he was substantially motivated to use force by way of punishment. However, an acquittal *by jury* would have been more satisfactory than that the trial should have been stopped for there being no case to answer.

In fact, simply establishing that recognising the culpable elements would make a greater range of evidence relevant is significant enough. More attention is likely to be paid to them in investigations. Even where there is still no cogent evidence of either culpable element, then a decision not to prosecute the officer *could be explained to the public on that basis* rather than a mere impotent reference to the fact that the making of the mistake could not be disproved (and, if such evidence is in fact available, then a judicial review of the decision not to

[64] See *Ashley v Chief Constable of Sussex Police* [2007] 1 WLR 398 [91].

[65] See www.independent.co.uk/news/uk/this-britain/secrets-lies-and-deceit-after-police-shoot-naked-man-in-bed-685719.html.

[66] See www.guardian.co.uk/uk/2001/may/23/ukcrime.nickdavies.

prosecute could more realistically be mounted[67]). If evidence is found, then the prosecutor will be able to present its case on an alternative basis. The prosecutor may argue primarily that D did not in fact make the claimed mistake, or that grossly excessive force was used; but, in the alternative, that *if* D might have made the mistake, or *if* the jury thinks the force was strictly unreasonable but not grossly excessive, then this was explicable substantially to the presence of one of the culpable elements. Evidence of a culpable motive may assist in other aspects. It may be, for example, that a jury, lacking practical experience, finds itself in doubt whether four or more men are needed physically to restrain an unarmed man during an arrest, but is fortified to decide that this in fact constitutes grossly excessive force when they become aware of the officers' indifference to several past independent complaints.

The overall conclusion is that recognising these elements may help to prove some strong cases whilst enabling the authorities to explain why the weaker (discontinued) cases really are (morally) weaker.

III NON-IMMINENT OFFENCES

In this part, we take a look at an issue which is easily regarded as a side-problem in self-defence, namely the use of force in the prevention of non-imminent crime. However, aside from being pertinent to a book on 'seeking security', it appears that this area further illustrates the impotence of the common law approach, which we have criticised for its reliance on cognition, and for its tendency to isolate the defendant when judging his or her actions.

We should be careful already to exclude certain types of case from this discussion. In some situations D may wonder whether he or she needs to shoot to prevent an imminent *or* a non-imminent threat, as may be the case when someone has taken hostages and is conducting a siege. Such situations should be considered as cases where D tries to prevent an imminent crime, provided that D *suspects* the possibility of the imminent commission of a threat. Also, if D acts to prevent an imminent crime (including the termination of a continuing offence), the commission of which may cause the long-term endangerment of life, then again no special rule is required. Here the possibility of future loss of life simply informs the proportionality test which relates to the crime that D is immediately preventing. Thus, a man who has been taken hostage may need to kill his captor whenever an opportunity arises to escape. Since he is already acting to terminate his (existing) false imprisonment,[68] we may decide that it was proportionate for him to kill by reference to his own belief about his own eventual murder.

[67] A judicial review was brought into the decision not to prosecute for any homicide offence over the shooting of de Menezes: *R (Armani de Silva v DPP* [2006] EWCA 3204 Admin, but was unsuccessful since there was no realistic prospect on which mistaken self-defence could be disproved.

[68] This is the key to the problem, first raised by A McColgan, 'In Defence of Battered Women who Kill' (1993) 13 *OJLS* 50, 517–18. For discussion of the more difficult case of the abusive husband who does not so clearly 'detain' his battered wife, see below.

Instead, we are concerned here with cases where V is not suspected of *any* immediate offence. Typically, V is a fleeing (terrorist) suspect, and the question arises whether V may be stopped now if the circumstances do not readily permit his or her capture at a later date. The main authority for permitting the use of force against non-imminent threats is *Attorney-General for Northern Ireland's Reference (No 1 of 1975)*.[69] Their Lordships held that it had been open to the Crown Court to find that D used 'reasonable force' in shooting a fleeing suspected terrorist, on the basis that, *qua* terrorist, it could readily be inferred that V would regroup and 'sooner or later' resume 'dealing in death and destruction'. It was by virtue of this that several innocent persons continued to be shot in Northern Ireland during the Troubles,[70] since simply running away when called to halt was often thought to be indicative of terrorist behaviour. These cases have been criticised as endorsing an 'extreme theory of preventive policing',[71] and it seems that firearms police have been told for some years now that force may only be used against imminent threats to life.[72] However, even if that is the standing instruction, at the higher levels the situation remains obscure. The firearms officers who shot de Menezes were found to have restrained him *as he was trying to leave the carriage*, and since the officer believed that he had been instructed to 'stop' the suspect at all costs, it seems that it is believed that force can be used to prevent crimes which will at least happen in the near future, even if not in the immediate future. In the de Menezes case it would have been feared that he would seize upon another opportunity to self-detonate in the nearby town, and probably sooner rather than later since he would know now that he was being hotly pursued.

Yet it is not clear what the law should be; how to distinguish the Northern Ireland scenario from the desperate suicide-bomber scenario? Some may wonder whether such cases are better thought of as necessity cases, assuming that such a general justification exists; but even if this is possible – and it seems unlikely since V still poses a threat – one would have the same difficulty of knowing where to draw the line. Some writers tend to think of non-imminent crimes as being the subject of force only if the anticipated offences are 'inevitable'[73] or at some other very high threshold of likelihood; and the point is made that the highness of the threshold should not matter because D can still rely on

[69] *Attorney-General for Northern Ireland's Reference (No 1 of 1975)* [1977] AC 105.

[70] *Farrell* (n 14 above); *Lynch v Ministry of Defence* [1983] NI 216; *Magill v Ministry of Defence* [1987] NI 194; *Kelly v Ministry of Defence* [1989] NI 341.

[71] The phrase is that of A Jennings, 'Shoot to Kill: The Final Courts of Justice' in A Jennings (ed), *Justice Under Fire* (London, Pluto, 1988) 109–10. See too the trenchant criticism of K Asmal, *Shoot to Kill? International Lawyers' Inquiry into the Lethal Use of Firearms by the Security Forces in Northern Ireland* (Dublin, Mercier Press, 1985) para 112, and of Professor Sir JC Smith, 'Using Force in Self-Defence and the Prevention of Crime' (1994) 47 *Current Legal Problems* 101, 118–20.

[72] The guidance from the Association of Chief Police Officers (ACPO) is that 'When it is considered necessary to open fire on a subject, using conventional ammunition, police officers need to shot to stop an imminent threat to life': ACPO, '*Manual of Guidance on Police Use of Firearms' (ACPO, 2003)* para 6.1 at www.statewatch.org/news/2005/jul/acpo-firearms-2003.pdf.

[73] See Leverick (n 32 above) 102 ff.

a mistaken belief that the threat is inevitable. However, relying on mistakes as to inevitability here is hardly helpful. It may exclude the person who has been briefed that V is 80 per cent likely to intend a suicide bombing in the near future. The disinclination of the law, and of some writers, to move beyond the familiar cognitive approach has no doubt led to the thoroughly obscure legal situation that we currently have today. Thus, the Metropolitan police refused to admit the possibility that Mr de Menezes might have been stopped as he was trying to escape from the carriage; and one wonders whether their apparent reluctance is connected to the legal uncertainty relating to the prevention of non-imminent crimes. Thus, they did not attempt to explain their tactics which involved shooting the suspected would-be suicide bomber unless there was an immediate and unconditional surrender. Without the benefit of argument on these crucial issues, and having rejected so much of the police evidence, it is hardly surprising that the inquest jury opted for an open verdict. Yet the shooting does appear to have been non-criminal, as one's intuitions might inform us and as we shall argue below.

The first matter to note is that we can never know for sure whether D's action *was* strictly necessary; and so at best, using force against non-imminent threats is permissible behaviour. Thus, if we start with the premise that D is trying to prevent a non-imminent offence and is not sure that it could be prevented in any other way, D still forfeits the defence if he or she was substantially motivated to punish V, or if D was indifferent to the reasonableness of his or her force. That may indeed often suffice to rule out many cases. If it were proven that soldiers would shoot fleeing terrorist suspects as much to assert their authority over the local population as to prevent future offending,[74] or if this became a matter of routine regardless of doubts about its propriety, then that should already be fatal to the defence.

Even so, it may be that applying such a rule is not enough. It should bother us that such decisions might be made 'on the ground' against a person who is 'known to be unknown'. In the absence of an imminent threat, the person who shoots is blameworthy for taking it upon him or herself to take the decision. Further, this may be so even if the person doesn't have any culpable motives and is prepared to account for his or her own decision; it is arguably not the person's decision to make alone. We allow officers to act according to their own responsibility when facing imminent threats because there is no choice; but we need not allow soldiers or officers to draw up their own idea that an unknown suspect poses an inevitable long-term threat and act accordingly. Thus, the proposed further rule is that where D wishes to rely on the prevention of non-imminent threats, he or she must believe that the suspect has been assessed by an agent of the state[75] as posing an ongoing (serious) threat to life. Thereby, D is no longer at liberty to act purely on

[74] That is, to communicate the message that, eg when a car is asked to stop at a roadblock, the occupants had better fear for their lives if they are not minded to comply.

[75] By this I mean normally the police, but also a court of law, the security services and probably anyone else who receives public funds for intelligence-related work.

his or her own beliefs; D must also believe that these are shared beliefs among responsible agents. Then we should be free from having to find that D thought the anticipated offence to be as high as 'inevitable': it is rather that the fact of official assessment of V's dangerousness should substitute for the need of high thresholds of likelihood. Further, it should be emphasised that we are not speaking of a back-door version of superior orders here. That the police believe that they have identified V as (say) a fleeing suicide-bomber does *not* mean that D is now somehow 'authorised' to kill. D must still use necessary force, and that will be judged on a case by case basis.

This rule would have enabled us to condemn those soldiers in Northern Ireland who shot persons whom they knew to be unknown to them on the basis that their decision to flee indicated that they may be terrorists. Even without taking into account their possible culpable motives, it seems clear that they cannot have believed that any of their superiors had carried out any kind of risk assessment about the victims. However, as for the shooting of de Menezes, we would find no evidence that the shooting officer was motivated to punish V or felt unaccountable for his actions; and the officer certainly believed that de Menezes had been identified by his superiors as a suicide bomber, who would pose an ongoing threat. Even on the facts as the inquest jury found them, the officer who shot de Menezes, fearing that he would soon arrange to self-detonate elsewhere, may have had *good* reason to shoot him whilst he had him in a controlled environment. It is suggested that the approach outlined here enables us to better explain why some contentious killings *are* in fact non-criminal.

IV STAGE AGENTS AND PRIVATE CITIZENS

So far, we have discussed reform in the context of state agents. Happily, however, no separate set of substantive legal principles is required for private citizens who use force in self-defence, etc. I once proposed something of the sort, so that more helpful precedents could be set where state agents act in typically recurring scenarios.[76] However, this tends to imply a tidiness of analysis that is likely to be missing in practice, and the search for clear rules (and precedents) leads one to maintain an unduly cognitive approach where the actor's motivations or attitude becomes unimportant. Moreover, it typically misses the problem that we should only want the defence to be unavailable in criminal law (as opposed to tort) where the defendant deserves to be *punished*, in the same way that we *should* want the defendant to be punished for mistakes or excesses of force if we *can* find him or her to be culpable. If we have succeeded in identifying ways in which D can be punished and labelled as an ordinary violent offender, then it would be less surprising that the same set of principles should apply to both state agents and private citizens.

[76] J Rogers, 'Justifying the Use of Firearms by Policemen and Soldiers: A Response to the Home Office's Review of the Law on the Use of Lethal Force' (1998) 18 *Legal Studies* 486.

There seems to be no a priori reason why it should be harder to prove that a private citizen who mistakes V's intentions, or uses excessive force, did so because he or she wanted to punish V or was indifferent to the reasonableness of what he or she was doing. Insofar as the private citizen is under no duty to intervene of his or her own volition in order to break up a fight or to prevent a crime, it may often be easier to infer that one who does so (and who uses excessive force) was motivated to do so to 'punish' a wrongdoer. So the differences between the related doctrines of self-defence and crime prevention may take on extra significance where private citizens are involved,[77] but it is a difference which is well recognised by the relevance of the motive to use force by way of punishment. In many cases, D may have made unguarded statements at or around the time of the incident from which his or her motives might be inferred. We may recall the appeal of Tony Martin, the Norfolk farmer who allegedly lay in wait on the ground floor of his farm in the expectation that burglars would one day target his property. The Court of Appeal, as though in passing, felt compelled to note that:

> On a number of occasions at meetings of the local Farm Watch and in discussions with neighbours and the local policeman Mr Martin was said to have made his dissatisfaction with the police very plain. He was heard to express the view repeatedly that self-help was the better way of dealing with criminals. He is said to have used such remarks as 'you know the best way to stop them – shoot the bastards'; that if a particular team of burglars returned he would 'blow their heads off'; and he was also said to have suggested that he would recommend putting such criminals in a field and using a machine gun on them.[78]

It seems that this evidence should have more prominence than was apparently afforded to it at trial and in the appeal. Since Martin did find the burglars in his own home, it is fair to assume that some fear and some element of self-defence informed his decision to shoot; but since the burglars were very clearly fleeing when shot, it is proper to inquire into his deeper motivations and it seems that the desire to punish must have substantially contributed to his decision to shoot. Thinking in terms of substantial motives to use violence for punishment would have led to a much more satisfactory outcome in *R v Faraj*[79] where D invited into his house an employee of a utility company (V) who had come to repair a fault. From the outset D had imagined V to be a would-be burglar and, once inside the house, D held him at knife point and threatened him repeatedly before letting him go. His conviction for false imprisonment was reversed because the jury had not been clearly instructed that he was entitled to act on his mistaken belief that V was a burglar for the purposes of arresting him.[80] However, even though

[77] See J Rogers, 'Have-a-go Heroes' (2008) 158 *NLJ* 318.

[78] *R v Martin* [2002] 1 Cr App R 27 [17].

[79] *R v Faraj* [2007] EWCA Crim 1033.

[80] Faraj was also relying on defence of his own property; there was perhaps an evidential basis for both defences, since he made some rudimentary efforts to phone the police while V was in his custody.

he does seem to have mistaken V for a burglar, his decision to invite him into the house (instead of simply refusing entry) and to promptly put a knife to his throat suggests that he wanted to punish the burglar for his attempted offence.[81]

It is even possible that a private citizen may be able to prevent a non-imminent crime. The proposal in part III that D should believe that V is a person who is thought by the authorities to pose an ongoing risk to life (or is a person employed or acting as an agent for another such person[82]), is capable of applying to private citizens too. The only difference is that their belief will arise not from a briefing from a superior but more likely from their status as a potential victim. Yet this is not far-fetched. Most police forces send '*Osman* warnings' to persons whom they believe to be at long-term risk, sometimes offering practical solutions (including relocation of witnesses to offences who are facing death threats from those close to the accused).[83] The most likely difference is that, unlike the state agent, the police may not routinely inform the potential victim of the identity of the potential assailant, but in some cases the source might be so obvious that D could still be said to have believed, by virtue of one of these warnings, that the police had identified a particular person or particular group of people known to him or her. One would expect form to triumph over substance here; a written '*Osman* warning' might be the best evidence but not the only possible evidence to support a belief in official identification of a long-term risk. This approach may assist the battered wife, who has contacted the police who agree that her ex-husband poses an ongoing risk to her life. However, as with state agents, none of this is to 'licence' the private citizen to use force to prevent the offence; the effect of official endorsement is merely that when D uses force he or she is not acting as though the suspect should be subject to D's own speculations about future events. It simply acts as a gateway to an assessment of the necessity and proportionality of his or her actions.[84]

To say that the same principles may apply to state and to private citizens is not to deny that crimes by state agents may, *ceteribus paribus*, be worse than crimes committed by private citizens, meaning also that more may be required to establish a justification or excuse from a state agent.[85] However, 'more' can be demanded in application of the same basic principles. The attitude of indifference, especially in cases where D believes that he or she is free to use force because D thinks that he or she is effectively immune from investigation, is, one should think, more likely to be provable against state agents. Moreover, thinking in terms of these principles may

[81] The facts suggest that Faraj only allowed V to go when V claimed to be a fellow Muslim.

[82] This may be relevant in cases where someone is thought to have 'taken out a contract' on D.

[83] The exact number of '*Osman* warnings' is perhaps higher than one might imagine. It seems that in 2007 alone, at least 1,028 people (including 177 women) were told by the police that they had intelligence that a particular person wished to kill them and was thought to have the means to do so: *The Times*, 9 June 2008.

[84] Some research has suggested that up to one half of abusive men follow and continue to harass their wives after they have left. See the discussion by Leverick (n 32 above) 105–07.

[85] For elaboration, see J Gardner, 'Criminals in Uniform' in R Duff, L Farmer, S Marshall and V Tadros (eds), *The Constitution of Criminal Law* (Oxford, Oxford University Press, forthcoming).

change our own perspectives to conflicts between the citizens and the police. One illustrative case is *Lindley v Rutter*,[86] where a drunken woman was arrested and officers sought to remove her brassiere in her cell, though there was no reason to suppose that the arrestee was at any risk of attempting suicide. The arrestee fought to prevent this, albeit unsuccessfully and without causing any injury. It was accepted that the police acted improperly and so Ms Lindley's conviction for assaulting a policewoman in the execution of her duty was set aside; but her conviction for assault was maintained, apparently on the basis that she used excessive force. The policewoman herself was not prosecuted. However, on the principles here, we would be more concerned at the actions of the officer, which seem to have been done out of routine and with some indifference as to the true necessity of what she was doing. Moreover, even if Ms Lindley acted in any way excessively, we would tend not to find her culpable because she surely did not act to 'punish' the officer for her intrusion, and was not (as far as we can tell[87]) indifferent to appraisal of her use of violence. The more natural inference is that, if she overreacted at all, then it was because she wanted to preserve her modesty and resented the 'routine' interference that was proposed. That is not an argument to the effect that the policewoman should have been prosecuted instead of Ms Lindley, but recognition that she was probably more culpable than Ms Lindley for her own excess of force should at least lead to a more balanced outcome than that which occurred (perhaps non-prosecution of both would have been quite defensible).

Further, it is politic to think in terms of the same set of principles for citizens and state agents; indeed it seems to be something on which politicians from both the right-wing and left-wing agree, albeit for different reasons.[88] The history of section 76 of the CJIA was inspired by the apparent desire to 'encourage' have-a-go heroes to tackle anti-social behaviour violence in the street. This was one political promise that was almost certainly made in haste,[89] and the section turned into a mere exercise in consolidation when the lawyers in the Ministry of Justice could apparently find no way to make the law even more favourable than it already was. It is however possible to be sceptical that 'private heros' were to be the real beneficiaries. The Ministry of Justice did not seek the counsel of the criminal law team of its own Law Commission on drafting section 76 CJIA, even though the Commission had recently started to make plans to look at the use of force.[90] However, it is unconceivable that the Ministry

[86] *Lindley v Rutter* [1981] 1 QB 128, criticised by Glanville Williams in his celebrated *Textbook of Criminal Law* (London, Steven & Sons, 1983) 512.

[87] The Court was told that 'before this night the defendant was a young lady of unblemished reputation and [her being arrested for being drunk and disorderly] was wholly out of character'.

[88] See J Rogers (n 76 above) 492–93.

[89] The then Minister for Justice, Jack Straw, promised the Labour Party Conference in October 2007 that the law of self-defence would be amended so that it would more clearly favour (indeed, even encourage) the public spirited defender of law and order. See J Rogers (n 77 above).

[90] The author was aware of this when he was asked to supply to the Law Commission a copy of the Home Office's review on the use of lethal force in 1996. The Home Office report had never been published, was very difficult to track down even immediately after it was compiled, and 10 years later apparently no one in Whitehall could lay their hands on a copy(!).

would not have consulted those who are duty bound to use force on the state's behalf, and equally it will be clear already why the police and the army must privately be very happy that the common law is now consolidated. It is presently unclear from where the political impetus for any change might come, but should the moment arrive, we should bear in mind that it would be put at risk by suggesting separate laws for private persons and state agents. Thus, thinking further in terms of culpable elements of occasions of self-defence bears a further politic advantage. Conceivably they could even be packaged as a way of dealing with private security companies who arguably use excessive force on a regular basis.[91]

V CONCLUSIONS

I have criticised the law of self-defence and related defences for not looking past the matter of D's subjective beliefs and whether D 'instinctively' thought that he or she acted reasonably. In cases where mistakes or excessive force were used (including the prevention of non-imminent crimes) we should develop a discourse of *why* D erred in the way that he or she did. Where D was also substantially motivated to use force by way of punishment against V, or had an attitude of indifference whether he or she was making a mistake or using reasonable force (as the jury perceives it) then D is culpable and should forfeit the defence. It is submitted that more troublesome cases (such as the shooting of James Ashley) could at least have gone to trial by jury by applying these rules, and that juries could apply these principles straightforwardly. There should also have been fewer of the problems that were encountered in the de Menezes inquest, since it should be clear that the officer would be availed in the absence of any substantial evidence of either culpable element, and that would have shaped the inquest tactics of the police more helpfully. There may be more convictions, too, eg, if juries are given the chance to ponder why a person who has had several complaints of violence levelled against him or she should continue to act in the same way, unless that person was truly indifferent to *their* possible assessment of his or her actions (as opposed to that of his or her immediate superiors or colleagues). Being able to lead a wider range of evidence (including an extraordinary pattern of similar though unsubstantiated complaints) may also help the prosecution to persuade a court that mistakes were not made at all. Such principles may apply profitably to private citizens too, perhaps especially those who work in 'private' law enforcement.

[91] In addition to the abuses at the privately run prison for juvenile offenders (n 37 above) one might consider the recent death of Jimmy Mubenga during his deportation by G4S staff. The men who restrained him are under suspicion for manslaughter, and investigators have heard from whistleblowers that the company management has repeatedly ignored previous warnings of the dangers of a restrain technique known as 'carpet karaoke'. See www.guardian.co.uk/uk/2011/mar/16/mubenga-g4s-face-charges-death.

The ideas developed have further implications. If accepted, they may prompt us to look more closely at how exculpatory defences differ between criminal and civil proceedings. Identifying culpable attitudes may be important in establishing culpability in other criminal law defences (we have already mentioned chastisement). However, it may be that the cognitive approach of the present law is reasonably well suited to civil proceedings, at least in cases of self-defence, etc if the burden is on the defendant to show that he or she made a reasonable mistake. More broadly, we should continue to seek reliable empirical data on the resolution of complaints against state agents. Under my proposal, even an officer who has been routinely vindicated on several independent complaints may potentially have this used as evidence of mounting indifference to his or her use of force. It may be in the officer's interests, and of the officer's superiors, to ensure that complaints against him or her are dealt with rigorously transparently such that it is unlikely those then exonerated are likely to feel able to use force with effective impunity. Should the picture be as depressing as it would seem, we should welcome substantive law proposals which may have a partially curative effect on current practice. However, even if the picture of internal police accountability is in robust health, that would still be no reason not to welcome a set of rules which seek to identify true moral culpability in self-defence cases.

13

The Hard Treatment of Innocent Persons in State Responses to the Threat of Large Scale, and Imminent Terrorist Violence: Examining the Legal Constraints

G R SULLIVAN*

I TERRORIST VIOLENCE: LARGE SCALE AND IMMINENT

FIRST, THE SCOPE of this chapter will be addressed. The central concern is to examine the legal constraints applicable to the hard treatment of innocent persons by state officials who are acting in order to avert or diminish a threat of large scale and imminent terrorist violence. The subsequent discussion will differentiate between classes of innocent person but all that need be said for now is that in this context an innocent person is a person who is not directly engaged in any violent terrorist activity, nor assisting, encouraging or supporting any violent terrorist activity. Not discussed here is the question of whether state officials have more latitude for the infliction of hard treatment where the person who is to suffer is not an innocent person in the sense described.

The legal constraints to be considered arise from the criminal laws of the United Kingdom,[1] although much of the discussion will have relevance for other jurisdictions. Further, an assumption will be made that the law to be considered is the peace-time criminal law. In other words, it will be assumed that without enabling legislation there are no special powers to be invoked in order to deal

* Many thanks to Ian Dennis for his helpful comments.

[1] There are no significant differences in the doctrines and rules applicable to the situations under discussion in the three separate criminal jurisdictions of England and Wales, Scotland and Northern Ireland. It will suffice to cite the relevant law from the largest jurisdiction, namely England and Wales.

with emergencies of the kind to be discussed.[2] Within the United Kingdom, terrorist violence means violence intended to influence or intimidate a government or the public or a section of the public, in order to advance a political, religious or ideological cause.[3] The definition is further extended by providing that violence or the threat of violence to persons or property involving firearms or explosives is to be regarded as terrorist violence even if there is no intention to influence government or the public.[4] This legal definition of terrorism and terrorist acts is undeniably extensive and has been subjected to considerable criticism on that account. Such criticism will not be addressed here. Provided the threat is a threat of large scale and imminent violence, we will assume uncritically that it is a threat associated with terrorism if on the face of it the defining conditions set out in section 1 of the Terrorism Act 2000 are met.[5]

There is considerable latitude allowed by the phrase 'large scale and imminent terrorist violence'. The idea informing this choice of phrase is to permit discussion of the full range of situations where the stakes for officials deciding to act (or not to act) can reasonably be said to be very high. Indeed we cannot rule out the threat of terrorist harms of horrendous magnitude. In the recently published 'United States Security Strategy', a document authorised and endorsed by President Obama in his capacity as president, there is the following passage: 'And there is no greater threat to the American people than weapons of mass destruction, particularly the danger posed by the pursuit of nuclear weapons by violent extremists'.[6] This statement will be taken as an evidenced based risk assessment (although there is inevitably a large element of conjecture as to if and when weapons of this kind will be possessed by terrorist groups) and it will be assumed that other countries face similar dangers. In addition to the threat of nuclear weapons, it will also be accepted that there are even more urgent threats in terms of the known capacities of terrorist groups arising from 'dirty' bombs and from chemical, biological and other toxic devices. Remaining at the forefront of terrorist possibilities are incidents involving use of conventional weapons and explosives capable of causing multiple deaths and many serious casualties, significant destruction of property and infrastructure, giving rise to general consternation. Threats of violence of this nature are also threats within the scope of the reference to large scale violence.

To be within the present discussion, the threat must be an imminent threat. The most clear cut instance of imminent threats would be dangers arising from an ongoing terrorist operation yet to be completed. Additionally, threats on the point of realisation are within the scope of this chapter. It will, however, be a

[2] Therefore ruled out of the scope of this discussion is the question of whether in the shadow of a truly existential emergency there are default prerogative powers which would legitimate the taking of drastic measures by state officials against the legally protected interests of innocent persons.

[3] Terrorism Act 2000 s 1.

[4] ibid s 1(3).

[5] Any complications that may arise for our discussion if a court should read down s 1 in a way that renders a threat of large scale violence a non-terrorist threat will not be discussed.

[6] 'National Security Strategy', (The Whitehouse, May 2010) 4.

rare occurrence for the police and other law enforcement agencies to be in possession of intelligence which enables them to intercept a threat at the very point of its implementation.[7] More usual will be situations where a group of terrorists are reasonably suspected of having resolved to attack a selected target in the near future but where circumstantial details are not to hand.[8] Measures taken to avert threats of this kind are within the notion of imminence used here. Outside the scope of our discussion will be state action directed at diminishing terrorist threats which have yet to resolve themselves into target directed plans. The focus is terrorist projects which are at the point of realisation or are in a state of readiness fit for implementation against a specific target.

If a sufficiently cohesive and stable polity faces the continuing threat of large scale terrorist activity, above all else, citizens will expect their government to be effective and resolute in its policy and practice regarding this threat. If a government is taken to have acquitted itself well in responding to terrorist attacks or in thwarting attacks, its prospects of re-election would be enhanced, particularly in a time of managerial, non-ideological politics. Of course, responsiveness to the wishes of the electorate is a large part of the point of democratic politics. Nonetheless, the democratic process does contain problematic dynamics, a process which may have cumulative and wide ranging effects on law and policy.

In the United Kingdom, the actuality and threat of modern terrorist operations has been present since the late 1960s[9] and seems set to continue indefinitely.[10] In response to the threat of terrorism, there has been resort to special

[7] Omand, *Securing the State* (London, Hurst and Company, 2010) 87–89.

[8] As when members of a terrorist group under surveillance cease email and telephone contact with each other and are not present at their usual places of abode.

[9] What may be considered the modern era of terrorism in the United Kingdom began when the Provisional IRA demonstrated a capacity to sustain a long term bombing campaign in mainland Britain. The threat of terrorism related to the Irish question has significantly diminished but 'dissident' Irish terrorist groups remain active. Recently (2 April 2011) a group believed to be the Continuity IRA killed a police officer in Omagh by exploding a bomb under his car. However, the most serious terrorist risk is currently perceived to come from what is sometimes termed jihadist terrorism which seems, in terms of the particular experience of the United Kingdom, to be a form of protest terrorism, executed mainly by UK nationals or residents, and which comes with a large component of cultural enmity. There was a major jihadist terrorist event in London on 7 July 2005 and there have been a number of unsuccessful attempts by jihadist terrorists to stage other large scale events. Apart from recent terrorist events occurring within the United Kingdom, there is a considerable institutional history of engagement with what were officially designated terrorist groups. Aside from Ireland, the imperialist history of the United Kingdom saw coercive measures taken by British agencies in the 20th century against movements officially portrayed as terrorists in what was then Palestine, and also Kenya, Malaysia, Cyprus and Aden. This colonial legacy was influential in terms of the formulation of law and policy implemented in Britain and Northern Ireland in matters such as special powers, interrogation techniques, and police/military relations: see further, Walker, *A Guide to the Anti-Terrorism Legislation* (Oxford, Oxford University Press, 2002).

[10] The cultural differences and power relations which shape the agenda of international jihadist terrorism have a long history and seemingly a long future: see for instance, Ruthven, *A Fury for God* (London, Granta Books, 2002); Lewis, *Where Did It All Go Wrong?* (New York, Oxford University Press, 2002); Burke, *Al-Qaeda* (London, Penguin Books, 2004) .

powers of search[11] and arrest,[12] pre-charge detention for interrogation,[13] reverse burdens of proof,[14] trials without juries,[15] offences based on a reasonable suspicion of facts rather than proof of facts,[16] widely drawn offences embracing conduct far removed from the commission or assistance of terrorist acts,[17] internment on ministerial order[18] and control orders imposed by a special tribunal, entailing a complete loss of liberty.[19] The enactment of some of this legislation has required derogations from the European Convention for Human Rights (ECHR).[20] Control orders, interrogation methods and 'shoot to kill'

[11] The Terrorism Act 2000 ss 44 and 45 allows unlimited powers of stop and search in designated areas for articles which could be used in connection with terrorism following authorisation by a police officer of at least the rank of Assistant Chief Constable, and confirmation by the Home Secretary within 48 hours. In deciding to stop and search, a police officer need not have reasonable grounds for suspicion that the person to be searched has terrorist related articles in his possession. The Coalition Government announced in its recent review of counter terrorism legislation (report 25 January 2011) that these provisions would be amended to limit stop and search to cases giving rise to reasonable suspicion.

[12] The Terrorism Act 2000 s 41 provides that suspicion of involvement in terrorism is a sufficient ground of arrest: a specific terrorist offence does not have to be specified.

[13] Terrorism Act 2000 s 41 and sch 8. Until recently pre-charge detention could extend to 28 days but the current limit is 14 days.

[14] Following successful challenges to reverse burdens invoking art 6(2) of the European Convention for Human Rights, for most terrorist offences, reverse burdens are reduced to an onus to produce evidence sufficient to raise an issue favouring the defence whereupon the burden of persuasion reverts to the prosecution: Terrorism Act 2000 s 118.

[15] Terrorism Act 2000 pt VII provides that for 'scheduled offences' a special court may be convened where a single judge acting as the sole arbiter of fact and law decides the case against the accused. There are appeals from the judge's verdict in the normal way. These special courts are confined to Northern Ireland and reflect the divided community and the difficulty of empanelling juries which would have the confidence of citizens regardless of their allegiances.

[16] For example, s 57 of the Terrorism Act 2000 which makes it an offence to possess an article in circumstances giving rise to a reasonable suspicion that it might be used in connection with assisting or perpetrating terrorist offences.

[17] See Terrorism Act 2006 s 5(1)(a): engaging in *any* conduct (emphasis supplied) in preparation for committing acts of terrorism.

[18] Civil Authorities (Special Powers) Act (Northern Ireland) 1922 reg 12 (SI 1956/191). Internment based on ministerial order has been confined to Northern Ireland.

[19] The genesis of control orders is to be found in pt 4 of the Anti-Terrorism, Crime and Security Act 2001. These provisions permitted the detention of foreign nationals suspected of involvement in terrorism but where there was insufficient admissible evidence for charging a terrorist offence and where deportation of the suspect was not possible because of the risk of torture in the receiving country. This regime was found to be unlawful by the House of Lords (see n 21 and associated text) on the basis of discrimination against foreign nationals. Subsequently, the Prevention of Terrorism Act 2005 replaced this scheme with the control order which allowed significant curtailment of the liberties of suspected terrorists present in the United Kingdom irrespective of nationality where deportation was not possible because of the risk of torture or where open trial would be inimical to general security. In its recent review (report 25 January 2011) of UK counter terrorism legislation, the Coalition Government announced that control orders would be replaced by terrorism prevention and investigation measures. The idea is to allow greater liberty for suspects but in circumstances which still make possible effective surveillance. See further Dennis in ch 8 of this volume.

[20] Derogations can be made from the Convention in conditions of general emergency. The United Kingdom has obtained derogations in respect of internment (for Northern Ireland), pre-charge detention and control orders.

arrest procedures have been found in breach of the ECHRin domestic courts and by the European Court of Human Rights (ECtHR).[21]

It is beyond the scope of this chapter to consider the efficacy and the legitimacy of these responses to the terrorist threat. The only point to be made here is that there has been no political cost attached to the passing of these measures, at least in mainland Britain,[22] even though they contravene some of the most fundamental features of the common law tradition. Rather, a political price would likely have been paid by a government which set its face against such things. By contrast to the plethora of legal measures regarding the background threat of terrorist activity, there has been no specific legislation relating to our topic, namely the hard treatment of innocent persons in order to avert or diminish the impact of imminent and large scale terrorist attacks. The legal materials to hand – the entitlement to use reasonable force in the prevention of crime; the doctrines of self-defence, necessity and duress; and the categorical ban on torture and inhuman and degrading treatment – leave much unsaid. The fears and pressures on the political class and associated officials that have given rise to the present corpus of terrorist legislation will be even more pressing in responding to the urgent situations about to be discussed. Of course, the operational decisions and the consequent acts/omissions to be considered here will be those of law enforcement and security officials rather than politicians and senior civil servants. However, the force of expectation will filter down the chain of command. Great tensions could arise between the fulfilment of Hobbesian imperatives and respecting the fundamental rights of innocent persons.

II INNOCENT PERSONS AND STATE ACTION

For this discussion the class of innocent persons comprises those persons who are not violent terrorists nor assisting, encouraging or otherwise giving material support to any violent terrorist activity. This class of innocent persons will be divided into the following three categories:

[21] *Secretary of State for Home Department v JJ and others* [2007] UKHL 45 (detention without trial of foreign nationals suspected of terrorism found in breach of art 15 of the ECHR); *Secretary of State for Home Department v AF (no 3)* [2009] UKHL 28(use of 'closed' material in imposing control order in breach of art 6 if D not given sufficient information to give effective instructions to his lawyers); (*Ireland v the United Kingdom* (1978) 2 EHRR 25 (five separate methods of interrogation each found to constitute inhuman and degrading treatment within the terms of art 3 of the ECHR); *McCann and others v the United Kingdom* (inadequate planning of procedures for using fatal force, entailing breach of art 2 of the ECHR).

[22] In Northern Ireland, anti-terrorist legislation was acutely controversial and divisive. This did not have any repercussions on the level or kind of support for the major political parties of mainland Britain. To date, law and policy related to the jihadist terrorist threat has been stressful for community relations and was one of the influences leading to the formation of the Respect party, but it has not been a political issue in terms of the level and kind of support for the main political parties.

(1) Persons harmed in the responses of state officials to imminent terrorist operations, such as passengers in hijacked planes, hostages in buildings under siege, or pedestrians caught in crossfire.
(2) Persons taken into custody by state officials but known to be innocent of any terrorist connection in the sense of committing terrorist acts or being complicit in terrorist acts, but whose hard treatment during interrogation may prevent or mitigate current attacks or the threat of an imminent attack.
(3) Persons taken into custody by state officials and mistakenly assumed to be terrorists, planning to carry out or in some way complicit in terrorist attacks, and who are assumed to have information which could prevent or mitigate an imminent attack.

Why this focus on innocent persons? Part of the answer is that the legal position regarding forceful interventions to prevent attacks or imminent terrorist attacks by persons who are in fact terrorists in operational mode and where the harmful effects of the interventions are confined to the terrorists themselves, is relatively straightforward. Invariably, such persons will be committing or be about to commit crimes and English law allows a person to use 'such force as is reasonable in the circumstances in the prevention of crime'.[23] If we remind ourselves that our concern is large scale terrorist acts, it is hard to envisage circumstances where the forceful, preventative interventions by state agents which are focused exclusively on the terrorists themselves, are likely to be found unreasonable by a jury.[24] (There may arise more difficult issues concerning the scope of permissible state action against a terrorist who is captured while engaged in acts of terrorism and who may possess valuable information about the ongoing operation or other imminent operations. These issues are not discussed here.)

Generally, where forceful interventions associated with terrorist threats are made against persons who are not terrorists, the legal position becomes considerably more uncertain. It is this uncertainty that requires examination, particularly discussion of what restraints should be imposed on state preventative action in such cases. Certainly, if expressions such as the 'war on terror' are more than rhetoric, concern must arise about the latitude that might be allowed to state agents in their treatment of innocent persons if the agent's actions can be likened to the prosecution of a just war. There is a wide, trans-cultural consensus against

[23] Criminal Law Act 1967 s 3. Criminal Justice and Immigration Act 2008 s 76 provides further guidance on when force used in the prevention of crime may be considered reasonable but it does not restrict or enlarge the general standard of reasonableness; the section is designed merely as an exercise in clarification informed by previous case law. See further, Simester and Sullivan, *Criminal Law: Theory and Doctrine*, 4th edn (Oxford, Hart Publishing, 2010) 766 *et seq*.

[24] The jury finds the primary facts and also resolves the normative issue. Merely because the defendant believes the force used to be reasonable does not raise a defence of mistaken belief as it is for the court, acting through the jury to impose the normative standard: *Owino* [1996] 2 Cr App R 128 explaining *Scarlett* [1993] 4 All ER 629 and confirmed by s 76(6) of the Criminal Justice and Immigration Act 2008. The courts frequently emphasise that juries, when judging the question of reasonableness, must seek to put themselves in the circumstances of the defendant, taking heed of all the pressures and fears that would have been present: see for instance *Palmer* [1971] 1 AC 814.

killing and harming non-threatening innocent persons, even in pursuit of outcomes highly beneficial for far greater numbers of people as compared to those killed or injured.[25] And yet such inhibitions may count for very little if a country takes itself to be facing an unjust, existential threat. One salient feature of debates about events such as Dresden and Hiroshima is that their moral status is still keenly disputed. No one can plausibly deny that thousands of non-threatening persons were intentionally killed as a means of expediting the defeat of the Axis powers.[26] Yet arguments are still put with great vigour that these killings of innocents were warranted responses to extreme circumstances.

The United Kingdom, as matters stand now, should not be regarded as being in a condition analogous to war because of the threat of terrorist violence.[27] Indeed the House of Lords has ruled that the ongoing threat of terrorist violence did not justify the discriminatory detention of foreign nationals, although it did consider that in the light of the terrorist threat article 5 could be derogated from if done in a proportionate and non discriminatory fashion.[28] Under the current dispensation, forceful reactions on the part of state officials to terrorist threats fall to be scrutinised within the ordinary terms of the criminal law. (Although terrorists captured during terrorist operations are outside the scope of our discussion.)

The constraints imposed by the criminal law on the hard treatment by state officials of subjects falling within one of the three categories of innocent person identified for discussion will shortly be examined. It will be seen that when applying the norms of the criminal law to particular state responses to terrorist threats there is no formal distinction made under the law to the acts, respectively, of officials and non officials.[29] When assessing the legality under the criminal law of a particular token of hard treatment by D of V, an innocent person, the same binary question is put irrespective of D's official or non-official capacity: is D guilty or not guilty of a criminal offence? Subsumed under a verdict of not guilty is a distinction used frequently by criminal law theorists, namely the

[25] Hauser, *Moral Minds* (Boston, Little, Brown, 2006) 121–31. Hauser and his associates administered a Moral Sense Test (moral.wjh.harvard.edu) to 60,000 subjects across 120 countries. With great consistency, subjects from a multiplicity of cultural backgrounds expressed strong sentiments against killing innocent, non threatening persons as a means to some societal good. The consistency also held for age and gender. There was far less consistency where the killing was a side effect of an otherwise good outcome.

[26] For an authoritative account of the nature and extent of the Allied bombing campaign in Germany in 1945, see http:www.anesi.com/ussbs02.htm *United States Strategic Bombing Survey* (1976) vol 4, 7–10.

[27] It has been argued of course that this 'business as usual' take on the terrorist threat is based on a profound misunderstanding of the nature and depth of the terrorist threat: see notably Bobbitt, *Terrorism and Consent* (London, Allen Lane, 2008).

[28] *A v Secretary of State for Home Department* [2005] 2 AC 68.

[29] The parameters of what constitutes lawful or excusable force are set by the statutory entitlement under s 3 of the Criminal Law Act 1967 to use reasonable force in the prevention of crime, the common law of self defence, the 'clarification' of s 3 and the law of self defence by s 76 of the Criminal Justice and Immigration Act 2008 and, to some extent, the common law defences of duress and necessity. This body of law does not distinguish between officials and private citizens.

distinction between justification and excuse. The distinction can be used to find that a particular use of force by D on V was entirely warranted and lawful in all dimensions, whereas the use of force by D(1) on V(1) may be considered something for which he or she should not be punished but which is not to be regarded as fully warranted when determining in the round the legality of D(1)'s use of force. Therefore, before particular cases involving hard treatment of innocent persons on the part of state officials are addressed, some preliminary remarks are in order on the distinction between justification and excuse in the context of terrorist emergencies because of the practical implications differing accounts of the distinction may have when assessing the overall legitimacy of state action.

III JUSTIFICATION, EXCUSE AND PERMISSIBILITY

Even forms of very hard treatment may not amount to crimes on the part of officials. The absence of criminal liability may hold constant over a range of circumstances, involving action taken against the terrorists themselves (beyond the scope of our main discussion) extending to cases where harm of the greatest magnitude is inflicted on wholly innocent persons. For instance, D, a male armed police officer, correctly identifies V as a man on the point of detonating a bomb on a crowded London tube train. D expertly kills V with minimum risk to passengers, and saves many lives. By contrast D(1), another armed officer unreasonably identifies V(1) as a man with a bomb and kills him. V(2), the man actually possessed of a bomb subsequently kills many people. It is certainly the case that D commits no offence in killing V; it would seem to be a clear-cut case of as using such force as is reasonable in the circumstances as permitted by section 3 of the Criminal Law Act 1967.[30] It may well be the case that D(1), even though a police officer trained in the use of fire-arms commits no offence when he kills V(1).[31] If through some quirk in the prosecution process both officers should be

[30] This is not a formal proposition of law. What constitutes reasonable force is for the jury, yet it is most unlikely that a jury would find that the force employed was unreasonable. Also, it would be appropriate for the judge to direct the jury to acquit if satisfied as to the primary facts, avoiding any prospect of a perverse verdict.

[31] Although D(1)'s belief that V(1) was a suicide bomber was unreasonable, he may yet be found to be using reasonable force within the meaning of s 3 of the Criminal Law Act 1967 because, 'the question whether the degree of force used by [D(1)] was reasonable in the circumstances is to be decided by reference to the circumstances as [D(1)] believed them to be' and furthermore 'if [D(1)] claims to have held a particular belief as regards the existence of any circumstances [D(1)] is entitled to rely on it . . . whether or not the mistake was a reasonable one to have made': Criminal Justice and Immigration Act 2008 s76(3);(4). It seems odd that a reasonable use of force can be based on an unreasonable belief as to the need to use force but at least, '[T]he degree of force used by [D(1)] is not to be regarded as reasonable in the circumstances as [D(1)] believed them to be if it was disproportionate to those circumstances' :s 76(6).

For an argument that art 2 (right to life) of the ECHR is incompatible with the acquittal of state officials who use fatal force when lacking a reasonable belief that in facts warranting the use of force of such gravity, see Leverick, 'Is English Self-Defence Law Incompatible with Article 2 of the ECHR?' (2002) *Criminal Law Review* 347. But see Smith, 'The Use of Force in Public and Private Defence and Article 2' (2002) *Criminal law Review* 958.

charged with murder, both would very likely be acquitted of that offence[32] and in terms of the verdict returned against them that would be that. Many criminal law theorists however would put D and D(1) in different cases. They would say that D was justified and that D(1) was merely excused. Does this distinction have practical implications when evaluating the legitimacy of official responses to terrorist threats?[33]

It is commonly said that a person who is justified is acting within the realm of right. On that view anyone who violently resists justified conduct will offend. As the justified agent is exercising a right to act in a certain way, the agent may call upon third parties to assist him or her and those third parties will act lawfully if they do so. By contrast, a person who is merely excused, leaves people at risk of harm from his actions with their full range of options. V(1), knowing himself to be innocent, may lawfully defend himself against D(1) and anyone who is assisting D(1). So the justification/excuse divide could matter very much in the ex post scrutiny of the conduct of officials.

Clearly, if the distinction is to be put to practical work a serviceable distinction between those actions of state agents which are justified, and those which are merely to be excused is required.[34] The distinction between justification and excuse is not settled doctrinally in England and Wales and if a doctrinal resolution were ever required it would have to be based on a choice between competing theories.

For some theorists, justification is to be found in improvements in the state of the world at T(1) by comparison with the state of the world at T. What counts as an improvement is strictly a fact of the matter thing which leaves out of account the motivations and dispositions of the agent whose actions have brought into being the improved state of affairs.[35] From this un-nuanced perspective, if V was killed by D before he or she could detonate the bomb, the saving of lives is the basis of a finding of justification. It is not to the point, say, that D had no reason to believe that V was a suicide bomber: it is fine if D acted on some 'sixth sense' provided D is vindicated by the facts. Indeed, all remains fine if D is turned into a private citizen who knows nothing of V's terrorist status, but kills V because he or she was a rival in love, provided V also happened to be a suicide bomber about to detonate a bomb. Also in the clear[36] would be D's friend S who came along to offer help and support in what he or she took to be purely a matter of revenge.

[32] If D(1)'s mistake was egregious, D(1) might be found guilty of gross negligence manslaughter.

[33] For argument supporting the importance of the distinction for the criminal law generally see Fletcher, *Rethinking Criminal Law* (Boston, Little, Brown, 1978) ch 10. For scepticism about the general utility of the distinction, see Simester and Sullivan (n 23 above) 665–69; Dennis, 'Necessity as a Defence to Crime: Possibilities, Problems and the Limits of Justification and Excuse' (2009) 3 *Criminal Law and Philosophy* 29.

[34] For an excellent account of the nuances of the distinction, see Greenawalt, 'The Perplexing Boundaries of Justification and Excuse' (1984) 84 *Columbia Law Review* 1897.

[35] Robinson, 'Competing Theories of Justification; Deeds v Reasons' in Simester and Smith (eds), *Harm and Culpability* (Oxford, Oxford University Press, 1996) 45.

[36] Some theorists allow that D and S can be liable for attempted murder.

Contrast D(1), an armed policeman who on this occasion has killed V(1), on the basis of superior orders instructing him that V(1) was a suicide bomber who must be killed immediately. If it turns out that V(1) is an innocent man, D(1)'s conduct is at best excused, however reasonable it was for D(1) to comply with the order. V(1) would act lawfully in defending him or herself against D(1) and so too any persons helping V(1) to defend him or herself.

These are questionable rules of engagement for state agents confronting or interrogating terrorists or those they reasonably take to be terrorists. Must we accept that justification is a fact of the matter thing and that the motivating reasons of agents are beside the point? On the contrary: there are no reasons of principle or policy mandating such a thin conception of justification.[37] To be sure, when things turn out for the best relief may temper vengeance. All things considered, it is a bad thing to shoot your wife's lover on a London tube train but this time the bad thing was in some senses a good thing as many lives were saved. However, was it justified conduct? Surely not. Once relief subsides, a cooler appraisal may conclude that D is a bad man who demonstrated how criminally bad he was by killing someone for reasons of revenge.[38]

Motivating reasons should not be left out of account when determining whether a particular act or omission of the agent was justified. Indeed a perfectionist account of justification could plausibly insist upon a conjunction of sound motivating reasons and a felicitous outcome. Indeed the perfectionist account of justification may be the best account.[39]A state agent may act reasonably and with the best of intentions yet bring about a catastrophe. It does not quite hit the right note to say that the agent's tragic act was a justified act, particularly from the perspective of persons gravely harmed by the action. And yet the act may have been a permissible act in that, all other things equal, the official should act in a similar fashion if placed once more in like circumstances. For example, in particular circumstances optimal outcomes may be best striven for by taking quick decisions, decisions which may require action necessarily based on incomplete information. Operational maxims such as 'observe; orientate; decide and act', however helpful, cannot eliminate the need for drastic decisions taken in a state of uncertainty.[40] When assessing ex post the legitimacy of such decisions in the light of their consequences, a decisional matrix of justified, excused or inexcusable may be too confined. A better question from an *ex ante* perspective would be whether the decision was a permissible or impermissible response for a competent official.[41]

[37] See Gardner, 'Justifications and Reasons' in Simester and Smith (n 35 above) 103.

[38] See further, Sullivan, 'Bad Thoughts and Bad Acts' (1990) *Criminal Law Review* 559.

[39] For a discussion of the layered nature of justification see Segev, 'Sub-Optimal Justification and Justificatory Defences' (2009) 4 *Criminal Law and Philosophy* 57.

[40] Omand (n 7 above) provides an informed account of the psychological pressures placed on security officials who out of necessity have to take decisions on the basis of incomplete information: ibid 173–98.

[41] Arguably the bounds of permissibility may be set too low for state officials who use fatal force following an unreasonable mistake: see n 31 above.

To return to D(1), the armed police officer who has received an order from a superior officer to kill V(1). If D(1) acted reasonably in following this order, his actions in killing V(1) should be considered permissible even should it turn out that V(1) was an innocent victim of circumstance (and even should it be the case that P, D(1)'s superior officer, made a bad mistake in identifying V(1) as a suicide bomber). There is something almost oxymoronic in asserting of the same token of conduct that it was a permissible, even mandatory thing to do (subordinate police officers should follow orders if their content is not patently illegal or obviously based on misinformation) and that D(1) should be merely excused for killing an innocent man. When we are excused for something we have done or failed to do, there is always the implication that we should try our best to avoid a similar mishap again. Excuses wear thin. However, all other things equal, D(1) should trust the judgment of his officers and follow his orders in the future. Decisions as drastic as a decision, say, to destroy a passenger plane in mid-air can only be based on the best risk assessment feasible in the circumstances and therefore permissible (though not necessarily mandatory) even if the decision takers are aware of the possibility that there may be an innocent explanation for the highly suspicious flight path.[42] Inevitably, emergency situations will arise where neither a choice for action nor inaction is guaranteed to be optimal.

It has been argued however that adopting a standard of permissibility based on the integrity of the agent's motivation and the reasonableness of the risk assessment rather than the felicitous results of the agent's conduct is illogical. This argument stipulates that inherent in the concept of justification and even in the notion of permissibility is the idea of right. Suppose a person who lacks any colour of justification, permissibility or excuse for his act, such as a suicide bomber. He cannot legitimately use force on anyone who would prevent him from detonating his bomb. This stricture will hold even for our fanciful example involving a vengeful husband who kills his wife's lover and unwittingly prevents many deaths. The fact that the bomber would commit an offence against the husband if he acted violently by way of self-defence is said to demonstrate that the latter has right on his side, a right constituted by the facts of harm prevention, and not on his motivation. However, the true explanation of why the bomber would commit an offence if he attacked the husband lies in the wrong that the bomber intends. If he intends to preserve his life in order to detonate his bomb in the immediate future, his acts need not be characterised as self-defence (he intends to die shortly by his own hand) but as force employed in order to be able to commit imminently the crime of murder. We need not be committed to

[42] There were press reports of a plane deviating from its Heathrow bound flight path and flying low along the route of the Thames toward Twickenham, where 70,000 spectators were watching a rugby international. Apparently, the lack of any imminent danger became clear (the pilot had lost his bearings) only shortly before intercept jets were due to take off. The incident has not been officially confirmed.

the strange idea that the homicidal husband had in some objective sense right on his side.[43]

Of course, the position of victims of violence will differ in cases where the victim is a wrongdoer and where he or she is not. If D reasonably suspects that V is about to detonate a bomb and V is truly about to detonate a bomb, then clearly V has no right to defend himself against D. Yet if V is an innocent man, a strong inclination arises to allow him to defend himself against D, however reasonable D's suspicion of V. To allow him to do so seems to raise again the spectre of logical impossibility. On the position argued for here, D's reasonable suspicion about V makes permissible D's forceful intervention against V. Moreover, this permissibility is not something restricted to D. If D is in a position to order S to assist in killing V, S too is permitted to assist D unless S has good reason to know that V is innocent. However, allowing V to defend himself does not require peeling away the permissibility of D's conduct. It is well established that there is a right of self-defence against innocent threats.[44] There is no good reason to confine the right to defend oneself against innocent threats, to threats made by innocent persons who are merely excused rather than exonerated.[45] Even if V is aware of the circumstances which make him a plausible suspect from the perspective of D, there is no duty of self sacrifice. To be sure, as D's conduct is permissible, it follows that as a state official he was acting within his authority. However, it does not follow that lawful authority cannot be lawfully resisted. To be sure, out of concern for the safety of its law enforcement officials, a state may, if it wishes, insist that lawful authority cannot be lawfully resisted. However, that would be to apply a policy rather than adopting a stance mandated by logic.

We will now go on to discuss in what circumstances drastic yet permissible action can be taken by state agents against innocent persons in the three classes we have identified. If certain drastic actions may be permissible if state agents are in possession of the true facts, we will also hold them to be permissible on the basis of facts they reasonably perceived and believed in good faith to be the case, even if their perceptions are at variance with the true facts. Further, we

[43] This analysis would not apply if the person killed was not carrying a bomb although the person intended to carry out a suicide bomb attack at some point in the future

[44] Simester and Sullivan (n 23 above) 775–77.

[45] The claim is made that unless an innocent threat is in some sense unlawful (tortious) or unjust there is no basis for the law to determine which innocent person can use force against or resist the other: Uniacke, *Permissible Killing-the Self- Defence Justification of Homicide* (Cambridge, Cambridge University Press, 1994) 158–93. However, if it is accepted, as it generally is, that if D's life depends on it, he may, for instance, remove by deadly means V who is blocking the route to safety through immobility caused, for example by fear, or a heart attack, the unlawfulness and injustice brought to the party by V are hard to discern. The position seems to be that if D is in mortal danger, he can use force against V if V is preventing, however blamelessly, D's escape unless D would be usurping a place of safety already lawfully obtained by V. Self preference is permissible in such deadly circumstances, a principle that applies to the situation of an innocent V about to be killed by an innocent D. Both parties are lawfully entitled to use proportionate force against the other, which is not tidy but it is not a logical contradiction. See further, Montague, 'Self-Defence and Choosing between Lives' (1981) 40 *Philosophical Studies* 207.

will regard action as permissible if it is taken in good faith on the basis of a reasonable risk assessment. In circumstances where effective action must be prompt action, it may be reasonable/permissible to act on the basis of information known to be incomplete.

IV HARD TREATMENT OF INNOCENT PERSONS

A Innocent Persons Harmed due to their Close Proximity to State Interventions Made against Terrorists

Police and other state agencies will confront situations where effective action against terrorists will almost certainly entail the death or injury of innocent persons who are in close proximity to terrorist operations. Examples are only too familiar: passengers on highjacked scheduled flights; hostages in aeroplanes, ships and buildings; pedestrians in the line of fire and so forth.

The discussion will be focused on passengers present in a plane which is under the control of terrorists. State authorities have what seems reliable information that the terrorists will crash the plane into a high-rise, densely occupied building, thereby killing everyone on the plane and many thousands of persons in the building. In such terrible circumstances the best response would be to divert the plane to a place where deaths and casualties are minimised. Given some form of tragic outcome seems inevitable, failure to minimise casualties is arguably a dereliction of duty.[46] To be sure, not everyone may be happy about what state officials decide to do. Those inhabitants of the small village who survived the impact of the crashing plane and survey a scene of death and destruction may well experience deep anger against the state officials who ordered fighter pilots to force a diversion on the terrorists controlling the passenger plane.[47] Yet none of the canonical objections to the taking of innocent life appear to have been breached by the state.[48]

Of course, the diversion option may not be available. The authorities may be confronted with a situation where a plane can only be prevented from crashing

[46] As well as the specific responsibilities that state officials will have under applicable legal and administrative regimes, art 2 of the ECHR places a responsibility on the state and its officials to take proportionate, anticipatory measures to minimise the loss of life in circumstances where state responsibility is engaged: *Osman v United Kingdom* (2000) 29 EHRR 245.

[47] Although the anger is understandable and should not be rebuked, it does not rest on any sound grievance against the state and its officials. The events leading to death and destruction imposed upon the state a general, impersonal duty to reduce the number of deaths. A ground of grievance might arise if the state fails to pay adequate compensation to those who have sustained personal and material losses as a result of the crash. Those adversely affected have paid a price exacted for the benefit of society as a whole and should be adequately compensated from public funds.

[48] Even if on some versions of causal salience the state can be portrayed as a causal agent in the deaths (and a deflection scenario can be interpreted in different ways), the deaths of the villagers are a side effect of the state's life saving strategy rather than a means to the saving of lives: Finnis, 'Intention and Side-Effects' in Frey and Morris (eds), *Liability and Responsibility* (Cambridge, Cambridge University Press, 1991) 32.

into the building by its destruction in flight. Under most understandings of what amounts to an intentional killing, the terrorists and the innocent passengers will be intentionally killed[49] should the plane be shot down by the authorities. Of course, the passengers were under grave risk of dying if the authorities had refrained from shooting down the plane. Inaction may also have allowed the terrorists to kill persons present in the building in addition to the passengers on the plane. Is this enough to undermine the very strong prohibition against intentionally killing innocent, non-threatening persons as a means of saving the lives of other innocent persons? For many deontologists, the prohibition is unyielding even in circumstances where the numbers saved will greatly exceed the numbers killed.

The German Federal Supreme Court has adamantly set its face against the intentional killing of innocent passengers by the state, even in the circumstances under discussion.[50] The Court was constitutionally reviewing a legislative provision authorising the Minister of Defence to order a passenger plane to be shot down if it could be assumed that the plane would be used against the lives of others and if shooting down the plane was the only way of averting that present danger.[51] The Court assumed that many innocent persons, in addition to the trapped passengers, would be killed when the plane was crashed by the terrorists. Yet the ruling was that no innocent, non-threatening lives could be taken to avert that catastrophe. It was not in point that the innocent passengers would be doomed in any event when the plane crashed. Neither did numbers matter. The proscription against the taking of innocent life holds if there is but one innocent passenger aboard however many lives will be lost in the building when the plane crashes. What mattered for the Court was that to intentionally kill an innocent person for the benefit of others was to treat that person as a means to someone else's end. The legislation was declared unconstitutional on the grounds that it violated the right to dignity (article 1 of the German Constitution) and the right to life (article 2 of the German Constitution).

What is the position for England and Wales? The starting point would be section 3 of the Criminal Law Act 1967 which allows the authorities (and anyone else) to use such force as is reasonable in the circumstances in the prevention of

[49] There is some English authority which would support the conclusion that the deaths of the terrorists are intended, whereas the deaths of the passengers are merely foreseen: *A (children)* [2001] 1 Fam 147 (Walker LJ). Yet even though the deaths of the terrorists do not conceptually entail the deaths of the passengers (there are possible worlds where the passengers float to earth unharmed) under our current understanding of the state of the world, it seems difficult to drive a wedge between the intentional destruction of a plane in mid-air and the intentional killing of everyone aboard, albeit some killings will be regretted more than others.

[50] Judgment of the German Federal Constitutional Court of 5 February,2006, www.bverfg.delentscheäidungen/rs20060215_1bvr035705.html. I am much indebted to Professor Michael Bohlander for conversations about this case and also his article, 'In *Extremis*? Hijacked Airplanes, "Collateral Damage" and the Limits of the Criminal Law' (2006) *Criminal Law Review* 579.

[51] The judgment was assessing the constitutional propriety of s 14(3) of the Air Traffic Security Act 2005 which provides: 'The direct use of weapons is only allowed if under the circumstances it must be assumed the airplane will be used against the lives of human beings and that such use is the only means of averting the present danger.' This provision was declared unconstitutional and void.

crime. It is well accepted that killings can be justified as reasonable if the preventative force is proportionate and directed against a wrongdoer. There is no direct guidance to be had whether an English appellate court would find that it is within the terms of section 3 to kill one or more non-threatening innocent persons, virtually certain to die in any event, to secure the lives of other innocent persons not doomed to die if state action is taken on their behalf. Some guidance can be obtained from cases concerned with the (in English law) fitfully recognised general defence of necessity,[52] where the preponderant assumption is that non-threatening lives cannot be lawfully taken,[53] but these circumstances have not yet arisen. Consideration would have to be given to article 2 of the ECHR (guarantee of right to life) which is now part of domestic English law.[54] There is not much guidance here. The article allows lives to be lawfully taken if 'absolutely necessary . . . in defence of any person from unlawful violence'. Yet, the right to life of the passengers and the right to life of the occupants of the building are equally protected by art 2. While the article 2 jurisprudence imposes in certain circumstances a pro-active duty on the state to install preventative measures that should assist in saving lives,[55] there is no hint in this jurisprudence whether these measures can encompass the taking of non-threatening innocent lives to save other innocent lives.

The fact of the matter is that if an event similar to 9/11 were on the radar in the United Kingdom, what reactions would be lawful reactions is a matter for conjecture. The nearest we have to any form of guidance is the case of *Pagett*[56] where the Court of Appeal found that a police officer had acted lawfully when he fatally shot a hostage when preventing the escape of the suspect who clasped the hostage to his body. However, the case does not really assist. The officer's objective was to shoot the suspect, albeit in circumstances where there was a very high risk of shooting the hostage. However, the killing of the hostage in *Pagett* is a side effect not a means to an end and therefore not categorically proscribed by all deontologists. Yet for our case the destruction of the plane and the immediate deaths of the terrorists and the passengers are inseparably bundled together. The German Federal Supreme Court correctly ruled that in these circumstances the taking of the passenger's lives is a means to saving of the lives of others.

[52] Simester and Sullivan (n 23 above) 779 *et seq*.

[53] Innocent life was taken under the head of necessity in *Re A (Children)* [2001] 1 Fam 147(Brooke LJ) but on the very particular facts of separating conjoined twins where one twin had excellent life prospects were she separated from a non-viable twin whose physiological demands would have entailed the deaths of both twins within approximately 18 months failing a separation operation. Although it is uncomfortable to describe the weaker twin as a threat to the stronger twin, the fact of the matter was that the life expectancy of the latter was radically diminished by the demands of the former. It was this consideration that led Ward LJ to characterise the separation operation as an act done in defence of the stronger twin. The case is of limited assistance to the plane scenario where the passengers are non-threatening in every sense.

[54] The Human Rights Act 1998 makes the ECHR a direct source of English law.

[55] See *Osman* (n 46 above).

[56] *Pagett* (1983) 76 Cr App R 279.

The lack of specific legislation in the United Kingdom dealing with 9/11 scenarios is highly unsatisfactory, not least for those whose duty it is to decide what to do and order others to do it. Specific legislation[57] is unlikely in the United Kingdom any time soon. Any forthcoming legislation should allow the taking of innocent lives to save other innocent lives when the set of innocents to be killed appear virtually certain to die in any event, on the basis of one or more reasonable assumptions. This empowerment should cover not only situations where the catastrophic terrorist event seems virtually certain, but also where it seems likely on a balance of probabilities on the basis of the best risk assessment that can be made in the circumstances. It is considered that this scheme is just as between the two sets of innocent persons. Although the state must be even-handed in affording protection to all innocent persons present in the jurisdiction, it should be entitled to take into account the fact that some persons are, unfortunately, beyond protection by the state. Arguably, it owes a duty under article 2 to focus its protection on those who can be saved. If allowing events to take their course will likely ensue in the deaths of both those who can and cannot be saved, it is not unreasonable to assert a breach of article 2 in respect of the failure to take measures in favour of those who could have been helped.[58]

We should emphasise that we are discussing state action. We should allow a defence, akin to conscientious objection, for any private citizen who refuses to participate in state action involving the taking of innocent life, even though it is arguable that they were legally obliged to participate.[59] However, the state's responsibility for the lives and safety of all innocent persons lawfully present within its jurisdiction entitles, if not obliges it, to consider measures of the kind argued for here.[60]

There are also strong reasons of policy for following this approach. Abstaining from intervention may allow the terrorists to carry out their project with all the set-backs to other legitimate interests and with all its propaganda value for them. The purist German approach gives terrorist groups a valuable trump card. If state authorities are aware that at least one innocent person is aboard the hijacked aeroplane, forms of diversion which abstain from taking any innocent lives or letting events take their course seem the only permissible responses.

[57] As has been done in a number of jurisdictions: see Bohlander (n 50 above) 588–90.

[58] This assumes that a non-denominational state with a population of different faiths and no faith should take decisions of this kind on the basis of what may be termed 'secular rationality' decisions which may well offend against the strictures of particular forms of religion; see further Sullivan, 'Ministering Death' (1997) 17 *Oxford Journal of Legal Studies* 123, 134.

[59] For instance, a civilian air traffic controller may find his or herself in a situation where contractually he or she is obliged to assist a process intended to result in the death of innocent passengers. If that should offend against the controller's deepest moral beliefs he or she should be entitled to disengage even though the state may be empowered by its general duty to its citizens to take some innocent lives.

[60] See note 46 above and associated text.

Further, this purist approach may inhibit effective responses to other forms of terrorist attack.[61]

B Innocent Persons known not to be Terrorists or Complicit with Terrorists but whose Harsh Treatment May Avert or Mitigate Imminent Terrorist Attacks

Consider the following facts. D and his terrorist group have bombed a London night club causing much death, serious injury and destruction. Shortly after, they bomb a Glasgow air terminal to like effect. D and his group have threatened other imminent bombings of public places. The current whereabouts of the group are not known but they are believed to be hiding somewhere in the United Kingdom ready to launch further attacks.

The police have taken into custody V, the wife of D, and E, their three-year-old daughter. The responsible officer P does not suspect V of any involvement in D's terrorist activities but the officer is convinced that V knows where D and his group are hiding. The officer proposes to use all means necessary, including torture of V and E, to find out where D is. In these circumstances there would be enormous pressure on the responsible authorities to bring the terrorist campaign to an end. There are other nightmare possibilities which the security forces are obliged to take seriously as future possibilities such as use of biological weapons or portable nuclear devices. However, we will stay with the example given, which is well within the range of the currently possible.[62]

There are some responses that cannot be endorsed by law or ethics, notwithstanding a reasonable assumption that the responses disallowed might have brought the bombings to an end. We will argue that the matters to be discussed are sufficiently discussed within the terms of legal and ethical debates. Putting for the moment truly existential threats to one side, we will resist the idea that when faced with momentous danger, we can leave law and morality behind because they have nothing useful to say when responding to very extreme circumstances.[63]

[61] It is easy to think of situations where protecting the public generally may require, say, the use of high ordinance weapons against a terrorist group in circumstances where the deaths of some innocent persons are not plausibly characterised as mere side effects as when targeting a building known to contain innocent hostages.

[62] In December 2007, a car parked outside a London nightclub crammed full of high grade explosives failed to detonate. Some days later, an attempt to drive a 4 by 4 vehicle primed with explosives into the crowded concourse of Glasgow air terminal was thwarted at the point of entry. Both incidents were the responsibility of the same terrorist group.

[63] See Williams, 'A Critique of Utilitarianism' in Smart and Williams, *Utilitarianism, For and Against* (Cambridge, Cambridge University Press, 1973) 93 questioning the appropriateness of moral appraisal in circumstances lacking 'minimum sanity'. For criticism see Bennett, *The Act Itself* (Oxford, Oxford University Press,1995) 167–71. See too Harel and Sharon, 'Necessity knows No Law: On Extreme Cases and Uncodifiable Necessities' discussed at n 95 and associated text below.

i What Can be Legitimately Done to V?

Under current English law, it is a criminal offence for any person to fail to disclose information which he or she knows or believes might help or prevent another person from carrying out an act of terrorism or might help bring a terrorist to justice in the UK.[64] The regime allowing pre-charge detention of those suspected of involvement in terrorism or terrorist related offences could be invoked to detain V for questioning.[65] What physical and psychological pressure could lawfully be brought to bear on V? As we have noted, English law permits the use of 'such force as is reasonable in the circumstances' in the prevention of crime.[66] Although, controversially, the use of fatal force to arrest someone taken to be a terrorist in order to prevent his or her escape and the commission of future terrorist offences (the man shot was merely a joy-rider failing to stop at a manned barrier) has been considered permissible,[67] it has never been claimed that any degree of force can be used when interrogating innocent persons about the whereabouts of dangerous and currently active terrorists.

The conventional view would be that an official who uses or even threatens force would commit a criminal offence. Furthermore, if serious violence were used and it could be said to be officially condoned or insufficiently safeguarded against, the United Kingdom would be in breach of the ECHRwhich proscribes in all circumstances the infliction of inhuman and degrading treatment.[68] It may well be that if the suffering endured by V is extreme, officials ordering and inflicting the treatment would be guilty of the crime of torture.[69] If the torture were officially condoned or insufficiently safeguarded against, the United Kingdom would be in breach of the European Convention and the United Nations Convention,[70] instruments which unequivocally ban recourse to torture by parties to these conventions. If the suffering endured by V in consequence of the imagined or real suffering of E reaches the requisite thresholds, inhuman treatment and torture may well occur against V, with the legal consequences outlined above including personal criminal liability on the part of officials ordering and inflicting such treatment.

There seems here a concordance between the legal position and the correct ethical response to V's situation. Failure to disclose knowledge of the whereabouts of a criminal who is about to commit a crime has never, without more,

[64] Anti-Terrorism, Crime and Security Act 2001 s 117.

[65] Terrorism Act 2000 s 41 and sch 8.

[66] Criminal Law Act 1977 s 3.

[67] *Kelly* [1989] NI 341. Surprisingly this decision was not taken to contravene art 2 of the European Convention: *Kelly v UK* (1993) 74 DR 139. As Sir John Smith remarked, how can a shooting carried out with intent to kill be characterised as an arrest? Essentially, it was an extreme use of preventative force, directed at crimes to be committed at some unascertained time and place: Smith, 'The Right to Life and the Right to Kill in Law Enforcement' (1994) 144 *NLJ* 354.

[68] ECHR art 3.

[69] Criminal Justice Act 1988 ss 134 and 135.

[70] Convention against Torture and other Inhuman and Degrading Treatment (entered into force 26 June 1987).

been regarded as a sufficient basis for liability in the offence as an accomplice.[71] As we have noted, V would be guilty of a lesser statutory offence than the principal's.[72] V could be vigorously questioned about where D is in order to lay the ground to charge this offence but that would be all. Were it otherwise, a radical shift in power between the state and its subjects would occur, a change quite incompatible with a system of criminal justice constrained liberal values. Apart from any offences committed against V, evidence obtained by force might well be inadmissible.[73] Of course, a liberal democracy enduring a series of terrorist attacks with the immediate prospect of yet more attacks is a democracy challenged by the most undemocratic of means. Are exceptional protective measures warranted here?

Michael S Moore for one would say that they were.[74] He regards a person withholding information useful in the prevention of terrorist acts as effectively in the same moral case as terrorists themselves. He claims that a person with information concerning a terrorist threat effectively becomes party to the threat if that person fails to make available information that would negate or mitigate the threat.[75] Although there may be some intuitive appeal to this broad conception of participation in terrorism, it goes beyond the boundaries of complicity recognised by English law.[76] There may be all manner of reasons falling well short of any parity of culpability with the perpetrators, why a person might not reveal details of what he or she knows of the crimes of others. Hence a specific and lesser offence of failing to disclose information about terrorists was created. From our perspective, V may be regarded as innocent of any terrorist connection if the most that can be proved against her is that she knows where D is. For Moore however, she is on a par with a terrorist and can be treated for the purpose of interrogation as a terrorist. He considers that a democracy under attack by terrorists is entitled to use all means against terrorists, including torture, to ward off terrorist attacks.

However, what of the cut and dried legal proscriptions, domestic and international, which deny recourse to torture (and inhuman and degrading treatment) against any person in any circumstances? In the extreme circumstances of terrorist attacks, he considers that the defence of necessity trumps these prohibitions and justify torture used to prevent or mitigate the death and injury of innocent people.[77] Moore's judgment of what kind of treatment can be meted out to V by interrogators is highly problematic. Any torture she endures will

[71] If a person has some special legal responsibility to control the conduct of another, a failure to exercise that control by way of encouragement or assistance to the principal offender is sufficient for complicity in the principal's offence but not otherwise: Simester and Sullivan (n 23 above) 204–07.

[72] See n 64.

[73] Under the Police and Criminal Evidence 1984 s78 the judge has a discretion to exclude any evidence if necessary to ensure the fairness of the proceedings. Only confessions of guilt obtained by force are categorically excluded: s 76(2).

[74] Moore, 'Torture and the Balance of Evils' (1989) 24 *Israel Law Review* 280.

[75] ibid 333.

[76] See n 71.

[77] Moore (n 74 above) 340–42.

involve suffering of intensity beyond any lawfully imposed criminal punishment. And, of course, she may not know where D is. The fact that P is convinced that she does may not be grounded in fact.

ii What Can be Legitimately Done to E?

We can be brief in terms of the position under English law. Taking E into custody for reasons unconnected with her health, safety or general welfare will constitute criminal offences on the part of those who ordered and maintained her detention.[78] Any physical or psychological mistreatment of E will constitute criminal offences. One would anticipate that English courts would summarily reject any argument that the mistreatment of E constituted reasonable force in the prevention of crime, and would not allow that justificatory claim to negate any crimes on the part of responsible officials *even if the mistreatment of E coerced V into revealing the whereabouts of D.* That children in the position of E should be left safe and unharmed is for all intents and purposes a moral absolute.

For Moore, the inviolability of E is not a moral absolute. He does lay great stress on the moral gravity of torturing innocent persons. Yet the anchor can be pulled up:[79]

> To justify torturing one innocent person requires that there are horrendous consequences attached to not torturing that person-the destruction of an entire city or, perhaps, of a lifeboat or a building full of people. On this view, in other words, there is a very high threshold of bad consequences that must be threatened before something as awful as torturing an innocent person can be justified.

It is suggested that Moore's threshold is not high enough, at least in terms of the realities, awful though they are, of terrorist violence to date. Although qualified by a 'perhaps', it seems that the threshold is not set at some truly existential threat but would cover circumstances such as our example. His views are of particular interest because are they are held not by someone with a utilitarian or consequentialist attitude to the criminal law but by someone who is a hard-edged retributivist, with a belief that moral values are firmly grounded in 'moral reality'.[80] Interestingly, he agrees that proscriptions of torture of innocent persons should be cast in absolutist terms.[81] And yet he takes the position that even an adherent to the principle that torture of innocents should be completely and unequivocally proscribed, can, consistent with that position, hold that that norms cast in absolute terms can be breached if the cost of keeping the norm becomes too high. He insists that he is not a deontologist who becomes a Shavian consequentialist when the cost of observance becomes too high. Rather,

[78] Child abduction; kidnapping.
[79] Moore (n 74 above) 330.
[80] Moore, 'Moral Reality' (1982) *Wisconsin Law Review* 1061.
[81] Moore (n 74 above), 340–42.

he claims his position rests on a true understanding of the nature of moral norms. For him, there is no such thing as a value which retains its value in all possible states of the world. If the cost of adhering to the value becomes too high in terms of horrendous consequences, we go beyond the field of application of that value. It becomes not worthwhile in terms of the best interpretation of a non-consequentialist morality to intransigently hold to one value if observance comes at too great a cost to other values, such as saving innocent lives. This is not to defect to a non-agent relativist consequentialism argues Moore. It is an avoidance of Kantian excess and an acceptance of the incommensurability of values which, when taken individually, may still be conceived in absolute terms.[82]

It is thought a tenable reading of Moore to state that the prospect of the further deaths and injury to innocent persons in our example would justify the torture of the innocent E, should all else fail in terms of yielding the information so desperately required.[83] Yet such a conclusion is enormously problematic in terms of principle and policy. A contrast between the deaths and injury of many hundreds of innocent persons on the one hand and the torture of one innocent person on the other, is too stark and atomised. For a liberal democracy, the proscription on torture is among other things a declaration of the terms on which we wish to live within a politically organised society. It is a decision which is taken *ex ante* and which is intended not to be revised while the form of life that, all things considered, we wish to live remains feasible. The possible loss of innocent life that may be entailed from abstaining from torture is factored into the decision to renounce its use. Similar decisions have been taken by many democracies in relation to renouncing the death penalty. To be sure, the number of innocent lives that are the price of these forms of abstinence is conjectural and contested. The effectiveness of torture as a source of reliable information and the efficacy of the death penalty as a deterrent are highly contested empirical questions. However it is incorrect to claim, as is sometimes claimed, that torture is always futile as well as cruel. On occasion torture will produce valuable, reliable information when all else has failed. Information extracted by torture has been used to good effect to increase the security of the United Kingdom.[84] Does this fact alter the balance of the argument? Not for the situation currently obtaining in the United Kingdom. To date terrorist violence has come nowhere close to existential levels. As matters stand now the horror

[82] It is hoped that this is a fair if brief rendition of a complex argument. In candour, I find the difference between Moore's deontological position and a consequentialism *in extremis* position, difficult to grasp.

[83] When elaborating his view that the avoidance of horrendous consequences may justify torture of the innocent, Moore does not make any age related exemptions. Earlier in his article (at 292) he states that the torture of children for consequentialist gains is 'morally repugnant' and that, 'No-one should torture innocent children-even when done to produce a sizeable gain in aggregate welfare.' It may be that Moore would hold to the impermissibility of torturing children in all circumstances despite his claim that there are no moral absolutes when the cost of observance is too high.

[84] Omand (n 7 above) 175.

that is torture can be dispensed with without threat to the overall fabric of existence.[85] An ethical commitment to abstaining from torture entails abstaining from its use even at the cost of innocent lives.

Arguments from policy give further support to the ban on torture. In our example, P, the responsible official, is 'convinced' that V knows where D is. Even if we accept that it is morally permissible to torture persons who are not themselves terrorists nor complicit with terrorists in an attempt to stymie imminent and large scale terrorist attacks (something we do not accept) it is in practice inevitable that many acts of torture will not produce useful information. P's conviction that V knows D's whereabouts and that torturing E will cause her to reveal them may be well founded and the torture of E may avert a serious terrorist attack. However, there are all manner of alternative possibilities which will entail that the torture is futile suffering and, among other things, a great disadvantage in the cultural struggle against terrorism. In the context of the United Kingdom, we may note that all the non-Irish terrorist attacks, either successful or thwarted, have involved persons who are UK citizens or persons lawfully present in the United Kingdom. If D falls within either class, there may well be many persons lawfully present here in addition to V, who may be reasonably suspected of knowing D's whereabouts or his plans. Consequently, there would be a considerable risk of repeated episodes of futile torture, increasing community tensions.

For the United Kingdom at least there are no grounds for changing the legal position with respect to the treatment of V or E.

C Persons who are Assumed by Officials to be Terrorists or Complicit with Terrorists but in Fact Have No Terrorist Connection and No Knowledge nor Influence on Future Terrorist Attacks

When D and his group successfully exploded a bomb at a London night club, causing much death and destruction, F just happened to be in the vicinity. He correctly guesses the nature of the incident and as a jihadist sympathiser he is in a state of exultation, a state that continues when he is arrested some moments later by the police, who have descended in numbers. On questioning in custody he falsely claims to be a member of the terrorist group that carried out the attack and assures his questioners that there are many attacks to come. Although in great sympathy with Islamist terrorism, he has been uninvolved in terrorist activity and has no knowledge of the plans of any terrorist group.

[85] The UK Government has published its national security strategy (www.guardian.co.uk/politics/2008/mar/19/terrorism.uk.security) where it is stated that the United Kingdom was estimated to face 30 known terrorist plots, with monitoring of 200 networks and 2,000 individuals. No reference is made to risks arising from terrorist operations involving nuclear or biological weapons. Of course, terrorist actions of such gravity cannot be dismissed as future possibilities. See n 6 and associated text.

i What can be legitimately done to F?

In assessing the propriety of anything done to F while he is in custody, we take as the basis for appraisal what it was reasonable for officials to believe concerning the terrorist proclivities of F. Our discussion will precede on the basis that it was reasonable for officials to adopt a working assumption that F is a member of D's terrorist group and that he has knowledge of the immediate plans of that group.

In terms of the formal legal position there is little to choose between the position of V and that of F. There is a legislative power to detain F before any charge is brought[86] and we can assume intensive and lengthy interrogation with little respite for sleep when he is first taken into custody. However, he cannot be physically mistreated in any way, nor put under psychological pressure which results in psychiatric harm. If working within these parameters produces no useful information (and F has no useful information to give) there are no coercive resources legally available to investigators, save for continued detention and questioning.

In the literature on responses to terrorism, there is a repeated claim that officials responsible for the interrogation of terrorists will not allow formal legal restraints to inhibit the use of effective means of investigation.[87] Furthermore, there is some support for the view that officials should not allow legal norms to hamper the investigation, particularly in cases where it is reasonable to assume that the suspect is an active terrorist possessed of information concerning imminent terrorist activity.[88] Certainly, for our case, if P was prepared to countenance the torture of V and E, it would be perverse if he did not order the torture of F, if he has a sense that there is information to be had and all else has failed to obtain it. As outlined above, under the explicit legal norms in play, the torture of F is unequivocally proscribed in English law. And yet explicit norms can be rendered inapplicable, if there a legally recognised form of exemption to block the application of the norm.[89]

The exemption might again be based on a claim that the torture of F to obtain information of imminent terrorist attacks would be 'reasonable force in the prevention of crime'. Nothing would change in substance if the ground of

[86] Terrorism Act 2000 s 41 and sch 8.

[87] For instance, the controversial proposal from Dershowitz for judicially authorised torture warrants is premised on a firm assumption that torture whether officially sanctioned or not is certain to occur where information is urgently required concerning terrorist attacks: Dershowitz, *Why Terrorism Works: Understanding the Threat, Responding to the Challenge* (Yale, Yale University Press, 2002).

[88] For a useful collection where considered statements favouring torture in certain circumstances are made by some distinguished contributors, see Levinson (ed), *Torture: A Collection* (Oxford, Oxford University Press, 2004).

[89] It is only when there is some legal mechanism blocking the application of the norm such as force used in the prevention of crime or necessity that we can say that the action of state officials is permissible. Arguably, defences such as duress by circumstances which do not block the norm but render the breach of the norm excusable are not available to state officials when acting in that capacity.

exemption claimed was general necessity.[90] We found that this justificatory claim failed in the cases of V and E. The failure was based on the implicit yet embedded right of innocent persons not to be used as a means to the end of crime prevention, however efficacious a means their bodily and mental mistreatment might be. The only way that V plausibly became a presumptive candidate for lawful mistreatment was to turn her silence into a form of collusion with the terrorist group, a move found to be unconvincing. From the vantage of our privileged access to the true facts of our case, we know that F too is innocent. However, that is not how he will be perceived by those officials responsible for obtaining information from him. From their perspective, he seems to be a member of a continuing terrorist conspiracy. He claims to have participated in a recent terrorist atrocity and to know about further atrocities. Do the reasonable assumptions of officials about F change the analysis in terms of his right not to be tortured?

English courts should resolutely protect F's right not to be tortured (we will leave lesser forms of mistreatment to one side). Two binding treaty obligations oblige the United Kingdom to ban recourse to torture in all circumstances and to make torture a criminal offence. History and morality make a compelling case for the unyielding proscription of torture. However, if it were wished to hollow out a commitment against torture yet retain the façade of proscription, recourse to necessity is the best implement to hand.[91] Necessity is essentially based on consequentialist assumptions, uncertainly trammelled by the current state of play within a jurisdiction regarding what interests constitute fundamental rights. F's entitlement to his right not to be tortured can be undermined by making his failure to reveal the whereabouts of D's terrorist group part of the continuing threat presented by the group. Though conceptually dubious when used as a means to enlarge the circle of complicity to include persons outside a terrorist group but who know something of its plans, such reasoning is more persuasive where a captured member of the group or someone who appears to be a member fails to tell the responsible authority what he or she knows of the ongoing terrorist plans of the group.

Justifying coercive measures taken against F can draw on affinities with forceful action taken to prevent crimes at the point of commission. Proportionate means to prevent serious crimes can include taking the life of a person whose danger to others entails forfeiture of the person's right to life. The ground is

[90] In the absence of a criminal code, there is no a statutory provision creating a necessity defence, but it is fitfully recognised at common law, *Simester and Sullivan,* (n 23 above) 713–23. As elsewhere, the defence rests on a balance of harms approach but with uncertain limits imposed by fundamental rights.

[91] Moore, (n 74 above) favours absolute provisions prohibiting torture which, as we have discussed yield to the defence of necessity. For a similar approach see Gross, 'Is Torture Warrant Warranted? Pragmatic Absolutism and Official Disobedience' (2004) 88 *Minnesota Law Review* 88. This approach is criticised above.

prepared for asserting the claim by analogy that F, by taking on the mantle of a terrorist, has forfeited his right not to be tortured.[92]

It will be argued in the next section that there are no grounds of principle that require the United Kingdom to renounce its proscription of torture at the present time. Additionally, there are strong prudential reasons for not doing so. We know that the torture of F will be a futile business in terms of providing useful information and there will be many cases of torture with the same outcome were the practice to be permitted. Moreover, should the practice be permitted for imminent risk cases, there is a risk that once the taboo is broken, it will become an investigatory tool for terrorism cases in general. The concept of necessity is a problematic concept in terms of legal stability in the hands of high powered appellate courts;[93] the boundaries of the concept are likely to be creatively explored by investigatory bodies under great institutional pressures to produce results. This conclusion, which will be more fully defended below, will be castigated in some quarters as naïve, even hypocritical. For those convinced in good faith that the future security of the United Kingdom may require in extreme circumstances recourse to torture, the way forward is not to sign up unequivocally to outright proscriptions of torture, yet brief responsible officials that individual cases of torture may be legitimised ex post if the circumstances facing the official were sufficiently dire. The way forward for those determined to allow recourse to torture as a last resort is to seek legislation which spells out what can be done by way of coercive interrogation and in what circumstances.[94] If such legislation is incompatible with a particular country's international commitments to ban torture in its jurisdiction, it should renounce those commitments. That route is not endorsed here, but it has the virtue of transparency.

In an interesting contribution to the torture debate, Harel and Sharon agree that countries committed to reducing the incidence of torture should bind

[92] Even commentators who reject recourse to a general defence of necessity as a means of undermining proscriptions against mistreatment in interrogation because such an approach may be used to mistreat wholly innocent persons, may allow recourse to self defence as a justification in the case of terrorists themselves: see for instance Gur-Aye, 'Can the War against Terror Justify the Use of Force in Interrogations?' in Levinson (n 88 above) 183. It should be noted that Gur-Aye does not endorse the use of torture, rather interrogative force against terrorists (not bystanders) if essential to obtain vital information about an imminent and concrete danger. The application of self-defence to legitimate forceful interrogation is not smooth. For cases where it is believed a man interrogated has himself planted or assisted others to plant some device primed to explode shortly, self- defence or defence of others seems apposite. However where, as in the case of F, a suspected terrorist has been arrested and is now non-operational but who may know of the imminent plans of his fellow terrorists, recourse to self-defence seems to add no limiting effect to that of general necessity. What is needed in this situation is information about the activities of persons other than the person interrogated. F is only in different case from someone like V in terms of eligibility for harsh interrogative treatment if a reasonable suspicion that he is a terrorist is reckoned to put him in different case and is not clear how invoking self-defence does this.

[93] The decision of the Supreme Court of Canada in *Perka* (1984) 13 DLR (4th) 1 contains excellent discussion of the difficulties of containing a necessity defence within manageable bounds.

[94] To this extent one must agree with Dershowitz (n 87 above) that if such things are ever to be done, knowledge of what is done should be in the public domain.

themselves to legal commitments which ban unequivocally any resort to torture in any circumstances.[95] They sharply disagree with the view that a deontological commitment to the banning of torture is compatible with provision of a necessity defence which can be invoked by state officials under pressure to avoid catastrophe. In a complex argument that cannot be done justice to here, they consider that to bring a necessity defence within a normative system will contaminate and weaken the force of the primary norm proscribing torture. They insist that the proscription against torture must be left inviolate within the system of norms. Yet, they expect officials to use all necessary means to avoid catastrophes including, should the stakes be high enough, resort to torture. Further, they think that the acts of such officials should not attract any censure. In their own words:

> Maintaining a normative distinction between acts performed under the direction of principles or rules and unprincipled context generated acts, acts performed under the force not of principles, but of circumstances, allows for accommodating the necessity of infringements in extreme cases within a deontological framework. The actions required in extreme cases are, we argue, permissible only when necessary. Moreover their permissibility is grounded in the necessity of the circumstances. Thus they ought to be performed strictly as acts of necessity, not as acts governed by principles.[96]

The sentiment reflected in this passage is not new.[97] The idea is that at some point in a desperate crisis normative constraints will lose their purchase and the exigencies of the moment will hold sway. It is certainly plausible that faced with the imminent prospect of some truly awful event, a nuclear explosion say, responsible officials will do whatever it takes to avert a catastrophe and among other things breach the ban on torture. For Harel and Sharon there would be no breach of the ban despite recourse to torture. For them the ban would no longer apply. An emergency of such magnitude creates a space where the only remaining imperative is to do what must be done.

There must be considerable doubt whether this 'lawless' conceptualisation of necessity would be accepted by courts on any occasion where an official who has tortured a suspect seeks to avoid a conviction by raising a defence of necessity. It would seem likely that a court would take itself to be remaining within the normative/legal system from whence it derives its jurisdiction and authority. The issue then would be whether the deontological proscription of torture can be overridden on consequentialist grounds if the price would otherwise be too high. Far better to try and resolve such matters *ex ante* and resolve what state officials should be permitted to do when faced with emergencies of the direst kind. In the UK at least it seems most unlikely that open Parliamentary debates

[95] 'Necessity Knows No Law: On Extreme Cases and Uncodifiable Necessities' http://www.law.utoronto.ca/documents/conferences2/Constitutionalism09-Harel.pdf and see too, Harel and Sharon, 'What is Really Wrong with Torture?' (2008) 6(2) *Journal of International Criminal Justice* 241.

[96] ibid 3.

[97] See Williams (n 63).

will be held on what official responses may be allowed in the case of dire emergencies.

V TERRORISM IN THE UNITED KINGDOM

It is not possible to state with anything close to precision the extent and nature of the terrorist threat that the United Kingdom faces. To an extent, this reflects the uncomfortable fact there is much that cannot be known even by those with the right expertise and access to all classified information. Faced with this uncertainty, it would be tempting to adopt a precautionary principle left to experts in terrorist risks to apply. However, that would be to withdraw crucial matters of normative and political judgment from the arena of public debate. To what extent particular institutional measures passed or proposed are a fitting response to the terrorist threat can only be judged by non-expert citizens on the basis of past history and facts made publicly available.

When in 1953, the United Kingdom became a party to the ECHR, which contains an outright proscription of torture and inhuman and degrading treatment, it is safe to assume the kind of terrorist activity and risk that subsequently materialised were not in contemplation. It would do us well to remember that what was in mind were the many terrible human rights abuses that occurred in Europe before and during the Second World War. The Convention is not intended to be something lightly set aside when civil peace and stability are threatened. When in 1988, the United Kingdom incorporated the United Nations Convention against Torture into its domestic law, making officially endorsed torture a crime, terrorist activity centred on the Irish question was a familiar reality but what we may loosely term jihadist terrorism had yet to take place within the jurisdiction. In the light of this current terrorist threat, should the United Kingdom rethink its commitments to the proscription and criminalisation of torture?

The reference to commitments is important, reflecting values to be kept even at a high consequentialist price. In the matter of its criminal justice policy, the United Kingdom has borrowed extensively from the penal practices of the United States. There is a great emphasis on assuring the electorate that crime and its associated risks will be firmly and effectively dealt with. Levels of imprisonment have increased markedly, in large part due to sentences which depart from a retributivist model and incarcerate on the basis of strong presumptions about the risk of future offending based on past convictions.[98] The influence of similar US models is palpable. However, there remain distinctively British, or, if you will, European strands to our penal policy. It is in point to mention in this

[98] Most notably a range of measures introduced by the Criminal Justice Act 2003, endorsing sentences premised on public protection where conclusive or strong presumptions about minimum terms of imprisonment are based on the nature of the offence and past convictions. For further discussion see this volume, chs 9, 10 and 11.

context the death penalty. Effectively, the death penalty was abolished in the United Kingdom in 1965.[99] The political commitment to the abolition of capital punishment has remained stable despite consistent and large majorities among the general population for its restoration. Indeed, the commitment to its abolition was recently fortified when the United Kingdom ratified the sixth protocol of the European Convention which obliges parties to renounce the death penalty. This demonstrates a resistance to populist pressure on the part of the political class and other influential elites when the issue is seen as sufficiently salient to the quality and tone of civil society. Within those classes, there remains a strong sentiment that peace time liberal democracies are in better civic condition if executions are remaindered to history.

Can there be the same level of confidence that there will be the same constancy in the political and official class to refrain from the use of torture? In the late 1970s the European Commission for Human Rights found that interrogation practices employed against suspected terrorists in Northern Ireland amounted to torture, although the ECtHR reduced the category of abuse to inhuman and degrading treatment.[100] From that time until the present, there have been no corroborated allegations concerning the torture of persons detained as terrorist suspects within the territory of the United Kingdom. There have been allegations that British troops serving abroad have participated in the rendition of combatants and non-combatants to places where they might be tortured. There have been further allegations of complicity on the part of British security officials in the interrogation of terrorist suspects who were tortured by officials of the holding state.[101] These allegations have led to civil cases still ongoing, police investigations and now a judicial inquiry. In announcing the inquiry, the Prime Minister, David Cameron, condemned unequivocally any recourse to torture whether directly or in association with other states.[102] In the matter of torture, there may be a greater alignment between the views of decision-making elites and the general population. Whereas there are overwhelming majorities in favour of the execution of convicted terrorists whose activities have caused deaths, there has been no general clamour for the introduction of torture and other forms of coercion to be used when interrogating suspected terrorists.

Of course, this state of affairs may change. If there were a series of successful terrorist attacks the sentiment against the abusive treatment of terrorist suspects could well alter. A change in sentiment would be even more likely if the prospect of truly awful events becomes credible. A recent decision of the House of Lords[103] relaxed the previously unyielding approach that English courts took

[99] Murder (Abolition of Death Penalty) Act 1965.

[100] *Ireland v the United Kingdom* (1978) 2 EHRR 25.

[101] Human Rights Joint Committee, 'Allegations of UK Complicity in Torture' (23rd report, 21 July 2009).

[102] *The Guardian*, 16 July 2010.

[103] *RB v Secretary of State for Home Department* [2009] UKHL 10.

to avoiding the prospect of torture for any person currently within the protection of English courts. Prior to this decision, appellate courts when reviewing decisions of lower tribunals to deport foreign nationals on the ground of national security would quash a decision to deport unless there was a 'high level of assurance' that the receiving country would not subject the deportee to torture or inhuman and degrading treatment.[104] The Appellate Committee in the *RB v Secretary of State for Home Department* case departed from this enhanced form of scrutiny and adopted the lower standard of 'irrationality'. Accordingly the unsuccessful appellants were subject to deportation to stand trial for terrorist offences in countries[105] known for using torture during interrogations and admitting evidence obtained from torture at trial. The orders for deportation were confirmed on the basis that it was not irrational for Special Immigration Appeals Commission (SIAC) to accept at face value assurances given at inter-governmental level by the receiving countries that the deportees would not be tortured.[106]

The fact that the United Kingdom has sought 'on the face' non-torture guarantees from regimes known to use torture, and that this practice has now withstood scrutiny at the highest appellate level, constitutes pragmatic rather than principled responses to an intractable problem. Further pragmatism might be in the offing if terrorist violence becomes large scale, frequent and rooted. One would hope that certain measures, such as the torture of persons such as E and V would never be contemplated come what may. One cannot rule out coercion against persons such as F, who was reasonably believed to be a terrorist with information concerning imminent attacks. If that route were ever taken, as argued already, it should be done *ex ante* under legislative provisions. Recourse should not be had to below the radar methods such as executive clemency. Neither should there be recourse to legal doctrines such as self-defence and necessity, while leaving in place the façade of outright proscription of torture.

VI CONCLUSION

At the present time there are no reasons of principle in favour of the United Kingdom abandoning or modifying the outright proscription of torture and inhuman and degrading treatment. It is hoped that this state of affairs can be maintained whatever the level of terrorist activity provided it is functionally possible for the United Kingdom to conduct itself as a liberal democracy. If at any time terrorist activity and the capacities of terrorist groups should threaten very large numbers of casualties and the destruction and contamination of major population centres, one would anticipate the deployment of all possible

[104] *Othman* [2008] 3WLR 798.

[105] Algeria and Jordan.

[106] 'At face value' is considered fair comment as the receiving countries refused any form of external monitoring of the custody conditions of the deportees.

means to avert catastrophes. One should hope for if not expect open public debate at the highest political level on what those means should be should there arise credible threats of the highest magnitude. However, at the present time even the worst terrorist incidents here or overseas have not been catastrophes of an existential dimension.

One matter found less than satisfactory was the legal position regarding the treatment of innocent persons caught up in life threatening terrorist acts. Using by way of illustration passengers aboard a hijacked airplane, it was argued that it would be legitimate even to intentionally kill such unfortunate and innocent persons if, on the best risk assessment that could be made in the circumstances, those passengers would very likely die in any event and that another set of innocent persons would be saved from a likely death. The complex legal and ethical issues arising in such circumstances should not be resolved under the question-begging formula 'such force as is reasonable in the circumstances in the prevention of crime'.

Index

www.ingramcontent.com/pod-product-compliance
Ingram Content Group UK Ltd.
Pitfield, Milton Keynes, MK11 3LW, UK
UKHW020906190926
475560UK00010B/295

9 781849 461665